To all those who protect and serve,
often far beyond the call of duty

# CONTENTS

# INTRODUCTION

*The people who know Scott and Laci have no doubt whatsoever that he has nothing to do with her disappearance. I mean, this was a couple everybody envied. They were just so much in love. I mean, they were a couple, they were partners, they were a team. . . .*

—Sharon Rocha, mother of Laci Peterson

Ever since Laci Peterson disappeared on December 24, 2002, and the public became galvanized by the story, people have asked me *Why?* Why was there so much interest in this single murder case? Why did it sustain our attention for so long? Women—even lovely, very pregnant women—go missing all too often in this country, and many of them are murdered. In fact, statistics show that homicide is the leading cause of death for pregnant women. And these deaths generally occur not at the hand of a stranger; they are usually the work of the person the woman loves and trusts most—the father of her child.

Often enough, I gave the pat response. It was a slow news day that Christmas Eve, when this beautiful young woman with the most engaging smile vanished from her quiet suburban neighborhood in a matter of minutes. No one saw anything untoward. She had no enemies. Most important, she apparently had the ideal marriage. Everyone described Scott and Laci Peterson as completely in love. In those first few days, no one mentioned any hints of tension or strife between them. Both sets of in-laws would contend that they were perfect together.

By all appearances, things were going well for Scott and Laci. Their finances were shaky, but that could be said of many young couples. The husband was charming, industrious, and obviously in love with his wife. The wife was a responsible, level-headed young woman, radiant in her happiness over the upcoming birth of their son.

Laci Peterson did wear expensive jewelry, even on her walks in a neighboring park. Early on, that seemed the only logical explanation for her disappearance: Someone must have kidnapped her for those gems. Or maybe, just maybe, some horrid soul had wanted the baby she was soon to deliver. After all, such hideous demons were out there, and the smallest quirk of fate could send an innocent into their terrible clutches.

As the story began to unfold, however, I had my doubts. After almost three decades studying, practicing, and reporting on the criminal justice system, I felt that something wasn't right in those first news stories about Laci Peterson. It was reported that her husband, Scott, had been fishing in the San Francisco Bay on that fateful day. Fishing, of course, seemed like an innocent activity.

And yet it was a cold, gray Christmas Eve. Laci was about to deliver their first child. The couple was having an elaborate brunch for their in-laws the next day. There was shopping and cooking to be done, presents yet to buy.

Why would Scott Peterson be fishing?

As I followed each new development and watched Scott's first fleeting appearances before the press, I noticed that he seemed rather removed from the tragedy unfolding around him. His emotional affect was flat. He did not jump onto the airwaves with pleas for the release or recovery of his beloved wife. His behavior was discordant and disturbing.

Nevertheless, in those first days there were plenty of pundits who scrambled to explain away Scott Peterson's behavior. Eminent defense attorneys stepped forward to proclaim that everyone grieves differently and that Scott's behavior displayed no evidence of a guilty mind. I disagreed. The more I looked into the story, the more fascinated I became with Scott's personality. Before long, I began to raise questions on the air about whether he was showing signs of a behavior disorder. Scott seemed to display many of the textbook qualities of a sociopath. He seemed relatively intelligent, was charming and gregarious, and claimed to be devastated by Laci's disappearance—yet beneath the superficial reactions, I sensed something else. Scott Peterson showed no normal signs or expressions of grief. He seemed to have no emotional insight into the extent of the tragedy unfolding around him. To put it plainly, he seemed insincere.

As the story developed, more and more evidence emerged to support this analysis. The inconsistencies in Scott's story failed to resolve themselves. There was little sign that he was leading, or even involved in, the search for Laci. Then came the explosive news about Scott's girlfriend, Amber Frey, whom he had hidden from Laci and her family. Scott's life, it appeared, had been entwined in a knot of outrageous lies, and now the lies were unraveling. His abnormal calm in the face of both families' unbearable sorrow, his self-serving, narcissistic manner, and his failure to lead the search all supported my initial hunch that this man, Scott Peterson, was a sociopath. In fact, the character he immediately brought to mind was Ted Bundy, the charming serial killer who murdered at least sixteen women in the 1970s. Of course, Scott hadn't roamed the country killing strangers the way Bundy did. Yet the defining element of a sociopath is not his record of violence; it is his character—that mix of charm and cold, emotionless calculation that I saw in both men. Sociopathic behavior can be found anywhere in our society; some of the most successful CEOs in our country could be classified as having sociopathic tendencies.

It's when such people turn violent that even the most insightful among us can be caught by surprise.

Such was the case, I believe, with Scott Peterson. And my conviction was only bolstered by the unparalleled access I have had to the inner workings of this investigation and trial. Many participants have given me in-depth interviews, often sharing with me stories that never made the news or reached the jury. My associate, Cole Thompson, and I have also had access to previously unseen police and Justice Department records, photographs, audiotapes, and forensic reports, all of which have contributed to the detailed account that follows in these pages.

But the most important purpose of this book is not merely to chronicle the events that this unforgettable case comprises. It is to take an intimate look at the character and psychology of a man convicted of the most heinous of crimes—the murders of his wife and his unborn son.

The question *Did he do it?* has now been answered by the people.

But that other question—*why?*—haunts us still.

# PROLOGUE

His look was California chic—jeans, a dark T-shirt, dress shoes. He turned to go, then paused. Removing his wedding ring, he slid the band into his pocket. Now he was ready.

Roses were his calling card; it was amazing how quickly young women fell for an armful. Janet Ilse was no different. An attractive sophomore at California Polytechnic Institute, she was taken by his dark good looks and soft, husky voice from the moment they first chatted on campus. When he arrived on her doorstep for their date, carrying twelve separate bouquets of a dozen roses apiece, she nearly melted.

Despite the six-year difference in their ages, and the fact that he was soon to graduate from Cal Poly, Janet was charmed by this courteous, self-assured young man. His sheepish grin was complemented by just enough of a swagger to set her pulse racing as he helped her into his black and gray Ford pickup for a night of eating and drinking in the lively college town of San Luis Obispo.

Aside from a few casual flirtations in class, Janet knew little about Scott Peterson before their first date. He was a senior agriculture student who shared a house with three male roommates somewhere off campus. During that first dinner, he described his love of fishing and hunting, but he revealed almost nothing of a personal nature. Instead he focused intently on everything the twenty-year-old had to say. She was flattered by how swiftly he made her the center of his attention, and apparently his admiration as well. As the expensive meal ended, he leaned back and lit up a cigar. He spoke of his future in terms of money and prestige, with the confidence of someone certain of his own success.

Their relationship flowered quickly. Scott was especially generous, thoughtfully planning each of their dates, taking her to nice restaurants and lavishing her with intimate presents—a delicate necklace with sparkly green gemstones, a fancy black designer dress. Janet was a vegetarian, and they hadn't been dating long when Scott announced that he had stopped eating meat. She was surprised and flattered. Scott Peterson seemed almost too good to be true.

As Scott began talking of their future together, Janet found herself falling in love. Yet every now and then something happened that didn't seem quite right. On one of their dates to a California rodeo, for instance, Janet giggled about the youngsters running around the fairground. Scott turned to her and announced emphatically that he did not want kids. They would simply get in the way of his intended lifestyle.

While she was smitten with Scott, Janet was uneasy about his quick intimacy. It wasn't long before he suggested they take an extended vacation to Mexico. To her, it all seemed too much, too soon. Yet Scott was polite and gracious, not only to her but also to her housemates, Tracy and Wendy; he often showed up at their apartment with small gifts and groceries, saying that he loved helping the cash-strapped college students.

Scott had just moved into a house with three others, Rob, Nando, and Juan, after responding to an ad on the Poly Union billboard. The four young men began as strangers but quickly became more like frat brothers, throwing barbecues and parties at their place. Janet enjoyed spending time there and her roommate Tracy often came along. For a while, Tracy was seeing one of Scott's roommates, and the two couples double-dated. On one occasion, both women stayed overnight at Scott's house.

Over the months, Janet and Scott's relationship grew stronger. Scott often brought his dog, McKenzie, along on their dates. The frisky golden retriever was just a puppy. As he parked himself happily on the rug in Janet's living room on Walnut Street, the couple talked about moving in together. They were acting more and more like a family.

Janet found it both exhilarating and scary to have someone so interested in her every thought and feeling. Scott expressed a desire to meet her relatives, but he rarely talked about his own, and he never asked her to meet his parents. Janet knew that Scott's dad lived in San Diego, but that was about all. She was reluctant to introduce him to her folks, especially her father. She feared that her dad would view Scott as slick or conceited. She found him a little cocky on occasion, and she knew some people might think he was nothing more than a smooth operator. Nevertheless, she was crazy about him, and their relationship continued to grow.

The couple had been dating for nearly five months when Janet decided to surprise Scott with a late-night romantic encounter at his place. It was after midnight when one of his roommates let her into the house. She quietly opened his bedroom door, held her breath, and tiptoed into the room.

Janet Ilse was stunned, dumbfounded, at what she saw. There on the bed, a dark-haired woman lay curled up next to Scott. Even more disturbing was Scott's reaction. When he saw her, he did not move. He did not jump up, or cry out, or beg her forgiveness. He just lay there coolly and stared as she lashed out at the two of them.

Only later would she realize that the man she was berating was someone else entirely—someone with a life in which she played no part.

"I'm sorry," was all Scott would say as his roommate burst in and pulled Janet away from the bed. Dazed, she allowed herself to be led outside and into a car. As they drove on the quiet streets back to her apartment, she found her voice again.

"I can't believe he cheated on me," Janet shouted.

"He's not cheating on you with her; he's cheating on her with you," the young man explained. "He's married."

"What?" Janet was flabbergasted.

It was true. When he moved in, the roommate explained, even his housemates had no idea that Scott was married. Not until a woman phoned the house identifying herself as Scott's wife did they realize the truth.

Janet did not hear from Scott for a week. Then, one afternoon, an apologetic Scott Peterson showed up on her doorstep.

"I'm sorry you found me in bed with Laci," was all he could say.

Janet made it clear that she did not want to hear from Scott again. The relationship was over.

Scott and Laci Peterson were newlyweds when he began his affair with Janet Ilse. It was just one link in an increasingly serious chain of dishonesty that marked Scott Peterson's life in the time before his wife's murder. His web of deceit would eventually trap everyone he knew, from virtual strangers to his closest family members. And over time, his deceptions would become far more sinister.

# CHAPTER ONE

# DECEMBER 24, 2002

Scott was running late. It was about 4:45 P.M. as he pulled into his driveway, parking next to his wife's Land Rover. In less than two hours, he was due for dinner at his in-laws' home. It had been a busy day already, and there was a long way to go.

Scott entered the backyard through the gate and patted McKenzie, the couple's beloved golden retriever, as the dog bounded out to meet him. He unclipped the dangling leash from the dog's collar and tossed it on the patio table. Passing through an unlocked back door, Scott moved through the dark, quiet house. Stopping to tidy up a bit, he carried a bucket of wash water and two mops outside. He tossed the water onto the lawn, then left the cleaning items by the door. He then headed for the fridge. Cold pizza and milk would pacify his growling stomach, empty since a bowl of cereal early that morning.

Carrying a veggie slice with him, Scott went over to the washing machine, hidden behind bifold doors in the den. He pulled out some dirty towels. Then, stripping down to his underwear, the young man loaded his green pullover, blue T-shirt, and jeans into the washer, covered them with detergent, and started the machine.

Then he was off to the bathroom, where he finished the pizza before stepping into the shower. Emerging in clean clothes, Scott checked his watch. It was 5:15 P.M. He picked up the phone.

Sharon Rocha was scrambling to finish preparations for her family dinner that evening when the telephone rang. It was already 5:17; her daughter Laci and son-in-law, Scott, would be arriving soon.

"Hi, Mom," Scott said. "Is Laci there?"

"No," Sharon replied.

"Laci's car is at the house, and McKenzie is in the backyard with his leash on," Scott said flatly. "Laci is missing."

*Missing?* The word took a moment to register. Her daughter would be pulling into the driveway with Scott any minute, she thought. Laci was a well-mannered, efficient young woman. She wouldn't be late for a family gathering.

Suddenly, a wave of fear washed over her. Laci was eight months pregnant. Had she gone into labor? Was she at the hospital? Trying not to panic, Sharon told Scott, "Call your friends. Ask them if they've seen her. Then call me back!"

Sharon put down the phone and turned to Laci's stepfather, Ron Grantski. His normally jovial face had turned serious as he listened to his wife's conversation.

"Laci's missing," Sharon said, echoing Scott's phrase.

Just two or three minutes went by before the phone rang again. Sharon grabbed it on the first ring, nervously running her fingers through her short blond hair.

"I checked with friends," Scott reported, "but nobody's seen her."

"Try the neighbors," Sharon commanded, her alarm escalating as she put down the receiver. Laci had sounded fine when they last spoke on the phone at 8:30 the previous evening. There was no reason for her to be missing, unless she was hurt or had been harmed.

The wait seemed endless before Scott called back, although phone records would show that only a few more minutes had passed. "I checked around," Scott said again. His tone remained even; the young man was not one for histrionics. "Nobody's seen her." Scott explained that Laci had planned to walk their dog that morning. Her usual path would have taken her through East La Loma Park, located at the end of their street on Covena Avenue. But he reminded Sharon that McKenzie had been at home when he arrived, trailing his leash.

By then it was 5:32 P.M., fifteen minutes since Scott's first call. In hindsight it seems surprising that Scott could have gathered information from so many people so quickly, but Sharon wasn't going to waste any more time. She told Scott to meet her in the park, then hung up, phoned her friend Sandy Rickard, and asked her to help search for Laci.

Moments later, Sandy pulled up in front of the house. "I'm going to look for her," Sharon yelled out to Ron. "Call the police." Then she raced out the front door.

For months, Laci had been taking McKenzie for morning walks in the nearby park. Sometimes Sharon went along, but in recent weeks, Laci had begun tiring easily, and Laci's yoga instructor and obstetrician had both recommended that she give up the walks until the baby was born. At first, Laci resisted—she was always headstrong—but now her body was insisting that she slow down. The narrow, sandy footpath that sloped down toward the park entrance no longer provided sure footing, and Laci was less inclined to complete her regular half-mile loop around the leafy grounds.

Sharon knew it was unlikely that Laci had taken that walk.

A t 5:47 P.M., Ron Grantski dialed 911.

"I'd like to report a missing person," he told the dispatcher.

It was Christmas Eve, so only a skeleton crew was on duty, but the Modesto Police Department knew the emergency line would probably stay busy. Many people find Christmas one of the loneliest times of the year, and the department often logged an especially large number of calls from people whose anxiety levels jumped during the holiday season.

Grantski gave his own address—1017 Marklee Way—then Laci's—523 Covena Avenue, between Encina Avenue and Edgebrook Drive. Their houses were less than two miles apart in the small city of Modesto, southeast of San Francisco and about ninety minutes from the Pacific coast.

Grantski told the dispatcher that he was relating information from his son-in-law, who had notified him that his stepdaughter, Laci Peterson, was missing.

The dispatcher who took the call made the following notes:

```
STEP-DAUGHTER, LACY [sic] PETERSON, PORTUGUESE/
WHITE FEMALE, 26 YEARS, LEFT TO WALK DOG AT DRY
CREEK PARK & NEVER RETURNED HOME. SUBJECT IS 5
FOOT 1, DARK HAIR & DARK EYES, 8 MONTHS PREGNANT,
UNKNOWN WHO LAST SEEN WITH. DOG RETURNED HOME WITH
LEASH & UNABLE TO LOCATE WOMAN ANYWHERE. REPORT
RECEIVED FROM WOMAN'S HUSBAND, SCOTT PETERSON.
HUSBAND IS NOW LOOKING FOR WIFE IN THE PARK. OFFI-
CER JOHN EVERS DISPATCHED TO THE PARK AT 17:48. AT
17:58, OFFICERS DERRICK LETSINGER AND MATT SPUR-
LOCK AND SGT. BYRON DUERFELDT DISPATCHED TO 523
COVENA AVENUE.
```

An adult missing person report rarely generates a major response within the first twenty-four hours, but the emergency operator recognized that Laci's condition made her situation different. The young woman might be injured or experiencing a problem with her advanced pregnancy. And, of course, there was always the possibility of foul play.

By 6:00 P.M., officers from the Modesto Police Department were en route to both the couple's home and East La Loma Park.

D ry Creek Park spans twelve city blocks and is parceled into several small mini-parks. East La Loma Park, barely three blocks from the Peterson home, was the area where Laci usually strolled with the dog. McKenzie had been a gangly, energetic puppy when Laci gave him to Scott for Christmas just a month after they met. He was almost eight years old now, sprouting white whiskers around his muzzle, but Scott still warned strangers that the retriever was very protective of Laci.

Sharon Rocha was growing increasingly worried as her friend Sandy steered them into a parking lot just west of El Vista Avenue. Jumping out of the vehicle, Sharon hurried across the stubby grass, Sandy trailing behind her.

During the short ride from her house, Sharon had called Scott and arranged to meet him at El Vista Bridge to begin the search. Now she raced through the park calling out, *"Laci!"* and peering into the shrubbery, checking trash cans lined along the pathway. She and Sandy were nearly breathless when they reached the site.

Sharon later recalled that it seemed like "forever" before Scott arrived, although he had said he was already in the park when she last called. She finally spotted Scott walking along the south side of Dry Creek with McKenzie at his side.

"Scott!" Sharon called, waving her arms. "Scott, we're over here!"

But Sharon couldn't get his attention. Scott seemed to be lost in his own world. Although he was just fifty feet away, he didn't seem to hear or see his mother-in-law. It wasn't until Sharon's nephew, Zachary Zwald, walked over to him that Scott actually acknowledged the other family members around him.

Sharon was surprised to find her son-in-law so calm. She later told police that Scott wouldn't look her in the eye as they spoke about Laci. Eventually the lights of a police cruiser distracted Sharon, and she headed over to meet the police; Scott and the others followed close behind.

The first uniformed officer on the scene, John Evers, had been on patrol for ninety minutes when the missing persons dispatch came over his radio. A sixteen-year veteran of the Modesto Police Department, Evers noted the darkening skies and dropping temperatures and quickly got down to business.

According to his radio call, the husband had been the last person to see the missing woman earlier that day. "When was the last time your saw your wife?" he asked Scott.

Scott told Evers that he'd last seen Laci around 9:30 that morning before he'd left home to go fishing. During their brief conversation, Scott said that Laci had planned to take their dog for a walk in the park that morning, then go grocery shopping for the dinner party at her mother's that evening. She planned to spend the afternoon baking gingerbread cookies.

When Scott left the house, he continued, his wife was mopping the floor. He returned in the afternoon to find McKenzie in the back-yard, his leash still attached. Entering through the unlocked patio door, he found the house empty.

"Is her purse at home?" Sharon interrupted.

"I don't remember," Scott said blankly.

"Where does she usually keep it?"

"On a coatrack by the front door."

"I'm going to the house to see if it's there," Sharon announced. Officer Evers stopped the anxious mother and told her he'd go check it out himself. She should remain at the park.

John Evers pulled up in front of Scott and Laci's home along with Officers Letsinger and Spurlock and Sergeant Duerfeldt in county patrol cars, and quickly established a command center for the missing persons investigation at 523 Covena Avenue.

The Petersons' home was a modest, single-story ranch with drab green shingles on the west side of the street. The couple had purchased their three-bedroom, two-bath home for $177,000 in 2000. In less than three years, its value had appreciated by $100,000. The peaceful neighborhood, with its well-kept houses, manicured front lawns, and flower beds, had a small-town feeling. Neighbors tended to stop and chat with one another, and children felt safe playing and riding their bicycles in the quiet streets. The Petersons' property was surrounded by an imposing six-foot wooden fence. The police noticed that several of their windows looked out on Covena Avenue, but heavy drapes covered the openings and blocked any view—in or out.

As Officer Matt Spurlock led the men down the brick walkway toward the Petersons' front door, Sergeant Byron Duerfeldt dialed the unit's on-call supervisor to alert him to the situation. Carter, the head of the Crimes Against Persons (CAP) unit that night, listened intently as Duerfeldt reported the details: A woman named Laci Peterson, age twenty-seven, eight months pregnant, was missing from her residence. The husband, Scott Peterson, age thirty, said he had left early that morning to go fishing for the day. When he returned home at 4:30, she was missing.

"Where is Peterson now?" Carter asked.

Duerfeldt reported that Scott was walking the neighborhood looking for his wife. Other family members were already gathering at the residence. No one seemed to know where Laci might be.

"I'm requesting the assistance of a CAP detective, sir," Duerfeldt said. The Crimes Against Persons unit had six full-time detectives assigned to investigate felony assaults, robberies, homicides, and missing person cases. Carter agreed, then instructed the field sergeant to locate the husband and bring him back to the house for a more in-depth interview. He also wanted calls made to area hospitals in case Laci had checked herself in without the family's knowledge.

"Call me back with any new information," Carter instructed.

Sergeant Duerfeldt left to find Scott Peterson while his three uniformed patrol officers examined the Peterson premises. Officer Spurlock led the way to the house.

Duerfeldt found the front door unlocked. Most of the interior lights were on. A carefully trimmed Christmas tree glimmered in a corner of the dining area next to the fireplace. The officers quickly inventoried the presents piled beneath the tree. One large box wrapped in deep blue paper was addressed from Scott to Laci; another gift, a Louis Vuitton wallet, was nestled in an open bag. Initial reports assumed that this was Scott's gift to his wife. However, a credit card receipt showed that Laci had purchased the wallet during a trip to Carmel the previous week, although whether it was for herself or someone else was never established.

In the galley-style kitchen, painted a cheery yellow, a chalkboard on the wall read *Merry Christmas*. There was some leftover pizza sitting on the kitchen counter in an open box, and an open container of ranch dressing nearby. A telephone book on the counter was open to a garish full-page ad showing a young man being handcuffed by a uniformed officer. "Criminal Defense—Former Deputy District Attorney," the ad read. Among the specialties the lawyer listed was murder.

The living room, painted a vibrant burnt orange, was furnished with overstuffed couches topped with fluffy throw pillows. But something seemed out of place in the carefully ordered environment. Evers noticed a tan-and-white throw rug bunched up on the floor against the patio door as if something had been dragged over the threshold.

The officers also walked through the nursery, with its deep blue walls and nautical theme. A small white crib was set up against one wall, its mattress covered with new baby clothes. Miniature sailboats dangled from the ceiling, and a decorative life preserver hung on the wall bearing the greeting WELCOME ABOARD!

The officers continued their examination, opening closet doors and pulling back the shower curtain, looking for anything out of the ordinary. After checking the rest of the house, the men moved to the backyard through the living room door. They carefully stepped over the bunched up rug, leaving it undisturbed.

Spurlock noticed that a mop bucket and two mops were leaning against an exterior wall just beside a side door. The bright blue bucket was still wet, apparently from recent use, as was the sidewalk nearby.

The police surveyed the area quickly, then left the residence. Evers saw Scott standing outside and asked him to check the house for any signs of a struggle or burglary.

The officers accompanied him back inside. Evers tossed out some questions as they walked. According to Scott, Laci had been wearing a white, long-sleeved crewneck shirt and black maternity pants when he left home that morning. She was barefoot at the time, but she usually wore white tennis shoes when walking McKenzie. He also told the officers that she had been wearing expensive jewelry—a diamond necklace, diamond earrings, and a gold-and-diamond Geneve wristwatch—when he last saw her.

"Is your wife's purse still in the house?" Evers asked.

In response, Scott went not to the hall coatrack he'd mentioned to Sharon in the park, but into the master bedroom. The bed was tidy. Hanging behind some scarves on a hook in the closet was Laci Peterson's purse. To most women, this might seem an unusual place to keep an everyday handbag, but Scott went straight there to find it. The blue pocketbook contained her wallet, keys, sunglasses, and other personal items. The young husband told the police that nothing seemed to be missing.

Although Scott seemed calm about the discovery, Evers knew that finding a woman's purse left behind like this was an ominous sign.

"Have you been working all day?" Evers asked.

"I went fishing," Scott replied. Pulling a piece of paper from his pocket, he volunteered it to the officer. It was a receipt from the Berkeley Marina for 12:54 P.M. that afternoon.

The officers exchanged glances. Scott was certainly quick to provide proof of his whereabouts without being asked.

"What time did you leave the house?" Spurlock inquired.

"Earlier this morning." Scott did not pinpoint an actual time.

"What did you go fishing for?"

No answer.

"What did you use for bait?" Spurlock persisted. He wasn't comfortable with Scott's awkward answers, and as an avid angler, the officer knew just what to ask.

"Some type of silver lure," was the best Scott could do.

"Where do you keep all your fishing gear?" Spurlock asked.

Finally, a direct response. "I keep it at my company's storage facility."

Scott began reciting his movements after leaving home that morning. First, he drove to his company's warehouse at 1027 North Emerald. Checking his e-mail and faxes, he sent a message to his boss in Portugal. After straightening up his work space, he spent some time assembling a mortiser—a woodworking tool—before finally hitching up the new boat to his truck.

I would later wonder about his use of time. Scott had decided to fish only two hours earlier, according to his own account. It was too cold to golf, he said, so he chose fishing in the bay as an alternative. He left home knowing he had errands to run before the dinner with his in-laws at six o'clock that evening, including picking up a Christmas gift basket by 3:00 P.M. for Laci's grandfather. Yet, when he arrived at the warehouse, he allegedly spent time cleaning up the interior, working on his computer, and casually assembling the mortiser, all before setting out on the ninety-mile trip to the Berkeley Marina to fish.

In describing his trip, Scott specifically mentioned that he'd made two calls to Laci from his cell phone during the drive home—one to her cell and another to the house. He left messages, he said, but he never reached her.

Once back in Modesto, Scott continued, he took a few minutes to unhook the boat and trailer at his warehouse, then drove straight home. It was after 4:30 when he pulled up to the house, saw his wife's vehicle in the driveway, and noticed the leash still hanging from McKenzie's collar.

Given all that, the next sequence of events seems even more peculiar. Scott casually described entering the unlocked back door to find the house dark and empty. There were no smells of baking gingerbread wafting through the kitchen, no groceries were stacked on the counter—in short, no sign of Laci anywhere. Scott dealt with the mops and water bucket in the entry hall. Then, having traveled all day without packing anything to eat or drink, he grabbed a snack from the refrigerator. He told the cops that he had assumed Laci was at "Mom's" to help with dinner that evening. Then, instead of checking his home answering machine or calling the Rochas to confirm this, Scott ran his clothes through the washing machine, since they were "wet from the rain and salt spray." He then showered and changed.

It was after five o'clock when he finally called the Rochas. It was only when Sharon told him Laci wasn't there that Scott became concerned. Laci had been planning to walk McKenzie in the park, he said; he now feared that something had happened to her. As Sharon later confirmed, he spent only a few minutes calling friends and neighbors in an attempt to locate her.

When the officers asked about the throw rug near the back door to the patio, Scott told them the cat and dog were most likely responsible for its crumpled state. As the officers watched, Scott placed his foot on one corner and straightened it out. Its original suspicious position was never photographed.

Returning to the kitchen, Scott announced that nothing appeared to be missing or out of place. Before leaving, the officers and sergeant officially secured the residence at 523 Covena Avenue. Just hours earlier, it had simply been the Peterson home. Now it was a potential crime scene.

The bald and bespectacled Sergeant Duerfeldt waited on the curb for a report from his officers, then called his supervisor, Sergeant Carter. Duerfeldt told Carter that his officers were uncomfortable with some of Scott's early answers—especially his eagerness to provide a receipt from the Berkeley Marina when asked what he had been doing that day. As Duerfeldt made clear, his men hadn't asked for any proof.

There was more. At first, Scott couldn't say what he was fishing for; moments later he declared he was fishing for sturgeon, but couldn't say what bait he used.

Duerfeldt was also bothered by the fact that Scott had washed his clothes and taken a shower before looking for his wife. It also appeared that he might have mopped the kitchen floor before calling Sharon Rocha. The officer noted that it was another relative, not Scott, who actually telephoned the police to report that Laci was missing.

Having checked local hospitals with no success, Duerfeldt told Carter that patrol units were searching the neighborhood and nearby East La Loma Park. He also reported that the Petersons' dog was actually running loose in the neighborhood earlier in the morning, trailing a dirty leash, and that a neighbor had returned the dog to the Petersons' yard.

Sergeant Carter thanked Duerfeldt, then quickly dialed Homicide Detective Al Brocchini and dispatched him to the scene. It had been less than an hour since Sharon Rocha had called 911, but Carter wanted a murder investigator on the scene immediately.

In the years since the O. J. Simpson case, the phrase *rush to judgment* has become an increasingly prominent notion in our culture, trotted out whenever cops quickly hone in on a particular suspect in the initial stages of an investigation. It is ironic that this expression became associated with Simpson, given the early evidence that clearly implicated him in his wife's murder: the blood trail from his white Bronco to the Rockingham front door and the infamous bloody glove outside Kato Kaelin's rear window. But Johnnie Cochran's "dream team" made "rush to judgment" one of its most successful slogans, and it captured the public's imagination.

Some of my guests and viewers accused me of a similar rush to judgment when I questioned Scott Peterson's story early in the investigation. As we were all reminded throughout the case, everyone is entitled to the presumption of innocence. But the presumption of innocence attaches during trial, not in the course of an investigation. When a person of interest emerges, the police *must* work to focus on that individual, to establish his involvement or exclude him from suspicion; they cannot merely assume his or her innocence. In my opinion, it would have amounted to investigatory malpractice if the Modesto police had failed to put Scott under the microscope from the beginning.

The police turned their attention to Scott despite some obvious reasons to look elsewhere. Laci Peterson's family certainly did not believe Scott had anything to do with her disappearance. There were no initial reports of trouble in the marriage. There were no reasons Laci would choose to disappear or do herself harm.

In cases of foul play, the culprit is statistically most likely to be a spouse or someone else known to the victim. A 2001 study conducted by doctors at the Maryland Department of Health and Medical Hygiene found homicide to be the leading cause of death among pregnant woman. In many cases, experts believe, fear of fatherhood may bring on such violence. Pregnancy is a life-changing event, especially for men, who may view the emotional and financial responsibilities as "huge stones around their necks," according to criminal profiler Pat Brown, president of the Sexual Homicide Exchange.

It's also important to note that Laci Peterson was a very low-risk candidate for a violent attack by a stranger. She was alone for an hour at most on that Christmas Eve morning after Scott left the house. The closed living room drapes prevented someone on the street from seeing Laci inside. In cases of kidnapping or sexually motivated crimes, the perpetrator has often conducted some sort of surveillance of the potential victim to determine vulnerability and availability. The window of opportunity in this residential neighborhood, when people were likely to be home preparing for the holidays, was almost nonexistent. Although the Petersons' back door was unlocked, there was no evidence whatsoever that someone entered the house and struggled with the young mother-to-be before forcibly removing her from the home. If burglary were the motive, it would be highly unusual to choose a house with a car parked out front. When the police arrived, they found expensive jewelry readily accessible in the master bedroom. And Scott and Laci's dog was found in the yard dragging his leash, another reason to believe that Laci was not accosted by a stranger inside the house.

Laci Peterson's advanced pregnancy had curbed her activities in the weeks before the murder. She limited herself to short walks, errands, and visits with friends. In her condition, she was not gallivanting about in dangerous places at odd hours. While Laci was an attractive young woman who might have been a target if she had gone walking in the park, she was not only eight months pregnant, but also accompanied by her large and protective companion, McKenzie. Whether it took place in the house or the park, Laci's daytime abduction from a populated location would have been highly risky for a stranger bent on harming her.

However, Scott Peterson's initial behavior gave the police real cause for concern. Why was he so sketchy in recalling the details of a fishing trip he had taken just that morning? Why did he wait so long to raise an alarm when he came home to find his wife missing and his dog trailing his leash? Why didn't he check with his wife's obstetrician, or the hospital where she was scheduled to give birth? Although Scott told Officer Evers that Laci was the one mopping when he left the house, his removal of the mops and dumping of the water suggested that Scott himself might have been cleaning up after some suspicious activity. Although a logical explanation would later emerge for the fact that the Peterson's phone book was open to an ad for a criminal defense attorney, no alert detective could have dismissed the discovery out of hand. Far more damning evidence would come to light as the police continued their investigation, and it was good police work—not a precipitous rush to judgment—that had police scrutinizing Scott's involvement in those early hours.

As time passed, the search for Laci Peterson intensified. The Stanislaus County Sheriff's Office sent its helicopter, Air 101, to traverse the area surrounding Dry Creek Park. On the ground, the Modesto Police Department's K-9 Officer, D. Gonzalez, responded with his search dog, Dino. They worked the area east of El Vista Bridge to La Loma Avenue, including the creek banks and brushy areas, up and down the trails, through the picnic and playground areas, and into the gully on the south side of Dry Creek. The team would also check the backyards of residents that bordered the park.

When Officers Letsinger and Spurlock left the Covena home, they headed over to Dry Creek Park to join the search. Upon arriving, they saw Laci's stepfather at the footbridge.

"Do you know where Scott's been all day?" Spurlock asked.

"I believe he went golfing this morning," Grantski responded.

"Are you sure?"

"Yes."

Officers Spurlock and Letsinger exchanged glances but said nothing. Excusing themselves, they proceeded with their search of the park, following the trail south to the pump station, then north past the footbridge and back again. By then it was quite dark, so they returned to the Peterson home.

Officer Evers was standing on the front lawn of the ranch house with Scott Peterson. "Find anything?"

"Not yet," Spurlock replied.

As the three men stood chatting, Scott's stepfather walked over. "Were you able to get in a game of golf this morning?" Grantski asked Scott.

Scott hesitated. Then, speaking a little too quickly, he said, "I didn't play golf today. It was too cold. I went fishing instead."

Grantski looked puzzled. He glanced at Spurlock and Evers, then turned back to his son-and-law. "Nine-thirty or ten o'clock in the morning is way too late for fishing," he said. "You should have gone earlier. What were you fishing for?"

There was no response.

# CHAPTER TWO

# DECEMBER 24, 2002, NIGHT

CAP Homicide Detective Al Brocchini could hear the helicopters as he sped down Route 108 toward the Peterson home. He was following the details via the police scanner bolted to the dashboard of his unmarked car. Friends and neighbors were already assisting in the search, and officers were calling in with bits of information: some gloves at Wilson and Encina Avenues, a burnt white shirt in one of the park fire pits where Jennie Street intersects North Morton Boulevard.

Brocchini had planned on a quiet Christmas with his family in the foothills of the Sierra Nevada Mountains, but he agreed to return to Modesto for this investigation. Sergeant Carter was comfortable calling on this detective on Christmas Eve. With seventeen years on the job, a son on the Modesto police force, and no young children at home, Brocchini was the obvious choice; Carter was confident that Brocchini's wife of twenty-five years would be more understanding than most spouses on that day.

Sergeant Carter wanted Brocchini to talk to Scott Peterson, to get a reading on whether Laci Peterson's disappearance seemed like a voluntary departure or something more sinister. There were other possibilities, such as an accident or kidnapping, but Brocchini was not working those angles.

"If Laci is not found by patrol or by investigation, you are to call Detective Craig Grogan to assist," Carter ordered.

Barely five foot six, with a youthful face and wide brown eyes that sparkled behind silver-rimmed glasses, the heavy-set Brocchini looked like a cop even in his business suit. Nine years with the MPD and eight before that with the Alameda County Sheriff's Department had left their mark; his rough-and-tumble demeanor contrasted sharply with his cherubic features.

Christmas lights illuminated the house numbers along the broad two-lane road that dead-ended at Thousand Oaks Park. Brocchini spotted police officers on the lawn of 523 Covena as he pulled up behind several patrol cars lining the curb. The frigid air hit him like a slap as he climbed out of the heated vehicle and onto the patchy grass, where Officer Evers, tall and lean in a navy-blue uniform, stood waiting. Brocchini joined Evers and the two walked over to the driveway, where Scott Peterson stood speaking with a friend.

"This is Detective Al Brocchini," Evers interrupted.

Looking down at the detective, Scott nodded, but expressed no outward concern.

"I'd like you to walk me through the house and point out anything that looks out of place," Brocchini said. As he led them up the concrete driveway, Brocchini noted that Scott Peterson didn't appear particularly worried.

Once inside, Brocchini immediately checked the home's entrances and exits. While nothing seemed amiss, he too was getting a bad vibe from the husband. He knew the feeling. His gut was telling him to slow down and pay close attention.

"This type of investigation has many different aspects," Brocchini told Scott as the three men strode across the shiny wood floors to the master bedroom. "There are officers canvassing the neighborhood and the park in search of your wife, but it's *my* job to interview you as the last person to see Laci alive.

"It's going to be uncomfortable for you because I have to ask difficult questions about your relationship with your wife," he continued. "It's been my experience that you'll end up not liking me very much. Keep in mind, I'm only doing my job."

"I understand," Scott nodded, agreeing to cooperate in "every way."

Brocchini sensed otherwise. Normally, police would wait at least twenty-four to forty-eight hours before initiating a full investigation in a missing person case, but Brocchini's instinct wouldn't let him wait. What he saw next, as he entered the bedroom, confirmed his feelings. A fluffy white comforter had been pulled up over the pillows, in what looked like an attempt to tidy the bed. Yet, at the foot of the bed, where one would normally fold back the covers, Brocchini noticed an indentation that spanned the width of the bed, as though a body had been laid out there. The detective did not note his observation in a police report, but a crime scene photographer later captured the suspicious impression on film.

"There's her purse," Evers announced, pointing to the blue handbag on the hook behind some scarves. "Her stuff is in there." Scott watched as the detective verified its contents. It was clear that Laci would not have left home voluntarily without her pocketbook.

The officers followed Scott across the hall to what appeared to be a guest room and secondary work space for Scott and Laci. The room had a double bed covered by a light blue blanket and a generic-looking desk, file cabinet, and bookshelves.

On the desk, next to two laptop computers, Brocchini spied an open pocket knife. On the floor, in front of a partially open closet, was a blue Nike duffle bag. It was unzipped and part of a green rain jacket was poking out.

"Did you take something from that bag?" Brocchini asked.

Scott said he'd removed a pair of white tennis shoes and placed them on the dining room wet bar before leaving for his fishing expedition that morning.

Brocchini noticed an open space on the top shelf of the closet where it appeared the bag had come from. A second duffle bag, which had apparently fallen off the top shelf, was resting on the clothing rack between the top shelf and the closet wall. It looked as though the second duffle bag had fallen when the Nike bag was taken down. When questioned about the bag's location, Scott claimed he was just "sloppy."

In another closet, the detectives found several rifles.

"Do you own any handguns?" Brocchini asked.

Scott said he owned a Glock, but it had been stolen from his car a few years earlier. "I've got a second handgun, a Llama .22-caliber that I've owned since before my eighteenth birthday. I normally keep it in the desk in the spare bedroom, but for the last month I've been keeping it in the glove box of my truck, since my last pheasant-hunting trip about a month ago. It's loaded with ammo."

Trailing Scott to the TV room/den that now occupied the converted garage, Brocchini noticed a washroom partially hidden behind bifold doors. He paused to examine a stack of stained white towels heaped on top of the washing machine. "The maid probably used those the other day," Scott volunteered. "They were in the washing machine. I took them out so I could put my clothes in."

Reaching inside, the detective pulled out a pair of blue jeans, a blue T-shirt, and a green pullover.

"Those are the clothes I wore fishing today," Scott said.

"Why did you wash them as soon as you got home?"

"They were wet from the bay and the rain."

Having spotted an overflowing laundry basket in the master bedroom, Brocchini wondered why Scott hadn't added these items to his small wash load. When he asked about the Petersons' maid, Scott explained that it had been her third time to the house. She was hired to clean every other Monday.

Breaking with protocol, Brocchini now decided to proceed with a full-blown investigation based on an assumption of foul play. "Can I get her phone number?" he asked Scott. "And can I get a look at your cell phone for the call history?"

Scott handed over his phone and watched as the detective copied down all of the incoming and outgoing calls.

At one point during the walk-through, Brocchini noticed the couple's golden retriever in the backyard. The dog hadn't barked when he and Evers first entered the house, and Brocchini was curious to see how McKenzie would respond to him. Stepping outside, he approached the retriever, who greeted him happily when the detective knelt down to pet him.

"That's unusual," Scott remarked.

"Is he your dog?"

"Yeah."

"How old is he?"

"He's about eight or nine years old. I've had him since before I was married."

"Is he protective of Laci?"

"Yeah, like around the pool man if I'm not here."

Outside the back door, Brocchini saw the bucket and two mops. Scott said that Laci had been cleaning that morning.

"I brought the bucket in and set it near the front door," Scott explained. "When I left to go fishing, Laci was mopping."

"How did the mops get outside?"

Scott explained that when he entered through the back door, his pets raced in ahead of him. When the cat ran toward the bucket, he said, he took it outside and dumped the water, afraid the cat might drink from it if he left it visible.

Leaving the house, Brocchini strode over to Scott's bronze-colored 2002 Ford pickup. It was backed in facing the street, next to a dark green Land Rover parked in the opposite direction.

"Can I look inside the car?"

"Yeah," Scott replied, unlocking the vehicle with a remote key.

In the cargo bed of the four-door F-150, there were five four-foot long patio umbrellas wrapped in a blue tarp. Scott said that he'd intended to store the umbrellas at his shop, but simply forgot to take them out on his two trips to the warehouse that day. The expensive umbrellas had been left in the open truck bed the entire time Scott was out on the bay. Next to the umbrellas was a toolbox containing some articles of clothing, a nylon rope, and a bag of shotgun shells. A light brown canvas tarp lay bunched up near the vehicle's tailgate.

Moving forward to the passenger compartment, the detective swung open the driver's door. When it bumped against Laci's vehicle, Scott immediately demanded he stop the search.

"I can move the truck forward," Scott said. Then, producing a glove, he offered to hold it between the door and the Land Rover.

Brocchini promised to be more careful, but he was surprised at Scott's reaction. Was this young man more interested in a scratch on his car than the safety of his wife? This was a moment worth noting. In my experience, a close family member who worries about protecting his property at a time like this is a suspect who should be watched. None of the items in Scott and Laci's home were damaged. Yet, even as the police were watching him, Scott let his proprietary interest in the SUV overwhelm both his concern for his wife and his common sense. In hindsight, Scott's behavior suggests control issues as well: From these early moments, he began posturing aggressively around the detective investigating his wife's disappearance.

Returning to his inspection, Brocchini saw the camouflage jacket Scott said he'd been wearing on his supposedly rainy fishing trip. The jacket was dry to the touch. A sports bag nearby contained two fishing lures, still in their package, and a store receipt. Two other sacks from shops in a nearby mall contained clothing, along with purchase slips dated several weeks earlier. In the glove box was the Llama .22-caliber handgun Scott had mentioned, loaded with a magazine of live ammo. There was no round in the chamber.

Without hesitation, Brocchini collected the pistol and marked it as evidence.

Shifting his focus to Laci's vehicle, a 1996 Land Rover Discovery, he saw a cell phone on the front seat still plugged into the dashboard. He tried to turn it on, but it flickered and immediately switched off. The phone's battery was dead.

As the two men stood in the driveway, Laci's mother was over on the front lawn watching. She had barely glimpsed Scott since their brief meeting in the park more than four hours ago. Now she tried to catch his eye again, but he still seemed to be avoiding her. Sharon thought his behavior was out of character but put it out of her mind when she realized that she'd never seen him under such stress.

The waiting was physically and emotionally exhausting, and Sharon finally sat down on the curb to rest. By that time, five marked police cars lined the street, and the number of people on the scene was increasing. Officers in navy blue uniforms and the investigation team in jeans and sneakers joined the detectives already on-site. Her friend Sandy was with her when Scott finally walked over.

"You know, if they find blood anywhere that doesn't mean anything," Scott told his mother-in-law. "I'm a sportsman. Just look at my hands. I could drop blood anywhere."

Sharon was too upset for the strange statement to register, but the exchange bothered Sandy, and later she reported it to the police. When I first heard this story, I wondered if Scott was simply taking a page out of O. J. Simpson's playbook. When questioned about blood drops appearing in his Bronco and on the walkway to his home, Simpson deftly explained that he had cut his knuckle twice—once before he left on his "alibi" trip to Chicago, and a second time on a glass in the Chicago hotel room when he was told about Nicole's death. He later revised this by saying he cut himself all the time.

As an avid equestrienne, I have four horses and six dogs; I'm always scuffing myself playing with the puppies or working in the barn—or, even more hazardous, while cooking in the kitchen. Nevertheless, I cannot imagine trying to convince anyone that major droplets of blood can be found around my home on a regular basis, as Scott did.

Just before 11:00 P.M., Detective Brocchini suggested that Laci's mother go home for the night. Then he turned to Scott. "Is it all right if the ID Tech people go inside to take photographs and collect evidence?" Taking crime scene photos and gathering evidence a few hours into a missing persons case is quite unusual, but Brocchini was following his instinct. He wanted the scene preserved as quickly as possible.

"That would be fine," Scott replied.

At 11:17, Brocchini and Evers drove Scott to his place of business, exactly four miles away. Scott sat in the passenger seat of the detective's unmarked sedan; Evers followed closely behind in a patrol car. Scott was a fertilizer salesman for Tradecorp, a company headquartered in Spain. His territory spanned California, Arizona, and New Mexico, but the base of operations was a one-story warehouse in an industrial area of Modesto, at 1027 North Emerald Avenue.

Just as they had searched the Petersons' home, the detectives intended to scrutinize Scott's place of business. They were particularly interested in the boat he had taken on his afternoon fishing expedition, a fourteen-foot aluminum Sears Gamefisher stored inside his warehouse.

The officers observed that there were two entrances to the warehouse, a single-car roll-up door and a door that led to an office area. "I'm the only one with the key, since I'm the only employee," Scott told them as he unlocked the office door.

"There's no electricity," he then announced as he led the men inside. Neither officer flipped the light switches to test his assertion. Although Brocchini would be criticized for fingering Scott as early as he did, at this point he was still willing to take Scott's word about the electricity. Grabbing a Streamline flashlight with a rechargeable battery, the detective spotted a computer and a fax machine with an incoming fax in the tray. He noted the date, December 24, and the time it had been sent, 14:28, or 2:28 P.M. "Tell me about this fax?" he asked Scott.

"I think I received it before I left to go fishing," Scott replied. "It's from New Jersey, so there's a three-hour time difference."

Once again, Scott's stories weren't making any sense. "If you got it at 11:28, that would have been kind of late to go to Berkeley." the detective mused. "It's cutting it kind of close leaving Modesto at 11:28 and arriving in Berkley at 12:54."

"Well, maybe I got it when I got back from Berkeley, but I remember getting it and reading it."

"Would you roll up the door so I can at least position my car in front of the shop, so I'll have some light besides this flashlight?" Brocchini requested.

"Sure." Striding to the warehouse area, Scott heaved open the roll-up door while the detective repositioned his vehicle, using his high beams to illuminate the boat. Only later did it occur to him that if Scott's computer and fax machine were working that morning, the electricity was certainly working then.

The boat sat atop its trailer. It appeared dry on the outside, but there was water visible in the bow. The detective noticed a chunk of concrete with a rebar hoop on one end on the floor of the boat. Scott identified it as a homemade anchor, but there was no rope attached. Brocchini paused for a moment to examine what appeared to be concrete debris along the rib line inside the boat. It was not on the actual rim, but on the edges inside of the vessel that ran horizontal to the bottom and up both sides. There did not appear to be any reason that concrete particles would be there or on the table nearby. He noticed scratches on one side as well.

A pair of yellow rubber gloves and a short red docking line lay inside the boat. Both were wet. One ultralight rod and reel, and a similar saltwater rig, were also in the boat. The freshwater rod was fitted with a small Mitchell reel spooled with braided line with a small lure tied to the end. The reel was missing its crank handle. The saltwater rig, a new-looking Master Brand rod and reel, was broken down into parts. The reel was spooled with what appeared to be seventeen-pound monofilament line. A small buzz lure, used for top water bass fishing, hung from the line. Both rod and reel had what appeared to be residue, possibly salt, on the exterior. A small tackle box sat nearby.

As Brocchini photographed the boat, Scott said, "I hope you don't show those to my boss," apparently worried that he would get in trouble for using the warehouse to store his boat. Even granting that different people react differently under stressful conditions, any good investigator would have noticed the behavior as odd. As Brocchini noted, "This appeared to be suspicious concern from a husband of a missing woman."

After the warehouse search, Detective Brocchini and Officer Evers took Scott to the Modesto Police Department headquarters at 600 Tenth Street for a formal interview. The downtown building was just minutes from the Peterson home, around the corner from the county jail.

"I haven't been taking notes all night," Brocchini told Scott as they pulled into the station house. "I'd like to sit down so I can take some notes and get a more thorough statement from you."

Scott agreed.

The men went upstairs to an interrogation room and began the taped conversation at midnight. They would not finish until 1:30 that morning.

What follows is the first complete rendering of the taped interview between Brocchini and Scott Peterson, including those portions not admitted at trial.

Detective Brocchini started a tape recorder, then began to speak. "Pretty much, Scott, we'll just go over what we already talked about so I can make some notes."

Scott mumbled his agreement.

"Tell me about the morning?"

Very matter-of-factly, Scott recited their activities. "Ah, okay. I don't know what time we got up," but he did say that Laci was up first and had cereal for breakfast. He noted that his pregnant wife got sick if she did not eat as soon as she got out of bed.

"I laid around in bed longer, I got up at, I don't know, eight o'clock or so." Brocchini noted that Scott made no mention of anybody making the bed. "I showered. We were watching her favorite show, *Martha Stewart* [*Living*]. Watched a little bit of that."

"You didn't watch the whole thing through?" Detective Brocchini interjected.

"No."

"You remember what part you saw?"

"I don't know, some cooking deal, cookies of some sort. They were talking about what to do with meringue." This trivial fact would become a crucial reference point at trial, one that would prove embarrassing for the prosecution but even more damning for Scott.

"I can't remember your house . . . the converted garage area, is that your TV room?" the detective asked.

"Yeah."

"Did you eat any breakfast?"

"I had a bowl of cereal."

The events Scott described in that first interview struck me as odd when I first reviewed the transcript of this conversation. Police photographs in the kitchen showed no cereal bowls or other breakfast dishes in the sink. There were bowls in the dishwater, but no one looked in the refrigerator to see if Laci had begun marinating French toast for her brunch the next day, as Scott would later claim. This item would have been evidence that she was alive in the morning hours on Christmas Eve. Of course, if Laci had cleaned the kitchen that morning, that would have been one more activity—along with mopping the floor and possibly making the bed—that would have delayed her walk with McKenzie.

"Okay," the detective prompted. "When did you realize you were gonna go fishing?"

"Ah, that was the morning decision, it either—"

"That's a morning decision?" Brocchini asked.

". . . Go play golf at the club or go fishin' . . ." Scott said.

"Okay."

"It seemed too cold to go play golf at the club." Scott chuckled. "So, ya know, decided might as well—"

"Uh-huh." For a passionate golfer, it is rarely too cold to play. However, Christmas Eve out on the bay in a fourteen-foot boat sounds awfully chilly.

"Laci told me what she was gonna do for the day," Scott volunteered.

"And what was that?"

"She was gonna finish cleaning up, like I said, she was mopping the kitchen floor, then take the dog for a walk and then she was going to the store to buy for Christmas morning breakfast tomorrow. That was gonna involve prepping the breakfast, and she was gonna make gingerbread cookies for tonight." Scott explained.

"What was she mopping?" Brocchini asked.

"The tile in the entryway area." When the detective pressed him to be precise, Scott specified that it was the back entryway area.

"Right where the mop was outside?" Brocchini asked, his dark eyes peering over his glasses to watch the young man's response.

"No, no, no." Scott said she was working in the area that led out to the back patio.

"There was a lotta places she planned to go," he continued. "She had me put the bucket by the front door."

"So she asked you to put the mop bucket by the front door?" Brocchini repeated.

"Yeah, she's, you know, eight months pregnant, can't pick it up for anything, so I filled it up for her, put it in, ah, I think that's the central place." Scott didn't seem aware of the mounting inconsistencies in his story. Laci wouldn't have been able to move the bucket, yet he left it some distance from where she was cleaning? For that matter, the mops would have been very difficult for her to use in her condition, as they required someone to bend over and wring out excess water by hand before moving around the house.

"Did you move the bucket back when you came home? How did it get outside?"

"Yeah, yeah."

"So you put it out there?"

Scott mumbled his agreement. "The dog and the cat ran in. Yeah, she wasn't about to lift anything heavy."

Brocchini shifted to another subject. "When you left, do you remember what she was wearing?" Scott described black pants and a white long-sleeved T-shirt without any printing on it. She had not been wearing a jacket or shoes at the time.

"No shoes?" Detective Brocchini asked.

"Uh-huh." Later, Scott said that she usually wore white tennis shoes on her walks with the dog. As for her jacket, he commented, "She usually steals my stuff."

"She uses your stuff?"

"Yeah, because you know. . . . Instead of maternity stuff, so I don't really know."

"You don't know?" Brocchini pressed.

"She could have had hers or mine or nothing, I don't know," Scott continued. Brocchini never asked if these items were missing; he later learned that Scott hadn't bothered to check.

Detective Brocchini touched upon several more topics before

turning to Scott's fishing trip. "Okay, then you hooked your boat up?"

Scott muttered in the affirmative.

"About what time did you leave Modesto?"

"Ah, gosh, I don't know. Extrapolate what time I got the—you know, noon, is that right?"

"Yeah . . . no, one."

"Which one is it, then?" Scott demanded, referring to the marina receipt he had provided earlier.

"Shit, I don't know," Detective Brocchini admitted. "Tuesday, time twelve fifty-four on December twenty-fourth. Okay, so you got there at one o'clock."

"I got there at one?" Scott repeated. "Ah, that should take at least an hour and a half."

"Yeah, okay, it would be eleven-thirty or about," Brocchini calculated.

"Probably longer than that 'cause you can't go over fifty-five with that trailer," Scott explained.

"Did you drive straight there?"

"I did."

"You stop for lunch?" Detective Brocchini asked.

"No."

"Did you buy bait?"

"Nope, I'm not a bait fisherman," Scott declared.

"You didn't buy no lunch, didn't eat nothing?" the investigator persisted.

"Nothin'," Scott insisted. "I was damn hungry with that pizza when I got home."

Having established that Scott had arrived at the marina at about five minutes to one, Brocchini asked how long he had stayed on the water.

Scott could only estimate. "About an hour and a half."

Did he take a chart of the area with him? Scott said no.

"What, you just winged it?" Brocchini asked.

Scott nodded.

"Did you go very far?"

"No—I mean, probably a couple miles. I went north, found a, like, a little island kinda deal there."

"Uh-huh," the detective nodded.

"An island that had a bunch of trash on it. I remember a big sign that said NO LANDING. Looked like some broken piers around it. I just assumed it would be a decent, you know, shallow area."

"Did you troll?"

"Little bit. I mean a lot of, lot of the reason I went was just to get that boat in the water to see, you know." Scott had told the police earlier that he was fishing for sturgeon, but they would soon learn that his experience with sturgeon fishing was limited at best. If that was truly what he'd been doing, he'd chosen the wrong season and the wrong equipment. Furthermore, it was actually illegal to troll for that fish.

Scott's cell phone rang. It was Laci's younger half sister, Amy, calling to say that she and several other family members were back at his house.

"Amy?" Brocchini inquired.

"Yeah," Scott replied without elaboration.

"Is it Laci's sister?"

"Uh-huh. Different mothers, same father," he said dryly.

Brocchini was struck that Scott did not ask his sister-in-law a single question about the search for his wife. Reading the transcript, so was I. If my family member was missing, the first words out of my mouth on any new phone call would have been, "Did you find her?" or "Have you heard anything?" Yet Scott didn't ask Amy a thing. He must have known the answers.

"Okay, so you fish ninety minutes, then what? You go back to the marina?" the detective continued.

"Uh-huh."

"You see anybody, you talk to anybody out there?"

"Talked to a couple guys fishing. They asked me, 'Did you catch anything?' They didn't either. Ah, the guys working, fixing ah, maintenance guys, got a good laugh from me trying to back down the trailer," he explained, grinning. These individuals, if real, never emerged to testify at trial.

"Okay, then what? You drive, how did you get there?"

Scott described his route to the Berkeley Marina along Highway 580 to 50 North.

"You come home the same way?"

"Yeah," Scott replied.

"You have to stop for gas?"

"Stop for gas in Livermore or Pleasanton . . . I think it was a Chevron station. There are buses around."

"How'd you pay?"

Scott told the officer he used a credit card, but he had no receipt.

"Debit or credit card?"

"I don't know which way they count it, debit or credit, when you stick it in there," Scott answered.

"Okay. When you got in the car, who did you call?"

"I called Laci, ah, just as I was leaving the marina."

"Home phone?" Brocchini asked.

Scott said he had called the home number and Laci's mobile phone, leaving messages on both. He gave Brocchini her cell number and password, but said he didn't know if the calls were time stamped. "Try it out," Scott said.

Brocchini listened to the messages, noting that the times were exactly as Scott said. He made no mention of his contemporaneous conversations with his father or his friend, Greg Reed. Both men enjoyed fishing, but Scott said nothing to them about his new boat or his trip to the bay.

After gassing up, Scott drove straight to the warehouse to drop off the boat and then went home.

Brocchini cleared his throat before asking the next question. "When you left, ah, what where you wearing?"

"Blue jeans and a blue T-shirt."

"And what shoes?"

"Ah, Timberland."

"Which jacket?"

Scott paused.

"Did you leave your jacket in the truck?" the detective interrupted.

"When I left the house, I didn't have a jacket on. But I had a, when I was in the warehouse, I had that green pullover on that was in my truck. When it started raining, I had a camo jacket on in the boat and, ah, tan hat."

"Okay, so then you went back to the shop, you unhooked the boat?"

"Uh-huh."

"Did you do anything else?"

"No. I . . . I guess I saw that fax. And I was late getting home so I went straight home," Scott responded.

"Did you try to call anymore?" Brocchini pressed.

"Just, ah, once from the marina, both phones, and then later on, I left a second message on her mobile."

"There was only one from you."

"Well, I left two at home, and I thought I left two on the mobile. Maybe I didn't leave the second one on the mobile," Scott conceded. "One was when I left Berkeley and the other one was, ah, when I was driving in Livermore. The traffic was pretty bad and I knew I wouldn't be home by four, so I gave her a call."

When he got home, Scott backed his car into the driveway next to Laci's SUV, then entered the house through the backyard. When he found McKenzie, dragging his leash, Scott removed the leash and placed it on the patio table. Entering the house through the French doors, he noticed that they were unlocked. He related his movements for Brocchini—dumping the mop water, then washing his clothes.

"Were you calling for Laci?" Brocchini wanted to know.

"Oh, yeah, of course," Scott assured him.

"But she wasn't home?"

"No, I assumed she was at her mom's."

"Okay, then what?"

"I grabbed some pizza from the fridge." He then went to take a shower.

"Did you call her mom?"

"After I got out of the shower, and put clothes on, that's when I checked the messages."

"Were there any?"

"Yeah."

"Yours?"

"There were three, two from me and one from Ron, her stepfather, asking for whipped cream when we came over." With an air of annoyance, he added, "That's when I said, hey man, he's calling me for whipped cream?"

"Did you erase them?"

"No."

The detective made a mental note. Most people would erase unnecessary messages unless there was some other reason to keep them . . . like an alibi. "Okay, so then you called over to her mom's?"

"That's right."

"Had they heard from her?"

"No. Not all day."

"Was that unusual?"

"No. I think we were supposed to be there for dinner at six or six-thirty."

"Okay, so you told Sharon, or did you talk to Ron?"

"Talked to, ah, talked to Mom, Sharon. I asked if Laci was there. She told me no."

"Who called us?" the detective asked.

"Ron."

"Did he tell you he was gonna call?"

"Yeah."

"Who all did you call, other people then?"

Scott said he had immediately called Laci's closest friends, Stacey and Renee. He pointed out that he'd opened the phone book to start calling hospitals when Sharon rang back, but admitted that he wasn't sure about the sequence. According to Scott, Sharon said they would call the police. He should check with the neighbors and then look in the park. "I mean, I may have checked the neighbors, then come back and got on the phone."

"Had any of your neighbors seen or heard anything?" Brocchini asked.

"Ah, first neighbor I checked with was directly across the street; her name's Amy." He was referring to Amy Krigbaum, who lived at 520 Covena Avenue with her roommate, Tara Venable. Scott left a note with his next-door neighbor, Karen Servas. She was the person who later told Scott about finding McKenzie running loose with his leash on. Whatever the actual order of events, less than fifteen minutes transpired between Scott's first call to Sharon and her insistence that he go to the park.

"Was there anything unusual, out of the ordinary in your house?"

"The only unusual things, ah, were the leash . . . and the door unlocked."

"How 'bout the gun? How, how long has that been in your car?"

Scott explained that the Llama .22-caliber had been in his glove box for about a month. Scott had brought the pistol on a trip to Lone Pine with his father to shoot pheasant. "I tried to shoot it once on the trip but it didn't go off."

The detective shifted the focus. "Have you guys had any problems, ah, marriage problems?"

"No," Scott assured him.

"Everything is good?"

"Uh-huh."

"And you have been married four years?"

"Yeah, four or five, I'm thinking. I think this is five. I got married in '97."

Shifting again, Brocchini asked about the park. "Times you've walked in the park you said that, ah, you have seen campers, bums or whatever. Has Laci ever complained to you about somebody bothering her?"

"Naw," Scott replied. "I mean, like I said, I don't think they'd come up to her and accost her in any way. You know, she has times she's felt uncomfortable and thankfully she has the dog. We've called the police a couple times about people down there just to get 'em to move on, you know, and it's not uncommon for Laci or my-self to wake one of these guys or ladies up and tell him to get lost." At this point, Scott still seemed convinced that McKenzie would have warded off any attackers. Later, he would change his story and assert that his wife was probably accosted in the park for her jewelry.

The interview moved on to the Peterson's housekeeper, Margarita.

"Maggie or Margarita, she was there on Monday . . . and obvi-ously she did a lotta work because the house wasn't filthy.

"Why was your wife mopping on Tuesday morning?"

"I don't know. Got me—I mean, she was pretty fastidious about it, though," Scott replied—describing his wife in the past tense.

"Was she?" Brocchini asked.

"With the dog and the cats and her doing, ah, the Christmas deal, that was pretty common." He added, "Yeah, she always had the vacuum or mop out." The past tense again.

"You haven't fired any guns today?" Detective Brocchini asked.

"No, it's been a month since the trip to Lone Pine."

Brocchini asked Scott if they could test for gunshot residue on his hands. Scott hesitated as the detective produced a Gun Shot Residue Kit. He asked, "Will boat motor exhaust register positive?"

"Would you be willing to take a polygraph?" Brocchini responded.

"Sure," Scott replied, but Brocchini noticed that Scott was shak-ing his head from side to side, indicating *No*.

"So what you're telling me, Scott, is you have no idea where Laci is."

"None."

"Just to eliminate you as a suspect, would you be willing to take a polygraph?" the detective repeated.

"Yeah. They're accurate, right?"

"Yeah, yeah," Brocchini assured him, "I mean, it's nothing that can be used against you, but yeah, I believe they're accurate."

"No, I'm certainly willing."

Brocchini added, "It wouldn't be now, it'd be, ya know, in a day or two. . . . It's just like the next step in this thing."

"Sure," Scott replied.

"Really," the detective concluded, "what's left is the flyers, the canvass tomorrow, the media coverage. What concerns me the most is the fact that your dog came home with the leash on. That bothers me."

"No question," Scott agreed.

The interview was wrapping up when Scott asked something quite surprising.

"The only question I have . . . what about resources available? You saw my mother-in-law tonight, um, anyway, you saw some of my friends, myself . . ."

"What do you mean?"

"Counseling and that kind of thing. Can you give us the numbers or do I have to search . . ."

"No, I can give you those numbers. I just don't know. You're probably not going to get any answers today. It's Christmas, I mean."

"Yeah, of course. And there is no need to call if we find Laci in the next days."

"Yeah, I agree. I'll give you those numbers."

"I will need them."

The question is chillingly obvious: How was Scott so sure that he would need counseling, only hours after Laci disappeared? Families of missing people are generally so caught up in the moment—and clinging so dearly to hope—that it's some time before counseling comes into play. Often the investigation and trial in a murder case so focuses the family that it's not until well after the verdict that members really acknowledge their grief and turn to counselors. Yet Scott was already sure he'd need that kind of assistance only hours into the search.

"I'll get you the number to the victim services." Brocchini replied.

The interview was over. It was almost 1:30 A.M.

Looking directly at Scott, Brocchini made a vow. "We'll get the bastard who did this to Laci." He wanted Scott to know that he didn't believe Laci had just wandered off. He already believed she was dead. And he was not going to let go of this case until he solved it.

I believe it was at that moment that the lines were drawn. Scott's deadly game now included the police.

Scott's demeanor was an issue from the start of the investigation. His family, attorneys, and a gaggle of television pundits would make their excuses about how we all respond to tragedy and argue that nothing should be read into the young husband's seemingly callous behavior. However, years of observing human nature would lead the experienced detectives to different conclusions. After the interview, Brocchini carefully recorded that Scott appeared "casual and nonchalant . . . bored, tired, and devoid of urgency."

I think most people would agree that an innocent husband whose pregnant wife is missing would show at least some emotion. Scott Peterson showed nothing of the kind. At the time, it might have been argued that he was simply trying to appear strong around the cops. But in the weeks that followed, he would demonstrate an extraordinary ability to turn his feelings on and off at will—in his private behavior with Amber Frey and during his public interviews with female members of the media.

It was Detective Al Brocchini who first noted Scott's strange behavior. Additionally, in his immediate search of Scott's truck, he spotted items that were removed only hours later, including the umbrellas, tarps, jacket, and lures. By acting fast, he managed to survey Scott's workplace before anyone could clean up the concrete particles or erase the computer hard drives. Had Detective Brocchini followed standard procedure and treated Laci's disappearance as a standard missing persons case, that valuable evidence might have been lost.

That Brocchini got Scott on tape at midnight, only seven hours after the initial call, was another important coup. By the next day, Lee Peterson was warning his son to refuse a polygraph. Had Brocchini delayed, it's likely that there would never have been a taped interview with Scott to show to a jury.

Scott returned to his home after 4:00 A.M. on Christmas Day, only to find the exterior completely encircled in yellow crime scene tape. As he entered the empty house, the phone rang. It was Laci's brother, Brent, asking him to come to his mother-in-law's house. Scott declined.

Why wouldn't he want to be with family at a time like this?

On Christmas morning, residents of the dusty Northern California city woke up to a front-page headline: "Woman Vanishes on Walk, Police Start Widespread Search." On television, local stations were reporting that the search for the missing Modesto woman was intensifying. As over two dozen police officers combed the La Loma neighborhood, Detective Brocchini was knocking on doors.

His first stop was 520 Covena, where he met with Scott and Laci's neighbor Amy Krigbaum, her roommate, Tara Venable, and Venable's twelve-year-old son, Michael Thomas.

When asked if they had seen anything out of the ordinary, Krigbaum spoke up. She recalled being awakened around 10:30 on Christmas Eve morning by a neighbor's dog barking. She could not be sure exactly whose dog was making the noise.

The women hadn't seen Laci walking in some time, they told the police; they assumed it was due to her advanced pregnancy. "We sometimes feel sorry for Laci because she is alone so often," Krigbaum said. Scott traveled a lot, and occasionally spent a night or more away from home on business.

In a second interview with Detective Brocchini, Krigbaum would recall that when Laci Peterson was at home and awake, her typical routine was to raise her two front window shades in the morning and lower them in the evening when the sun went down. On Christmas Eve morning, Krigbaum observed, the shades were not raised. She simply assumed that Laci and Scott were away. When she put her Christmas turkey in the oven around 1:15 that afternoon, Scott's truck was not in the driveway and the shades on the house were still drawn.

Around 4:25 P.M., Krigbaum went to the Save Mart for marshmallows. She estimated she was gone about twenty minutes. When she returned home, Scott's pickup was backed into the Petersons' driveway—an unusual way for him to park.

At 5:30, Scott appeared at her door, asking if she had seen Laci. Scott said he'd been trying to call his wife all day on her cell, but never got an answer. He appeared nervous and volunteered that he had been out golfing all day. She watched Scott walk over to another neighbor's home, then saw him return home a few minutes later.

Brocchini next interviewed the Petersons' maid, Margarita Nava, at her home on Jarena Drive. As Scott said, she was hired only six weeks earlier; the twenty-third was her third visit to the residence. She arrived at 8:45 A.M. and finished her chores about two o'clock that afternoon.

Laci was in the house that day, and according to Nava she complained about feeling extremely tired. The housekeeper didn't believe that Laci would have walked the dog in her fatigued condition, but she didn't believe the Petersons were having any trouble in their marriage. Having watched the couple work together on the nursery, she thought they were both very excited at the prospect of a baby.

Brocchini asked about the very dirty towels he had observed atop the Petersons' washing machine. Nava explained that she'd used them to clean the outside of the window frames and the inside of the fireplace screen.

"Where did you leave the towels?" he asked.

"I left them in a bucket so they could be washed at a later date."

Yet Scott had told the police he'd found the towels inside the washing machine. A seemingly minor discrepancy, but *someone* took them out of that bucket to fill it with water. Was this at Laci's request, or did Scott have some cleaning of his own to do?

By 11:30 A.M., Brocchini called Detective Craig Grogan and requested that the Homicide Division become officially involved in the investigation.

Modesto cops would see it as a lucky break that Grogan was next up on the rotation. Like Brocchini, Grogan was a seasoned professional. Fellow officers in the department had nothing but praise for the stocky detective with the thinning hair and bushy moustache who'd joined Modesto's Crimes Against Persons Unit in 1998 after thirteen years in policing. Besides investigating homicides, kidnappings, sexual assaults, and other violent crimes, Grogan's duties included missing persons cases.

Technically, Grogan shouldn't have been available to take the Peterson case. Two days earlier, a storeowner had shot and killed a robber, but Grogan knew it was a case requiring little or no investigation, so instead of taking it himself, he let a patrol officer handle it. Many investigators would have wanted the open-and-shut case to "get off the bubble"—that is, to move to the end of the rotation. Interestingly, the next officer on the rotation was in the middle of a contentious divorce. It would have been difficult for him to commit the time and attention the Peterson case would require. What Grogan didn't foresee was just how much the intense investigation would test his marriage. Grogan, who lived on a ranch a good distance out of town with his wife and two small children, would miss his children's birthdays while working on the case. On countless occasions, he was forced to tell his wife he was too busy to take her calls. Outside observers rarely understand the toll these cases take on the officers and their own families.

As Grogan caught up on the details of Laci's disappearance, other investigators hit the pavement. Detective Jon Buehler knocked on Karen Servas's door just before noon. Servas, the Petersons' next-door neighbor, had already told police how she'd discovered McKenzie the previous morning. Now she gave her official report.

Around 10:30 that morning, about the same time that the other neighbors, Amy Krigbaum and Tara Venable, had heard a dog barking, Servas was backing out of her driveway. She spotted the golden retriever standing near the street. Checking his tags to make sure it was McKenzie, she decided to take him home.

The Petersons' front gate was locked, so Servas circled around to the second gate near the swimming pool. Seeing nothing unusual, she left the dog in the yard. She did notice that his leash was very dirty, so much so that she went back into her own home to wash her hands before getting back in her car to go run errands. She recalled a man walking near her car at the time, but noticed nothing unusual or alarming about him.

Concerned for Laci's safety, Buehler pressed Servas for more information. From what he'd learned about her family and life, it just didn't seem likely that she would simply leave home without notice.

Servas described her relationship with Scott Peterson as warm and friendly. She and her ten-year-old son were frequently invited to swim in the Petersons' pool; from time to time, Scott helped her with chores and repairs around her house. She described the couple as active and upbeat. They enjoyed entertaining at their home and appeared to have a good relationship. Servas had last seen Laci and Scott on Sunday, the twenty-second, when they told her that their baby was a boy. They were planning to name him Conner.

When he finished with Karen Servas, Detective Buehler joined Al Brocchini to check out several homeless encampments along the south side of Dry Creek Park. The area was a scattering of small tents, with clothing hanging from the trees, bags of rubbish, old wet mattresses, and plastic tarps amid the camping supplies and broken-down barbecues. When nothing appeared to be related to Laci's disappearance, the officers left the area and went their separate ways.

At 1:00 P.M., Buehler joined Grogan and Doug Mansfield, an agent from the California Department of Justice, at the division office. Scott Peterson's polygraph was scheduled for that afternoon, and Mansfield was there to assist with the test.

As the men talked, Buehler received a phone call. Scott Peterson had changed his mind, claiming that his father, Lee, suggested the exam wasn't a good idea.

It was one of many promises Scott would make during the case that he failed to keep. I suspect that Scott never intended to take the polygraph, and that his father merely provided the perfect excuse when he advised him against it. Scott never seemed concerned that he would have to face up to his lies, sometimes only hours after making them. Whatever new problem he'd created for himself, it seemed his only concern was to put off any reckoning just a little longer.

Knowing that Scott was at police headquarters attending a press conference that afternoon, the officers walked over to confront him in person. Once inside, Grogan strode over to Scott Peterson and introduced himself. Grogan said he'd just been assigned as lead investigator in the case, and wanted to familiarize himself "with him and members of Laci's family." Whether or not Scott decided to take the polygraph, Grogan added, there were additional questions the detective needed to ask. Scott didn't have to agree to an interview and was free to leave, but his assistance would be appreciated. Scott said he would stay, telling Grogan that he wanted to help.

Scott followed Grogan, Detective Buehler, and Agent Mansfield to an interrogation room to talk. Some of the rooms had audio and video facilities, but since Scott had already completed a taped interview with Brocchini, Grogan chose a regular conference room. This was likely a misstep on Grogan's part. From the start, I've believed that Scott's own words—and his inconsistencies—were the most damning things against him. Every time Scott was recorded, his words and mannerisms would come back to haunt him. Sadly, taped interviews have become especially critical today, as the public has grown increasingly suspicious of the police. Once upon a time, when an officer took the stand, his uniform gave him instant credibility. Nowadays, it seems that police testimony is considered suspect until substantiated by clear forensic evidence or audiovisual corroboration. At trial Grogan would rely on his notes, but if this interview had been on tape, I believe his testimony would have been unimpeachable.

Scott was asked to give the officers some background about his relationship with Laci. He told them about meeting her at California Polytechnic University in San Luis Obispo. They were married on August 9, 1997, and moved to Modesto two years ago. Laci was pregnant with their first child, a boy.

Scott appeared to be close to Laci's family; he referred to Sharon Rocha as "Mom." But Laci's biological father, Dennis Rocha, who lived in Escalon, California, had little contact with the family. Scott described his wife as "outgoing," and told the investigators that she'd recently left her job as a substitute teacher in the Sylvan School District. He gave the police the names of two of her closest friends, Stacey Boyers and Renee Tomlinson.

As a manager and fertilizer salesman for Tradecorp, Scott traveled extensively. Although his hours were flexible, he generally left for work around 9:30 every morning. Tradecorp had wanted him to work from an office in Fresno, but he and Laci had selected Modesto because her family was nearby.

Next, Scott described the three days leading up to Laci's disappearance. He could recall nothing out of the ordinary, he said. He'd occupied himself with yard work, a little golf, and some gym time at the tony Del Rio Country Club, eating at home, and renting movies.

On Monday, December 23, Scott arrived at his office about ten o'clock and worked until two in the afternoon. Laci went to her noon maternity yoga class, and later that afternoon Scott joined her for an OB/GYN appointment. Scott told the police that the baby's heart rate was 150 beats per minute. They'd asked the doctor to reveal the child's sex months earlier because "Laci could not wait." Scott dropped Laci at home, went to the gym from four to five in the afternoon, stopped by his office for the mail, then returned home.

Early that evening, they'd taken a trip to Salon Salon, where Laci's sister worked as a stylist. Amy cut Scott's hair while showing Laci how to trim his hair at home. Scott didn't mention that Laci had brought her own curling iron along to the salon for some individual instruction—seemingly a minor detail, yet one that would become relevant at trial in determining whether Laci was alive the next morning: The Petersons' housekeeper told police that she'd put the curling iron in the cabinet when she cleaned on the twenty-third, yet official photographs revealed that it was resting on the sink the morning Laci disappeared. Scott's defense team would use the picture to argue that Laci was obviously alive that morning, and used the iron to style her hair. Yet the prosecution was able to show that she'd actually removed it from the cabinet the night before when she took it to the salon.

After the haircut, the couple got some pizza at Mountain Mike's, watched *The Rookie* on tape, and were in bed at the usual time.

Scott then described the crucial morning hours on December 24. Laci was already up, he said, when he got out of bed around 8 A.M. Scott recalled that she was marinating French toast in Grand Marnier for the Christmas brunch. Remember, there was never any testimony about the contents of the Peterson refrigerator to confirm or deny this assertion. Had the officers checked the refrigerator, it could have helped to prove or disprove Scott's story about their activities that morning.

Scott told the investigators that Laci was wearing a plain white long-sleeved pullover shirt with a crew neck, and black maternity pants with an elastic waistband. Once again he repeated her schedule—the plan to walk McKenzie, go grocery shopping, then bake gingerbread that afternoon.

Despite her casual attire, Scott said, Laci was wearing a pair of diamond earrings, a gold and diamond wristwatch, and a diamond solitaire around her neck; some of the items, he said, she'd recently inherited from her grandmother. Her wedding ring was at a local jewelry store being reworked to include her grandmother's stones. The cost of this work was to be one of Scott's Christmas gifts to Laci. If there were other presents, they were never found. The police who'd checked the presents under the Petersons' tree were especially attentive to any gifts from Scott to Laci. After all, if you're planning to kill your wife, why spend money on presents she'd never open?

Scott next described Laci's normal exercise routine to the officers. She would walk in the morning after "the frost." Entering the park from the north end of Covena Avenue, she would turn right or eastbound toward the tennis courts, then complete a half-mile loop before returning home. The walk generally took about forty-five minutes, he said, and she always took McKenzie with her. The dog wasn't particularly protective of Scott, but Laci was a different story. He told Brocchini that he'd once warned the "pool guy" not to get between her and the dog. Laci didn't generally carry pepper spray or a cell phone with her when she walked. Although he'd already told Brocchini that it was unusual for her to leave the house without locking the door, he now said that Laci sometimes left the door unlocked.

It was after breakfast when Scott decided to go fishing at Berkeley Marina. He'd researched the area on the Internet after purchasing his boat two weeks earlier. When asked if Laci had ever gone fishing with him, Scott said "only once." On their very first date about eight years ago, he had taken her out on the water for a deep-sea fishing trip, and she became very seasick. Laci refused to ever go boating again. This incident would give rise to one of the most poignant statements made by Sharon Rocha during the sentencing phase of Scott's trial.

Scott told the cops he was sure he'd left the house around 9:30; Martha Stewart was on TV at the time, talking about meringue and cookies. This fact would prove embarrassing to the prosecution at trial, but would also provide a devastating time line to be used against the defense.

That Tuesday morning was his first outing with the new boat. On the twenty-second, he had obtained a two-day license and some fishing lures at Big 5 Sporting Goods. Just hours before, Scott had been unable to give Officer Evers even the sketchiest account of his plans. Now, with Grogan, he was very detailed. He would be fishing for sturgeon and striper in the bay.

When he got to the warehouse, Scott said, he checked his e-mail; there was a reminder to ship a golf bag he recently sold on eBay. Scott also sent a holiday note to his employer. As he'd said before, he then assembled a woodworking tool called a mortiser—a strange use of his time for a man heading off on a fishing trip. Finally, he cleaned up the office, unloaded tools from his toolbox, and hooked up his boat. He left for the bay shortly after eleven o'clock. When Agent Mansfield asked if he'd called Laci before leaving the office, Scott replied that he "never spoke to his wife while at work."

While the timing of the e-mails could be determined, there was never any proof that Scott was cleaning or assembling tools while at his office. The prosecution would argue that he used these moments to hide Laci's body between the boat seats, then covered the boat with the brown tarp originally discovered in the back of his pickup.

Once again, Scott described his drive along Highway 132 to 580 and the I-80 North Interchange. He recalled reaching the Berkeley Marina at about one o'clock, putting five dollars into the "Iron Ranger" automated parking meter, and collecting a timed parking receipt. He loaded two fishing rods and a tackle box into the boat, but forgot the brand new lures he had purchased only two days earlier. When questioned why he hadn't brought any food or water, Scott said he knew time was limited; his main mission was simply to get the boat in the water.

Scott claimed that he'd stayed out for about an hour. Powered by a fifteen-horsepower engine, he motored northwest until he reached a shallow area along "a trash-filled island with a posting that read, NO LANDING. " He had no problems trolling for sturgeon, although he had forgotten the saltwater lures.

According to Scott, the weather turned bad and it began to rain, so he returned to the marina. While loading his boat, he ran the trailer into the dock, giving several bystanders a laugh. Once on the road, he called his wife. It was 2:15 when he left the "Hey, beautiful" message at home, then another on Laci's cell phone with the dead battery.

Traffic delays in Pleasanton and Livermore slowed his return. He wasted more time by stopping for thirteen dollars' worth of gas, duly noted on his debit card. Realizing he would never make it back in time to pick up the gift basket before four o'clock, he placed another call to Laci—again, no answer.

Driving at 55 mph because he was towing the trailer, Scott said, he arrived at the warehouse about 4:30. Quickly disconnecting the boat, he was back on the road within five minutes. Moments later, he arrived home to find McKenzie still wearing his leash and the back door unlocked.

For the second time in less than twenty-four hours, Scott described what he did next—an account that still doesn't make sense to me. The dark, empty house set off no alarms in the young man's mind. Instead of looking around for Laci, he had a casual snack, washed some clothes, and took a shower. Were these the actions of a father-to-be with a seriously pregnant wife who should have been home to greet him?

Before he could describe his call to Sharon Rocha, the investigators asked Scott about his overall relationship with Laci. It was good, he responded. The couple never shouted at each other or fought. They were both in good physical health. Laci took only prenatal pills; neither had any medical problems or history of mental illness. They lived on a budget and saved money by eating most meals at home. The local Barnes & Noble bookstore was a favorite haunt. Just two weekends before his wife's disappearance, the couple had stopped there to buy children's books for their unborn son.

While Scott took care of finances and paid the household bills, Laci was a "good money manager." She didn't make extravagant purchases. He added that she was pleased he'd bought the boat and become a member of the Del Rio Country Club.

When Scott laid out the family finances, however, the picture was one of a couple living from paycheck to paycheck. Scott's current monthly income was around $5,000, plus roughly $1,400 in travel reimbursements. Yet his regular expenses, as he outlined, nearly equaled his salary:

$1,250/mo.—House payment

650/mo.—Truck payment

750/mo.—Credit card payment

500/mo.—Home improvement payment

600/mo.—Food bill

390/mo.—Club payment

300/mo.—Retirement installment

240/mo.—Life insurance bill

$150/mo.—Utilities

50/mo.—Cell phone bill

The Petersons' monthly outlay totaled at least $4,880—just two hundred dollars less than Scott's salary. Their savings account hovered around $2,000. Laci had quit working and expressed no desire to resume an outside job. Although testimony at trial did not support a financial motive for murder, the young couple was spending almost everything they brought in. Their accumulated savings left little to pay for a new infant . . . especially when it became clear how much money Scott was spending on his extracurricular activities.

Asked to elaborate about the life insurance expense, Scott told police that he had a Whole Life Plan, and immediately recited his agent's name and phone number. Laci had a separate policy, but he couldn't remember the payout amount.

Although Scott traveled extensively on his own, he and Laci did vacation together on occasion. In August, Scott went to The Cliffs, a resort at Avila Beach in San Luis Obispo with a friend; four months earlier, he and Laci had gone to Hawaii with another couple. The couple spent a few days in Carmel with Scott's parents just a week before she disappeared, and he described three overseas business trips he'd taken himself that year, all for corporate meetings.

The investigators also asked Scott about visitors to the Covena home in the last week. Their housekeeper Margarita, who came Monday mornings at 9:30 and left around 2:00 in the afternoon, was the only person Scott recalled. Before her, his in-laws, Sharon and Ron, had been the last people to visit.

Scott told the officers he had never been in a fight in his life and had no criminal history. "What about all the guns?" Brocchini asked. Scott listed his weapons:

.22-caliber Llama semiautomatic handgun (which Detective Brocchini confiscated)

20-gauge Browning

.22 Ruger

.223 Ruger

12-gauge semiautomatic Browning

12-gauge semiautomatic Mossberg

12-gauge side-by-side Ithaca

20-gauge semiautomatic Smith & Wesson

Scott said he last fired a gun while pheasant hunting in November. The .22 was confiscated by Brocchini from his glove box. Scott reported the 9-millimeter Glock as stolen from his car outside a Firestone tire store in 2001. Scott sued the store over the theft, his first small claims suit, and collected seven hundred dollars from the company.

The detectives finally asked what Scott thought had happened to Laci. By then, Scott had settled on the idea that a transient had assaulted her in the park, probably because of her expensive jewelry. Recently, he told detectives, his wife had become concerned about stories of rapes and assaults in the park. She'd started thinking about carrying pepper spray on her walks, but she never did.

The two investigators tried to keep Scott talking. Did the couple have any future plans? Scott said he and Laci intended to move to San Luis Obispo when Conner began school. He wanted to buy an olive ranch. Grogan remarked that Scott seemed very poised in social settings; he must be a very successful salesman. Scott smiled and thanked him, saying it was important to have those skills in the sales business. Did Laci ever embarrass him in social situations? Not at all, Scott replied; she was actually quite helpful.

The interview concluded around 4:30 P.M., when Detective Grogan learned that Scott's parents were downstairs demanding to see their son. Grogan accompanied Scott to the waiting room. Lee Peterson told the detective they had just driven up from San Diego to help their son. Tall, slender, and slightly stooped, Lee said that Scott should not be interviewed without an attorney present. Grogan responded that his son had declined to take a polygraph that might exclude him as a suspect. Before his father could speak, Scott again refused the test.

What did Lee Peterson know? Cops sensed he was suspicious of his son.

Leaving the Petersons, Grogan returned to the bureau to compare notes with Brocchini and Buehler. The detectives found several inconsistencies in their respective conversations with the young man. Their suspicions were heightened when Brocchini added that a boat patrol officer at the Berkeley Marina reported that there'd been absolutely no rain on Christmas Eve.

It was time to put Scott under a microscope.

Grogan prepared a search warrant for Scott's home, business, vehicles, and boat. They would serve the warrants the very next day. Then, at 4:30 P.M., Brocchini's cell phone rang. It was Scott Peterson, wanting a progress report.

"Officers did a grid search last night and then repeated it today," Detective Brocchini said. "There are three dog teams there, and mounted sheriffs are coming over. The sheriff's helicopter has also searched the area with a heat detector."

"Have you used cadaver dogs yet?" Scott asked.

The detective was shocked.

"Cadaver dogs are used for sniffing out dead bodies," Brocchini explained. "Have you already given up on finding Laci alive?"

# CHAPTER THREE

# SCOTT AND LACI

Despite their heightened suspicions, the Modesto police had little to go on during the first few days of the investigation. But one thing was clear: They needed to know more about Scott and Laci's background. Through countless interviews with friends and family and analysis by the California Department of Justice, investigators began to stitch together a "victimology" report that would provide a look into the lives of Scott and Laci Peterson. Many aspects of this report have never before been disclosed.

Thirty years old at the time his wife vanished, Scott Peterson was born in San Diego's Sharp Hospital on October 24, 1972. He was the only child of Lee and Jackie Peterson, who had married the previous year. Both of Scott's parents had children from previous relationships. When Scott was born, his father, Lee, already had two sons and a daughter from his first marriage to Mary Kamanski. Mark, Joe, and Susan lived with their mother in San Diego, but visited with their dad on weekends.

Jackie Peterson had three children from previous relationships, but she had given up two of them, Anne Bird and Don Chapman, for adoption soon after their birth, and Scott didn't learn about them until he was an adult. Their fathers' identities remain unknown.

One source close to the family told me that Jackie reportedly considered giving up her third child, John, as she had done with the previous two children. When her doctor advised against it, however, Jackie raised John as a single mother, and Lee adopted John after he married Jackie.

John was six years old when Scott was born. At the time, Lee worked for a trucking company, and Jackie had a small dress boutique. Before Scott's arrival, the family was somewhat estranged. However, the new baby became a focal point for their love and attention, and was said to have reunited the "fractured family"—a phrase that would be used many times in Scott's trial.

Scott's half-siblings, John and Susan, would later testify about those early years. They were both thrilled to have a little brother. He was carried around so much that family members joked about being afraid that "he might not learn how to walk." Scott's childhood nickname, Scooter, captured his upbeat charm perfectly. Always smiling, always quiet and well behaved, Scott apparently could do no wrong. John could think of only one incident where the boy displayed a temper. At age four, after a light spanking by his father, Scott left the room. A moment later he came back and punched his father in the stomach.

That was the only memorable disturbance in Scott's gentle demeanor until Christmas Eve 2002.

When the fair-haired boy turned four, his family moved to Scripps Ranch, a neighborly middle-class suburb in northeast San Diego. Scott's father began a shipping and packing business nearby, and his young son would often accompany him on deliveries. Witness after witness described their close father-son relationship. Together they enjoyed fishing and pheasant hunting on the weekends, and from the age of five Scott went along with his father to the local driving range to learn golf. He practiced with a special sawed-off driver his father made for him. Lee had saved the homemade club in the basement of the family's home as a memento of those days. By age seven, Scott joined the Peterson clan on golf outings at a local country club. Yet he rarely made it to the eighteenth hole, opting instead to take his small fishing pole to a nearby river.

Lee described Scott as a happy, "shiny" baby who rarely cried. His own childhood hadn't been as bright as the one he gave his children. Lee's grandmother had immigrated to the United States from Lithuania, settling in Minnesota, where the family lived without running water. Just as Scott accompanied his father on deliveries, Lee had followed his mother on her housekeeping jobs. As a young man, he joined his father on his rounds repairing typewriters. Lee eventually joined the business.

Lee wanted his family to enjoy a better lifestyle, and for years he had struggled financially to make it happen. The family finally turned the corner when they moved to Rancho Santa Fe. When Scott was ten, the family headed to Poway, an inland city of about 50,000, where he attended Painted Rock Middle School. He went on to the University of San Diego High School, a Catholic preparatory school set high above the city overlooking the Pacific Ocean. While there, Scott honed his passion for golf. When he got his driver's license at sixteen, his parents rewarded him with a used Peugeot sedan.

Police learned that Scott had at least two high school girlfriends. The first was Stephanie Smith, who began dating Scott when he was a senior and she was in the tenth grade. When the police interviewed Stephanie, she described how Scott had lavished her with gifts and flowers. He picked up the tab on all their dates, and even presented her with a special ring for Valentine's Day.

The two had been dating for nearly four months when Stephanie heard rumors about a classmate named Dawn Hood. Friends were saying that Dawn had been seen driving Scott's new car and holding hands with the young man.

When Stephanie confronted him about the rumors, however, she found his response hard to believe. Dawn and he had swapped cars, he said, so she could try out his new wheels. When pressed, Scott vehemently denied there was anything going on with Dawn. The two were just "friends."

Stephanie asked about the hand-holding.

"I hold hands with lots of my friends," he responded.

"That was the last straw," Stephanie told the police. She asked Scott to return the items she had given him, and immediately called it quits. Not long after, Scott began seeing Dawn Hood exclusively.

The police also located Dawn, who confirmed that she and Scott had dated for about eight months, beginning in the spring of 1990.

They were "health freaks," she said, and refrained from alcohol and drugs. She and Stephanie both described Scott as a gentleman.

Dawn told investigators that she performed community service for one of her high school classes, and that Scott frequently accompanied her to a facility for children with disabilities. Scott also did volunteer work at a homeless shelter as part of a school course.

Dawn and Scott broke up in the fall of 1990, when Scott moved to Arizona to attend college. Dawn remembered Scott as "a loner." Her family was friendly with Scott while they were dating, and he sometimes stayed with her parents, even when Dawn wasn't there. Dawn had never noticed any violent or strange behavior during the entire time she knew him, and she couldn't imagine that Scott had anything to do with his wife's disappearance.

Scott spent one semester at Arizona State University, but he told police that he'd grown disillusioned with the school after deciding he didn't like the golf coach. The facts are probably quite different. One of his teammates was the now-famous golfer Phil Mikelson. When reporters asked him about his relationship with Scott, he couldn't really remember him because they were never "in the same league." Phil was a rising star; Scott was not. It is far more likely that Scott retreated to Cuesta Junior College in San Luis Obispo when he realized that a PGA career wasn't in his future.

Perched above the Pacific Ocean, halfway between Los Angeles and San Francisco, San Luis Obispo welcomes thousands of tourists every year. Scenic Hearst Castle, the palace-like estate of publishing magnate William Randolph Hearst, is located nearby. Scott attended the junior college for about eighteen months, made the Dean's List, and played on the school's golf team. He paid for school by working. According to his mother, he never asked his parents for financial assistance. He surprised them both when he announced that he was moving out of their house to room with two golfing teammates. Lee Peterson told a local reporter that his son and his friends surfaced the flat roof of their new home with artificial grass. From there, they would hit golf balls into a neighboring cow pasture. According to friends, Scott dated while attending school there, but he was never seriously involved with anyone. They said he liked things his own way.

In 1994 Scott transferred again, this time to California Polytechnic State University, a four-year-college in San Luis Obispo. There he earned a bachelor of science in agriculture. Scott's friends described him as laid-back, focused, and someone who rarely displayed emotion.

While he was at Cal Poly, Scott cut back his studies, taking just two courses each quarter while working at a golf club and waiting tables downtown at the Pacific Café. There, he met a young waitress named Michelle. After they'd been dating for about eighteen months, Michelle told police, Scott started talking about getting married. When he became jealous and overbearing, she broke off the relationship—but only after a fight.

"Scott did not want to take no for an answer," Michelle recalled. "He would hold all his emotions in for a long time, and then have an emotional breakdown." Scott cried on a number of occasions, begging her for another chance. Even after they split, Scott would come to Michelle's house, eager to woo her back, trying to rekindle their sexual relationship.

Still, it was only a few weeks after Scott and Michelle split up in 1995 that he began dating Laci Rocha.

Laci was also attending Cal Poly. One of her friends was employed at the Pacific Café, and Laci would occasionally come in to visit. Scott, always charming and well mannered, caught her attention, and she asked her friend about him. Scott, in turn, had noticed the petite, curvy former cheerleader with the engaging smile.

Laci asked her friend to give Scott her phone number. When handed the slip, Scott assumed his coworker was playing a trick and tossed the paper in the trash. When he realized it wasn't a joke, he retrieved the number.

From the moment she wrote the note, Laci was confident that Scott would call her. Indeed, she'd already told her mother she'd met the man she wanted to marry—that she'd fallen in love with Scott on sight. Sharon asked if she'd gone out with him yet. Laci said no, but predicted that they'd go out together soon. This was entirely in character for Laci. A confident young woman, she could also be headstrong and was used to getting her way. Both her mother and her sister, Amy, said the same thing: *If Laci put her mind to something, look out.*

Before long, Scott did ask her out—on the deep-sea fishing trip he'd mentioned to the police. Laci became seasick, however, and the excursion ended sooner than planned. Still, the attraction between Scott and Laci was strong and the two continued dating. Laci told her mother that she'd found her lifelong partner.

Several weeks later, Scott invited both women to the Pacific Café. He greeted them politely as they entered the trendy restaurant, and led them to their table, where he had specially arranged a dozen white roses at Sharon's place setting and a dozen red ones for her daughter.

Scott's parents also met Laci soon after the two began dating. The Petersons liked the bubbly, dark-haired beauty from the start. But their other children found it surprising that Scott had picked a girl with a colorful sunflower tattooed on her left ankle. They thought it was "outrageous."

What Laci didn't realize was that, while all this was going on, her new boyfriend was still pleading with his ex, Michelle, to take him back. Scott brought Laci into the Pacific Café during Michelle's shift to try to make her jealous, and even introduced the two women. At some point, Laci apparently caught on and became upset, but in the end she prevailed. Michelle moved away from San Luis Obispo about two months after their breakup and never saw or spoke to Scott again.

By Christmas 1995, Laci had moved into Scott's apartment. Her holiday gift to him was the auburn-haired puppy they named McKenzie. Laci graduated from Cal Poly the following spring with a degree in ornamental horticulture. Scott had avoided alcohol in high school, while dating Dawn Hood, but with Laci, he developed a taste for good wine. Indeed, Scott's parents told investigators that when they dined with Scott and Laci, they insisted that the younger couple pay for their own bottles because they had such expensive taste.

When I started reading about the couple's early years together, Scott's personality traits began making sense to me. A sociopath is quite capable of morphing into the very person his companion needs. It is this ability to manipulate, ultimately for selfish reasons, that is a hallmark of this behavior disorder.

Just as he had with Stephanie the health nut, and then again with Janet Ilse the vegetarian, Scott seemed to get through life by mirroring the needs of his companions. He quickly became, at least on the surface, the person Laci wanted him to be: the rising young entrepreneur and suburban father, who spent time remodeling the home, working in the yard, and joining her to entertain friends and neighbors. Later, with Amber Frey, Scott would go from a man who never attended church, to one who professed in a letter from jail that he hoped to get out and "do the work of the Lord."

Shortly after Scott met Laci, he learned about his two siblings who had been given up for adoption before his birth. Don Chapman of Pennsylvania and Anne Bird of San Francisco were first reunited with each other and then with their biological mother, Jackie Peterson. As he seemingly did with every other aspect of his life, Scott took the news quite calmly and quickly developed a relationship with his additional siblings.

In researching this book, I had the opportunity to sit down with Anne Bird, a bright, articulate, well-spoken woman with a highly defined sense of ethics and integrity. She seemed concerned that she might know something important to this case, and out of a need to "tell the truth," as she put it, she spoke out in detail for the first time over dinner at a California restaurant.

Anne came into the Peterson family in 1996 when her half brother, Don Chapman, contacted her to ask whether she wanted to meet her biological mother. After conducting a search on his own behalf, Don located Jackie Peterson and sent her a certified letter saying that he was her son. Jackie reportedly opened the letter in front of her family, and then "freaked out" because no one else, including Lee, had ever heard about Don and Anne.

Anne was hesitant, but eventually green-lighted Jackie to contact her. She first met Scott when he rang the doorbell at Jackie's home and she let him in. He could not stop staring at her all evening. She was thinner then, and the two looked very much alike, especially their eyes.

Anne believes that Scott was immediately taken with her. She was worldly and well-traveled, having spent seven years in London, where she attended Oxford University. She'd also been to Brussels and other European cities, experiences Scott had only wished for. Her adoptive parents were wealthy and Anne had a lot of well-to-do friends. At twenty-two, she had landed a great job at the Golden Door Fitness Resort and Spa in Escondido, and then later at a spa in Mexico. Scott was impressed with the life Anne had lived—so much so that his sister, Susan Caudillo, grew envious of their relationship. Later, when Scott became a suspect, she carefully monitored everything Anne would say, as though she was concerned that Anne might slip up and mention something that would help the police.

Over time, Anne learned a great deal about Jackie and her background, but the stories her biological mother told changed continually. She recalled several different versions of Jackie's upbringing, including the one Jackie later recited at Scott's trial. In that version, Scott's mother told the court that her father had been killed on December 24—the same date Laci disappeared. He was struck in the head with a lead pipe for the $800 in his pocket. Jackie was just eight years old at the time. Apparently the murder took a toll on Jackie's mother. Some of her children were sent to live with various relatives, and Jackie was placed in an orphanage.

Jackie's story did include some truths, but Anne learned from other family members that it also contained some fiction. For one thing, her father had been killed on December 23, not December 24, as Jackie testified in court. There were other embellishments, but like Scott, Jackie always stayed close to the truth.

There were other things about Jackie that disturbed Anne. When they first met, Scott's mother, who had lifelong lung problems and often relied on oxygen to help with her breathing, had spent some time talking to Anne about lung transplants and how hard it was to find a donor. Anne couldn't help wondering whether she was being sized up as a potential organ donor.

According to Anne, Jackie's husband was introduced to her as "Pete." Only later, after the case broke, did Anne learn that Lee Peterson had started going by "Pete" in the wake of some money troubles in the 1980s. At the time, Lee and Jackie were reportedly living high in Rancho Santa Fe. Jackie was driving a Rolls Royce, and Lee a Ferrari. They owned an expensive home that was mortgaged to the hilt. It seemed the couple had a penchant for expensive things "whatever the cost . . . even if they couldn't pay for them."

Eventually, Anne was told, the Petersons moved to Morro Bay, where Lee began using the name Pete. While she was already in the picture at the time of Laci and Scott's wedding, Anne reported, she wasn't invited to attend. Laci didn't want to be upstaged on "her day," Anne felt, by a new member of the family everyone would want to meet.

On August 9, 1997, Scott and Laci were married at the Sycamore Mineral Springs Resort in San Luis Obispo, where Laci later worked as a banquet coordinator. Nestled in the lush wooded hillsides of the Avila Valley, the luxurious resort was a popular spot for weddings, family reunions, conferences, and retreats. The grounds were densely planted with bougainvillea and other brilliant tropical flowers, lush sycamores, and oak trees.

Laci's parents, Sharon and Ron, gave the couple about $7,000 for their wedding; Scott's parents, Jackie and Lee, contributed a similar amount, and Scott and Laci covered the rest of the expenses. The ceremony was private but well attended; it was a glorious, sunlit day, and Laci was resplendent in a sleeveless wedding gown with a square-cut neck. She wore her dark hair in a sweep adorned with an elaborate headpiece and flowing white veil. Their wedding day was a mix of the traditional and the personal: The three-tiered wedding cake was dotted with exquisite flowers, and the couple celebrated their nuptials with a champagne toast. Scott raised a glass to his new in-laws, Sharon and Ron, thanking them for their "perfect daughter."

Yet beneath the surface, as investigators later learned, the wedding day was less than perfect. The resort's general manager, Roger Wightman, told police that before the wedding he saw Scott sitting at the bar, drinking and "hitting on" the waitress. Wightman described Scott's behavior as inappropriate. It also seemed strange that Scott asked a new acquaintance, Mike Richardson, to be his best man, despite his supposedly close relationship with his brothers.

Scott wasn't the only one behaving badly on the night of his wedding. According to the manager, Laci's biological father, Dennis Rocha, arrived there late, and was so intoxicated that he needed help putting on his pants. Then he fell and ripped the seat of his pants. Wightman said he took the slacks, stapled them together, and helped him get dressed again.

It isn't uncommon for a daughter to marry a man like her father. Scott and Dennis both drank to excess that day, and as we'll see, Scott continued to drink heavily throughout the marriage.

Sharon and Dennis Rocha were married for only seven years. They had two children, Brent in 1971 and Laci four years later. Dennis left Sharon when Laci was only a year old, and Laci's relationship with her natural father was reportedly somewhat "strained." The two had little contact, mostly on holidays and family events.

Dennis's parents, Helen and Robert Rocha, owned a 325-acre ranch and dairy farm in Escalon, California, and as a girl Laci spent weekends living the country life. The ranch included four houses, a mobile home, four or five barns, and a working dairy. The couple also owned a smaller 40-acre ranch nearby. As a younger man, Dennis had worked diligently on the farm. But after years of irresponsible behavior from Dennis, the senior Rochas drew up a trust naming Laci's brother, Brent, and Dennis's sister, Robin, as executors of the estate. The ranch was sold in 1995, and the new owner leased a small parcel to Laci's father, where he still lives.

After Laci's biological parents split up, Ron Grantski embraced the role of father to Laci and Brent. Grantski had a son from a previous relationship, Darryl, who lived in Oregon with his mother. When Brent was nine, he went to live with his father in Escalon. Laci remained in Modesto, attending Sonoma Elementary, La Loma Junior High, and Downey High School, before graduating in 1993. She was extremely popular in school, joining numerous clubs and participating in sports like softball and basketball. She was also a cheerleader for a youth program, Pop Warner Football. In high school, she held part-time jobs at a local market, a restaurant, and a doctor's office. In college, she worked at a flower shop and then a winery, and she was named Outstanding Freshman of the Year at Cal Poly.

Sharon Rocha described Laci as "headstrong," noting that her birth sign was Taurus, the bull. This description would be echoed by friends and neighbors after her disappearance: One girlfriend suggested Laci "wore the pants" in the family, interrupting Scott when he was speaking and directing him to take out the trash in front of company. According to another friend, Laci even followed Scott to the bathroom, where he sometimes retreated from her chatter, and just kept talking to him through the door. Ron Grantski, who described Laci as "outgoing," "happy," and "cheerful," conceded that her nickname was "J. J.," for "Jabber Jaws."

Speaking later with *Today*'s Katie Couric, Grantski recalled a family trip to the caverns near Sonora. "She was talking all the way up there," Ron smiled. "And I said, 'Laci, do you think you could be quiet for thirty seconds?' "

" 'Sure,' she said. 'How long is thirty seconds? Is it thirty seconds yet?' "

According to Grantski, Laci was very social and found it easy to converse with people she'd just met. He and Laci's mother agreed that she was extremely trusting, but not reckless or foolish. Grantski's only complaint was about Scott, who he felt did too much around the house. Ron was concerned that Sharon might expect the same from him.

By December 2002, Laci had made it clear she intended to be a stay-at-home mom. She wanted a bigger house, a new car, and more children, and no one doubted she would get it all. She was quite vivacious, but according to her sister, also bossy and eager to climb the social ladder.

Laci was a big fan of Martha Stewart, and in many ways she worked to emulate her. She baked special birthday cakes for her friends, and surprised them with elegantly wrapped gifts. She was passionate about good food, and hosted dinner parties with fancy fare and expensive wines. All were welcome at the Petersons' soirees, as long as they followed Laci's rules. Guests were required to dress for dinner, and tardiness was not tolerated. Everybody knew to be on time, or else.

"Laci wanted to be sure, each and every time we were all together, that we would have fun," one friend said. "Laci not only taught us proper etiquette, but how to laugh. And not just giggle, but to laugh loud and often."

After she and Scott married, they briefly lived apart—with Laci working in Prunedale and Scott going to school in Morro Bay some 130 miles away. What seemed like an innocent separation would set the stage for Scott's later infidelities: His first extramarital affair, with Janet Ilse, would be followed by a second, serious, but reportedly nonsexual relationship with another Cal Poly student, Katy Hansen. Both women dated Scott during the time he lived in San Luis Obispo.

Janet Ilse came forward during the investigation, but Katy Hansen's relationship was reported to police by a friend of hers. When contacted, Katy said that she and Scott studied together, and soon started dating casually. On several occasions, they double-dated with their roommates. Katy recalled Scott as very bright, congenial, and courtly, and told the police that he never appeared stressed, even under the intense pressures of college exams. Scott started his senior project two days before the due date, yet bragged that he had aced it with an A. (His college transcripts confirmed the claim.) Scott's overall GPA was 3.387 when he graduated in the spring of 1998.

Katy and Scott dated for about two and a half months. Scott enjoyed dancing; he liked going to martini bars, smoking cigars, and playing golf. The two also went on romantic hikes along trails that crisscrossed the scenic coastal desert town. Scott often brought along his dog, McKenzie—the golden retriever his wife, Laci, had given him on their first Christmas together. His pattern with women was solidifying.

One evening, Scott confided to Katy that he aspired to become the mayor of Fillmore, a small city northwest of Los Angeles, but first he intended to travel. He also dreamed of working at the Newhall Land and Farming Company, a large, privately held corporation in eastern Ventura County. Katy never met any of Scott's family or friends, outside of his three roommates. Until she learned of Scott's brothers and sisters on the news after Laci disappeared, she assumed he was an only child.

Katy told police that she'd once asked Scott if he'd ever been engaged or married. He told her no. The following day he called to apologize, admitting that he'd lied. He had been married in the past, but was now alone; his ex lived in Salinas. Katy had no reason to doubt him. After all, Scott lived in a house with his roommates, and he didn't wear a wedding band. She had been to his home for dinner, and never once saw any women's clothing or other feminine items in Scott's room. Katy told police that their relationship was never intimate, but she believed it was growing more serious.

As graduation day neared, Katy thought the romance would continue. There was no talk of breaking up once Scott graduated. But all that changed on graduation day. Katy was seated next to Scott during the college's closing ceremonies when suddenly a dark-haired woman walked up to him, placed a lei of flowers around his neck, and planted a kiss on him that telegraphed, "this woman and Scott were *seriously* involved."

Katy was bewildered as Scott calmly introduced the woman as Laci. When Laci walked away, Scott reacted as he had when Janet Ilse caught him with his wife. He did not utter another word to Katy that afternoon. She didn't ask any questions; she merely counted her blessings that their relationship had gone no further, for it was obvious that Scott was still married after all.

A few weeks later, Katy received one dozen pink roses. Scott attached an odd message, saying that he had "no job, no home." Katy never contacted Scott after receiving the peculiar delivery.

The picture of Scott that emerges from these episodes is fascinating. This was a man who was used to being appreciated simply for himself. He was never going to make it as a pro golfer, a rocket scientist, or a captain of industry, but he viewed himself as an exceptional citizen, and expected others to do the same. He accepted things as they came, at least on the surface, but later the world would see the double life he led. One Scott was a gentle, responsible, tolerant husband full of love for his spirited wife. The other was someone having reckless affairs and displaying emotional mood swings, even crying jags, with his various mistresses. He was able to lie with abandon, and no one was the wiser. At tremendously upsetting moments, he was capable of turning completely cold, dismissing the upheaval with a half-hearted "I'm sorry." He seemed to have no empathy with those who suffered from his behavior.

Roses, courtly behavior, wining and dining; at least Scott was consistent, in these and many other ways that would become clear over time. He obviously cared a great deal about his public image. Even on the meager income of a college student, he would lavish flowers, gifts, and expensive meals on his girlfriends. All the women, including Amber Frey, described Scott as a man who went out of his way to be special for them. They all witnessed his charm and apparent sincerity when he wanted something, but also his extraordinary callousness when things didn't go his way. Like others, Janet and Katy were wooed to the brink by Scott, then unceremoniously dropped when his game was over.

Scott was truly a player. He would display whatever emotion seemed "appropriate" at a given moment, but could drop the façade in an instant and move on with no trouble. This would be quite apparent during press interviews in late January, interviews that would become important weapons for the prosecution at trial.

He was also a phenomenal and apparently pathological liar. Most people pay a price for lying, if not externally, then internally. Not Scott Peterson. He lied again and again, often about trivial matters or when it was completely unnecessary. Outside of the occasional anguished performance for a girlfriend, he showed no guilt or remorse when caught in deceptions, large or small.

He also perceived himself as a special case. Whether dropping out of school because he didn't feel sufficiently appreciated by a golf coach, or leading a blatantly promiscuous double life, Scott found countless ways to flagrantly violate social norms and demonstrate that the rules simply did not apply to him.

Despite his overtly gregarious nature, Scott was actually quite a loner. Whether shallow or secretive, he remained a relative unknown to friends and associates. Few people professed to know him well. He seemed to adapt to most situations, making those around him feel comfortable, but in hindsight, he never truly let them in.

He did have some insecurities. Although Scott moved through several colleges, taking extra time to graduate, he made it known that he thought himself very bright. During the murder investigation, when he heard that an old college professor had been quoted as saying Scott "was kind of smart," he retorted angrily, "Kind of smart? I'm *real* smart."

This was another characteristic that would work against Scott as the murder investigation got under way—inflated sense of self-worth and intelligence. There's no doubt that Scott Peterson is intelligent, but to my mind, his brash lies and flagrant conduct indicated that he truly believed he was a match for the detectives who were investigating him. I'm certain that he expected to survive their scrutiny unscathed.

About two months before Scott's graduation, around Easter 1998, Laci moved back in with Scott. Yet I suspect that Laci knew in her heart what was going on with Scott, especially after the episode with Janet Ilse. Yet apparently she was willing to accept it. Being from a divorced home, perhaps Laci was desperate to avoid failure in her own marriage.

In August, Laci took a position as a banquet coordinator at Gardens of Avila Restaurant at the Sycamore Springs Resort, where she and Scott had been married the previous year. Records indicate that she resigned after only two months. In an exit interview, Laci told the general manager that she was dissatisfied with the woman who was supposed to be training her. She complained that she was "constantly belittling to me and was anything but respectful." She also voiced dissatisfaction with two other employees, saying that she had received calls "with stupid questions—questions that a little common sense should have answered." She explained that she was "offended" by her $9 hourly rate, even though she knew the salary when she accepted the position. When asked if she would stay on to train an incoming banquet coordinator, she said no. She was "reactivating her substitute teaching status" on the first of the month.

Meanwhile, Scott's parents had made him a partner in Lee's corrugated box business. Lee had proudly assumed his son would run the enterprise for years to come, but two years later Scott bought out his father's share, then quickly and callously sold the company. Once again he did what he wanted to do, regardless of the pain inflicted on those who loved him.

Scott used the profits from the sale to renovate a vacant building in San Luis Obispo near the Cal Poly campus. There he opened a restaurant he called the Shack, serving beer, wine, and sandwiches. Scott's father characterized the Shack as a "sports bar." It seemed to be a success and was voted one of the best happy-hour restaurants in the area.

Laci and Scott ran the business for about two years. Over time, however, they grew increasingly frustrated. It was difficult to find good help. The employees constantly interrupted their days off. Two years after the Shack opened its doors, Scott and Laci opted to sell. Their relatives didn't know how much they received for it; indeed, no one could say for sure whether the new owner ever fully paid Scott. Still, he seemed relieved to be out of the business.

The young couple didn't stay in San Luis Obispo much longer.

After her grandmother died in 1999, Laci wanted to move closer to her parents. The couple lived with Sharon and Ron for about two weeks before moving to temporary quarters on Mesquite Road. In October 2000, with a $30,000 gift from Scott's parents, they purchased the house on Covena Avenue.

The pair often complained that there was little to do in Modesto. Still, they had many friends, and they kept their social calendar full entertaining friends and family. Scott soon began making improvements to their home, adding a swimming pool and brickwork in the backyard in early 2002. He also built a brick barbecue and retiled a bathroom, which he would later claim explained his considerable use of concrete late that year.

By summertime, Scott had joined the West Coast division of Tradecorp, for whom he sold fertilizers, plant nutrients, and other agricultural products. Traveling to serve his customers kept Scott away from home at least one day each week. After Laci's disappearance, he told investigators that his business had lost roughly one hundred thousand dollars over the past year. Documents retrieved from his office confirmed that the new division was far from profitable.

Around this time, Laci Peterson began talking more seriously about having a baby. She had been trying to get pregnant for two years with no luck and was beginning to wonder if it was possible. As a child, she had an eight-pound tumor removed from her lower abdomen. During the surgery doctors had to remove one of her Fallopian tubes as well. At the time, doctors told her she should have no trouble becoming pregnant. Now she was losing hope.

She and Scott discussed fertility tests, but before they could pursue the idea, Laci got the news she'd been waiting for: She was pregnant at last. She was overjoyed, and Scott seemed to share her feelings. Laci's mother recalled watching Scott hurry over to feel Laci's stomach when she said the baby was kicking. He seemed as excited as she was.

"I assume if he didn't want to have a child, he wouldn't have allowed it to happen," Sharon told investigators.

Not everyone had the same impression. Laci's sister-in-law, Rosemarie Rocha, told police about a conversation in the summer of 2001 regarding children and pregnancy. "I was kind of hoping for infertility," Scott told her. Although he seemed "uncomfortable" and "hesitant" around children, Rocha was heartened by the fact that Scott attended some of Laci's medical appointments after the pregnancy was announced.

Around the time Laci discovered her pregnancy, Scott commented to Sharon that he had just turned thirty, and here he was becoming a father the same year. He thought he was having "a midlife crisis." Sharon took it as a joke. Maybe it wasn't.

Police subpoenaed Laci's medical records as part of the investigation. Laci's first visit to the HERA obstetrics group in Modesto was for an annual exam in June 2001. Medical records show that she had stopped using oral contraceptives in December 2000. "At this time, she is planning to get pregnant at the end of this year," the office report noted. At the time of her initial appointment, the report noted Laci's height and weight as 5' 1" and 125 pounds.

According to records I obtained in my investigation, Laci's pregnancy was normal. There were several notations about her excessive weight gain, and she was advised to watch her diet and increase her level of exercise. On November 6 and again on November 8, Laci called the doctor's office. "She said she was experiencing shortness of breath after a twenty minute walk and was concerned. She was advised to eat first and take the walks later in the day," the record stated.

Laci was described as a social drinker, yet she apparently stopped drinking once she became pregnant. She had no known enemies, did not use illicit drugs, and had no history of mental illness. A police check showed that Laci had never been the victim of a violent crime. However, friends revealed that her high school sweetheart had "pushed her" once during an argument—and when the police examined the relationship further, it was apparently more violent than Laci ever admitted. Early in the investigation, Brent Rocha would tell police about this troubled relationship and ask them to investigate. In a twist of irony, that boyfriend, William "Kent" Gain, later attempted to murder another girlfriend. By the time Laci disappeared he was incarcerated in a Washington State Prison, serving a fifteen-year prison term for the crime. Gain would later send heartfelt missives to a Laci Peterson tribute website, professing grief and love for his former girlfriend. Even today, he reportedly keeps pictures of Laci posted in his cell.

Laci Peterson, then, had already endured one encounter with domestic violence. Yet, as the Department of Justice's missing person report pointed out, even though "persons close to her believed under normal circumstances she would have physically resisted an assault . . . her advanced stage of pregnancy and resultant limitations would have likely hampered any attempt to defend herself."

In November, Laci began attending a maternity yoga class, which met Mondays at noon. People in the neighborhood told investigators that they saw her walking her dog during that period, but as the pregnancy advanced, Laci complained of exhaustion. Relatives told police that she even used a wheelchair while visiting Disneyland with Scott's parents and half sister, Anne Bird, although Bird would later say this chair was just a gag to please Laci.

In our interview, Anne told me that Laci looked radiant during that trip. She was excited about having the baby and talked a lot about how much she loved her mother, Sharon. Anne first met Laci in March 1998, about seven months after the wedding. She liked her immediately. Laci filled up the room, loved being the center of attention, and rarely let anyone else get a word in edgewise. Like Laci's other girlfriends, Anne agreed that Laci did boss Scott around. And, like those women, Anne wished she had a husband like Scott, who did everything his wife told him with a smile.

Anne also attended Laci's baby shower, along with nearly fifty other women. At one point, she recalled, Laci was stifling laughter over a close friend of Jackie's who turned up in go-go boots. Anne recognized the woman from several pictures hanging in Jackie's house. "Weird people," she mouthed to Anne, as her sister-in-law tried to keep a straight face.

By the time the due date approached, Scott and Laci were spending money quite freely. They went all-out decorating the inside of their home, splurging on new furnishings, especially in the nursery. From the outside, however, the house looked unkempt and in need of repairs.

Scott still played golf regularly, and when his parents ponied up the $23,000 admission fee on December 1, he joined the Del Rio Country Club. (The $390 monthly dues were Scott's responsibility.)

The couple enjoyed entertaining. Their friends knew Laci to be a gourmet cook. According to her friends, Laci put a great deal of effort into her appearance. Spa treatments, manicures, and pedicures were part of her normal routine. She also loved shopping, and was described as a clotheshorse. She used the Internet to search for Christmas presents, and scoped out the local malls on a regular basis. While she loved finding a bargain, she didn't hesitate to pay full price if she wanted a particular item.

Laci kept a running list of new objects the couple had agreed to buy for their home. Her long-range goals included having more children and buying a larger house and new vehicle—even as she planned to remain a stay-at-home mom. During one conversation with Sharon, Scott joked that they might have to pitch a tent in his mother-in-law's driveway if their spending habits were not restrained.

Two days before her disappearance, Laci's brother Brent phoned from his home in Elk Grove to find out about the couple's plans for Christmas. He asked if he could bring their grandfather, Robert Rocha, down from his nursing home in Sacramento on Christmas morning. Laci readily agreed. After her 10:30 brunch, everyone could open presents. She and Scott would purchase a fruit basket or something similar for their grandfather.

In hindsight, it all seems like a charade: Scott spent so much time and money decorating Conner's room, taking Laci's ring in to the jeweler for Christmas, rushing over to feel his baby kick, despite telling others that he was "hoping for infertility."

But on December 23, 2002, Scott seemed to be planning nothing more than a quiet holiday entertaining family and enjoying his wife's company.

# CHAPTER FOUR

# SEARCHES

Over the next three days, police conducted a number of searches of Scott's house, warehouse, and boat. They initiated grid searches by air, and bloodhound searches on the ground. And their work yielded valuable clues, only some of which the jury heard about during the trial. The following pages are based on the complete record of those searches, along with unpublished conversations between police and Scott Peterson.

By December 26, 2002, Scott's office on Emerald Street was under surveillance. No one could enter the business until the pending search warrant had been served. "I felt that if evidence was present at the Emerald Avenue location, evidence destruction at that location could be completed without witnesses in the remote and mostly unoccupied industrial area in the late evening and early morning hours," Detective Craig Grogan reported.

Members of the Modesto Fire Department were combing the Tuolumne River area of Dry Creek Park, and a neighborhood canvas was underway, with officers going from house to house looking for individuals who may have seen anything out of the ordinary.

As per Grogan's instruction, police also compiled a list of potential suspects, focusing on prior offenders and known sex offenders in the area. He told Officer Tom Rhea to highlight any transients with violent backgrounds.

Just before ten, Detective Grogan received a call. An officer in the field had just interviewed a woman who claimed to have seen a female in the early morning hours of December 24, dressed in black pants and white shirt. She said the woman was pregnant and walking a dog.

Another tip came in from a woman named Diana Campos, a 46-year-old custodian at Stanislaus County Hospital. At 10:45 A.M., while on a smoking break outside the hospital, Campos said she had seen three people and a dog together in the park, heading west. She watched the three as they walked roughly the distance of a football field. The dog, a golden retriever, was barking incessantly, and the female was tugging on the lead as if trying to calm him. One of the men, who had what Campos described as a "beanie cap" atop his head, shouted, "Shut the fucking dog up."

Campos watched them as she puffed on her cigarette but did not sense any serious conflict among the individuals. In fact, she thought nothing of the sighting until December 26, when she saw a flyer describing Laci Peterson.

"When I looked at the flyer, I said to myself, 'I know the girl.'" She insisted that the woman she had seen in Moose Park was Laci Peterson, and told Detective Owen that she would not have called the police unless she was sure. Yet, Campos backpedaled slightly a few minutes later, saying only that she was "pretty sure." "I am real good with faces," she told the detective.

Campos described the woman as wearing a white top and sweatpants, with dark shoulder-length hair; she appeared to be six or seven months pregnant. The golden retriever was medium in size, with brownish red fur, but Campos could not recall the color of its leash. She described both men as in their thirties, 5'7", with medium builds. One wore a beanie-style cap, dirty clothes, a dark shirt and blue jeans. The second man had short brown hair and was dressed in jeans and a torn denim jacket. Campos said she was about fifty feet away from the group.

Over the course of the investigation there would be several more reports like these, but no time line was ever established. While Scott's defense lawyer, Mark Geragos, promised to produce these folks at trial, he never did. He was able to inject some of the information during cross-examination of police officers, but during his case in chief, none of these people took the stand.

Around noon, Detective Al Brocchini began tracking Scott's alibi. When he spoke with the Berkeley Marina Harbormaster, Ray Foresberg, the man was adamant: It had not rained at the marina on December 24. This information directly contradicted the story Scott had told Brocchini only twenty-four hours before, and prompted the men to secure a search warrant.

After hearing Foresberg's report, Brocchini went straight to police headquarters, where he and Detective Grogan completed search warrant applications for 523 Covena Avenue and 1027 Emerald Avenue. On the surface, these two officers seemed cut from the same cloth: short and stocky, each of them sporting the business suit of a plainclothes detective. Yet there were critical differences between the two. Brocchini, his dark hair cut in a military style, had a well-defined chin, broad facial features, and frameless eyeglasses; he was quicker to react, and to confront or challenge a witness. Grogan, whose brown hair was tinged with red, sported a thick mustache and bright observant eyes; the more seasoned of the two, he was much more low-key. Early in the investigation, Scott would accuse Brocchini of trying to "trick" him. Grogan was much more likely to assume the "good cop" role, and it was he who proved better able to engage Scott in the cat-and-mouse game they would play in the coming days.

Applications in hand, the two investigators hurried to the courthouse to obtain a judge's approval for the searches. As they arrived, Grogan's cell phone rang. A detective posted outside Scott's warehouse was calling to let him know that a man driving a bronze Ford F150 had pulled up, wanting to retrieve a computer from the office.

The man, whom the police turned away, was Scott Peterson. The officer told him to contact Grogan or Brocchini for more information.

At 3:10, Judge Nancy Ashley signed the warrants, clearing the way for the search. Before Brocchini could get out of the room, his phone rang as well. It was Scott, asking why a warrant was necessary.

The detective explained that it was just a precaution, reminding Scott that he'd reneged on his agreement to take a polygraph just moments before it was scheduled. Scott suggested that the detectives meet him at headquarters for the 3:30 press briefing; they could discuss the search then.

Moments later, the officers were standing in the hallway outside the press room. Then Scott called again, changing the rules. He'd left the news conference early, he said; now he wanted the men to come to his house. Before they could leave, Laci's stepfather approached. Grantski said that his son-in-law had just gotten up and walked out of the press conference, obviously angry at reporter's questions about his behavior.

At four o'clock, the officers edged their vehicle around a line of media satellite trucks and pulled up to the Peterson house. Dozens of journalists had staked out the home, waiting for updates on the case. The media was there at Scott's disposal, but he had no intention of using them to find Laci. In fact, he was clearly avoiding them.

Cordoned behind Modesto Police Department sawhorses, the reporters all missed what happened next. The jury was never allowed to hear what Scott and the officers discussed that afternoon—including a telling conversation with Jackie Peterson, Scott's antics over the search warrant for 523 Covena, and the full details of the bloodhound searches conducted at his home and warehouse.

Through a window, the detectives could see Scott sitting alone at the dining room table, calmly perusing a newspaper. They knocked, and without rising Scott yelled "Come in." He invited them to join him at the long wood table.

Scott had gone to the warehouse, he said, to get a photograph of Laci off his office computer for a flyer he was preparing. He was perturbed that he wasn't told about the lockdown of his office or the pending search, and reiterated that he would have given permission if the detectives had simply asked. Just thirty-six hours into the investigation, Scott was already displaying his arrogance, trying to seize the upper hand and setting up confrontations with the very people who were there to help find Laci. He was telegraphing a message: This is my territory—I'm in charge here.

Grogan interjected, redirecting the conversation to the importance of a timely search. There might be evidence of a stranger entering the home, then cleaning up to eliminate signs of an attack. He also explained that searching Scott's place of business, his vehicles, and his computers might provide clues of a stalker, or even Laci's possible involvement with another man. Scott listened intently, nodding his head as if agreeing with the comments. From his demeanor, the investigators assumed he would agree to the searches. Producing waivers that eliminated the need for a warrant, the detectives asked Scott for his signature.

Scott read the papers intently, then looked up. "You don't expect me to sign these right now, do you? I'm going to have to consult with an attorney before I sign anything."

Grogan shrugged. "Have you retained an attorney?"

Handing back the waivers, Scott replied, "I've made some calls but have not hired anyone yet."

At that point, Sergeant Ron Cloward entered the room and interrupted the exchange. He needed an article of Laci's clothing to use in the canine search. Scott allowed him to take Laci's brown hairbrush, a pink Jones of New York slipper, a pair of Ralph Lauren sunglasses, and a brown eyeglass case. Cloward also retrieved an item of Scott's, a green and blue slipper from the Gap.

"Are you writing down the items that you're taking?" Scott asked.

"Yes," Grogan replied.

As a uniformed officer prepared the slip, Scott interrupted, sliding some papers across the table to prevent the cop from scratching the wooden tabletop as he wrote. As Detective Brocchini noted, it was just like Scott's behavior with Laci's Land Rover: However disengaged he may have seemed from his wife's disappearance, he was clearly eager to protect property that had value to him. As the detective made another note of Scott's "unusual concerns," Cloward offered Scott his receipt for the borrowed items, and Scott readily accepted.

Around 4:30, Jackie and Lee Peterson arrived at the house.

Scott's mother had just left the news conference. She was complaining about Chief Wasden's comment that it would be strange for Laci to go walking without her cell phone. "Everybody knows Laci's cell phone had been dead for weeks," she griped. "So why would she be taking it on walks with her?"

When I read this in the police report, I wondered why Jackie was interpreting this comment as an indictment of her son. She was already feeling the need to protect him. Was this because she knew something about Laci, or simply because she had done it so often in the past?

Brocchini knew that Laci's cell phone was dead. He had checked it the previous evening. If what Jackie Peterson was saying was true, he asked, "then why did Scott leave a message on that cell phone Christmas Eve?"

"I was just repeating what other people said," she snapped.

As the afternoon wore on, more officers were dispatched to 523 Covena to assist with crowd control. They were setting up wooden sawhorses to contain the growing throng when a woman ran out of the house across the street, screaming that she'd been robbed. Susan Medina excitedly explained that she and her husband, Rodolfo, had just returned from their holiday in Los Angeles to find their home ransacked. Officers Fainter and Meyers followed her to investigate.

The point of entry was clearly the south side of the Medinas' home at 516 Covena, where a set of French doors had been kicked in. A shoeprint was visible on the right door below the handle. Drawers were open and closets tossed throughout the dwelling. Rodolfo Medina told the officers that a personal safe in the master bedroom, which had been concealed by maroon bedsheets, was missing.

A hammer and a glove were found inside the master suite; the burglar had apparently used the hammer to crack the safe. A hand truck stored inside the owner's tool shop behind the house was now on the porch. The intruder must have used it to transport the safe to the front of the house. In the backyard, police found items taken from the toolshed, including an air compressor and a gas-powered leaf blower. A number of power tools were missing.

Officers wanted a list of people who knew about the Medinas' holiday plans, and the names of businesses and persons who had been to the residence. They fingerprinted family members before leaving. This burglary would become important to Scott's defense in the months to come.

Across the way at the Peterson residence, an attorney named Ross Lee was meeting with Scott in a rear bedroom. When Lee emerged, he introduced himself as Tradecorp's corporate attorney, and told the officers that he had referred Scott to a criminal lawyer, Kirk McAllister.

Scott returned to the dining room and said he'd left a message for McAllister. He pulled up a chair at the table where his father, Lee, and his sister, Susan Caudillo, were talking with Captain Christopher Boyer. Boyer headed up the Contra Costa County Emergency Services Search and Rescue and was in charge of the canine team assigned to search the area around the Petersons' home. Linda Valentin, a dog handler, was also present.

While everyone waited for a call from Scott's attorney, Captain Boyer interviewed Scott in preparation for the bloodhound search. Brocchini listened quietly as Scott responded to Boyer's questions. He paid close attention as Scott detailed the items of clothing he said his wife had been wearing on the morning of her disappearance—the black maternity pants and white long-sleeved blouse with a crew neck.

"What type of shoes was Laci wearing?" Boyer inquired

Scott replied that his wife was barefoot when he left.

"What shoes does Laci normally wear before she goes walking?"

"White tennis shoes," he replied.

"Were any tennis shoes missing?"

Brocchini was surprised to hear Scott say he hadn't yet checked. Nor had he looked to see if any of her jackets were missing. This critical information could help determine whether she had gone for a walk or was abducted from inside the home.

Captain Boyer left the residence to begin the search, and Brocchini followed him outside. Boyer commented that in his twenty years of experience, this was the first time he had ever been asked for a receipt for items taken to help locate a missing person. Brocchini just nodded.

It was five o'clock before Grogan again asked Scott if he had talked to a lawyer about the search waivers.

"Not yet," he replied.

Grogan then pulled some papers from his pocket and began to recite. "I have prepared a search warrant that covers your home, vehicles, boat, and place of work. The searches·will be carried out over a period of a few days in a very slow and methodical way to hopefully find evidence that will aid in our investigation of Laci's disappearance."

Scott's reaction was immediate. "Where's the trust?" he demanded, looking directly at Brocchini. "Why did you fill out those forms and ask if you could search, if you already had a warrant?"

It was then that Scott accused Brocchini of tricking him on Christmas Eve. Brocchini had left his keys in Scott's car that first night, and his notebook in Scott's boat. Now Scott was suggesting that Brocchini had staged the whole thing to give him an excuse to go back and take a second look.

"Scott said I took his gun out of his car, and took his mop, mop bucket, and wet towels on Christmas Eve without telling him. I reminded Scott that he consented to the evidence search on Christmas Eve, and I apologized [that] I did not immediately tell him what I had taken. Scott agreed, but said he felt betrayed since I did not tell him about the items I took until he asked," Brocchini noted in his ongoing police report.

Grogan explained that he wasn't confident Scott would allow the search, but had wanted to give him the opportunity to consent. Scott's change of heart over the polygraph, after all, was the only behavior Grogan had to go on. Now the detective told Scott he would have to vacate the house within fifteen minutes, and would need permission to remove anything when he left.

With warrant in hand, Scott strode to the kitchen counter, grabbed a piece of paper, and thrust it at Brocchini. "Here," Scott said. It was a two-day fishing license dated December 23 and 24,

2002. He must have seen the item listed on the warrant. As the investigator placed it in his folder, the telephone rang. It was Kirk McAllister, the attorney. Scott took the call in a back bedroom. Moments later he returned, telling Detective Grogan that the lawyer wanted to speak with him.

McAllister informed Grogan that he now represented Peterson, and had informed his client not to speak further without an attorney present. McAllister knew there were questions his client should address, and Scott would make himself readily available. However, he had advised Scott not to take a polygraph.

Just before six o'clock, Scott Peterson and his family gathered their belongings and headed to the front door. Grogan stopped Scott and asked for a set of keys to his truck, home, and business. Scott handed them over, then quickly left the house. Brocchini and Grogan secured the premises, then left as well.

Grogan and Brocchini then joined Captain Boyer and the other dog handlers in Dry Creek Park, and Grogan listened as Boyer detailed his current findings. Based on the dogs' behavior, he believed that Laci had left the residence in a vehicle, not on foot. After the dogs picked up her scent, they ran right down the middle of Covena Avenue following the trail, rather than tracking on the sidewalk. The primary tracker, a bloodhound named Merlin, started at the Petersons' house, then headed north on Covena Avenue, west on Edgebrook Drive, and then south on Highland Drive. At Santa Barbara Avenue, he turned east until he reached La Loma Avenue. The animal went to the rear of a check-cashing establishment at the corner of La Loma and Yosemite Boulevard, then continued westbound on Yosemite. He stopped in the area of Santa Rosa Avenue, where he turned south.

At that point, Merlin's handler, Cindee Valentin, wasn't sure if the dog was still following the trail. The dog's behavior was now different from when he had the earlier distinct alert, she told Grogan. A deputy lieutenant with the Contra Costa Sheriff's Department, Valentin had joined the Search Dog Steering Committee of the State's Office of Emergency Services a year ago. The agency was responsible for the development and publication of statewide guidelines for all search and rescue dogs in California. Valentin worked as a horse trainer before expanding to professional dog training in 1991. Her unique background also included positions as an evaluator and trainer for several state certifying agencies for working dogs.

Valentin explained that the dog tracking Laci "ran in a manner consistent with a vehicle trail as opposed to a trail left by a person that was walking." Grogan asked Valentin to take Merlin to Scott's warehouse. Valentin agreed, but requested that the pair start at a nearby intersection. She wanted to see where, if at all, Merlin would pick up Laci's scent.

At 9:30 P.M., Detective Brocchini, Lieutenant Valentin, and Merlin were standing at the intersection of Kansas Avenue and Emerald, about three miles south of Scott's business. Valentin herself did not know where Scott's business was. Brocchini watched as the animal sniffed Laci's sunglasses case to pick up the scent, walked around in a circle on Emerald Avenue, then after only a few seconds began trotting south on Emerald.

Brocchini followed Valentin and Boyer as they chased Merlin through the intersection at Kansas. The dog's tail was up as he trotted at a steady pace down the center of the street. Merlin ran into the parking lot of a Laundromat on the southeast corner of Kansas and Emerald, slowing slightly, then trotted back onto southbound Emerald. Merlin continued south on Emerald to Loletta, when Brocchini asked Valentin to stop the dog.

The dog was then returned to the initial starting point. Again he ran south through the intersection, following the exact route he had just taken. The officers stopped Merlin on southbound Emerald near Loletta. The dog handler told Brocchini that there was no doubt in her mind that Merlin was following Laci's strongest scent. That scent was leading him southbound on Emerald. The dog was tracking away from Scott's business, not toward it.

He asked Valentine and Boyer to explain what the "strongest scent" would be if Laci had been driven to a location, remained at that site for an hour or more, then was driven away. They explained that the most recent scent, when Laci left the location, would be the strongest. Lieutenant Valentin then asked Brocchini to take her to the business. She explained that she needed to have a starting place or a stopping place when conducting a bloodhound scent search to testify in court.

Brocchini took Valentin and Boyer to the parking lot of Scott's warehouse at 1027 Emerald, and showed them suite B. The detective watched as she let Merlin out in the center of the parking lot and walked him toward Scott's place of business. Once the dog neared the suite, his tail immediately went up, indicating that he had picked up Laci's scent.

Merlin immediately began trotting eastbound away from the business, down the north driveway. The detective trailed Valentin and her dog east through the parking lot, and followed as the dog again took off southbound on Emerald right down the middle of the street.

The group continued south past Kansas Avenue until they reached the intersection of Emerald and Highway 132. Merlin slowed down at the intersection, appearing to have lost Laci's scent. Deputy Boyer explained that a large intersection with heavy traffic such as this one sometimes mixed up the scent. Valentin said it would take the dog a short time to relocate the scent.

Next they did an exercise called "the four corners," walking the dog around the entire intersection. In the process Merlin relocated Laci's scent, and took off westbound down the center of Highway 132. Brocchini and the others followed the dog about four hundred yards before pulling up. It appeared that the dog would have continued running on the highway if they hadn't stopped him.

Valentin told Brocchini she could testify that Merlin followed Laci's scent from 1027 N. Emerald southbound, then westbound on Highway 132. "I told him again that this trail was consistent with a vehicle trail," Valentin later wrote in her official report. Brocchini realized that the path Merlin had taken was the exact route Scott Peterson had driven to go fishing. The detective later measured the distance from Scott's place of business to the spot where the dog was pulled up. Merlin had trailed Laci Peterson's scent 1.1 miles.

It was after 10:30 in the evening when Lieutenant Valentin and Merlin completed the search around 1027 Emerald Avenue. Captain Boyer gave the detective all the items they had used: Laci's pink slipper, her Ralph Lauren sunglasses and case, her brown hairbrush, and her husband's Gap slipper.

It had been a very long day, but Brocchini went back to headquarters to examine Scott's truck, impounded earlier that evening. His search proved fruitless. "During this search I did not see Peterson's tan camouflage jacket that I had seen in the truck on 12/24/02. I also did not see the Big 5 bag containing two fishing lures, the backyard umbrellas that were wrapped in the blue tarp, the tan-colored tarp that had been bunched up in the back of the truck, or the shotgun shells I saw in the green toolbox," Brocchini later wrote. "It appeared that Scott Peterson had removed several items from the truck between 12/24/02 and the time the search warrant was served."

Brocchini did find a partial roll of chicken wire and a small hand tool that had a gardening fork on one side, and a hoe on the other. "The tool was coated with dry cement," he wrote. "It looked like it was used to mix ready-mix cement. There was loose ready-mix cement in the bed of the truck."

In a subsequent search, police found what appeared to be four small bloodstains on the interior side of the driver's door. A suspected bloodstain was also collected from the back of the steering wheel.

Following a preliminary inspection, the pickup was turned over to the FBI Forensic Evidence Team, which had traveled from Sacramento to assist the police. Members of the team sprayed the questionable stains with Hemo-Glow, a fluid used to detect bloodstains. All the areas fluoresced. In addition, an area of the interior door pocket and on the vehicle's door handle tested positive.

At 10:45, Detective Grogan received a call from Scott Peterson asking about the bloodhound search. The detective advised him that the dogs had tracked away from his home through a series of residential streets down to Yosemite Boulevard, then turned west. During the five-minute conversation, Grogan admitted that the dog had lost the scent after traveling a distance on Yosemite.

"Have you been able to get any sleep?" Grogan asked before hanging up that night.

The detective recorded Scott's reply, "He did not sleep well in a different bed. He now had the comfort in his own home with the 'smell of Laci' in their bed."

Within twenty-four hours of Laci's disappearance, her family and friends set up a command center at a local inn, the Red Lion Hotel, to assist police in their search for Laci. The general manager, Brad Saltzman, donated rooms for the effort. Thousands of fliers with Laci's photo and reward information were printed. Hundreds of people hit the streets in those first days, distributing the materials and searching the Modesto area for signs of Laci.

Sharon and Ron Grantski and Jackie and Lee Peterson were out before the cameras in these early days, but Scott was nowhere to be found. The young husband and father-to-be was declining all requests for television appearances, telling journalists that he wanted to keep the focus on Laci—not on him. This was unusual behavior for anyone in Scott's position, and in fact it brought about the opposite result: Scott's absence quickly became a topic of interest in the press.

Ironically, I later learned that it was one of Scott's parents, either Jackie or Lee, who had alerted the national media to the story through a connection with the Associated Press. It is my belief that Scott never expected the media attention that this case drew. I think he also miscalculated the abilities of the 270-member Modesto Police Department. He probably thought that some small-town cops on Christmas Eve were no match for him, and expected the story to disappear rapidly from the news when Laci's body could not be found. If so, Scott Peterson chose the wrong small-town cops. The MPD has a 90 percent homicide clearance rate, almost a third better than the national average.

Detective Craig Grogan dispatched officers to the Berkeley

Marina, where Scott Peterson said he had launched his boat on the day Laci disappeared. The temperature was a cool 52 degrees, the December air humid, as Sergeant Andy Schlenker and Detective Rick Armedariz pulled into the marina parking area at 201 University Avenue on December 27. The Golden Gate Bridge and San Francisco skyline were buried in a dense layer of morning fog as the officers stepped out of their car.

The marina, owned and operated by the City of Berkeley, is administered by the Parks and Waterfront Department. The expansive facility encompasses fifty-two acres of water and includes 975 berths. Also on the grounds are several restaurants, a Double Tree Hotel, and a 3,000-foot-long public fishing pier. The parking lot immediately north of the marina's boat basin includes a four-lane launch ramp that is open to the public. An automated Iron Ranger ticket machine stands next to the boat ramp, providing customers a receipt upon payment of the $5 launch fee.

As Detective Armendariz snapped photos of the area, Sergeant Schlenker located groundskeeper Mike Ilvesta. Ilvesta confirmed that members of the press had been canvassing the landing pier, trying to find anyone who had seen Scott on December 24.

Ilvesta was working that day from about six-thirty in the morning to 2:00 in the afternoon. He recalled that there were few visitors to the marina that day, and although the day was "cloudy and overcast," it had not rained, despite what Scott had told the police.

Over the gentle clanging of sailboat riggings, Ilvesta described seeing "a new, full-size, dark green, Ford 4 × 4 extended cab pick-up truck with a small boat trailer" arrive around 12:45 P.M. on December 24. The Ford's trailer was empty, and the vehicle was backing into the ramp area. The driver was a white male in his thirties, with sandy colored hair, wearing what looked like a polo shirt. The Ford was blocking Ilvesta's path, and the driver was having trouble backing the trailer down the ramp. Ilvesta waited while the man drove back and forth, trying to align the truck and trailer. After several minutes, the driver succeeded and Ilvesta was able to pass. Ilvesta left the area and continued with his workday.

Producing a photograph of Scott's bronze pickup, Armendariz showed it to Ilvesta. The groundskeeper said that while the truck he had seen looked similar, he couldn't be certain it was the same one. The detective next showed Ilvesta a photo lineup that included a picture of Scott.

Ilvesta studied the images but didn't recognize the driver of the Ford. Armendariz then produced a picture of Laci, and asked if he had ever seen her at the marina. He had not.

The investigators next interviewed the marina's waterfront manager, Cliff Marchetti. Marchetti had spent much of December 24 working in the office on the south shore of the grounds, across the boat-filled marina. He did not go over to the boat-launch area, and he had not seen any customers. He did confirm Ilvesta's account of the weather as "cloudy with overcast" but no rain.

Marchetti said it would be unusual for a fisherman to take a fourteen-foot aluminum boat out on the bay in late December because of weather conditions and the fishing season. He explained that crab fishing was the only type of fishing a person could do in a boat at this time of the year. "All other fishing is out of season," he explained.

Two workers at the marina's bait shop said they did not remember seeing anybody in the boat launch area on December 24. They, too, remembered it as a cloudy but not rainy day. In addition to crab, they said, the only fish likely to be caught were "sand dabs," a flat fish, and possibly perch and sturgeon.

The detectives next drove to a Chevron gas station on Frontage Road in the city of Livermore, trying to establish where Scott allegedly bought fuel. The assistant manager told them he had worked Christmas Eve, and provided police with the surveillance tape for that day. He then directed the officers to another Chevron station on North Vasco Road, where they retrieved another surveillance tape.

Meanwhile, at the adobe-style police headquarters in downtown Modesto, Detective Buehler was interviewing two of Laci's friends, Stacey Boyers and Lori Ellsworth. Laci's friends had briefly met the tall, rugged detective at the Red Lion Hotel on Christmas Day. He'd been working round the clock since the case broke. For

Buehler, the Peterson case came on the heels of a double homicide he had been assigned ten days earlier. The long hours were taxing on the divorced dad. While his ex-wife cared for their daughter, Buehler had full custody of his teenage son and needed to be home for him.

Buehler had been managing well enough thus far—his boy was getting A's and B's in school—but the night calls were hard. When his son was younger, Buehler sometimes bundled him up in a blanket and took him along to crime scenes, leaving him to sleep in the back of the unmarked car while he conducted his investigation. He'd gotten the scare of his life one night when he returned to his vehicle to find the boy gone. He combed the area frantically, until moments later he found his son in the CSI truck talking with the guys. With only that brief but terrifying experience to go by, he knew he could not imagine how the Rochas were coping.

Buehler gave Laci's friends an update on the case. Police were examining several possible scenarios: one based on the assumption that a stranger had entered the Petersons' house, committed an act of violence, and taken Laci's body away, the second involving Scott. Both Stacey and Lori told Buehler they thought it was more likely that Scott was responsible. They were growing increasingly suspicious as the days passed.

Stacey had been at the Peterson home on Christmas Day, and observed Scott "doing an unusual amount of vacuuming" in the laundry room and the living room near the chairs and couch. When she questioned him, he said he was just trying to occupy himself. If Laci were there, he said, she would be doing the same thing because she was "extremely clean." Both women found his remark strange. They knew Laci and Scott quite well, and while Laci was a big fan of Martha Stewart's entertaining style, neither she nor Scott seemed like "clean freaks."

Stacey also told Buehler that on Thursday evening, when Scott and his family were told to leave the residence before the search, Scott announced that he was growing "angry." He didn't like being taken out of his "comfort zone," he told Stacey. Yet, neither woman believed there was any trouble in the couple's relationship and could not direct Buehler to anyone who might disagree.

As Buehler took notes, Stacey told the officer that she and Laci had been best friends since the third grade. She'd last spoken with her on December 23 at around 4:45 in the afternoon, when Laci called to talk about the holidays and her pregnancy. The mom-to-be complained that she was physically uncomfortable but said she was excited about becoming a mother. Stacey knew that Laci had experienced "female problems" in the past and confirmed that she was overjoyed with her pregnancy. Laci had recently begun complaining about her breathing, and Stacey suggested that she give up her walks in Dry Creek Park. It seemed "unlikely that she went walking in the area of Thousand Oaks Park," Detective Buehler concluded after speaking with Laci's friends. "This location would require one to walk down and return up several grades."

Despite Scott's overnight trips, Stacey had never heard Laci express any mistrust of her husband. Laci was not the jealous type, she said. She had never heard the two quarrel or complain.

Then, around 5:15 P.M. on December 24, Scott had called Stacey in a panic. (Stacey probably got the time wrong by a few minutes; at 5:17 Scott was just talking to Sharon Rocha.) He told Stacey that the police were on the way and said something about his dog being found by a neighbor in the front yard. He asked Stacey if she knew anyone who drove a white Ranger, but she had no idea what that question meant.

Lori Ellsworth spoke up next. She and Laci were close; they spoke every couple of weeks, and she often attended dinner parties at the Petersons. Lori confirmed that Laci had seemed tired in recent days. It made no sense that she would have been walking McKenzie in the park on Christmas Eve. Nor did Lori believe that Laci would leave home without her cell phone at this stage in her pregnancy. Lori also described the couple's golden retriever as a "barker," and believed McKenzie would make noise if someone tried to approach his mistress.

Both women said they had never heard Laci discuss the couple's finances but thought that she and Scott were doing fine, assuming that between them they were earning more than $80,000 a year. The women described the jewelry that Laci had recently inherited. The pieces were very important to Laci. She'd been wearing several of them in late November, when the women got together to watch *The Bachelor*. The jewelry was not really Laci's style, but she refused to leave the pieces at home because she feared they might be stolen.

The detective asked about Laci's mental state. He had heard rumors that Laci had been depressed. Both women disagreed. Although she was struggling with her physical limitations, which kept her from enjoying the holidays as much as she normally would, she knew the pregnancy would soon be over and her health would return to normal.

Both Stacey and Lori conceded that their family members' opinions of Scott were becoming more divided as time went by, particularly as Scott's flat affect contrasted ever more dramatically with Sharon Rocha's fear and grief.

Buehler also interviewed Jake Zimmeht, a retired highway patrol officer, and Stacey's boyfriend for the past four months. When he and Stacey had thrown a holiday party on December 14, he noted, Laci arrived alone. Her husband was at a business function, she said, and couldn't attend. A photograph taken at that party of a very pregnant Laci in a festive red pantsuit would become a mainstay of media reports throughout this case. Although she was smiling brightly for the camera, I found something very sad about her eyes in that picture, as she sat alone in the large wicker armchair. As that photo was taken, another camera was snapping what would become an equally famous image—that of Amber Frey and Scott in formal attire at an event ninety-six miles away.

Zimmeht didn't meet Scott until the day Laci went missing. When Scott phoned Stacey a second time that afternoon, the retired policeman remembered, he was weeping hysterically. Yet when they arrived at the Petersons' a short time later, Zimmeht was surprised to see no sign that Scott had been crying. His eyes were not red or watery, nor did his face appear flushed. Zimmeht also got the impression that Scott was avoiding him, possibly because of his status as a former cop. Zimmeht expressed uneasiness about Scott, but he was sure Laci's family would stand by their son-in-law in the absence of any clear proof that he was involved.

The search of the Peterson home was in full swing when Detective Al Brocchini arrived there at eleven o'clock on the morning of December 27. Officers in protective hairnets, booties, and latex gloves were combing each room, looking for blood or other trace evidence that might suggest a struggle. Crime Scene Manager Rudy Skultety had instructed investigators to check baseboards, crevices, and lower portions of all furniture, since "there was a possibility that the house could have been cleaned."

Upon entering the house, Brocchini gave detectives the two-day fishing license Scott handed over the previous evening. The issue date, 12/20/02, was written in red ink. The license had the numeral 2, indicating it was valid for two days. The effective dates, December 23 and 24, were obviously filled in at a later time. Detectives recorded the license into the crime scene evidence log along with dozens of other items they had seized.

Brocchini was anxious to locate the clothing that Scott had worn during his fishing trip. In the laundry area, he spied a green, long-sleeved shirt folded on top of a laundry basket. He recognized the article as the same green pullover he had seen in the washing machine on Christmas Eve. Underneath the shirt was the blue T-shirt he had observed, but the pair of blue jeans Scott had worn were not there.

Brocchini asked his team if they'd come across a pair of men's denim jeans. One officer said he'd found a pair in the washing machine. The pants were dry, as if they had not yet gone through the wash cycle. Brocchini asked that they be processed as evidence.

Moving to the guest bedroom, where Scott kept his clothes, Brocchini checked inside the armoire. He found a second pair of jeans folded on top of several articles of clean clothing. The location suggested that this might be the pair Scott had just laundered. A closer inspection revealed "suspicious stains" on the front portion of the leg, and Brocchini also seized them as evidence.

He next looked for the tan camouflage jacket he had seen in Scott's truck on Christmas Eve, but he could find neither the camouflage jacket nor the fishing lures. He did, however, locate the umbrellas that were wrapped in the tarp in the back of the truck. They were now in Scott's backyard, leaning against a fence at the far end of the property. Three large umbrella stands were nearby. Brocchini wondered why Scott would load up the umbrellas in his truck but not the stands. The blue tarp that had been wrapped around the umbrellas was now in the patio shed, spread out beneath a power sprayer.

In a second, smaller shed on the south side of the residence, Brocchini found the tan canvas tarp among the garden tools. It seemed odd that Scott would risk damaging what looked like a valuable new boat cover by leaving a power tool on top of it. Sure enough, fuel had leaked onto the cover, and a strong gasoline odor permeated the air.

Brocchini knew that Scott had admitted making at least one additional trip to his workshop since Christmas Eve. "If he had planned on placing the umbrellas in his workshop on 12/24/02, why did he change his mind on 12/26/02?" Brocchini wrote. "It's also unusual that this brand new boat tarp that was in the back of Scott's truck on 12/24/02 was now placed in a shed under a leaking gas motor. This appeared completely out of character since most of Scott's things are in very good condition and well cared for."

When the canine units arrived, one possible motive for this "careless behavior" became apparent—the destruction of forensic evidence. The dogs searched the premises, including the front and backyards, the patio and large storage shed, and the crawl space below the house, but this produced no new leads. The smaller shed where the boat cover was stored could not be searched. "The interior of the shed reeked of gasoline even after the tarp had been removed," Detective Rick House recorded. The dog handler told House that "absent a significant body part, the source of the odor would have to be removed and the shed would need to sit open for at least two days before the cadaver dog, Twist, would be effective in a search."

Inside the residence, officers were confiscating items listed in the search warrant. A Dirt Devil vacuum cleaner was taken from the hallway closet and an upright vacuum was carefully wrapped to prevent any debris from escaping undetected.

In the master bedroom, sparsely decorated with wood and wicker, officers noticed several jewelry boxes atop the couple's six-drawer dresser. They contained pieces of jewelry that matched items Scott said his wife was wearing at the time she disappeared, including two gold chains with clear stones, one gold watch with numerous clear stones on the face, and a white metal ring with blue and clear stones. All of these items were seized as well.

In a dresser drawer, investigators found five jewelry appraisals in the name of Robert Rocha, along with passports for Scott and Laci and her diary. The first entry was made on July 16, 2002, the last on December 1, 2002. What appeared to be a ripped up credit report from Experian was also catalogued.

Mosquito netting dangled from the ceiling above the Petersons' queen-size bed. The fine, loosely knotted mesh was obviously more decorative than functional. A crime scene officer photographed the bed, capturing the chilling indentation in the duvet cover Brocchini had observed that first night. Pulling the feathery white comforter from the couple's bed, the detectives observed two small spots that might be blood. They collected samples, then marked the cover as evidence.

Police also observed a wood and canvas hamper next to the dresser, but did not collect any of the dirty clothes it contained.

The double closet was filled with women's clothes. Hanging in the left corner were two shoe trees. Detectives had been advised that Laci would have worn white tennis shoes when walking the dog. A pair of ladies' Ralph Lauren slip-on tennis shoes was in the closet. They were marked as evidence.

The guest bedroom closet was full of Scott's clothes and his gun collection. Six rifles were removed from the closet, along with three ammo magazines and a number of twelve-gauge shotgun shells.

Investigators confiscated a second credit report from the trash, a TraveLodge envelope containing handwritten letters from the night-stand, and a notebook from atop the desk. The couple's marriage license, mortgage files, and checkbooks were removed from the file cabinet, as was an insurance binder dated 6/25/01.

The officers seized two laptop computers, a Dell and a Compaq. A second Dell PC and an IBM Thinkpad laptop had already been collected from Scott's warehouse. Computer forensic investigator Kirk Stockham would later identify the sites visited by both Scott and Laci and the different e-mail accounts they used. He would find that the two had visited a variety of websites, including eBay, remodeling sites, and new baby research. The other three computers were apparently used by Scott exclusively; they contained Scott's pornography bookmarks, including bestiality and bondage-themed websites. Some of the titles were so prejudicial that they would never have been admitted at trial, including "Raping the Teacher" and "The Wife Confesses." Given that Laci had worked as a teacher, the first title is especially chilling.

The forensic search of Scott's computers would also reveal two websites Scott had visited on December 8, 2002. Stockham was able to retrieve a map that Peterson had called up—depicting a topical map of the currents and depths of the San Francisco Bay around Brooks Island.

"Peterson said after he launched his fourteen-foot aluminum boat with a fifteen-horse motor, he drove north out of the marina roughly two miles," Brocchini later wrote. "Peterson claimed he could see Brooks Island from his boat. Peterson described Brooks Island as having a lot of debris and trash around it with a large sign indicating NO LANDINGS. Peterson said he was in the water between 45 minutes and an hour. The area Peterson described going [to] in his boat was the same area that Peterson had brought up on his computer on 12/8/2002."

Investigators moved to the bright blue nursery, pausing momentarily over the tiny infant clothing laid out inside the crib, most with the price tags still attached. A white bag in a corner of the small room was full of women's clothes. Some of the items appeared to be new; others looked like they were marked for the dry cleaner. Two pairs of stretch maternity pants were collected as evidence, as was a Sonogram picture, presumably of their son, Conner.

Four hairbrushes were collected from the bathroom, along with two Oral-B toothbrush heads.

In the dining room, a photographers' flash illuminated the presents that lay wrapped beneath the Petersons' Christmas tree. The Louis Vuitton wallet, nestled in a fancy brown gift bag, was the only gift taken for examination by crime lab personnel.

On top of the polished dining table, police found a Louis Vuitton purse containing a wallet and identification in the name of Laci Peterson. Officers collected the pocketbook as evidence.

In the bright yellow kitchen, the message light on the answering machine was flashing. The officers listened to two new messages and eleven saved ones. One of the detectives used a cassette player to preserve them. Once the messages were copied, the machine was unplugged and taken as evidence. Handwritten notes and jewelry receipts found on the counter were also seized, along with a wall calendar and a yoga schedule pinned to the refrigerator.

The popular book for soon-to-be mothers, *What to Expect When You're Expecting,* was on the coffee table in the family room. Crime Scene Officer Doug Lovell vacuumed around the tables with special debris-collecting equipment.

The FBI Forensic Search Team examined the Petersons' family room and the area near the washing machine for trace evidence. The investigators observed a small brownish-colored stain, believed to be a blood transfer, on the interior French door leading to the rear yard, and a brownish-colored spatter on the lower half of the water heater door. Two stains were found inside the door jamb. A presumptive test on two of the spots tested negative for the presence of blood, but police elected to collect all the samples anyway. Squares of all the carpets were also clipped.

Just outside the rear door was a built-in sink; there police found McKenzie's brown leash. Two pairs of shoes, Timberland tennis shoes on the back porch and Donner work boots from the front porch, were tagged.

At 4:15 P.M., Detective Brocchini joined detectives at Scott's warehouse office. The overhead fluorescent lights illuminating the office space grabbed the detective's attention. "On 12/24/02 at 2300 hours, when I was at the business with Scott Peterson, Peterson told me there was no electricity and I would have to use my flashlight or headlights to see inside," Brocchini wrote in his report. "Det. [Henry 'Dodge'] Hendee showed me two light switches, one inside the office and one inside the warehouse that turned on the fluorescent lights overhead making the whole inside of this business well-lit." To Brocchini, it was another sign of Scott's bad faith. "I found it highly suspicious that Scott Peterson would not want me to have the lights on in the business when I was there inspecting his boat."

The warehouse contained three distinct sections. The first was the office area, with a cluttered desk, two computers, a fax, and a phone. The second area was a large, open warehouse space, containing a large flat trailer, Scott's fourteen-foot Sears fishing boat on its own trailer, a forklift, and numerous wooden pallets stacked high with a fertilizer product in plastic jars. It was impossible to get to the small bathroom in the rear of the business without climbing over pallets.

Brocchini observed "fresh dry ready-mix" concrete on the flatbed trailer. A one-gallon pitcher containing water and a mallet was nearby. More was on the floor in front of the trailer.

Checking inside the fourteen-foot aluminum boat, the investigator found the tan camouflage jacket he had seen in Scott's truck on Christmas Eve. The jacket was now stuffed inside a green duffel in the bow of the boat, along with long lengths of nylon line and the two new fishing lures that he had seen on December 24. The shotgun shells from the truck's toolbox were also inside the bag. He found the missing Big 5 bag and the sales receipt for the fishing tackle in a trash pail. It was clear Scott had been there after the taped interview the previous night. Brocchini wondered what else he might have done during his return trip. He was surprised he had not cleaned up the cement debris before police blocked access to the warehouse.

Examining the flatbed trailer in more detail, he noticed what appeared to be "four distinctive round impressions in the dry ready-mix." The one anchor he found in the boat seemed to match the size of a water pitcher that was on the flatbed. The pitcher was about one-third full with murky water and ringed with gray residue, apparently from the ready-mix concrete.

"It appeared adding ready-mix to the water made these anchors," Brocchini noted. "After the cement mold set, they were removed from the pitcher and set on the flatbed trailer. From the distinct circles on the trailer, it appeared at least four anchors were made. We could only find the one anchor that was inside the boat."

That anchor had no line attached. It consisted of two separate and distinct colors, as if the cement was not properly mixed. The upper portion was gray, and seemed consistent with the powder sprinkled around the pitcher. The lower half was white, resembling the mix found inside the shop vacuum in the warehouse. Reexamining the rib line of the boat's interior, he could come up with no reason the cement particles would be there, unless Scott had used the cement anchors to weigh Laci's body down and cement had crumbled off as she went over the side.

Detectives also discovered a pair of yellow needle-nosed pliers beneath the boat's bench seat; clamped in the pliers was a black hair. A piece of red line was lying on the floor nearby. Detective Hendee, the crime scene manager, observed that the hair in the pliers appeared to be human. Placing the items into sealed bags, he marked them into evidence to be sent for DNA testing. "It's unknown whose hair it was, but it was my understanding that Laci Peterson had black hair," Detective Hendee noted.

During the search, Captain Chris Boyer waited outside the building with Deputy Eloise Anderson and the cadaver dog, Twist. Brocchini wanted them to examine the interior of the warehouse. Once inside, the animal "hit" on an area on the south side of the workshop, next to the boat. Brocchini watched as the canine "made a strong hit on the three milk crates that were on the ground against the south wall." One of the crates contained a large roll of shrink-wrap; the other two held tie-down straps and other assorted items. The dog also had an "indication" on the bow of the boat, along the starboard, or right, side.

As the officers discussed the dog's reaction, Brocchini saw someone open the garage next door and drive his truck inside. He walked over to speak with the man, who identified himself as Ron Prater.

Prater had been Scott's neighbor on Emerald Avenue since August 2002. Although he knew Peterson by sight, he did not know his name. Scott kept to himself. In fact, although they worked mere feet away from each other, Prater said the two had never actually acknowledged each other. It was another example of a Scott Peterson many might not recognize: the supposedly congenial, neighborly young man who had never introduced himself to someone he saw on a regular basis. Maybe Prater just didn't have anything Scott wanted or needed.

Prater and his boss were both working on the mornings of December 23 and December 24. He wasn't certain which day he had seen Scott there, but thought it was either Monday or Tuesday. When he arrived for work between 8:30 and 9:00, Scott's truck was parked, facing north, in front of his open garage door. Prater observed three green and white sacks stacked in the bed of the pickup, along the left side. He assumed they were some sort of fertilizer product.

The detective asked if the bags could have been ready-mix cement. Prater could only say that the sacks were the right size. Prater also noticed a pair of brown shoes on the open tailgate. Brocchini recalled seeing a pair of brown shoes when he was surveying the shop, and went back inside to retrieve them. When Prater identified them as the pair he had seen, Brocchini marked them into evidence. While inside, the detective also checked for the bags, but he found nothing matching Prater's description. The detective was convinced Scott had made the anchors on that very day; they would have set up in plenty of time for the "fishing trip" the next morning. When asked about Scott's boat, Prater told the detective he had seen it parked, but never actually hitched to Scott's pickup.

At 5:40 P.M., Detective Grogan called, asking Brocchini to return to the Peterson residence and collect a small sample of what appeared to be fresh concrete on the north side of the driveway. Grogan thought it might be leftover concrete that had washed into the dirt along the driveway.

Meanwhile, another detective on the case, George Stough, was following up on a lead from a woman named Diane Jackson, who had reported witnessing the burglary across the street from the Petersons. At 11:40 on December 24, Jackson was driving along Covena Avenue. As she passed the Medina residence, she saw three "short of stature, dark-skinned, but not African American guys" standing in the front yard near a van. As she passed, the men turned and looked at her. Two of the men were standing at the rear of the vehicle, and a third person was in the front yard. At the time, she thought they were landscapers, but when she noticed them staring as she passed, she changed her mind. At first she said the van was white, but then decided it might have been a darker color.

"Try to remember back as you were driving by and see if you can visualize the van in your mind," the detective told her.

"It might have been tan or brown," she replied. In any event, she said, it was an older model, with a door or doors that opened at the rear. She couldn't remember anything else.

After the interview with Jackson, Detective Stough phoned the Medinas again, related what Jackson had told them, and asked if that description "rang any bells." Mr. Medina said it did not. He asked the detective to speak with his wife. Susan Medina listened intently, then asked if the men were Vietnamese.

"All I have is short in stature, dark hair, dark-skinned, but not African American," the detective said.

Mrs. Medina recalled a Vietnamese crew that had poured some cement at their home in July, but those workers had a construction truck, she told Stough, not a van.

A t 7:30 P.M., Scott Peterson phoned Detective Grogan and told him he was sitting in his pickup outside his home. Members of the press were there, interviewing a uniformed police officer. Scott wanted Grogan to stop the cop from speaking to the media and have the journalists leave the neighborhood so he could return home for the night.

"As long as the members of the press are not on your property, I cannot force them to leave the area," Grogan told him. "However, I could have the officer remove the crime scene tape and leave the area. You can possibly return home if the media loses interest and leaves the scene."

Scott opted to have the officer removed from the scene. The detective explained to him that his house was not secured and he would be taking responsibility for it if he returned. Scott agreed.

The press is a ravenous animal; it will chase a story until fed. And the meal doesn't always have to be the truth. In fact, if a tale is good enough, complete enough, the media can become satiated and bored, leaving of its own accord. But Scott approached this inevitable part of the search as a guilty man from the inception, and his behavior piqued the press's interest. Although his mantra was "I want the focus to be on Laci," he never explained persuasively how a husband's pleas and or press appearances could have a negative impact on the search. Meanwhile, Sharon, Ron, Brent, and even his own parents were benefiting the cause with their press conferences.

Furthermore, in his private dealings with the police, Scott still didn't seem very curious about the progress of the investigation. "Scott's demeanor was courteous throughout our telephone conversation," Grogan noted in a police report several days after Laci disappeared, but "he did not inquire as to the result of the search warrants. As I received this telephone call, Detective Buehler and Detective Brocchini gave me a recording device for my cellular telephone. A portion of our conversation was captured on audiotape."

At 10:00 P.M., Detective Brocchini contacted Captain Boyer and asked to have the Brooks Island area of the San Francisco Bay searched by cadaver dogs and the marina parking lot searched by tracking dogs. Boyer asked for Laci's sunglasses and pink slipper to be delivered as scent objects, then scheduled three patrol boats, two cadaver dogs, one dive team, and a helicopter for nine o'clock the next morning. The police also made available a team of specialized cadaver dogs with the ability to smell bodies in the water.

Members of the Contra Costa County Search and Rescue team initiated the search an hour early on December 28. It was a nippy 53 degrees, and the air was thick with moisture as the three orange crafts were launched. Police did not limit themselves to Brooks Island, but widened their scope to include forty miles of shoreline in nearby Richmond.

Later that morning, Detective Brocchini called Deputy Chris Boyer and told him that two trailing dogs had searched the parking lot. The first dog, from Alameda County Emergency Services, was unable to detect any scent in the lot area. The second dog, Trimble, had begun searching at the northeast entrance of the launch area. After turning north, he ran approximately ten feet, turned and circled several times in the immediate area, then stopped by his handler's side, indicating that she had no scent. Eloise Anderson then moved Trimble closer to the launch area and directed her to check that section of the parking lot. Again, the dog circled, sniffed the nearby foliage, and returned.

Trimble was next walked to the northwest entrance of the boat launch area, where she was again given Laci's items to smell. This time, the dog turned north and trotted about thirty feet. "She then turned, circled and headed south towards the launch area with a steady pull on her harness," Anderson later wrote in her report. "She took me to the western-most point of the pier at the launch area, and pulled steadily to a pole pylon where the pier took a sharp right and then a sharp left turn. She went approximately 15 feet past the sharp left turn, turned around and returned to the pylon where she again checked out over the water, turned and stopped, indicating the end of the trail."

"Deputy Boyer said this is not a conclusive search," Brocchini noted in his report. Yet, "in his and the handler's opinion, the dog was reacting to Laci Peterson's scent as it ran through the parking lot and down the right side of the boat ramp."

Meanwhile, Detective Grogan had been working at headquarters almost nonstop since Christmas Eve. Although his suspicions about the case were growing, he had no hard evidence or material leads. Then the phone rang.

An officer was calling to report a strange conversation with a sexual assault counselor, Jill Smith. Smith said she had counseled a "confidential victim of a sexual assault" about two weeks earlier who claimed to have been lured into a brown van, either a Chevy or Ford, by the woman's ex-girlfriend.

"While in the van, two men and two women raped the victim, and a satanic ritual was conducted," the officer related. "The victim told Smith that the group frequented area parks and was currently living at Woodward Reservoir. Smith stated that during the ritual the group mentioned a Christmas Day death, and that she would read about it in the paper."

After news of the brown van broke in the press, the Modesto PD found itself racing with Scott's defense team to gain control of the vehicle. A private investigator hired by Mark Geragos was reportedly offering two thousand dollars for information about the van, and police feared the defense team might get hold of it first and "find" evidence that Laci had been inside.

Grogan immediately dispatched two officers to the Woodward Reservoir to search for the van. Theories about the brown van and satanic cult were quickly seized upon by the media, many of whom seem to have read too many detective novels. Satanic murders have been reported in contemporary America, to be sure. However, almost without exception they prove to be the work of a single demented individual, not a collective action by some cult or coven.

When the Modesto officers ultimately located the brown Chevy van, the human occupants—Rayoune Miranda, 33, Sherry Miranda, 36, Mary Renfrow, 63, and Donnie Renfrow, 55—were carefully interviewed. They had been camping at Woodward for about three weeks, they said. One of the four, Rayoune Miranda, told the officers that he had been in Modesto the previous week when Yosemite Boulevard was blocked off with police vehicles. The officers were given permission to search their trailer, tent, and van, but nothing of significance was found.

However, the van was also home to six resident mice. When the vehicle was turned over to the DOJ for examination, the rodents escaped into that office for a time. The van was never reclaimed by its owners, and when the MPD and District Attorney decided to sell it for scrap, Geragos immediately purchased it. Many reporters thought he must have a real lead that might exonerate Scott, but the van was never produced at trial. Its current location is unknown.

In another part of the station house, a call was coming in to the Laci Peterson Hotline from Laci's prenatal yoga instructor, Debbie Wolski.

Wolski, part owner of the Village Yoga Center in Modesto's McHenry Village, told an investigator that Laci had begun classes during her first trimester, but soon quit because she wasn't feeling well. Laci resumed classes in her second trimester, and attended regularly on Wednesdays and Fridays for the next five months.

On one Wednesday in December, either the fourth or the eleventh, Laci had attended a session wearing about fifty thousand dollars' worth of diamonds. Wolski described the pieces as a pair of one-carat solitaire diamond earrings, a single brilliant cut two- to three-carat diamond necklace, and a large diamond ring with a three-carat stone in the center, a diamond stone on either side, and a row of half-carats in a platinum or white gold setting. On her left ring finger, Laci wore her wedding rings. Asked if the pieces were real, Laci blushed and said yes, explaining that the diamonds had belonged to her grandmother. Laci hinted that the rings only fit her because her fingers had swollen during her pregnancy.

Laci told Wolski that she was planning to "break" the ring into smaller pieces, including an engagement ring for her sister. She had worn them to class because she was going to have them appraised afterward, and she didn't want to leave the gems in her car.

During the chat, Laci also mentioned that she was in the process of putting her grandfather in a nursing home, and that the family was going to sell his house and his furnishings. Laci said the house contained a number of antiques, and inquired if Debbie would be interested in purchasing anything.

Laci told her that her exercise consisted of walking her dog every morning. The instructor remembered Laci describing a day in early

December when she was starting to feel dizzy and lightheaded. The feeling was like a "hot flash," she said, and she had to turn back early.

The last time Wolski had seen Laci was on December 13. Scott was "very excited" about the baby, Laci had told her. "I got the impression they were very happy," Wolski reported.

Another friend of Laci's, Terri Western, spoke with Detective Jon Buehler that afternoon at the Detective Division on F Street. Western, a fifty-four-year-old real estate agent and mother of Laci's girlfriend Stacey Boyers, was the broker who sold the couple their Covena home. She had known the "outgoing" Laci since she was a child. She noted that Scott was the quiet one in the couple's relationship, but the couple "always appeared to be on their honeymoon."

Scott seemed to adore her, Western said. "He would stand up as she entered a room or get up from the table and seemed like a gentleman who was in love with his wife."

Western had last seen Laci at Stacey's holiday party on December 14. That night, Laci told her that Scott could not attend because his boss had flown into San Francisco from Europe unexpectedly and Scott had to go to the city to meet him. Western found the story "extremely difficult to believe." As a businesswoman herself, she found it implausible that a boss would fly from Europe unexpectedly and require an employee to meet with him on such short notice.

As the police would soon learn, Western was right on target.

# CHAPTER FIVE

# DECEMBER 29, 2002

O n day five of the investigation, Detective Grogan began his shift with a telephone call to Laci's parents, Sharon Rocha and Ron Grantski. Grogan needed to know more about the couple's missing daughter. He asked them to meet him at noon at Modesto's Tenth Street police headquarters, about a five-minute drive from their home on Marklee Way.

As Grogan worked, a woman named Kim Peterson showed up at headquarters. No relation to Scott and Laci, Peterson was a representative from the Carol Sund/Carrington Memorial Reward Foundation, a victim's assistance group that was helping members of Laci's family cope with the traumatic events.

Kim brought with her a videotape she had been given by Laci's parents. Sharon and Ron wanted to release the footage to the media, but first wanted official approval. Kim also had some information she wanted to share with the detectives.

First, she told the officers that Scott Peterson had requested that no images of him be distributed to the media. Beyond that, in viewing the video herself, she "saw some behavior that indicated Scott may not have been excited about having a child."

The three sat down and watched the video together. In one segment, dated Christmas Eve 2001, Laci is seen repeatedly coaxing Scott to hold a friend's baby. Her voice can be heard telling her husband to hold the child for "five minutes," "one minute," then "two minutes." Finally, he relents.

An image of Scott cradling the infant shows up on the video, and Scott can be heard saying, "This isn't that much fun."

Laci's voice is again heard on the video. "This is your one and only time you'll see him do this," she lamented. Grogan made a note in his case file.

Kim Peterson had been actively involved in criminal cases since the horrific murder of Carole Sund and her daughter, Juli, by a serial killer. In February 1999, Carole, Juli, and a young woman named Silvina Pelosso went missing on a trip to Yosemite National Park. Desperate to locate them, Carole Sund's parents, Francis and Carole Carrington, established rewards for any information about the case. The couple was convinced that the reward money and media attention were instrumental in locating their daughter's rental car—the first break in the case. Although the case ended tragically when the women were found violently murdered, the Carringtons resolved thereafter to help others in similar circumstances. They established the Carole Sund/Carrington Memorial Reward Foundation to help families without economic means offer rewards for information that might help police locate missing loved ones.

As executive director of the organization, Kim Peterson might be expected to suspect foul play. Yet it was her experience, coupled with everything she had learned thus far about the case, that made Kim suspicious of Scott Peterson.

Later that morning, Grogan met with Laci's parents. As Sharon sat nervously on the edge of her chair, listening purposefully, the detective probed for more details about their daughter's life, from her childhood through the day she disappeared.

Sharon and Ron had been all over the talk shows, pleading for news about their missing daughter. The last time Sharon had seen Laci was on December 15, nearly ten days before she disappeared.

"Mom, come quick," Laci had excitedly urged her. "Put your hand on my stomach to feel the baby kick."

Sharon rushed over, placing a hand on Laci's belly. She held it there for a long time, but when she didn't feel anything she put her ear to her daughter's stomach instead. "Hello, little Conner," she said. "Your Nana loves you. I'm waiting to see you."

"We haven't completely decided on Conner yet," Laci replied. "We're thinking we might name him Logan."

"And then that was the last we had talked about it," Sharon explained. Laci's parents thought Laci and Scott had a good marriage. "Even when Scott should have been mad at Laci, he wasn't," Ron told the detective. The couple had never separated according to Sharon and Ron, and they spent up to 90 percent of their time together. They shared the same goals, including having a child and buying a larger home.

Grogan was taking notes. "Neither Sharon nor Ron ever heard Scott or Laci become involved in an argument, raise their voices at each other, or complain about any problems with their relationship," he noted.

On the surface, it sounded like the kind of relationship most people dream of having. But human nature rarely affords such perfection. A keen observer might have drawn a different conclusion from Scott's behavior: that he simply wasn't invested, wasn't emotionally involved in his marriage. It's easy enough to do whatever your wife wants, after all, if you just don't care one way or the other.

Sharon and Ron were both surprised when Grogan asked them about Scott's boat. Neither of them knew that Scott had purchased a boat, or that he was even thinking about it. They were both visibly upset to hear that Scott had been fishing in this boat the very day Laci disappeared.

Detective Grogan was back at headquarters early on December 30 when he received a call from Scott Peterson. Scott wanted the cell phone number for Sergeant Cloward.

Grogan said he'd find it and call back. When he did, the tape recorder was rolling. Grogan gave Scott the number, then asked for the name of the delivery person who had dropped off a parcel at the Peterson home on the morning Laci disappeared.

"Oh, sure, hold on. Let me dig out that paper."

Grogan could hear papers rustling in the background.

"Oh, ah, Russell Graybill." Consulting the receipt, Scott said that the driver had been at the house between 10:35 and 10:50 A.M. "I'll hang on to this until I see ya or you send someone for it."

Grogan then asked about the jewelry Laci was wearing the morning she disappeared. "She had on the diamond earrings, right?"

"Yeah."

"And she had on a wristwatch that is diamond encrusted . . ."

"I believe so."

"Around the side, what's the metal on that though, is it gold or silver or . . . ?"

"Um, I don't know, she had a couple of 'em—I think she has a silver one and a gold one. A couple of gold ones."

"She had two gold ones?" the detective asked.

"Think so."

Just as Scott had failed to check for Laci's purse, shoes, or jacket in the hours immediately following her disappearance, he still was unsure about the jewelry she was wearing. If Laci had frequently changed her jewelry, of course, this might be understandable. Yet in photographs taken in the weeks before she disappeared, Laci's jewelry was consistent: the diamond earrings, the Geneve watch, and her diamond pendant. By this time, her grandmother's expensive ring was already at the jewelers' being divided into several pieces, including an addition to Laci's own wedding ring.

"What about the dental records?" Grogan asked. He had already asked Scott twice for the name of Laci's dentist. Scott had said he didn't know the name but knew where the office was and promised to call him with the information. Now, two days later, Scott still hadn't bothered. "Oh yeah, I meant to go," he said. "I'll go by there today and get the name of it."

"One of the things I noticed when I was at the house is you had like ah, four degrees or something up on the wall," Grogan said. "Are all those yours?"

"Well, that was a joke from Laci," Scott explained, "a running joke because I went to school for so long."

When police investigated this "joke," they weren't convinced. Three of the diplomas were phony, including a BA in religious studies from Arizona State University dated June 1, 1992, and two from the University of San Diego: a BS in psychology from June 21, 1994, and a BS in business dated June 12, 1996. The diplomas were beautifully matted, framed, and displayed in the Peterson home as if they were legitimate. As the police soon learned, they had been ordered on December 16, 2002, from a website called phonydiplomas.com. It was Scott's credit card, not Laci's, that reflected the $269.85 charge, and Scott's shipping and e-mail address that appeared on the order.

The diplomas received little attention in the press, yet to me it was obvious that Scott had ordered the diplomas for himself, that they were part of his plan to create a new persona. They wouldn't have fooled Laci, of course, but others, like Amber Frey, might be deceived. The religious studies diploma, I believe, must have been purchased with Amber in mind.

Next, Grogan asked Scott whether Laci had ever driven Scott's truck.

"She liked it," Scott told him.

"Either one of you ever been injured in the truck or anything? You ever been in an accident in it?"

"No, never been in an accident. Find probably blood climbing [sic] in it but . . ."

"You know what that was from?" The detective interrupted, referring to the blood in the truck that Scott just mentioned.

"But I mean I—cut my hands every day."

"You cut your hand that day? How'd that happen?" Grogan asked.

"Um, reached in that side pocket in the door."

"What cut you?" Grogan asked.

"I mean, I know, Alan looked at my hands and I know he noticed cuts on my hands so—he knows." Scott was referring to the first night, when Detective Brocchini had inspected his hands.

"What was in there that cut you?"

"I don't know, probably just a door or the pocket or something." He said he bled slightly. "Still my hand, I, you know, I keep cutting it handing out flyers so, that's the reason I—I keep remembering it." Scott was not making sense.

Scott's injury fueled police speculation that Laci scratched him when he was strangling or smothering her. The other drops of blood, found on the couple's duvet cover, supported this conclusion.

As I learned later, one theory police entertained seriously was that Scott strangled Laci in the bedroom, laying her body out at the foot of the bed where Brocchini saw the indentation in the covers. As he was strangling her, Laci reached up and scratched Scott on the knuckle, causing the tiny blood spatter on the duvet cover near the indentation. Scott could have dripped blood from that cut into the side pocket of his truck when he transported Laci's lifeless body, hidden beneath the umbrellas, to the warehouse, where he loaded it in the boat and covered it with the tarp.

As he had with Sharon and Sandy on Christmas Eve, Scott knew he needed to explain how he had cut himself the very day Laci went missing. Since no one could know exactly how it happened, why was he worried?

"So you just had like a scuff on your knuckle or something?"

"Yeah, yeah. Still here."

"Which hand?"

"Ah, left hand, index finger—"

Grogan shifted the subject again. "Did Laci know you had that boat?"

"Of course," Scott retorted. "Can't go out and buy something, you know, without telling your wife."

"She's been at the warehouse before?"

"Yeah, I don't know, I mean I had it for a few days before she came and saw it," Scott offered.

"Can you say when the last time she was in there was?" Grogan asked.

"Ah, it's probably Friday."

"Just a few days before she disappeared."

"Yeah, I don't know if she was down there the weekend or not. It's pretty much a common stop for us going to Home Depot—it's on the way—stop and get a tool or whatever," Scott said.

"So on Friday, did she stop by and have lunch with you or what?"

"No, no, not lunch on Friday. [I] remember that. Well, I'm not sure if she did or not. I mean, I know we'd have lunch, but I don't know if she came by to say hi or not."

"You're not sure if she came by or not." Grogan inquired.

"No, I think so, but I'm not sure, you know, I don't—make a note of it or anything." While he had assured Brocchini just days ago that he and Laci never spoke when he was at work, now he had them lunching there regularly. "Craig, I'm sorry, I've gotta go," Scott said. "I've got an interview—I'm gonna talk to some press here." The call ended abruptly, but there is no record that Scott had an impending interview with any members of the press.

At 10:15, Detective Tom Blake gave Grogan a report on the boat purchase. Blake had tracked down the previous owner, a man named Bruce Peterson (again, no relation). Peterson told police that he'd run an ad in a local newspaper to advertise his fourteen-foot Sears aluminum fishing boat, with a fifteen-horsepower outboard motor, a fish finder, and other accessories for $1,500.

On Sunday, December 8, Scott came by to see the boat. Bruce Peterson told him he had only used it a few times in freshwater; the last time was about three months earlier, in September. Scott asked a few questions, then told Bruce Peterson he would take it for $1,400. The owner wanted cash, and Scott promised to return with the money the following day. Bruce Peterson said he did not show Scott how to start the motor.

Scott came back the following day, cash in hand. According to the owner, Scott was polite and gracious throughout their dealings.

Later that afternoon, detectives reexamined Scott's boat. They had been unable to start the boat when they first examined it on December 26. Water tests confirmed the presence of salt, indicating that the boat had been used in saltwater.

Just after 2:30 P.M. police interviewed a woman named Peggy O'Donnell. O'Donnell worked at a business called Adventures in Advertising that was located in the same industrial park as Scott's office on North Emerald. O'Donnell claimed that Laci Peterson had visited the complex several days before her disappearance, either December 20 or December 23, and asked to use the bathroom. O'Donnell's remarks fueled speculation that Laci may have known about the boat, just as Scott claimed, and that she could have left her hair in the boat when she visited the warehouse that day.

Based on the condition of the office when Brocchini saw it that first night, police do not believe that Laci ever entered the warehouse that day. It would have been impossible for her, in her condition, to get to the bathroom area. Pallets of product were stacked floor to ceiling. Even the police had trouble moving about in the cluttered space.

Later on the afternoon of December 30, Scott called Grogan with the information on Laci's dentist. When Scott admitted, after days of delay, that both he and Laci shared the same dentist, Grogan's eyebrows shot up.

He listened attentively to Scott as the tape recorder whirred quietly on his desk, capturing a conversation that the public and jury never heard.

"Scott, are you there?" Grogan asked.

"Yeah."

"On the press issue," Grogan began. "Obviously, you've been going to the press conferences."

"No," Scott responded flatly.

"You have not?" Grogan was surprised.

"I went to one." Scot explained.

"All right, the chief's been getting a lot of inquiries since the beginning of this thing about the polygraph." Journalists were asking whether Scott had taken a polygraph examination. "I mean every day they ask him about that and every day he doesn't really lie, but he doesn't really tell the truth either," Grogan said. "You know what I'm saying?"

"Yeah, I'm shook up." Scott said.

"It's going to make things a little bit uncomfortable, but, we're probably going to release . . ."

"Okay," Scott interrupted.

"Okay? I wanted to talk to you about that up front and tell you man-to-man cause I don't want you to be knocked down by that."

"I appreciate that, sir." Scott then asked about getting his vehicles back, along with the keys to his house and office.

Grogan promised to check with the crime scene investigators about the keys. He then asked a series of questions about the anchor police found in his warehouse.

"When you told us you made a homemade anchor . . . it looks like you made that right there at the shop?"

Scott answered in the affirmative.

"Did you just make one?"

"Yeah."

"Okay," Grogan sighed. ". . . the boat didn't come with one?"

"No, the guy wanted to keep the anvil mushroom," Scott explained. "Did um, Kirk McAllister call you?" McAllister was the criminal attorney he'd retained.

"No." Grogan responded.

"Okay, I don't mind answering your questions."

"All right. Can you tell me when you made that?"

"When?"

"Yeah." Grogan answered.

"Ah, I don't know, Friday, Saturday, Thursday, Friday, Saturday, maybe, somewhere in there," Scott said. "Maybe it might have been before that, no, wouldn't have been before that because I was in Carmel."

"It looked to me like you made it in that ah, pitcher."

"I used a plastic bucket," Scott responded.

"Okay. And then poured it in the pitcher or something?"

"I just used the plastic bucket, little painter's bucket." While the pitcher was quickly located by officers, the little white painter's bucket was never found, nor could Scott explain its absence. Police suspected that Scott had left it on the last anchor and pushed it overboard with Laci's body.

"Is that what it was set up in?"

"Yeah," Scott responded.

"Okay. And that's just rebar or something on the top?"

"Yeah, exactly." Scott explained that he'd placed the rebar in the anchor to use in affixing a rope.

"Okay. There's chicken wire in your truck," Grogan asked. "What was that for?"

"Ah, little trees at my house. See those little stakes I've staked up?"

"Okay . . ."

"Cat keeps scratching the hell out of 'em."

"All right. Why was it in your truck?"

"Well I bought it, had it in the back of the truck, taking it home to put around the trees," Scott told the detective.

"Okay, you hadn't put any up yet?"

"No, no." Scott told Grogan that he had bought the chicken wire at Home Depot about two weeks earlier; he had left it sitting in the car trailer in his office, and he had just decided to bring it home. While the umbrellas never made it to the warehouse, the chicken wire came home.

"All right that sounds good. Ah, any questions you got for me, Scott?"

"No, no, you've been, you've been, you know, real good to me so, you've been real fair, I appreciate it." Scott responded. He asked not one question about Laci or the police investigation.

"At some point tomorrow, and this is up to the chief, if they ask about the polygraph," Grogan started. "We're gonna say that, you know, you didn't take the exam. We're not going to say that you've been totally uncooperative 'cause that's not true either."

"Right," Scott answered dryly. ". . . All right and if I can get one of those cars back, it'll be a big help in finding Laci."

"Okay, all right, thanks a lot."

"Thanks Craig."

It was 5:30 P.M. on December 30 when Detective Grogan stepped into a private ninety-minute debriefing at headquarters. Only those officers closest to the investigation were invited to attend.

The topic was a phone call that had come in on the Laci Peterson tip line from a woman claiming she was Scott Peterson's lover. Her name was Amber Frey.

# CHAPTER SIX

# DECEMBER 30, 2002

At police headquarters, Detective Al Brocchini was checking on leads coming in to the tip line when a conversation between a member of his team and a female caller grabbed his attention. Brocchini was standing directly behind Beverly Valdivia as she took notes on her desktop computer; his eyes were riveted to the screen.

A woman named Amber Frey from Madera, California, was calling to claim that she was Scott Peterson's current girlfriend. She sounded credible. She gave a list of specific dates when she claimed to have spent the night with him, and related details of several phone conversations between the two since Laci's disappearance.

Taking the receiver, Brocchini identified himself, then listened intently as the woman told her story. After seeing a news report about a man named Scott Peterson who had reported his wife missing in Modesto, Amber had attempted to call Brocchini the previous evening. When she couldn't reach the detective, she dialed headquarters and spoke with a dispatcher, who confirmed that her boyfriend had the same birth date as the Scott Peterson in the news. Upon hearing that, Amber decided to call the tip line.

Amber told the police that she'd been seeing Scott Peterson since November 20, 2002, five weeks before Laci's disappearance, and had spoken with him on the phone virtually every day since then. Grabbing pen and paper off Valdivia's desk, Brocchini scribbled furiously as Amber told him about her "single" boyfriend. The two of them had even discussed the subject of marriage. Just as with Janet Isle and Katy Hansen, Peterson first told Amber that he'd never been married, but later changed his story and confessed something quite different.

Amber related the conversation. It occurred on December 9, just a couple of weeks into their relationship, at her home in Madera, ninety miles south of Modesto. Soon after Scott arrived, she recalled, he suddenly broke down sobbing. He had "lost his wife." He offered no specifics, and Amber felt uncomfortable asking for more. His anguish led her to believe that Scott was either divorced or a widower. Scott sobbed that "this would be the first holiday without her." He "did not want to talk about it," Amber said, so she pressed him no further.

Brocchini asked if the young woman would assist in the investigation by maintaining contact with Scott without revealing that she had spoken with the police. Amber agreed. Promising to call her right back with a meeting time, Brocchini hung up, raced upstairs to find Grogan and Buehler, and called an emergency meeting.

As Brocchini excitedly briefed his colleagues on the call, Grogan quickly realized that December 9 was the very day that Scott Peterson had plunked down $1,400 to buy Bruce Peterson's aluminum fishing boat. He immediately dispatched Brocchini and Buehler to Amber's home. This could be the break they needed.

The late December sun peeked through patchy clouds as the officers made the nearly two-hour drive to Madera, a small city in the heart of California's Central Valley. Home to a portion of Yosemite National Park, Madera County is largely rural. Yet Madera itself is a fast-growing town of 43,000, dominated by young people. The average age is just twenty-six.

It was almost 11:00 A.M. when the detectives pulled up to Amber Frey's house in Rolling Hills. Standing in front of the cottage were two women, tall and slender, with fair skin and long blond hair. They looked very much alike.

Pulling badges and photo ID from their pockets, the men identified themselves and handed over their business cards. Amber Frey identified herself and her friend, Shawn Sibley, the woman who had introduced her to Scott Peterson.

For Brocchini, the name *Shawn* rang a bell. Two days earlier, he had heard the same name while interviewing a fellow employee of Scott's named Eric Olsen.

The police had first learned of Olsen through an e-mail they found on Scott's computer, in which Olsen informed Scott that he was resigning from Tradecorp. In a subsequent phone interview, the thirty-two-year-old Olsen told police that he had traveled with Scott on several business trips, and that on those occasions Scott was always generous, wining and dining clients and splurging on expensive bottles of wine. Still, he said, he had grown unhappy because Scott had made him financial promises that were never fulfilled.

Olsen also told the police that he'd never seen Scott abuse alcohol or pick up women on those business trips. But there was one troubling incident that stuck in his mind. Near the end of the conversation, Olsen mentioned that a woman named Shawn had contacted him several weeks earlier asking about Scott's marital status. Olsen told the woman he did not want to be involved in Scott's personal affairs, and that she should contact Scott directly. As the detectives entered Amber Frey's residence, Brocchini wondered if this could be the same Shawn whom Olsen had mentioned.

Amber invited the officers into her large, open living room. Although sparsely furnished, the one-bedroom cottage was tastefully decorated. She may not have had much money, the police judged, but Amber Frey was a neat and meticulous young woman who was trying to provide a good home for her young daughter, Ayiana.

As they sat down, Amber showed the officers several items to prove that she and Scott Peterson had been dating. One was a Star Theater 2 home planetarium, a Christmas gift she had received from him on December 26. The gift was purchased by mail order and was accompanied by a receipt and a special message from Scott written in Spanish. Then Amber pulled out three corks from bottles of wine and champagne she said the couple had shared during their dates. The corks were signed and dated and bore the couples' names. As the officers examined the items, Amber handed them a formal invitation for a black tie Christmas party on December 14. She told police that she and Scott had attended the party together, and then presented the officers with a receipt for the tuxedo Scott had rented for the formal affair.

Amber wore an awkward smile as she next presented the detectives with a strip of unused condoms that she said would have Scott's fingerprints on them. She also turned over a wrapped Christmas gift that she had intended to give him, with the words FOR MY LOVE inscribed on the wrapping paper.

After the show-and-tell session, Brocchini pulled out a tape recorder, and explained that he wanted to record their conversations as part of the investigation. Both Amber and Shawn consented.

"Okay, it's ah, Monday, December 30 of 2002," Detective Buehler began, as the tape recorder on the table whirred. "Present is Detective Brocchini, along with myself, Detective Jon Buehler. We are here with Amber Frey and Shawn Sibley and the time we are starting is 11:02. We're going to do two interviews here. Probably the first thing we oughta start—ah, I guess Shawn you were the first one to meet Scott?"

"Yes," Shawn confirmed.

"And if you wanna just go into that and start telling us about how you met him, where you met him, how long ago it was, and under what circumstances," Buehler instructed.

Adjusting herself in the chair, Shawn Sibley began her story. Shawn had met Eric Olsen and his boss, Scott Peterson, in October at a California Association of Pest Control Advisers trade show in Anaheim. One evening, they all enjoyed a Monday night baseball game in the lounge at the Disneyland Hotel bar, with another man named Dave whose last name she didn't know.

Shawn and Scott spoke briefly about business. He was polite and engaging. Although the men would view it differently, Shawn insisted that Scott did not hit on her. She was wearing an engagement ring and made it known that she was in a committed relationship. Shawn decided to stay on for dinner with Scott, Eric, and Dave, and the four walked to Blue's restaurant on the Disneyland strip. During the stroll, Scott removed his conference name tag and asked Shawn, "What can I write on the back of this that would attract a woman to me?"

"I took it and wrote, 'I'm rich,'" Shawn recalled.

Scott smiled, and suggested the initials, "H. B. for Horny Bastard."

Scott picked up the tab for dinner and all the drinks. After the meal, Eric and Dave went back to their hotel while Scott and Shawn went back to the Disneyland Hotel and drank at the bar until it closed. They then sat in the hotel's courtyard and talked until the security guards told them to leave. Scott followed Shawn to her hotel room, where they sat in the hallway chatting until 3:30 A.M. She was sharing a room with her coworker, she said, so they couldn't go inside.

Although Sibley maintained that Scott never came on to her, they did talk about relationships. "He asked me," she said, "'do you think there is only that one person who you are meant to be with forever?' There's probably a thousand people out there on this earth that we could be compatible with; I don't think there's necessarily just one." Scott "wanted to find the one person who would make him happy," she explained. He told her that he thought he'd found the right person, but it didn't work out, and now he was looking for someone "intelligent." Shawn said Peterson claimed he was "sick of bimbos," and "he didn't like one-night stands." He was "looking for someone he could spend the rest of his life with," she said. Scott asked Shawn if she had any friends who might fit the bill, but Shawn had nobody in mind.

Since Scott had been drinking, he wound up sleeping in his truck in the parking lot instead of driving back to his hotel. When Shawn ran into him the following morning, the two continued their discussion. He told Shawn that he lived in Sacramento and had a condominium in San Diego. His office was in Modesto, but he was rarely there. He also told her that he traveled extensively, in and out of the United States, and at the end of the conference the two exchanged business cards and went their separate ways.

About a month later, Shawn received a message at her office from Scott. Assuming it was business-related, she returned the call.

Scott immediately started talking about "personal stuff." After the conference, Scott told Shawn, he did not check out of his hotel; instead he had driven straight back to his home, and the hotel mailed him his packed bag. With that Shawn and Scott began a phone friendship, speaking two or three times a week on both her business line and cell phone.

Shawn said the charming young man always wanted to talk about personal things before they discussed business. She liked Scott, and eventually she decided to introduce him to her friend, Amber Frey, if he was "serious" about meeting a smart girl and settling down. Shawn told Scott that Amber had been hurt before, but Scott assured her that he was not a cad. "Scott insisted he would do nothing to hurt her," Shawn told the officers. The introduction was made, and Amber and Scott began dating.

In early December, however, Shawn had learned that Scott Peterson might be married. Brocchini leaned forward and readjusted himself in the chair, paying close attention as Shawn recalled a December 6 conversation with an ex-employee named Feras Almasari, also known as Mike. Almasari told her that he had recently applied for a job with Scott Peterson at Tradecorp. Scott told Mike quite a story: Having sold his business in Europe, he said, he had retired and come to the United States to launch Tradecorp.

According to Almasari, Scott claimed to have so much money that his wife just "went ahead and bought" a house in Modesto.

Shawn was shocked to hear that Scott was married. She continued to question Almasari to make sure that they were talking about the same man.

"It's Scott Peterson, the owner of Tradecorp," Almasari told her.

"Did you confront Scott that same day?" Buehler asked, shifting in his seat.

"Immediately," Shawn recalled, her voice rising. "I mean Amber is my best friend in the whole world. I was freaked. Here I'm thinking, Oh, my God, I set her up with a married guy. How horrible is that?"

When Shawn got Scott on the phone, he vehemently denied ever being married. But she hung up feeling unsatisfied by his explanations, and soon thereafter she called Olsen. Shawn's account of her conversation with Eric Olsen corroborated what Olsen had told Brocchini during their interview on December 28.

Shawn called Scott again and accused him of having a wife. "He denied it," she said. Several hours later, Scott called her back and left a message on her answering machine. "I listened to the message. It was him, and he's all crying on it and said, you know, 'Shawn I'm sorry, I lied to you, ah, I know, when I said I have never been married.' He said, 'It's been very painful for me to talk about it. I lost my wife. Just give me a call, please don't tell Amber anything, you know, I wanna tell her in person.'"

When Shawn returned Scott's call, he said that he'd told people different stories, but still insisted he wasn't married. He told Shawn that he "lost" his wife—the same line he had used on Katy Hansen . . . and that he would use on Amber.

When Shawn threatened to go to Amber, Scott implored her not to. By this time he was sobbing.

"Are you currently married?" she demanded. "I need to know. He said, 'No, no, no. I'm not currently married.' His wording was 'I lost my wife,' but I didn't really know what that meant."

Scott was still begging her to let him tell Amber. "I need to know that you've told her," Shawn told Scott. "You need to call me immediately when you tell her because if this evening she doesn't know, I'm calling and telling her."

On Monday, December 9, Shawn received another call from Scott. He told her that Amber "knew everything." Shawn did not immediately call her friend to confirm this was true. Two days later, when Amber and Scott attended a birthday party for Shawn's fiancé, Scott was introduced to Amber's friends and treated everybody to drinks.

"What does Scott drink?" Buehler inquired.

"He drinks a mix of wine, tequila, vodka, and gin." Shawn said everybody liked Scott after meeting him that night.

"He's a likable guy," Buehler stated.

"Uh-huh," Amber chimed in.

"No doubt," Buehler continued. "I mean, that's what everybody has said. But, you know, we look a little past that when we're working something like this. Don't feel bad that you guys ended up in this kind of situation."

"He's a con man," Brocchini interjected.

"He's a salesman. He's very convincing," Buehler added. "He appears very sincere."

"Can you relate some of the stories Scott has told you since you met him?" Brocchini asked Shawn.

Shawn said that Scott had told her that he'd become a vegetarian for six months during college when he was dating a "vegan." He stated that it was "worth it to stop eating meat because the sex with her was great."

On the day he dropped his girlfriend off at the airport, Scott told her, he drove straight to a restaurant and "had a nice big, fat, juicy hamburger."

Scott talked of his travels to Europe, particularly Spain, and about skiing and sailing and spending time in Alaska. He told Shawn that his uncle owned a cabin there, where he and his brother often went to fish.

The majority of Scott's conversations revolved around "finding that special person." He talked about his hopes for the future and thanked her for introducing him to Amber. Scott often told Shawn how "nice and understanding" Amber was. She was "special." "He was not dating her for 'sport,'" he said. Scott had been searching for an "intelligent person" like Amber his entire life, she remembered him saying.

"Did he tell you any of his hopes, did he talk about family or kids?" Brocchini asked Shawn.

"I finally asked him, 'If my friend [Amber] has a child, would that bother you?' He said, 'Oh, no, that wouldn't bother me at all.' That's a whole 'nother story that Amber can tell you," Shawn giggled.

It was 12:41 P.M. when Brocchini switched off the tape recorder. The two detectives stood up to stretch their legs before continuing their session with Amber Frey, who asked Shawn to leave the room, saying that she was uncomfortable discussing her romantic relationship with Scott in Shawn's presence.

"Okay, we are starting again here on December 30 of 2002 on Monday at 11:50 A.M.," Buehler said as the taped interview began again. "Just start from the first time you heard about him, first time you met him, and any detail you think of that . . ." Buehler instructed. What follows is the first complete published account of the initial police interview with Amber Frey.

"First time I heard about him, I can give a date. It was early November," Amber began nervously. "Shawn told me about this guy she met, and he was absolutely wonderful. She said that we would be a good match. It was November 19 when he called me. He left me a message, and said 'Amber, this is Scott Peterson, I'm friends with Shawn Sibley, and I'd like to meet you.'

"He left his number, and I called him back. He didn't answer, so I called again and said, 'Well, Shawn said you're not very good with the phone,'" Amber explained. "He reached me on November 20, and I said, 'Oh, we finally caught up.' We talked briefly, and he said, 'Well, I'm going to be in town, can I, I would like to take you to dinner, if that's okay, or if you'd like to go,' and I said sure . . ."

Amber continued, in a rambling fashion, to recount the details of her first conversation with Scott. At one point she asked Scott how she would identify him in the restaurant, and he jokingly described himself as six feet tall, with a big belly. He then asked Amber how he would be able to recognize her.

"I said, I'm a thin woman, small-framed, five-seven, somewhere in there . . . you know, blond hair. And he goes, 'Well, Shawn didn't describe me to you?' I said, no, not really. He goes, 'Well I won't have a problem asking every attractive blonde I see, *Are you Amber?*'"

They arranged to meet at 7:00 P.M. at the Elephant Bar on North Blackstone Avenue in Fresno. Amber arrived early and went inside. "A gentleman came in. I thought it was him. We made eye contact, and he somewhat fit the description, but I said, 'Oh please, not him.'" Buehler chuckled.

"He passed, and I sat down, looked up, and saw a good-looking man in a suit with a big smile on his face, and he said 'Amber? I'm Scott,' and he gave me a little peck on the cheek and a hug.' "

Scott was staying at the Radisson Hotel in downtown Fresno. He'd been in a suit all day, he said, and he wanted to check in, change, and have a shower before dinner. Cynical women might have hesitated at this, but not Amber, who was already finding Scott charming.

"So we go in, and he carried all his luggage. He had emptied it from that truck. He said 'This is kinda embarrassing because I almost live out of my truck.' So we get in the hotel, he pulls out two glasses and a bottle of sparkling wine, or no, cha—actually it was either sparkling wine or champagne. At this point I, I don't recall the difference. I was like, 'Oh.' "

After he cleaned up, Scott placed a strawberry in each glass and poured wine in each glass. After their drinks, the two set off for dinner at Edo-Ya, a local Japanese restaurant. The two were shown to a table, but Scott didn't remain seated for long. Instead, he left to talk to the maitre d'. Few restaurants accommodate private seating these days, yet somehow Scott managed to secure a private room. There he promptly ordered another bottle of champagne. Amber listened, entranced, as Scott talked about himself and his travels to Africa, Ireland, and Spain. She had no idea that the grandiose self-portrait he was painting was pure fiction, apparently improvised on the spot.

The conversation turned to the upcoming holidays. Scott told Amber that he was going to Alaska for a weeklong trip with his brother and father for Thanksgiving.

"And then for Christmas, he said, 'my parents always go to Maine. From there, the twenty-eighth, I'll leave for Paris, 'cause I have some business there.' "

"So when will you be back?" she asked. He told her he would return at the end of January.

"We talked about my daughter briefly," Amber recalled. "I said, today she is twenty-one months old. He goes, 'Wow, so her birthday is in February.' I said February 20. Mine is the tenth, I told him, and he is like, 'Oh wow, that's just, you know, coming up.'"

Amber told the detectives that she and Scott remained in the private room until the restaurant closed. "We were having a good time eating and enjoying each other's company." After dinner they went to B.B.'s, a karaoke bar next door. Amber said that she and Scott both got up and did a karaoke number.

"He asked me if I smoked, and I said no. And he goes, 'Oh good' and he leaned over and gave me a kiss and said, 'Oh no, you don't smoke.' It was just a simple innocent kiss."

The two danced to Frank Sinatra tunes before heading back to Scott's hotel. On the way, they stopped at a local convenience store where Scott purchased a bottle of Tanqueray gin and some tonic water.

"Then we went back to the hotel . . . and then we started kissing, and everything else. We ended up having sex that night—protected," the twenty-seven-year-old blonde added.

The next morning, Scott drove Amber back to her car. He said he would be traveling for the next week, but would try to call. He did call her twice while he was away—both times supposedly from an airport. They got together again on December 2.

"It was his first time coming to my house," Amber said; it was only their second date. "He got here and picked me up and hugged me and said, 'Where's the little one?' And I said, 'Oh, she's at school. . . . I thought we could pick her up.'"

"He was really excited about getting to meet her," Amber said. Scott brought gifts with him that day, including a house plant and a bag of groceries. She still had the plant, although its leaves were wilted.

"He brought in a bag, and he also brought dinner and wine for that night. 'Everything else is packed; all we need to do is get the little one,' he told her. And I said okay. And so, he just kinda hung out and then we went to the school, and he walked with me into her class and got her and we left."

Outside, Scott and Amber struggled to get Ayiana's car seat safely installed in his Ford pickup. "That's terrible," Scott exclaimed.

"My car is not even baby-proofed." Amber had no idea that Scott had his own baby on the way.

Eventually Scott secured the car seat, and they headed to the park. The threesome strolled through the park and began to bond that day, even as the pregnant Laci Peterson prepared for the arrival of her unborn son.

Amber told the detectives that her two-year-old daughter seemed to be drawn to Scott. As the three were crossing over a walking bridge, however, little Ayiana reached out to hold hands with both adults, and for some reason Scott declined to take the girl's hand. Mixing up her medical terms, Amber told the detectives that she thought that Scott said he had "rigor mortis" in his hands—a possible reference to arthritis.

Nevertheless, she recounted, "He had a smile plastered on his face." "I just can't stop smiling," he told her, beaming. "This is just so awesome." Finding a spot in the park for their picnic, the three of them relaxed together until dusk, when they returned to Amber's apartment.

When they got there, Scott presented a gift he'd brought for Ayiana. It was a child's pop-up version of *The Night Before Christmas*. During an interview with police, Scott volunteered that he and Laci had spent time at Barnes & Noble two weeks before her disappearance and that they had purchased children's books. Did Scott purchase Ayiana's present on that trip? Or, as Scott's half sister, Anne Bird, suspects, could this have been the very gift Anne gave Laci at her baby shower?

After Ayiana went to bed, Amber and Scott stayed up talking. In a tender moment, Amber showed Scott pictures of herself when she was pregnant, just ten days before Ayiana was born. Back home, Scott's own wife had only weeks to go with her pregnancy. Her due date was February 10—Amber Frey's birthday.

Scott offered to get a hotel room that night rather than staying with her, but Amber encouraged him to stay, and he did. They were intimate again that night.

The following day, Scott called Amber to tell her that he'd be in town around four or five o'clock. "Seeing as you are going to be in town anyway . . . would you mind picking my daughter up for me so that I'm not late?" Amber asked. "And he goes, 'Oh, I'd be honored to. Do you think she would come with me?' And I go, 'Yeah. You know, we spent the day yesterday.'"

Brocchini and Buehler sat silently as Amber detailed the events of her third date with Scott.

"When I came home," she said, "it was six o'clock, probably almost six-thirty. Ayiana was in her high chair eating, he was in the kitchen. There was wine on the table. There was bread—he cut the bread and spread the pesto on it—and he had dinner in the oven, and I was like, 'Wow.'" The perfect man had waltzed into her life.

Amber and Scott took Ayiana out later that evening to pick out a Christmas tree. When he was interviewed later by police, the worker at Cobbs Ranch Christmas Tree Farm commented that Ayiana's "parents" had dressed the little girl more warmly than themselves. Scott grinned the whole time.

When they got home, Scott, Amber, and Ayiana began trimming the tree. At one point, Amber asked Scott if he had ever been married. Not surprisingly, Scott said no.

"Ever been close?" Amber asked Scott.

"No," he replied.

Scott shared Amber's bed again that evening, and the two talked about trust. He left in the morning, telling Amber that he was headed to San Francisco.

During those first few days, Amber said, there was almost no indication of anything amiss. The one exception, she said, was when Scott's cell phone rang on either December 2 or December 3, and he had to "step outside" to take the call. Scott implied that the call was business-related and said there was "gonna be a lot of yelling."

Scott called Amber a couple of times before their next meeting on December 9. That day he telephoned, saying he was attending a meeting in nearby Merced. Was she free to see him?

Scott arrived dressed in a conservative blue suit, an International

Rotary Club pin fastened to his lapel. "When he came to my house, he was very upset," Amber recounted. "Very distraught about something he had done that was very devastating to what possibly could be a beautiful relationship. He said, 'I need you to come in here.' He moved the chairs. He sat in that chair. . . . I was sitting there. He was pretty mad, was up pacing a little bit, and I was like, 'Okay, what is it?' And he said, 'It'd be so much easier if you just hated me and you didn't wanna see me again and I just, I hate myself so much right now.'

"Then he talked to me about lying and then he goes, 'I just had such a horrible weekend this week and it wasn't fun for anybody 'cause I—this was on my mind.' And I was like, 'What?' I'm holding his hand and he was crying, his stomach kept churning and he was having trouble swallowing and tears were pouring down out of his eyes. And he said, 'I lied to you about being, you asked me if I'd been married and I have. But it's, he goes, 'in my past and it's so hard for me because I just, I've had such a hard time dealing with' . . . and I said okay."

"I'm thinking, well, she passed away. And he goes . . . 'I haven't said very much, but obviously you know that she's not with me. And I wanted to be able to talk to you about this and I was going to talk to you about this when I came back from Europe.' He goes, 'This was on my mind and I had to let it all out.' And I was like, 'Okay. I'm sorry this was so hard for you to tell me and I thank you for sharing this with me. And, I, you know, there will be time for you to share more.' And he's like . . ." Amber paused, then sighed, ". . . taking breaths and having trouble swallowing."

Scott asked, "You're not mad?" "How can I be mad?" she asked. "That's understandable if you have a loss. I said, 'Were you ready for me?' and he said, 'Oh, yes, Amber, absolutely yes,' then he said, 'This will be the first holidays without her.'"

Still sobbing, Scott announced, "'Well, I should go. You need time to think about this.' And I go, 'Why would I need time to think?' And he goes, 'Well because it's new, you know. And I lied to you.'"

Scott seemed to be suggesting that their relationship was in trouble. He was headed to Europe on business, and when he returned they could talk again and see how things were between them.

Amber confessed to Brocchini and Buehler that she had no idea Scott was lying to her. His intense, emotional explanation was just that convincing. Rather than relive the pain of his past situation, Scott said, he would often tell people he was never married. Still, she remained concerned that he was not telling her everything.

They had already made plans to go to a birthday party for Shawn's fiancé on December 11, as well as to attend a formal Christmas party on December 14. Amber asked if he still intended to accompany her to the party on the eleventh, as planned.

"Do you still want me to go with you?" Scott asked.

Amber said her response was affirmative. "Absolutely, yes, I want you to be there," she said she told Scott.

It was then, Amber explained, that Scott seemed to have a change of heart and decided to stay that evening. She said he sat down on the couch and they chatted. She sought to soothe his nerves.

"You are just amazing . . ." Scott told her. "I am just so intrigued by you."

On Wednesday, December 11, Scott came back to Madera, and he and Amber went to the Fashion Fair Mall in Fresno to pick up a tuxedo.

"You know how he paid?" Brocchini asked.

"Credit card," Amber responded.

Scott told her he had business in San Francisco on the night of the twelfth, but would be back on the fourteenth for the party. Amber arranged for her mother to baby-sit. "He came to my door with a dozen red roses," Amber explained. "He gave me a big hug and a kiss and [said], 'Oh, I missed you,' and he goes, 'Well, I hope you have more vases.' I said, 'Why?' And he said, 'Because these are for you, too.' And he pulls out two more dozen roses."

"If it's ever too good to be true, it is," Brocchini chuckled.

"I know," Amber responded. "So, I'm not done. So we get to the intimate details?"

"No, not yet, go ahead, you're going in good order there," Brocchini instructed.

Amber explained that the intimate details were next.

"Oh okay, yeah."

"I looked down and there was a single rose that was odd from all of 'em, and I pulled it out and I said, 'What's with this single rose?' and he said, 'Well, you have a candle?' And I said, yeah. He said, 'Can you get the candle?' Sure. So I get the candle, he shuts the light out and lights it and says, 'Well, I, this is all I could think about in San Francisco when I woke up today.' So he cuts the rose, the stem off, and it's just, you know, a short stem at this point with the rose.

"He started—he starts rubbing the rose on my face and kissing me, and he said that . . . ah, he was just talking about his dream that he had. And then he leaned me up against the wall and was rubbing the rose down my neck and he was saying, 'I don't know how it feels to have a rose rubbed all over me, but this is how I woke up.' His dream, apparently, that he was having. And he unzipped my top that I had on and was kissing me and ah, it was pretty, you know, intense.

"I was gonna take, he had a jacket on still and he goes, 'You know how this dream ends?' I'm like, *Oh*. It was very sexual. There was not intercourse at this point and then he got up and said, 'You know I kept trying to go back to sleep to finish it, but I couldn't.' "

Before Amber and Scott left for the formal, however, she confronted Scott again about his marriage. She told him that she now knew that he'd explained his marital status to her two days before because Shawn had confronted him. "Well, I was gonna come to you after I came back from Europe, was gonna see where things were with us . . . but then she confronted me," Amber quoted Scott as saying.

"That bothers me," Amber told him. "And he goes, 'I know, I'm sorry, but that was—it was wrong.' "

Scott continued. "There's things that I've been thinking about that I just hope that you can trust me enough that in a decision that would affect you and Ayiana, that you would be able to say yes, and trust me in that.' . . . And I said . . . 'Can I trust you with my heart?' And he goes, 'Well, that's up to you in being able to trust me and make decisions about things,' " Amber said.

Amber was wearing a form-fitting red dress, her highlighted blond hair swept up on her head, and Scott was handsomely attired in his tuxedo when the two left Amber's house for the party. As they stepped outside, she told the detectives, it started to "sprinkle," so Scott swept her up and carried her to the truck.

At the formal, the couple mingled, drank, ate, and posed for photos. It was around 3:00 A.M. when they returned to Amber's place. "I don't think we slept that night, 'cause we were intimate and [at] one point, early morning, there was no protection at all," she told the detectives.

"I've already talked to him about being on birth control," Amber explained. "That was something I hadn't been on for years. . . . He was aware of that and the possibilities, and he said, 'Oh, that's not fair of me to do that.' And then he starts telling me about vasectomy. And I said what? You don't want to have children? And he goes, 'No, Amber. Assuming we're together, I can only think of one child, which would be Ayiana.'" Scott's desire for a vasectomy at the age of thirty troubled her.

"That was, ah, the fifteenth?" Buehler inquired.

"The fifteenth," Amber confirmed.

The day after the party, she and Scott dropped off the tuxedo and went over his schedule for upcoming business trips. Scott said he was on his way to San Francisco, with stops in Arizona and Stockton, California, for meetings before he returned to Sacramento. But those meetings were still open-ended, he cautioned, leaving Amber the impression that there was a chance they could get to see each other again soon. "I go, 'Wow, then I might get to see you again.' And he goes, 'Yeah.'"

Scott called Amber on December 19 and told her he was in Arizona, near the New Mexico border. During the call, Amber told Scott that she had an appointment with the gynecologist later that week to ask about getting back on birth control, but Scott did not want to talk about such a personal subject over the phone. They could discuss it when he returned from his travels.

"Assuming we are together, I only want to think of one child and that would be Ayiana," Scott said again.

Their next phone conversation was on the twenty-third. Scott claimed he was in Maine, duck hunting with his dad. Amber told police she thought Scott was calling from the shower because she could hear water running in the background.

"I go, 'You in water?' . . . And he goes, 'Yeah, you caught me again, I'm in the bathtub.' "

Amber thought this was odd, but she speculated that the shower may have been one of the few places in his home Scott could call without family or friends hearing him.

Scott didn't call on Christmas Eve. But on the twenty-fifth "he called me in the morning and then again at night," said Amber.

"We talked a little while and there was a woman in the background," Amber recounted. "He told me it was his mom." At one point, she recalled, Scott told the woman that she couldn't come sit down next to him. "But he didn't say my name when he said that to her."

"On the twenty-seventh, he called me from Boston," Amber continued. Scott claimed he was flying out the next morning on a 7:45 A.M. flight to Europe.

"On the twenty-eighth, I decided to call him around four-something P.M., and he answered his phone."

"Hum," Buehler commented.

"I was, like, thinking, *God, he's supposed to be in Paris right now. His phone wouldn't work.* He goes, 'Hello? Hello?' " Then he hung up the phone and called her back right away.

"I said, 'Where are you?' And he said, 'I'm in New York. The plane was delayed, and I missed the 8:30.' And I was like, 'Why didn't you call me earlier? It's already the end of the day here.' And he goes, 'You're right, I shoulda called you. I wasn't being considerate. I'm sorry.' "

"There will be a lot of holidays where you and I will spend together," Scott told her. Amber said Scott expressed a desire to spend a winter in New York with her, telling her "it would be so romantic."

Amber asked Scott if he was "a promiscuous international traveler."

"'Outside of a relationship, when I'm not exclusive or seeing anyone . . . but there's only one person I call sweetheart,' and that's what he always calls me, his sweetheart," Amber said. When she related the conversation to a male friend later, her friend said that Scott sounded like a player, who probably used the term "sweetheart" so that he wouldn't confuse the names of his various lovers.

Then Amber made a suggestion to the police: Perhaps she could tell Scott that she was pregnant? "I have had my period," she said. "He doesn't know that, though."

"So, you're suggesting that we could probably use that as a ruse or something like that?" Buehler asked.

"Yes," Amber responded. "Because we were unprotected after . . . so it, it could have been possible, I could have gotten pregnant. Very possible."

"Um, hum, okay," Buehler nodded. The detectives did not pursue Amber's suggestion. Detective Buehler quickly changed the subject, and there's no indication from other police records that the idea was ever seriously discussed.

Buehler wanted to know exactly when Amber learned of Laci Peterson.

On Saturday, December 28, Amber had gotten together with her friend Denise Lane. Amber was already curious about Scott's marital status, so she and Denise conducted an Internet search using his name. They got a number of hits for Scott Peterson in San Luis Obispo and Sacramento.

The next day she got a call from her friend Richard Byrd, a police officer in Fresno. He suspected that Scott Peterson from the Laci Peterson missing persons case in Modesto was the same man she was dating. "Richard read me a little article about him and his wife and what he is going through and about him being a nice guy," Amber said, clearing her throat. "And friends and family are out; he's not ruled out, but he's not . . ."

"Uh-huh," Buehler responded. "He's a big suspect."

"Well, the paper's not saying that," Brocchini noted.

"That's true, we're not telling 'em that," Buehler replied.

## CHAPTER SEVEN

# DECEMBER 31, 2002,
# NEW YEAR'S EVE

The day after her first meeting with the police, Amber and Scott exchanged messages before speaking at 4:18 P.M.

"Amber?"

"Hi." Amber remained composed.

"Amber, if you can hear me, it's New Year's." Scott spoke over the static on the line. As he spoke, a tiny recorder attached to Amber's cell phone hummed away, capturing every word he said.

"I know, I can hear you," Amber responded.

"Amber, are you there?" Scott spoke into the phone.

"Are you having a good time?"

"Amber, hey, Happy New Year," Scott said.

"Happy New Year," Amber replied.

Scott began to spin an amazing story for his girlfriend. "I'm near the Eiffel Tower for the New Year's celebration," he said. "It's unreal, the crowd is huge." It was another of the grandiose lies that Scott seemed to use to bolster his ego. He did not realize that the composed young woman on the other end knew she was being scammed.

He told Amber that he had been trying to find a quiet place to call her. With all the celebratory noise, he claimed, it was hard to hear. Of course, he had never left California.

"The crowd's huge?" Amber asked.

"Amber, if you are there, I can't hear you right now, but I'll call you on your New Year's," Scott told her. There was crackling on the line, as if the caller were actually thousands of miles away.

"Okay, I'll hear from you then." Amber responded.

"Amber, Amber, I miss ya. I'll see ya soon," Scott said, before the call clicked off.

The phone rang again. It was Scott calling back.

"Hello." Amber eyed the tape recorder to confirm that it was still whirring.

"Baby?" It was Scott. "Can you hear me?"

"Yes," Amber replied.

"I found a quiet place; it's pretty good, huh?" Scott said, referring to the phone's reception.

"How was your New Year's?" Amber asked.

"It's pretty awesome fireworks," Scott said with a laugh. "The Eiffel Tower . . ."

"Uh-huh," Amber acknowledged. "Well, that's good. I'm glad you guys decided to go out."

Elaborating on his tall tale, Scott listed his companions by name: Jeff, François, and Pasqual, a friend from Spain.

"Good," Amber said. "Did you make any New Year's resolutions?"

"What should my New Year's resolution be?"

"Oh, I don't know, that was my question," Amber retorted.

"I'll come up with something good," Scott responded with a chuckle. "So, um, if you can hear me, I miss you and I'll try to call you back. It will be nine o'clock here in the morning, but I'm going to call you back for your New Year's. Talk to you soon, baby."


At police headquarters, a press conference was under way. Sergeant Cloward read from a prepared statement: "As we continue to profile Laci's background, gather witness statements, recognize her close relationship with family and friends, investigate the circumstances of her disappearance and, in view of the timing with the holiday season, it is becoming more apparent that her disappearance is the result of foul play. The investigation is progressing forward with that as the main focus, but we have not ruled out other possibilities."

What he didn't say was that the investigation was beginning to focus on Scott Peterson as the chief suspect.

In the glare of TV camera lights, officers announced a $1,000 reward for information leading to the identification of the person or persons responsible for the burglary of the home across the street from the Petersons on Covena Avenue. The break-in, they noted, took place some time between December 24 and 26. Information in that case could be relevant to Laci's disappearance because of the timing and proximity to the Petersons' home. Officials repeated the eyewitness description of the suspects as three dark-skinned, although not African American males, short in stature. They were also looking for an older model full-size van, tan or light brown in color, with one or possibly two doors in the rear.

As the press conference continued, Detective Grogan was in an upstairs interview room with Scott's parents, Lee and Jackie Peterson. The fifty-nine-year-old Jackie's chronic lung disorder was reportedly the product of repeated bouts of pneumonia as a child, and she used supplemental oxygen throughout the interview.

The Petersons told Grogan that they lived in Solano Beach, near San Diego, and that they had driven to Modesto as soon as they learned that Laci was missing. During the interview, they provided the police with more background information on their son.

In response to questions, the couple told Grogan that Scott had landed his job with Tradecorp through one of his professors at Cal Poly. Scott tested for a managerial position and was hired soon after. At first he had worked out of his home in Modesto, until he was able to get a client base and rent a warehouse. The company knew that it would take some time for him to show a profit, Lee explained.

When asked if they were aware that Scott had recently purchased a boat, Lee and Jackie Peterson shook their heads. Although they knew that Laci was no longer bringing home a check, and there was a baby on the way, neither of Scott's parents questioned the investment. The boat was clearly an indulgence of his own, as Scott certainly knew Laci's motion sickness would keep her off the water. But Lee Peterson said that the purchase didn't surprise him because his son "liked to experiment with things." Apparently Scott had made similar purchases—a car, a motorcycle—without mentioning them to his father. On its own such behavior might appear harmless, of course, but in hindsight it seems impulsive, irresponsible, and selfish.

Scott's parents said that both Scott and his wife wanted to have a child. Jackie believed they had been trying to get pregnant for about three years. The frustrated couple had just begun researching fertility testing when Laci announced that she was expecting.

Grogan did not dare ask the Petersons about Scott's affair with Amber Frey.

At the East La Loma Park, more than a thousand people gathered for a New Year's Eve candlelight vigil. Scores of Laci's friends, former classmates, and teachers packed a grassy knoll around a makeshift stage, a flatbed trailer adjacent to the police department's mobile command center.

As dozens of satellite news trucks surrounded the perimeter, reporters and cameramen grabbed sound bites from those closest to Scott and Laci. Scott Peterson was in attendance that night. Yet many observers found it odd that Scott never spoke with the press and was avoiding the TV cameras. Furthermore, he chose not to join the other family members on the stage, staying instead on the ground— and away from the spotlight.

Lee and Jackie Peterson joined Laci's parents and siblings on the podium, where they took turns speaking, urging the swelling crowd to continue the search for Laci. Hundreds of people, their shoes wet from standing in the soggy grass, raised glowing candles as Sharon Rocha took the microphone. Many in the crowd wore pale yellow and blue ribbons pinned to their clothes: the yellow to symbolize hope, the blue for the baby boy Laci was carrying. Applause rang out as Laci's mother pleaded with the crowd to "just keep looking" for her daughter.

"Don't give up," a teary Sharon told the onlookers, her voice cracking as she uttered the words.

Standing beside her was Modesto's chief of police, Roy Wasden. "Wherever the search takes us, let's keep looking for Laci," Wasden told the crush of participants, as a sea of flickering candles danced in the wind.

Laci's father, Dennis Rocha, came to the vigil from Detective Grogan's office. Like the Petersons, Laci's dad sat down for an interview with the police that day. Rocha looked as though he'd been through hard times. His skin appeared wrinkled and leathery from exposure to the elements, and from the difficult life he had led. Rocha wore his thick salt and pepper hair combed to one side, and a bushy mustache curled upward toward his cheeks. Behind dark-rimmed glasses his eyes were red and swollen, no doubt from crying.

Dennis told Grogan that he was Laci's natural father. He and Laci's mother had been married for seven years; having "married young," he said, they had lived on his parents' ranch in Escalon during the early years together. After the two divorced, he visited with Laci every other weekend until she was sixteen. Once his daughter got a car, she wanted to spend more time with her friends and pursue other interests. He understood and didn't force her to make the trip.

Dennis told the police that his mother, Helen Rocha, had been "very helpful" with Laci and his two other children, Brent and Amy. She had recently passed away and had left Laci some of her fine jewelry. She was a "lady," Dennis said.

"About how much was your father's estate worth?" Grogan inquired.

Dennis said the ranch was sold for about $500,000, and that there was an equal amount in stock.

After the divorce, Dennis paid child support regularly, and noted that he and his ex were still friends. He described Sharon as a bit "prissy" but "very attractive" when the two started dating. Like Laci, his ex-wife was a cheerleader during high school. In Dennis's opinion, however, all of his children were somewhat "spoiled." Sharon had indulged both Laci and Brent, he said, as did their paternal grandparents.

Dennis admitted that he and his older daughter had grown estranged after Laci went off to college. Since her move to Modesto, he had seen her only about a dozen times, on holidays and birthdays. Eight months earlier, on May 4, Dennis was with the family as Laci turned twenty-seven. That birthday would be her last.

During the interview, Dennis Rocha also expressed concern about his son-in-law, Scott Peterson. While he had never heard Laci complain about her husband, he felt that Scott always "acted like he was too good for us." He also ventured that "something doesn't sound right in his story." As he told Grogan, "You don't go fishing by yourself."

Dennis also told Grogan that Scott had been "giving me the cold shoulder." And he said he was convinced that his son-in-law's emotional outbursts were nothing more than an act. "He has not attended a press briefing since the press started asking questions about him. He got up and ran out and hasn't been back since."

"I think he was jealous of the baby, that's what made him do it," Rocha told the detective.

Hurrying to the park, Dennis Rocha joined his son, Brent, and daughter, Amy, on the stage, where Sharon Rocha, Ron Grantski, and Scott's parents were already gathered. All of them made public, heartfelt pleas for Laci's safe return.

Scott Peterson was conspicuously silent. He insisted that he wanted the focus of the evening to be on his missing wife—not him. At one point, Scott was nowhere to be found. Yet photographers captured his image mingling—and smiling—with friends. Months later, that picture would be juxtaposed with the grieving faces of other attendees on a large screen in a California courtroom.

At the stroke of midnight, Amber's phone rang. Celebrating at Shawn Sibley's New Year's Eve party, she stepped outside to take the call.

"Happy New Year's," Amber said.

"Happy New Year," Scott responded.

"So tell me, what's your New Year's resolution?" Amber asked, picking up a theme from their last call a few hours before. It was an interesting question. Amber was attempting to elicit some information about Scott's future plans. She would continue her performance, as both confidante and inquisitor, for more than a month.

"Ah, I didn't even think of one."

"You didn't think of one?" Amber retorted. "You had nine hours to think of one. My New Year's resolution is, and actually I thought of one for you—which one do you want me to share first?"

"Uh, first . . ."

"Yours first," Amber continued. "My New Year's resolution for you would be to not travel so much . . . and spend more time with me and Ayiana. What do you think of that? Is that something on your mind or anywhere close?"

"Oh yeah, for a long time . . . I could care for you . . . care for each other and . . . we could fulfill each other."

"And Ayiana, what?"

"We could be together, could care for her, and you know, raise Ayiana."

"Uh-huh."

"We could fulfill each other . . . forever."

"So," Amber cleared her throat. "I know you said before you'll be back by my birthday so . . . anticipate any plans . . . do you have anything in mind?"

"For your birthday? Yeah, I'll have to come up with something good."

"I haven't even thought about what should we do for Ayiana's birthday party. . . . So how would you feel about meeting Ayiana's grandparents? Not my parents, Ayiana's father's parents."

Scott said he thought it would be fine; he didn't see anything "weird" about it.

"You'd be okay," she said.

"I can't think of any reason why I wouldn't be," he agreed.

Yet, when pressed by Amber, Scott cited several differences between them that could cause their relationship not to work. "Like, I've never gone to church much. . . . And that you know could be a point for you, and would we see eye to eye on raising Ayiana? And how would you accept our role . . . I can think of others but those are major right now."

"Mm-hum . . ."

"The fact that you want another child . . ."

"Right . . . Do you still feel that you're very adamant about not having another child?"

"Ah, I wouldn't say adamant, but it's just not my thought . . ."

Later in the conversation, Amber tried once more to pin Scott down on his travel plans. "Do you even know when you're coming back?"

Scott said he would be in Guadalajara from January 28 through February 2.

"That's certainly something for me to look forward to," Amber replied.

"Yeah, but you know, what we need to do, sweetheart, is not analyze our relationship."

"I'm not analyzing."

"You know what I mean," Scott said. "We just need to spend a little time together and let it grow."

At one point, Amber asked Scott about a book he had been reading. "What book was that?"

"Jack Kerouac it was, um . . . hitchhiking across the country . . . oh, shoot, what's his book? Late sixties movie, hitchhike New York to San Francisco . . . I can't think of the name of it right now." Scott seems to have been thinking of Kerouac's *On the Road*—and perhaps confusing it with the 1967 film *Easy Rider*.

"That's okay. Good book, though? Did you enjoy it?"

"Yeah, it was interesting cause it's a . . . it was interesting because I never had a prolonged period of freedom like that from responsibility, you know . . ."

Here was another telling statement from Scott—a clear suggestion that he had been thinking about the burdens of adult life . . . responsibilities, in his case, that included caring for Laci and their baby. He was dreaming about being free—free to travel, and pursue other women, and to become an entirely different person from the doting husband and fertilizer salesman that he had become.

The conversation turned to religion and then to banter about their ages. Amber told Scott that she was looking forward to her thirties.

"You're really cute," Scott laughed. He told Amber he was already old, already in midlife.

"You're not old, you're so young, Scott. . . . You're not even at midlife. You're in great shape and you have an awesome body."

"My knees are cracking," Scott said.

"That's nothing, my knees crack. It's nothing. So tell me, do you think I'm intelligent?" Amber asked.

"Yeah, that was one quality I was thinking of. You know what the quality was that I'm thinking about now?"

"No, tell me."

Scott's response was inaudible.

"Me?" Amber replied. "How is that?"

"You have good self-esteem and it's difficult to find in people. And it makes you incredibly sexy and appealing to me."

"That's something I've had to work very hard on Scott, not something that came easy to me."

"You've done a great job."

"There's always been something that I always keep it to the surface," Amber said; she was beginning to cry. "'Cause everything in its time, and everything in its time serves a purpose."

"Yeah."

"I'm sorry."

"Oh God, don't ever say that, don't ever say you're sorry for sharing."

"What?"

"I'm here for you?"

"What was that?" Amber wept.

"I'm here for you."

"I wish you were."

"But I am, and I will be," Scott consoled. As he spoke, a dog—probably McKenzie—barked in the background.

"I'm smearing my mascara down my face," Amber giggled.

"You're wonderful," Scott said.

"I'm drinking a Guinness Extra Stout on top of my three cranberry lime twists."

"You're having breakfast."

"Yeah, that's a good way to look at it," Amber giggled. "So when do I get to hear from you again, Scott?"

"I'll call when it's the nighttime."

"When's your nighttime?"

"There's nine hours' difference, I will take the train late tonight from here to Brussels. . . . Then I'll be in Brussels for at least four days."

"All I'm saying is, I don't know when you go to sleep."

"Oh, probably midnight or one."

"So that would be?"

"Three or four your time . . . and, um, okay, you go to bed at nine, it's six o'clock my time."

"I don't go to bed until eleven. So eight your time."

"Okay, I might be up then. I'd like to talk to you at that time. To me it's the most intimate time."

"The most intimate time because . . . ?"

"Just because that time of day our psyches are in . . . focused on relationships, as opposed to getting up in the morning and doing things or going to pick up the dry cleaning," Scott said. "You go back to that party."

"Okay."

"And our relationship will grow. I have confidence in that."

Scott's call to Amber lasted seventy minutes. Before it was through, Detective Buehler noted, Amber had "confirmed many details that had been brought up in the interview Brocchini and I conducted with her on Monday, 12/30/02." Among these were his supposed travel arrangements: "She was able to get him talking about plans for his return from Europe and his travel to Mexico, returning to the United States on January 25. An agreement was made to continue phone contact around the same time each night."

As soon as this relationship became public, commentators and onlookers speculated that Amber Frey was the motive for Laci's murder. However, this explanation has never resonated with me. Scott's pattern of extraneous lies and narcissistic behavior overrode any sincere love for this woman.

Rather, the one thing Scott Peterson seemed to care about was rejecting his life as a small-time fertilizer salesman in Modesto, saddled with a suburban wife and the eighteen-year obligation she was about to bear. He preferred to think of himself as an international playboy, who swept into town from time to time to entertain his mistresses with fine meals and grandiose tales of his escapades and glorious future.

His stories, and his actions, were not for Amber Frey; they were simply for Scott.

# CHAPTER EIGHT

# JANUARY 1, 2003, NEW YEAR'S DAY

Detective Jon Buehler spent much of New Year's Day 2003 on the road, driving to and from Madera. Buehler had been officially appointed to "handle" Amber Frey, and it was a good choice for many reasons. Buehler was kind, eager, and enthusiastic. He was also divorced, which meant he didn't have a wife at home to feel uneasy about the many phone calls he would be receiving from this attractive but very needy young woman. Buehler's assignment would require a lot of hand-holding. In the coming weeks his phone would ring repeatedly, interrupting precious time with his son and daughter. But in the end, his efforts did not go unappreciated by the woman who bravely stepped in to help solve the crime.

Buehler was not the only officer whose private life would come to a grinding halt when Laci went missing. Detectives followed up on countless leads that arose during the almost two-year investigation. There were calls from people saying that Laci had been taken for her unborn child; others from psychics purporting to have visions of the missing woman in various locations; and still more from tipsters anxious to report sightings of a pregnant woman fitting Laci's description. The calls came in from all over the country.

One fact that was ignored by the press is that the six detectives on the case were juggling thirty-four other homicides at the same time. Many of them missed holidays with their families, and in some cases their long absences created problems at home. The personal sacrifices made by Detective Grogan, District Attorney Investigator Steven Bertalotto, and prosecutors Rick DiStaso and Dave Harris— all of whom have young children—were enormous.

Buehler arrived at Amber Frey's residence around 1:30 P.M. to take custody of the tapes of the previous night's conversations. Once inside, Amber told Detective Buehler that Scott preferred that she send mail to a post office box while he was overseas. Somehow, he claimed, he would be able to access the letters through his e-mail. Amber didn't think that made sense, but she jotted down the address anyway: Scott Peterson, P.O. Box 290, 1811 H Street, Suite B5, Modesto, California.

Later that day, Amber listened as Scott shared more stories of his supposed European adventures. Now he was in Brussels, about to take a morning jog over the quaint cobblestone streets. All the French food and wine was making him pudgy, he claimed.

"And last night . . . well, this morning too, there is this fucking dog next to this hotel," Scott said.

"This what?"

"This dog that just keeps barking. I want to kill it," he snapped. The dog, of course, was McKenzie.

He switched subjects. "I got here, like, at two o'clock this morning, but I'm going to fight the pudge."

"So, you're gonna go jogging at seven o'clock in the morning?"

"It is so cold outside," Scott told her. "It is freezing. There's no snow on the ground, but it . . . oh, it was so cold last night."

"So how long a distance are you going? . . . Are you just gonna jog around the streets, or . . ." Amber asked.

"Yeah, pretty much, yeah. I don't know. I'm just gonna run. I don't . . . I kind of remember the area here," Scott said. "I'll jog down to the main square, which is kind of neat, with all the big churches in the background."

"Yeah, I don't even really, you know—I mean, the only times I've really seen Paris is, you know . . ." Amber struggled to get the words out.

"I'm in Brussels now," Scott corrected her.

"Oh, you're . . . that's right, you did the change at Brussels. You're in Europe, though, right?" Amber queried.

"Oh yeah," Scott confirmed again.

Scott attempted to explain the time difference to Amber. While she was getting ready to turn in for the night, he was already starting a new day. Where he was, he said, it was nine hours ahead of Madera.

"Yeah, that's just so confusing to me," Amber giggled. "And I hope by the time, you know, by the end of this month, I'll finally get the hang of it."

"And then I'll be back. Then we won't have to worry about it again," Scott told her. Even now, with the investigation heating up around him, Scott was still convinced he had nothing to fear. Just as he told Amber weeks before, he thought he would be free by the close of January. Did he think detectives would simply quit when Laci's body did not turn up, or was he convinced he had already won the game?

"Right," Amber agreed.

"Okay, so you got to go to bed, huh?"

"Yeah, I'm just jabbering now."

"Okay. Good night, sweetie," Scott said. "I'll talk to you maybe tomorrow, okay?" Amber hung up the phone knowing that Scott was only ninety miles away.

Over the next several days, Scott's employers confirmed the detectives' suspicions. In a phone interview from Madrid, his boss, Eric Van Innis, said that he hadn't seen Scott on December 14. That was the day he told Laci he had to pick up his boss in San Francisco—a lie to cover his date with Amber at her Christmas formal. Van Innis told police that the last time he'd come to the United States was in January or February 2002, when he flew into San Francisco Airport from Mexico.

Another executive from Tradecorp, Nuno Loureiro, a member of the company's board, told police he received an e-mail from Scott on December 26, relating that his wife was missing and he was assisting law enforcement in looking for her.

In the e-mail, Scott stated that he would "need a few days off." Scott didn't seem to think the case would take much time from his busy schedule.

After receiving the message, Loureiro spoke to Scott twice by phone. Scott explained to Louriero that his wife had gone for a walk with their dog on December 24, 2002. He said that someone may have seen her in a parking lot, and mentioned that a nearby home had been burglarized. It was all very matter-of-fact.

Loureiro agreed to cooperate with the investigation, and promised not to mention their conversation or the fact that police intended to review the company records.

Grogan, meanwhile, was alerted to a rumor that Laci Peterson may have been involved in an affair of her own. The rumor was bolstered by a second source, a caller to the Laci Peterson tip line, who stated that the expectant mother was dating a personal trainer from her gym. A third tip came in by e-mail that same morning, also indicating that Laci had been dating another man. Grogan turned the information over to Detective Bertalotto of the District Attorney's Office and asked him to follow up. It is not unusual for such allegations to arise in a case of this sort, but no evidence was ever found to substantiate these claims.

As he delegated duties, Grogan's cell phone vibrated. It was Scott, asking for the keys to his home and business, and requesting access to some business checks that he said were in the glove box of his truck. He needed to deposit those checks, he said, in order to make payroll.

Grogan told Scott that he would make inquiries. He called Scott back about an hour later to let him know that the keys would be at the reception desk at headquarters after 1:30 P.M. He then moved quickly to get a court-approved GPS tracking system installed on Laci's Land Rover before returning it. This would allow the police to survey Scott's movements without him knowing it.

Grogan called back to alert Scott that the police intended to release photos of his vehicle and boat in an attempt to verify his trip to the Berkeley Marina on December 24. When Scott didn't answer, he left a detailed voicemail. To Scott, it was all part of the game; threatening him with the pictures was just Grogan's way of trying to get a rise out of him.

Two hours later, Scott Peterson made the next move. Striding into the lobby of the police station, he requested to speak to Grogan. Moments later, the stocky detective greeted him with a firm handshake, and presented Scott with his wallet. In his hand, he held Scott's keys. Given Scott's previous concern about inventory receipts, he forestalled any challenge by reviewing each key carefully and returning them one by one. He did not mention that police had made copies. Grogan intended to keep the keys to Scott's 2002 Ford pickup and the toolbox in the truck's rear, and the remote for his car alarm.

Scott nodded, then told Grogan that he needed to retrieve two business checks from his truck. He also asked if police had taken any checks from the business office. Grogan told him no, but explained that a number of Scott's business records had been seized as part of the search warrant. Scott requested that Grogan find out which checks police had taken as evidence and arrange for their return.

Grogan told him that he could not release them without a court order.

Scott pressed the detective, telling him that it would be helpful if he could pay his employees, and instructed Grogan to do what he could to get them released.

"I told Scott I felt he may have more time to contact the businesses who wrote the checks and have those checks stopped and a new check issued rather than have me stop working on the investigation of his missing wife to write court orders," Grogan wrote. Seeming to back off a bit, Scott said, "Sure, you're right. You should be working on the case.'"

It was Scott's move. If Grogan wasn't going to give him the checks, then he wasn't going to give the detective his debit card. Instead, he pulled out a piece of paper that read "Chevron Parthian, Livermore, 932498575. $13.08." He had downloaded the receipt from the Internet rather than let the detectives have his card to collect the information. Changing the subject back to his wife, Scott asked if Grogan believed that Laci was kidnapped for the baby. "Do you think when she has the baby, I'll get half my family back?" Scott asked flatly.

Just reading that question sends chills up my spine.

"I told Scott that we had investigated any leads with similar themes; however, I found the probability that Laci was kidnapped for the baby to be unlikely," Grogan logged in his daily report. "I also explained to him that we had asked all local law enforcement agencies to notify Modesto Police Department regarding any calls from hospitals about infants who are accompanied by females that do not medically appear likely to be the child's mother."

Scott next asked the detective if he thought that Laci had died.

"I told Scott that with each passing day, the likelihood that Laci would be returned unharmed diminished," Grogan wrote. Then, at last, "Scott appeared to have tears well in his eyes," the detective noted. But "Scott did not cry, and I did not hear him sniffing."

At 5:30 that afternoon, there was an apparent break in the case. Detectives George Stough and Sebron Banks went into a briefing about the burglary that occurred at 516 Covena Avenue. An anonymous tipster had informed Detective Stough that items stolen from the Medina home—and one of the men who allegedly pulled off the burglary—were at a house on Tenaya Avenue. The caller also stated that additional property taken during the heist was at a second residence on the same block.

At 6:00 P.M., police knocked on the door of 1406 Tenaya Avenue. A woman answered, and told police she lived at the residence. Inside, officers saw several small children.

Officer Hicks told the woman that he was following up on a burglary, and asked if he could speak with her further. She invited him in. The officers explained that they had received information that led them to believe that items stolen from a nearby house were in her residence. The woman gave police permission to search the premises, and signed a search warrant waiver.

While the search was under way, forty-two-year-old Donald Pearce pulled into the driveway. A background check of the home's residents prior to arriving on the scene revealed that Pearce had an outstanding traffic warrant from neighboring San Bernadino County. Officers standing in the driveway placed him under arrest.

Pearce told the investigators that he had resided with his mother in her home on Tenaya Avenue for the past sixteen years. He was unemployed, and worked on cars in his mother's driveway for income. He explained that he was the primary caregiver of his two young children; they lived in the main house with his mother, while he resided in a trailer in the back.

Another man, Steven Wayne Todd, also lived in a shed in his mother's backyard. When asked about the burglary on Covena Avenue, Pearce revealed these unreported details:

On the morning of December 26, 2002, Steven Todd came into his trailer between the hours of six-thirty and seven o'clock. He told Pearce that he had been inside the home all night, and that there was now a safe sitting on the home's front porch. Todd told him that he needed a vehicle to transport the heavy safe back to his shed. According to Pearce, the two men climbed into his four-door white truck, drove to 516 Covena, then used a dolly to transport the "very large, cream-colored safe" to their vehicle.

Pearce described how Todd had shoved the safe into the front seat and closed the passenger door, then climbed in the rear passenger side, leaving the dolly on the grass near the curb. The two drove back to their place on Tenaya, and then carried the safe, which Pearce said weighed about 250 pounds, to Todd's shed. The safe was so heavy that at one point they dropped it, and wound up rolling it to the front door of Todd's room. Todd retrieved a sledgehammer and other prying tools, and pounded on the safe's dial until it caved in and the door popped open. Inside there were two blue money bags, a box of jewelry, and a Tech 9 handgun, accompanied by a "very large magazine and bullets." Pearce told Todd he would get rid of the gun. A second gun was also among the stolen goods.

The two men sifted through the jewelry, then looked inside the blue money bags. They were empty, Pearce claimed. Susan Medina had told police they contained $50,000 in cash, but Pearce said that the jewelry and the handgun were the only items of value inside the safe. The pieces included a woman's gold and emerald ring, a jade and gold ring, a woman's diamond wedding set, ruby earrings, and miscellaneous rings and necklaces containing precious gems.

When police located Todd, he admitted to committing the burglary—he said he was on a bicycle at the time—but told police he had nothing to do with "the woman." When officers asked him to clarify, he said he was referring to "the missing woman with the baby."

Todd was no stranger to the arresting officers; he had been booked on similar charges in the past. He claimed that he had sold most of the jewelry and one of the handguns to a relative of a friend, and gave the rest of the pieces away to female friends. As for the tools stolen from the shed, he sold them at a swap meet that past Saturday. During a later interview with cops, Pearce admitted to selling the second gun for two hundred dollars.

Both men were booked into the Stanislaus County Jail. The detectives never believed that Todd and Pearce had any involvement with Laci's disappearance. After the two men submitted to polygraphs later in the day, the police issued a press release stating that the burglary and Laci's disappearance were in no way connected. Todd later pleaded guilty to one burglary charge and received an eight-year sentence; Pearce pleaded no contest to a lesser charge and got 180 days.

The police were still receiving reports from the Red Lion Hotel. Sergeant Ed Steele, the police liaison assigned to Laci Peterson's family, recalled that on the night of December 30, 2002, around 7:30 or 8:00 P.M., Scott Peterson had returned to the hotel, sat down in a chair, and began sobbing. Several of Laci's friends noticed his outburst and jumped up to comfort him. Scott's "crying jag" lasted for about thirty minutes. He then got up and helped himself to food donated by the local restaurants for the search teams.

"Sergeant Steele advised that Scott had no apparent loss of appetite and based on his breakdown earlier, he found it odd that he was able to eat within such a short time," Grogan recorded.

Grogan's next move was to leave Scott a voicemail message, telling him that the Land Rover was ready to be picked up. He didn't say that he intended to ask Scott for DNA samples, or that he would present evidence of his affair with Amber Frey.

"All of the information that I had provided Scott Peterson was true," Grogan noted in his report. "However, I did plan to return the vehicle with a tracking device installed in it, and I also planned to serve a search warrant completed by Detective Al Brocchini for blood, cheek cell samples, hair sample, and full body photographs."

Scott called Grogan back and said he would swing by headquarters in about half an hour to pick up the Land Rover. "Hey, um, I heard about the robbery—did we—get any leads out of those guys?" Scott asked.

"Well, we got all the burglars in custody and, ah, we're working on clearing those guys out now, but they just appear to be just a bunch of burglars," Grogan stated.

"Yeah?"

"I mean there's nothing . . . they're with us now and we're working on that angle of it, but it's not like, you know, any of them have been arrested for some heinous thing in the past or something."

"Yeah, I just hope they saw something." Scott told the detective.

A little while later, Scott arrived at the Detective Division with his father. Grogan met the men in the lobby and gave Scott the keys to his wife's SUV. He then asked if he could show him something. Scott consented. He and Lee started walking toward the interview room in the Investigative Services Building. Grogan motioned for Lee Peterson to remain behind, advising that he wanted to meet with Scott alone.

"You're free to leave, and you don't have to talk to me if you don't want to," Grogan advised Scott as they entered the small, well-lit room. Most of what happened next has never been reported in the press.

Scott sat down. He watched as the detective produced a photocopy of a fax the police had received—it was the photo of Scott and

Amber posing at the Christmas formal that Amber's mother had sent over the night before.

Grogan had other, better photographs of Scott and Amber in his possession, but decided not to produce them. Instead, he simply said that police had received "a copy of one faxed photograph" sent in anonymously. Looking directly at Scott, he slid the grainy black-and-white fax across the table. "Can you explain this?"

"Is that supposed to be me?" Scott asked impassively.

"It looks like you."

Scott insisted that the man in the picture was not him, nor did he recognize the woman. Was this another stalling tactic? Why else would he deny this, when police would surely be able to confirm it?

"Are you certain you have never seen her before?" Grogan asked. Scott said she resembled a girl he once knew in college.

Changing the subject, Grogan told Scott about the burglary investigation. Both men had taken polygraph exams and passed, he said. The police were certain that the suspects in custody had nothing to do with his wife's disappearance.

"Good," Scott said.

The detective then asked about some of the items that police had taken from his house and business during the searches. When, Grogan wanted to know, did Scott make the anchor for his boat?

"Again, Scott told me it was Thursday, Friday, or Saturday, prior to Laci's disappearance," Grogan recorded. "I asked Scott where he purchased the bag of cement and he told me he bought it at Home Depot, and once he had made the anchor, he threw the bag away. I asked how large a bag he made and he held his hands apart a distance of approximately two feet, indicating the approximate size of a 90-pound bag of cement."

"I asked Scott why he chose to make an anchor out of cement rather than buy an anchor from a store. He told me a bag of cement cost approximately $3 in a store and an anchor would cost $30 or more to purchase. Scott looked at several boats on December 9 before buying the nicest, most expensive one. His other activities, like wining and dining Amber Frey, did not support the notion that he would make some puny concrete weight to take to the Bay rather than spending just thirty bucks on a good, substantial anchor.

"I told Scott I had never seen a cement anchor previously and asked where he had gotten the idea. Scott told me he had seen them in rental boats in the San Diego area in the past and believed they would be easy to make. Scott told me the standard anchor is called a 'Danforth' but a mushroom anchor was the type on the boat when he first viewed it. Scott said the owner of the boat did not want to sell the anchor, so Scott decided to make his own.

"I asked Scott if he looked at any other boats. Scott said he had looked at two other boats on the *Modesto Bee* online. Scott again confirmed that Laci was the only person who was aware that he planned to purchase a boat. She did not go with him to look at the boats as she had no real interest in them," Grogan later wrote.

"I explained to Scott that in reviewing my report and Detective Brocchini's report, I saw a difference in his statement. I asked Scott to confirm when he first saw McKenzie on 12/24/2002 after returning home from fishing. Scott confirmed that he first saw McKenzie when he arrived home, prior to entering the house.

"I asked Scott why he had put the umbrellas in the back of his truck. Scott said he had wrapped them in a tarp to take them to the shop but had forgotten to take them out on two occasions. I asked Scott where their current location was and he told me he had taken them out of his vehicle and put them in a shed behind his house."

Eventually, however, Scott began to bristle. When Grogan started asking Scott about the tarp that he had moved from his truck to the shed, he wrote, "Scott said, 'I don't know if it's appropriate I'm talking to you without my attorney, Mr. McAllister.' I told Scott that was fine, but I wanted to explain one thing to him."

Grogan recorded what he told Scott next. "I was aware he was a young man with a job requiring his travel and he was a 'good looking guy' that would have no difficulty meeting women. I told Scott if there had been infidelities in his marriage, it would not necessarily mean he had done anything wrong to Laci and he should tell me if he had been seeing other girls. Scott said the last time he dated anyone aside from Laci was prior to his marriage to her."

Even as Grogan was having this conversation, police were learning that Amber was not the only woman claiming an intimate relationship with Scott while he was married to Laci. At that moment Scott's ex-girlfriend Janet Ilse was on the phone with one of Grogan's assistants, describing her 1998 affair with Scott while the two attended Cal Poly. Ilse, the woman who had walked in on Scott and Laci in bed together, had finally called police to share that story. Although what she and Brocchini discussed was not admitted at trial, it helped to fill in the detectives' portrait of Scott Peterson.

One detail Janet shared with the police was that Scott liked to hunt and fish. She knew he had been to Lake Lopez and Lake San Antonio—both freshwater locations—but as far as she knew, he had never fished in saltwater. She was also not aware of any other women Scott dated that year and admitted that she avoided him after their confrontation. She also knew that Scott owned the Shack. The only time she'd gone there, she spotted him and left immediately.

Janet also told the police that she was a vegetarian, and that while they were dating Scott had stopped eating meat—a statement that corroborated Amber's story about Scott becoming a vegan for some girlfriend because "the sex was great."

"I asked Janet about their intimate relationship," Brocchini later wrote. "Janet said, 'He had issues.' Janet said Peterson did some weird things at a bar after they broke up. It was only second-hand information from Peterson's roommates. However, Janet heard Peterson got real drunk and began exposing his penis in the bar. Janet said Peterson was very self-conscious about the size of his penis, and whether he could please a woman."

Size did appear to be an issue for Scott Peterson. While investigating the case, I learned that he had developed names for Brocchini and Grogan that suggested a fixation with sexual performance. Sources close to the investigation told me that Scott role-played a cross-examination of the two detectives, addressing them as "half-pints," "runts," "little five-foot-nothings," and "pricks." His questions were wildly immature, focusing on the size of their penises and their sexual abilities.

Janet Ilse told Brocchini that Scott had expressed a desire to meet her family and friends, but that he rarely talked about his own family. Janet said her friends all liked Scott, but she had never introduced him to her dad. "She said her father does not like people who are 'slick,'" Brocchini noted. "Janet told me Peterson thinks he is real smooth." Still, Janet had been in love with Scott. She still had photos, gifts, jewelry, and clothes that Scott had given her.

"I asked Janet how sure she was [that] Laci knew Peterson was in an intimate relationship with her" after the bedroom incident, Brocchini wrote. "Janet said [that she had] made it obvious to Laci that Scott and Janet were in an intimate relationship."

Checking the dates, the detective realized that Scott and Laci had been married less than a year when Scott began his affair with Janet.

In the coming weeks, Janet Ilse would continue to cooperate with police, sending them a package that contained a necklace Scott had given her and photos from the time they were dating. She enclosed six color pictures, including one of McKenzie at Janet's home, a snapshot of Scott relaxing beside Janet's coffee table, and one of Janet posing with the twelve dozen roses Scott had presented her on their first date. In an accompanying letter, Janet explained that she only kept a handful of the photos. She had angrily thrown the rest away after their breakup. In a moment reminiscent of Monica Lewinsky, Janet would later forward to Brocchini a black Hugo Buscati dress that Scott had given her as additional proof of their relationship.

Looking for more insight into this period of Scott's life, Detective Brocchini also interviewed a housemate of Scott's, but Robert Aguirre had little to offer. Rob had not known Scott before he moved into the house in 1998, and even after he moved in Scott revealed little about himself. It wasn't until three weeks after Scott moved in that Laci called the house and Rob discovered that Scott was married.

During that time, Rob said, Scott "associated" with women other than Laci, but he could not—or would not—say whether Scott had been sexually involved with any of them. He described Scott more as a "big brother" than a peer.

Aguirre told the detective that there were "many" nights during college when women stayed over at the house. When pressed further, he simply said that he couldn't recall any specific woman who spent the night with Scott. Even after Brocchini showed him a photo of Scott arm-in-arm with Janet Ilse, Rob said that he "would not or could not" recall this woman spending the night with his roommate.

Brocchini then asked if he could remember any woman discovering Scott and Laci in bed together. "It could have happened," Rob told the detective. "I just don't remember."

As the conversation between Scott and Detective Grogan drew to a close, the detective asked Scott to consent to a collection of blood and DNA evidence and full body photographs. Scott replied that he was sure that the detective had a search warrant for this. When Grogan produced the warrant, Scott did not read it; he simply went along without further comment. Scott was fingerprinted and photographed that afternoon, and technicians also collected cells from the inside of his cheek for DNA testing.

Detective Buehler soon joined Scott and Grogan, and together the three drove to Doctor's Medical Center to draw blood samples. During the twenty-minute ride, Scott sat up front next to Buehler. Grogan sat in the back seat and listened. Unbeknownst to Scott, a tape recorder was capturing his remarks about his mother's ill health, snowboarding, his wife's Land Rover, and the detectives working overtime.

Once at the hospital, the technicians took about fifteen minutes to collect blood samples from Scott. During the return trip, Grogan asked Scott if he had talked to his attorney about taking the polygraph.

"Yeah," Scott replied.

"What's his feeling on it?"

After hesitating, Scott told Grogan that his lawyer, Kirk McAllister, had some issues with the DOJ polygrapher, Doug Mansfield.

"I know he's very opposed to Mansfield, but I don't know if he's opposed to somebody else or not. I mean, that would help kind of put some of this stuff to an end. But . . . I don't know, it's something to discuss with him anyway and see what he thinks," Scott said.

Changing subjects, Scott began chatting about the media's role in the search for his wife. He also inquired about using a psychic who had contacted him to assist in the search for Laci.

Buehler told Scott that he could not recall a case in the past several years in which a psychic played a role in the recovery of a crime victim.

Arriving back at headquarters, Grogan once again suggested that Scott consider taking the polygraph.

Scott told the police that his attorney regarded polygraphs as "police voodoo."


The day ended dramatically with Laci's mother Sharon Rocha appearing on CNN's *Larry King Live*. Lee and Jackie Peterson were also guests on the program.

Larry was off that night, and Court TV's Nancy Grace was filling in. A video clip of Officer Ridenour opened the show.

"We still have hope that Laci Peterson is out there and alive," he said. "And so we think it's critical. And as long as the media wants to continue to cover this, we're going to be here to provide as much information as we can and get the community support."

Next, Nancy Grace introduced Jackie Peterson. "Where is Scott tonight?" she asked. "I would imagine he would be out begging the viewers to help in the search for his wife."

"He is," Jackie Peterson told viewers. "And he has. And he is with friends this evening that have been searching all day. We go out every day. We have many volunteers. We're headquartered at the Red Lion Inn. It's so many nice people and such work. But, it's so . . . we need more. And we're not going to give up hope."

Grace asked Jackie about the police saying that Scott had "cooperated to an extent." "Now, what did they mean by that? To an extent?"

"We don't know," Jackie conceded. "We don't know what they mean."

"Has he taken a polygraph?" asked Grace.

"I don't know if that's . . . if he's been asked to do that. He's been cooperative. They've . . . he's made available to them everything they've asked for," Mrs. Peterson responded.

Next, Nancy turned to Sharon Rocha. "Do they have any leads so far? Anything at all?"

"To the best of our knowledge at this point, there was a robbery or a burglary across the street from their home," Sharon told Nancy. "And they've actually made two arrests today. We were hoping that would be connected, but at this point, we're being told that it's not, so . . ."

Lee Peterson got the final word.

"If you knew Scott," he said, "as far as him being implicated, it's a nonissue."

# CHAPTER NINE

# JANUARY 4, 2003

In the wee hours of January 4, members of the Modesto Narcotics Enforcement Team, in cooperation with the Department of Justice, began twenty-four-hour surveillance of Scott Peterson. This, along with the tracking device affixed to his car, gave the police real-time access to Scott's actions.

As the surveillance teams followed Scott, scuba divers were busy searching the waters of the San Francisco Bay and the shoreline near the Berkeley Marina. Over the next several days, police would reinterview witnesses and work to narrow down Scott's time line by calling the numbers taken from Scott's cell phone.

Brocchini's first call was to Karen Servas, the Covena Avenue neighbor who'd found McKenzie running loose on the morning Laci disappeared. The detective had already interviewed her, but when her number showed up on Scott's call list, he talked to her for a second time.

Servas confirmed that she had received a call from Scott on December 24 at around 8:00 P.M. Scott asked her if she had seen Laci that day. When Scott phoned again several days later, she was in New Mexico. He left her a message asking exactly what time she had found the dog. Servas called back and told him that she had found a receipt from the store she had gone to right after returning McKenzie to his yard. It was stamped 10:34 A.M. Retracing her steps, Servas determined that she must have returned McKenzie to the couple's yard at about 10:20 that morning. Scott claimed that he left home at around 9:30 that morning. If that were true, that meant that the frame during which Laci disappeared spanned about fifty minutes.

Servas also mentioned to Brocchini that another couple who lived around the corner, Greg and Kristin Reed, told her that they had seen Scott's truck parked in his driveway around 9:40 A.M. on Christmas Eve. Servas told Brocchini that the Reeds were on holiday in Carmel and would not be back until early the following week.

"I asked Servas if she could remember anything suspicious or concerning to her," Brocchini noted in a report.

The chilling account that Servas gave next has never been reported.

Servas told the detective that she does not receive any of the national news channels on her television. On Christmas Day at about 5:00 P.M., she went over to Scott's to watch the news. While there, she heard some things that alarmed her.

Servas recalled that Scott and his parents, Lee and Jackie, were in the dining room with another couple. Scott invited her to stay for turkey dinner, but she declined, saying that she had to go home to pack for her trip to New Mexico in the morning. Besides, she mentioned, as a vegetarian she did not eat turkey.

About ten minutes after Servas returned home, Scott called and asked her to reconsider, telling her that he had added tortellini to the menu. Servas agreed and walked back over to the Petersons'. Scott and his parents were still there, but the other couple had left. Taking a seat at the dining room table, Servas noticed that Lee and Jackie Peterson seemed distraught. As they chatted, Scott told his parents that the police had taken a gun and some white rags out of the washing machine on Christmas Eve. He seemed upset that the officers had not immediately told him that they were seizing the items.

Upon hearing that police had taken the gun and the rags, Scott's mother made a comment that struck Servas as odd: "At least you didn't go shooting that night."

Servas then opened a bottle of wine and started preparing the tortellini. A Christmas message from Laci was still printed on the chalkboard tacked on the room's bright yellow wall, she noticed, and "Scott was acting like everything was fine."

As Brocchini jotted later in his report, "Servas said Scott mentioned three or four times that he was willing to take a polygraph. However, because the officers thought he was too emotional, they thought he should not take it." None of this had happened, of course. Scott seemed to be rehearsing a new batch of stories. "Later, Servas heard Scott saying, 'Too much time had gone by, so he couldn't take a polygraph.'"

Servas told Brocchini that she had seen Jackie Peterson on *Larry King Live* the previous night. "Servas said Jackie told Larry King the police had not asked her son to take a polygraph," Brocchini noted. "Servas said Jackie knew that was a lie when she said it because Jackie was present when Scott was talking about the polygraph at least three or four times in the house."

Servas told Brocchini that she was staying with friends and wasn't intending to return home. When he asked her why, she explained that she had a "weird feeling."

"Servas told me that she has looked directly into Scott Peterson's eyes on at least two occasions and Peterson looked back," Brocchini wrote. "Servas said she is not returning home because she is afraid of what she'll see the next time she looks into Scott Peterson's eyes."

"I don't want to see him," she said.

At the conclusion of the interview with Servas, Brocchini wrote the following notes:

> From reviewing Servas' statement, I noticed the following false statements:
> 1) Peterson told his parents and Karen Servas that police had removed the handgun from inside his residence rather than the glove compartment of his truck.
> 2) Peterson advised his parents and Karen Servas at least four times that he volunteered to take a polygraph. However, officers told him not to because of his emotional state and because too much time had passed since the incident.
> 3) Greg and Kristin Reed told Servas they saw Scott Peterson's truck parked in the driveway of his residence at 0940 hours [9:40 A.M.] on Christmas Eve when Peterson claimed he had left at 0930 hours.

Brocchini also talked to Brian Argain, a real estate agent and friend of Scott's. Argain had been introduced to the Petersons by his former girlfriend Stacey Boyer. He and Scott played golf together often, and he considered Scott a good friend.

Argain learned about Laci's disappearance when Guy Miligi, a mutual friend, called him on December 24 to say that "Laci was missing." That first night, Argain walked the neighborhood with Scott, looking for Laci. Scott simply told him he had returned home from fishing, and Laci was gone. Argain did not press for more details because Scott seemed upset.

Argain had seen Scott several times after that night, but the two never spoke about what happened. He was with Scott during New Year's Eve vigil at Dry Creek Park on New Year's Eve and was quite surprised when Scott would not join Laci's brother, Brent, on the stage. He advised Scott to get in front of the cameras, but Scott insisted that the vigil was for his wife, and not for the family. Argain urged Scott to talk to the media to clear his name, but again Scott told him he didn't like the attention because "this isn't about me." Argain became really upset when Brent urged Scott to come up on stage, and Scott replied, "I'm here with my friends."

"What is suspicious to you?" Brocchini asked Argain.

"Number one, Scott is not talking to the media. Number two, Scott's fishing story is fishy," Argain replied. "I'm good friends with Scott but his story isn't making sense."

Brocchini then contacted Guy Miligi directly. Miligi told the detective that he wouldn't be acting the way Scott Peterson was acting if his wife were missing. Miligi explained that he would be "much more vocal" and "out in front of the press." But he said that he wasn't faulting his friend, and vowed to continue to assist in the search for Laci.

Brocchini also reinterviewed Bruce Peterson, the man who sold Scott the fourteen-foot aluminum boat. Peterson confirmed Scott's claim that he didn't want to sell him the anchors with the boat, telling the detective that he asked Scott if he could keep them because he planned on buying another boat later in the year.

As Brocchini continued down the list of Scott's calls, Detective Grogan was meeting with Brent Rocha at the Investigative Services Bureau. Like his younger sister, Brent was attractive, with clear olive skin, thick black hair, and dark, full eyebrows. He worked in Sacramento as a project analyst for the California Department of Justice Division of Gambling Control.

The two men sat in a downstairs conference room and began to review the documentation gathered regarding the inheritance for the three Rocha children, Brent, Laci, and Amy. While the police were focusing on Scott, they had not rejected the possibility that Laci's disappearance was linked to the family finances. Grogan wanted to get a handle on that angle, to help support or eliminate theories having to do with Laci's inheritance.

He learned that Laci's grandparents' rambling ranch in the small agricultural town of Escalon had been sold in 1995. Another forty-acre tract, where Dennis Rocha still lives, housed a second residence that produced rental income. The Oakdale home of Laci's grandfather, Robert Rocha, was currently on the market, listed at almost $500,000. The family had recently moved the elderly Mr. Rocha to a skilled nursing home in Sacramento, where he was being treated for diabetes, dementia, and heart problems. His wife, Helen, had died in 1999. Since Robert Rocha's dementia precluded him from running the estate, Brent was appointed executor in 1999. He and his aunt, Robin, shared control of the living trust and estate, which were valued at $2.36 million in 1999.

When Helen Rocha passed away, the estate received $500,000 from her life insurance policy. Brent Rocha could have used the money as he saw fit, but chose to honor the primary goals of the trust, which were to care for his grandfather and father, Dennis. The money was currently being used for his grandfather's care, he said.

Grogan asked Brent what would happen once his grandfather passed away. Half of the estate would go to Robin, Brent said, and the remainder would be paid to the Dennis Rocha family trust. As executor, Brent would distribute funds to his dad as needed. He cited his father's irresponsible spending habits, and the fact that Brent had graduated from law school with a degree in tax law, as the reasons that his grandparents had appointed him to the role.

Once his grandfather died, Brent said, he planned to care for his father until his death. Then, whatever remained in the estate would be divided among Dennis's three children. If his father were to die in the near future, the three would receive about $400,000 apiece, but that number would diminish with each passing year.

Laci knew very little about the trust. She had spoken to her brother about three weeks before her disappearance and was told that she would probably not receive anything for a minimum of three years, until she turned thirty. And even then she might not receive a penny until after her grandfather and father had both passed away.

Brent described his sister as fun, outgoing, happy, determined, and strong. He was not aware of any problems in her marriage to Scott. He knew that she wanted to be a stay-at-home mom, and believed that both she and Scott were excited about having a baby. Scott did whatever Laci asked him to, Brent said, although he acknowledged that he saw the couple only infrequently.

"What do you think could have happened to Laci?" Grogan asked.

Brent said his first thought had been that she was abducted or assaulted by a homeless person. But he said that scenario seemed more unlikely as time passed. Once it became clear that her disappearance wasn't linked to the burglary across the street, he theorized that maybe someone had taken her for the baby or as part of a sexual crime.

Brent told Grogan that he didn't think Scott was capable of hurting his wife. He also said he doubted that either Dennis Rocha or Ron Grantski could ever harm Laci.

Instead, Brent told Grogan about Laci's old high-school boyfriend, telling the detective that Kent Gain had been verbally abusive during their relationship. He admitted that he had not seen Kent in seven years, but found it strange that Kent had not turned up to assist in finding Laci. Brent indicated that he did not know where Kent was living or what he was doing now.

Brent also raised the possibility that Laci may have been harmed because of her vocal opposition to a proposed street project planned for her neighborhood.

Amy Rocha was in the lobby waiting to speak to Grogan next. As she followed the stocky lead investigator down the stairs to the conference room, Amy explained that she and Laci were half sisters. They shared the same father, but Amy's mother was Nancy Galati of Escalon.

Amy's complexion was fairer than Laci's, her reddish-brown hair not as thick or dark as her sister's. A cosmetologist at Salon Salon in Modesto, Amy was six years younger than Laci. As he had with Sharon, Dennis Rocha left Amy's mother, Nancy, when Amy was just two. Amy lived with her mom until 1998, in her junior year of high school, when she moved in with her dad.

During her childhood, Amy, Brent, and Laci had stayed with their father on weekends. Amy first met Scott while she was in the eighth grade, when Laci was invited to teach Amy's cheerleading squad a new cheer, and she brought Scott along. She and Laci had grown close after Laci returned to Modesto in 2000.

Amy described her sister's relationship with her husband as a good one. The two seemed very much in love, she said. She never heard them argue, and Laci had never confided anything negative about Scott to her. She characterized Laci as easily excited, a "talker" who was often "antsy" and "high energy." Scott, however, was calm and relaxed. He never appeared stressed or ruffled, and always seemed "laid-back." Amy also described Laci as "a little spoiled." She usually got her way by asking for things nicely, but wasn't a brat. "She got anything she wanted because Scott tried to give it to her," Amy explained.

Grogan asked her about Laci's visit to Salon Salon on December 23. Scott had an appointment with her to get his hair cut after work that day. Laci and Scott arrived at around 5:30 and stayed for about an hour.

That day, Amy said, her sister was wearing a pair of cream-colored maternity pants and a black top with flowers. Laci sat on one of the salon's cherry-colored couches talking, while Amy cut Scott's hair. The two discussed Laci's brunch, planned for Christmas Day. Laci would be serving French toast, and she and Amy were both looking forward to having their grandfather and brother at the gathering. They agreed to chip in for a special gift basket of almonds, crackers, trail mix, and fruit from the local Vella Farms fruit market for their grandfather.

When Amy called in the order on December 23, she was told that the basket wouldn't be ready for pickup until noon the next day. Since the shop was closing early on Christmas Eve, the clerk said, the order would have to be picked up by three o'clock.

Scott offered to swing by to get it, since he would be going by there on his way to the Del Rio Country Club to play golf. Amy warned him that he would have to be at the store between twelve and three.

Amy went to work on Christmas Eve, but left early. When she arrived home some time after three o'clock, she found a message from Vella Farms on her machine: It was three o'clock and no one had come to pick up the basket. Around 3:45 P.M. she tried to reach Scott on his cell phone. When he didn't answer, she called Scott and Laci's home number, but again got no response. She then drove to Vella Farms, collected the basket, and returned home.

Some time after five o'clock, she received a call from Scott. "Is Laci there?" he asked. "Is your sister there?" When Amy told him no, he announced, "I can't find her, I got home, and she's not there." She said Scott sounded "frantic and excited."

After she hung up, Amy checked her answering machine and heard two messages from him. "Call me back as soon as you get this. I'm looking for your sister," he said on both messages. Amy canceled plans with her father, and began calling local hospitals. When she talked to Scott later that night, he claimed that he'd gone fishing that day. She was surprised, since he had told her the night before that he would be golfing at Del Rio that day. Amy had no idea Scott had bought a boat until she heard about his fishing trip that day, and she told Grogan she was sure her sister would have told her if she knew that Scott had purchased a boat.

After establishing Amy's whereabouts on the day of the disappearance, thus eliminating her as a suspect, Grogan laid out the photos of Laci's jewelry and asked Amy if anything seemed to be missing. The only item Amy could identify as missing was a pair of diamond earrings that she had seen her sister wearing.

"Based on Amy's statements, it appears the jewelry that Scott Peterson claimed Laci was wearing on the morning of December 24, 2002, while mopping the floor, is in fact in Laci's jewelry box, which Modesto Police Department collected as evidence," Grogan wrote in his report.

That evening, Scott returned home and dialed Amber before turning in for the night. He had to rush to get packed, he told her, because he was off to Madrid.

"What's in Madrid?" Amber inquired, as the tape rolled in the recorder.

"That's where the production office is," Scott explained. "I'll be saying *hola* a lot more, instead of *bonjour.*"

"So how are you doing this New Year?" Amber asked. Scott had claimed this would be his first New Year's alone.

"Um . . . happy at times, sad at others . . ."

"Yeah, I just yeah, you know, I just know you, that this was gonna be a hard holiday for you."

"No, I don't think about it," Scott told Amber. "You go to sleep now. I miss you. And I'll see you soon, huh?"

# CHAPTER TEN

# JANUARY 5, 2003

When the shift of officers arrived at 5:00 A.M. on January 5, there were four cars parked outside the Peterson home. They included Laci's Land Rover Discovery, which was outfitted with a covert police tracking device, and a nondescript gray Subaru.

The surveillance team trailed Scott as he left the house shortly before eight, dressed casually in blue jeans and a blue shirt. He drove the Discovery to the Red Lion, where search volunteers had gathered. He stayed there for about two hours before joining another man to distribute Laci posters in Moose Park and at several churches around town. In the interim, police observed, Scott had changed his clothes; he was now wearing a blue sweater with white stripes and a blue-and-yellow ribbon pin. Just before eleven, he headed home in the Discovery.

He emerged from the house again about ninety minutes later. Instead of taking the Land Rover, he jumped into the gray Subaru and headed westbound on Highway 132.

With no tracking system to aid them, the officers anxiously followed Scott in their unmarked vehicle. He drove westbound on Highway 580 toward the coast, passing under Highway 680.

It was exactly 2:00 P.M. when Scott, thinking he was in the clear, drove into the parking lot of the Berkeley Marina. At a press conference the night before, the Modesto police had announced that search teams would be at the marina the following day, and officers would be combing the shoreline and waters of the San Francisco Bay for clues concerning Laci's disappearance. But Scott didn't stop to speak with any of the searchers. Instead, as the officers watched, he drove around the boat launch area.

While Scott's defense team would make light of this at trial, I thought I'd never seen a more classic case of a criminal returning to the scene of the crime. At no time did Scott park and walk down to the search sites. Nor did he stop to thank the officers who were braving the bay to look for Laci. Instead, it was reasonable to conclude, he was gauging their progress.

"We were only there approximately five minutes before we left" on Scott Peterson's trail, the surveilling officers wrote in their report. By this time, Peterson was driving erratically. As the cops headed back on 580 toward Modesto, "Peterson was driving extremely fast. He was driving in and out of traffic at approximately eighty-five to ninety-five miles per hour in heavy traffic."

Scott raced past San Leandro and sped along Highway 580 through Livermore. "Peterson exited in Livermore and went to a Chevron," the report continued, and "drove up to the gas pumps as if to get gas. Peterson kept driving past several vacant pumps and got back on the freeway."

The game was on. Suddenly the cops were on notice: Scott was playing to win.

"Peterson then took another off ramp and drove through two gas station lots before finally stopping. It appeared Peterson forgot which side the gas tank was on and drove in circles until he properly pulled up next to a gas pump.

"Peterson went into the gas station," the report continued, but noted that something had changed about his attire: Scott was no longer wearing his blue-and-yellow ribbon.

Once he was back in Modesto, Scott slowed down, obeying the speed limit. By 3:35 he was back at his house on Covena Avenue, where he remained for an hour before climbing into another car with a male driver and driving to the Del Rio Country Club.

Back at headquarters, Brocchini was working the phones. His first call was to Renee Garza, who had known Laci since kindergarten. Renee and her husband, Brian, still socialized with the Petersons. Renee told Brocchini she'd never sensed any problems in the Petersons' marriage, and that Laci spoke as though she and Scott had a "very good sex life" and a great relationship.

About two years ago, Laci had stopped taking birth control pills and bought an ovulation kit in hopes of conceiving a child. Renee remembered the day that Laci excitedly phoned to tell her, "I think I'm pregnant."

Brocchini asked if Renee had discussed the case with any of Laci's other friends. She said she had. After the candlelight vigil on New Year's Eve, she invited their friend Rene Tomlinson to her home. The two agreed that it was troubling that Scott was shying away from the media, a sentiment that many friends now shared.

A short time later, Brocchini reached Laci's maid of honor, Heather Richardson, on her cell phone. Heather quickly dispelled rumors that Laci had been dating another man. She was certain that Scott was the father of the couple's unborn child. The last time she heard from Laci was either December 23 or 24, when Laci left a holiday greeting on her voicemail. After Laci's disappearance, Scott told Heather that Laci had gone to bed around 9:00 P.M. on December 23, and that when he left to go fishing the next morning she was wearing her diamond earrings and her grandmother's watch.

"What's your gut feeling?" Heather asked, turning the tables on the detective.

Brocchini explained that he was keeping an open mind. Still, he expressed concern that he had been unable to eliminate Scott as a suspect.

In a subsequent call, Brocchini asked Heather's husband, Mike Richardson, to help the investigation by asking Scott about his activities on Christmas Eve. Mike agreed, and in mid-January he talked with Scott. Scott told Mike that after reading an article saying that sturgeon were running in the bay, he'd decided to go fishing Christmas Eve. Scott remembered speaking with five people at the marina that day.

Despite the efforts of the Modesto officers and Scott's own private investigator, none of these people was ever located. By now, the police suspected that Scott had changed his alibi from golfing to fishing after he realized that he'd been sighted at the marina that afternoon. Detectives were convinced that he'd made the decision during his ride back to Modesto that day, then quickly placed "cover-up" calls to Laci, leaving messages for his wife at home and on her cell phone.

Mike told Brocchini that Scott didn't appear worried about Laci being found in the San Francisco Bay. As for the fishing boat he'd recently purchased, Scott told Mike Richardson that he'd planned to surprise his father-in-law, fellow fisherman Ron Grantski, with it after Christmas. This seems to be the first and only time Scott ever floated this story. In all the thousands of documents and countless interviews I've conducted in covering this case, I never heard anyone suggest there was any real camaraderie between Scott and Ron. They were not fishing buddies. The whole thing was another one of Scott Peterson's lies.

When Brocchini asked Greg Reed about a message Scott left on his answering machine. "Have you or Kristen seen or talked to Laci today or yesterday? I can't find her," was the exact message Scott left Greg that Christmas Eve. Scott must have been in the car when he phoned, Greg told Brocchini; he could hear road noises in the background. Scott never told Greg where he was, and Greg never asked.

"Are you certain that's what he said?" Brocchini responded. It was the phrase "yesterday or today" that seemed strange to the detective. "Yesterday" would have been December 23, and Scott told police that his wife had disappeared on Christmas Eve. Greg had saved the message on his voice mail, and offered to let the detective listen to it.

Greg and his wife, Kristin, lived around the corner from Scott and Laci, and Greg's mother was the couple's next-door neighbor. He and Scott were good friends, and they spoke at least once or

twice a week. Laci was in his wife's Lamaze class, which Kristen conducted at their home on Edgebrook Drive.

Greg also told the detective that Scott had called him on the afternoon of December 24. The two discussed an upcoming New
Year's party. He and Scott often talked about hunting and fishing, so
when he learned later that Scott had bought a boat he was surprised
that he hadn't mentioned it—or his fishing trip—on the call.

Nor had he mentioned his wife.

"What do you think about this case?" Brocchini asked Greg.

"I don't know what to think anymore," Greg told the detective.
Several things bothered him. He couldn't understand why Scott was
refusing to speak to the press. Nor could he understand why Scott
had asked about hearing from Laci "yesterday or today" in his message. For me, this remains one of the unsolved mysteries of the case.
Was Scott worried about something Laci might have told the Reeds
before she disappeared? Or was he revealing, inadvertently, that she
hadn't lived through the night?

Greg recalled something else unusual. He recounted a conversation he had with Scott the year before about a fence between Scott's
house and his mother's place that needed to be replaced. At the time,
Scott said he had no money for a new one. A month later, he installed a swimming pool in his backyard. If Scott had been telling the
truth about not having the money to replace a simple fence, Greg
wondered, how did he find the money for an expensive pool a
month later?

In the days ahead, Brocchini also interviewed an employee of
Scott's named Rob Weaver. Weaver told the investigator, he and Eric
Olsen met with Scott at a restaurant in Fresno. Olsen, who was resigning from Tradecorp, came to the meeting to return the company
fax machine. With Olsen's departure, Weaver was now Scott's sole
employee. Scott talked about Laci's disappearance, telling them that
he was a suspect in the case, and he didn't know what to do about it.
He also said that he'd had a private meeting with Geraldo Rivera, but
never revealed what the two discussed.

Next, a former classmate from Cuesta Junior College, Richard Reynolds, spoke with the detective. Reynolds said he and Scott had played on the school's golf team together. Like several of Scott's other friends, Reynolds described his buddy as a "loner." During college, he would date women just two or three times before moving on. Reynolds said that his wife, Lisa, had never cared for Scott, mainly because she didn't like his sense of humor. Reynolds recalled that Scott had once sent him a suggestive photo of a woman standing next to a bed with a caption that read, "This is my wife." From the photo, it was obvious that Scott wasn't married to the female posing in the photo. Reynolds's wife thought the joke was in bad taste.

In early January, Lee Peterson called the Modesto Police Department tip line to alert officers that he'd heard of a Modesto satanic cult called the Order of the Silver Crescent that sacrificed babies. The group, he said, was headquartered at 701 I Street.

A detective assigned to check out the tip learned that 701 I Street was occupied by a commercial business, and neither the business owner nor the others he spoke to there had ever heard of the Order of the Silver Crescent. A check of police records showed that officers had been called to the address twice that year, once for a discarded license plate and once for an alarm going off. There was no indication of any criminal activity, and nothing to suggest that a satanic cult was operating from that address. Still, the detective decided to check further.

The previous year, there had been four calls to the police from that address—three for an alarm sounding and the fourth for a burglary. When the detective checked with the police department's gang unit, he was told that none of its members had ever heard of a group called the Order of the Silver Crescent.

"I determined there was no validity to this tip," the detective wrote in his report.

Later, once Scott hired Mark Geragos to lead his defense, stories about satanic cults gained widespread attention. But these early tips suggest that more than a few people were ready to believe that such cults were operating in their midst.

A more realistic tip came from a woman named Kristen Dempewolf, who told the clerk that she'd seen a man she believed to be Scott Peterson on Christmas Eve morning in front of his house. He was in the driveway, and said "Good morning" to her as she walked by the house on her way home from the park. Dempewolf said the man was "putting things in the bed of his truck, small things, but I didn't see any of the items. He was moving things around."

Dempewolf, a petite brunette eight months pregnant, explained that at 8:45 that morning she was walking her chocolate Lab in East La Loma Park. She had already called police on December 25 to alert them that she was in the park between 9:00 and 9:30 on Christmas Eve morning and hadn't seen Laci there.

Dempewolf said she walked from East La Loma Park up to the bridge at Kerwin and then left the park at the easement by the 1000 Oaks Lift Station. From there, she walked by the Petersons' residence. Dempewolf told police that during the walk, she encountered a man and two women walking with a golden retriever that wasn't on a leash. Between 9:20 and 9:40, while she was walking on Covena, she'd seen Scott Peterson standing in the bed of his pickup truck. She said she typically heard a dog barking when she passed that house, but that there was no barking on that day. She observed an "older white utility van parked across the street" from the house. Her tip was passed upstairs to Detective Brocchini.

At least five people, including Diane Jackson, Rudy Medina, and Kristen Dempewolf, reported seeing a strange van in the neighborhood around the time of Laci's disappearance. Several of the sightings occurred on or near Covena Avenue at the very time Scott was loading his pickup in the driveway. Yet, I found it curious that Scott never mentioned seeing a van that morning.

Two explanations for this have been suggested to me. The first is that Scott did not act alone and the van was somehow linked to an accomplice.

The other is that Scott was too busy loading Laci's body into the truck to notice.

As the investigation progressed, Scott remained under twenty-four-hour watch. On January 5, the surveillance team reported, Scott paid a visit to his attorney, Kirk McAllister. When Scott entered the Eleventh Street office, he was dressed in a red-checkered shirt and blue jeans, with a business-card-sized photo of Laci pinned to his lapel. When he emerged, the photo was no longer there.

At 10:20, the team followed Scott to the Enterprise Rent-a-Car office in Modesto, where he parked Laci's Discovery in the lot and rented a 2002 Honda. He retrieved something from the back seat of the Land Rover and put it in the red Accord. Scott then unknowingly led officers on a ninety-minute ride to the Berkeley Marina. He parked for a total of ten minutes, and then "contacted an unidentified subject in the parking lot." Sources close to the investigation believe this man could have been an accomplice, and one source even told me that it's possible money was exchanged that day. The police report revealed nothing further about this clandestine meeting; the officers reported only that they lost track of Scott as he left the parking lot.

Some pundits have argued that a single individual could not have committed this crime, and have pointed to this meeting as evidence of a conspiracy. It does seem clear that the officers should have noted the license plate of the man Scott met that day and followed up on the contact. They did not. Yet, I have never seen any evidence that would support a second participant in this crime, and to this day I find it highly doubtful that this loose end would have led to such a discovery.

After losing him at the marina, the police set up mobile units at Scott's house, his business, and the Red Lion, hoping to resume their surveillance when he returned. Officials from Enterprise Rent-a-Car promised to alert the team as soon as Scott brought back the red Accord or rented another vehicle.

That evening, Sharon Rocha appeared on the Fox News Channel's *On the Record with Greta Van Susteren.* The distraught mother continued to support her son-in-law.

"If you knew Scott, you wouldn't have any doubts," Sharon Rocha assured viewers. "If you saw the way the two of them are together, and always have been together, I mean, I've never even known the two of them to have an argument or harsh words with each other. They've just always been a team."

"Oh, my God, I'm so glad that . . . to hear from you," Amber told Scott when he phoned that evening.

"Why?" Scott asked.

"Oh well, something uh . . . strange happened today."

"Amber?" Scott asked, as if he couldn't hear her through the static on the line.

"I'm here," Amber replied.

"Yeah, what's up?"

"I don't know," Amber stated. "Sauki called and left me a message and said she was worried about me. She was in between flights and she said she needed to talk to me when she got back into town, and I have no idea."

Amber was referring to a message her friend Sauki had left on her answering machine earlier that day. She said that she was at the airport and had just read the latest edition of *People* magazine. "There's something in it that just at this moment, it just shocks me and if I don't talk to you before I get on the plane . . . I will call you as soon as I get in . . . I really hope you're okay," Sauki said in her recorded message.

"Huh? Weird," Scott responded. "She left like a cryptic message?"

"I have no idea," Amber said. "I'm scared, I have no idea what she's talking about." Amber—and the police—were hoping that Scott would pick up on the subtle cue and tell Amber about Laci. The latest issue of *People* did contain a story about the Laci Peterson case. Only later did Amber learn that Sauki herself had supplied the magazine with a photograph for the story in *People*. Amber suspected that her friend had phoned to alert her because she was feeling guilty for what she had done.

"Weird," Scott repeated, but offered no explanation.

It was just after eleven on January 6 when Scott Peterson dialed Amber's cell phone again. This time, unbeknownst to Scott, the young woman was sitting in an interview room at the Modesto Police Department's Detective Division with criminal profiler Sharon Hagan and Detective Jon Buehler. Hagan and Buehler planned the phone call, even giving Amber specific questions to ask Scott. It was in this taped phone call that Scott confessed to lying to Amber about "everything."

"I'm so sorry that this has happened," Scott began. "And I'm so sorry that I've hurt you in this way. I don't want to do this over the phone. I want to tell you this. I want to be there in person to tell you this. But I'm sure that's why Sauki called you."

"What?" Amber asked.

"You haven't been watching the news, obviously," Scott stated.

"No," Amber replied.

Scott hesitated. "I have not been traveling during the last couple of weeks. I have, I've lied to you that I've been traveling."

"Okay," Amber replied.

"The girl I'm married to, her name is Laci. She disappeared just before Christmas. . . . For the past two weeks, I've been in Modesto with her family and mine searching for her. She just disappeared, and no one knows where she's been," Scott explained. "I can't tell you more because I need you to be protected from the media and Ayiana."

"Okay," Amber said. "Scott, are you listening?"

"Yeah, I am," Scott replied.

"You came to me earlier in December and told me that you had lost your wife. What was that about?"

"She . . . she's alive," Scott said.

"What?"

"She's alive," Scott repeated.

"Where? She's alive? Where?"

"In Modesto. Now, I know, I this is the hardest, I wanted to tell you in person. I . . . you need to protect yourself from the media."

"Okay," Amber replied.

"If you even watch the news at all . . . well, you haven't. Um, the media has been telling everyone that I had something to do with her disappearance. So, the past two weeks, I've been hunted by the media. And I just . . . I don't want you to be involved and to protect yourself. I know that I am, I'm destroyed. And God, I hope . . . I hope so much that this doesn't hurt you."

It was amazing: only two weeks into this investigation, long before the media coalesced around Scott as the suspect, Scott was telegraphing his fear of detection to Amber.

"How could it not affect me?" Amber asked, her voice rising.

"It does, and I just . . ." Scott started.

Amber sighed.

"But I . . . I . . . I . . . have just been torn up the last two weeks wanting to tell you, and I'm so weak that I haven't. And I just, I just hope that, um, I had to call you and tell you that."

"You never . . . you never answered my question, Scott." Amber said.

"Sweetie, you don't, I can't, I can't say anymore," Scott told her.

"I think I deserve . . ." Amber started.

"You deserve so much better," Scott interrupted.

"Yeah, and I deserve an explanation of why you told me you lost your wife. And this was the first holidays you'd spend without her." Amber asked. "That was December 9, you told me this, and now all of a sudden your wife's missing. Are you kidding me? Did you hear me?"

Scott repeated that he could not give her any more information.

"Well, you know, you told me you lost your wife. You sat there in front of me and cried and broke down. I sat there and held your hand, Scott, and comforted you and you've lied to me."

"Yeah," Scott admitted.

"Lying to me about lying," Amber continued.

"I lied to you about traveling," Scott said.

"But didn't you say, 'Amber, I will do anything for you to trust me?' 'Baby, we have, I feel we have a future together.' What was that about?" Amber demanded.

"I never said anything to you that I didn't mean," Scott replied.

"You never told me anything you didn't mean?" Amber repeated in an angry tone.

"I lied to you about things, I did," Scott insisted. "And you don't deserve the things that I've done to you, but . . . there's no *but*. Hey, I agree with that. I want to explain everything to you, but I can't."

Scott would repeat this damning phrase again and again in his conversations with Amber. I find this extraordinary. Even as he protested his innocence, Scott was insisting that he knew much more than he was telling. If he had nothing to do with Laci's disappearance, why would he say such a thing?

"Why?" Amber asked.

"Primarily, well, I've got a lot of reasons. Primarily protection for everyone."

"Protection of who?" Amber inquired.

"Everyone," Scott restated.

"Who is everyone?"

"Everyone is . . . you, me, our families," Scott explained.

"I asked if there was anybody else. 'Oh no, I'm monogamous as far as I'm concerned,'" Amber mocked.

"I never cheated on you," Scott declared.

"Ha, ha."

"I never did."

"You're married," Amber announced. "How do you figure you never cheated on me? Explain that one to me."

"I want to explain to you Amber," Scott stated.

"And you're going to, right? Is that . . ."

"I will. No, no, I will," Scott promised.

"When?" Amber asked.

"I hope . . . God, I hope the hell that you will listen to me and I can. I want to explain it to you so badly, but I can't now. And I . . . I can never ask you to . . . to trust me or to even listen to me again."

"You know what, that . . . that makes a lot more sense to me now, Scott," Amber said.

"What's that?" Scott asked, confused.

"Of course you couldn't tell me the story about your wife, because it hadn't happened yet," Amber declared, "and you were hoping to resolve [it] in January, that it would be resolved, and you'd have a story to tell me."

"Sweetie, you think I had something to do with her disappearance? Amber, do you believe that?" Notice how many times Scott answers a question or challenge with another question. He seems to believe he can deflect inquiry with this tactic—as, no doubt, he had done throughout his life.

"Well, let's see, how can I believe that? How can I believe anything?"

"I am not evil like that," Scott insisted.

"I would hope not," Amber said. "You know you've lied to me now and, do you know how many people I've given your picture to, or of us in Christmas cards? So, you're telling me that you want to keep me out of this, and Ayiana, and you want to protect me from that. I'm just at a loss.

"But isn't it ironic how, Scott, when I first met you on our date, how you told me you were going to Maine with your family, and you were going to Paris and Europe and all these things," Amber continued. "And then you came to me after Shawn found out that you were married and you came and told me this elaborate lie about her missing and this tragedy and that . . . this will be the first holidays without her."

"I . . . God, I don't want to fight with you. I never said tragedy or missing," Scott insisted.

"Oh yes, you said you've lost your wife," Amber recounted.

"I said that I lost my wife," Scott agreed.

She had it! The phrase Scott used on December 9, long before a tape recorder could capture it, was now preserved for trial. Either he was guilty as sin, or those four words made Scott Peterson the unluckiest man alive.

"Yes, you did . . . How did you lose her before she was lost? Explain that," Amber insisted.

"There's different kinds of loss, Amber," Scott said.

"Then explain *your* loss."

"I can't [explain it] to you now," Scott said.

"When can you?" Amber asked.

"I can once there's . . ."

"When my name has been smeared all over tabloids and everything else, because I'm the, the lover, I'm the girlfriend. When you've been married to this woman," Amber interjected.

"You don't deserve that," Scott told Amber.

"No, I don't deserve this," Amber retorted.

"And you said you've been safe with me. 'Oh, some people I tell I've been married, and other people I say I never have because it's so painful for me,'" Amber jeered.

"I've lied to you," Scott admitted.

"So, Scott, what about your baby? Laci's . . . missing woman, pregnant, is that what you just said?"

Scott would not address Amber's question. He did everything he could to avoid talking about Conner. "I want to explain all of this to you, and I . . . I just am not able to."

"Why?"

"I can't ask you to trust me, but you will . . . if you give me a chance to later to explain it," Scott pleaded.

"Yeah, is that why you said you didn't want to have any children and Ayiana was the only child you ever see of having and . . . and at that point assuming we're together she would be . . . you would have her as your own? Why would you tell me that when you were expecting a baby?"

"Sweetie, I . . . I'm sorry that I can't tell you everything right now," Scott said.

"Why can't you tell me everything? Why?"

"It just has entirely too many repercussions and they're not all for me. Okay, there's a lot . . . and the repercussions don't deal with me," Scott said, without offering any explanation. No sufficient explanation has ever surfaced for these comments.

"Tell me the coincidence of Laci, your wife, disappearing and your stories earlier in December? And then you . . . you're carrying on this elaborate lie with me that you're in Europe and you're in Maine with your folks? Explain that to me?"

"I wanted to tell you about this," Scott contended.

"But of course you couldn't because you were in Maine with your folks," Amber said sarcastically.

"No, I didn't make that trip," Scott sighed.

"You and I, assuming we'd be together, how would you have explained a new baby that you brought into this world?" Amber questioned. "How would you explain your baby to me?"

"Sweetie, you don't know everything," Scott continued.

"Well, is this child yours?" Amber confronted Scott.

There was a long silence on the line before Scott finally said, "Sweetie . . . I'm sorry. Amber, I cannot tell you." Astonishingly, Scott was now suggesting Conner was not his baby. As this conversation played out in court, mental daggers were being thrown by prosecutors and jurors alike. How could anyone be so cold and callous? How could he angle for advantage with his girlfriend by disowning his own child? It seemed clearer than ever that Scott Peterson could not feel empathy or pain for others—that he would say or do whatever was necessary to ensure his self-preservation.

"Is this child yours?" Amber repeated.

"I can't tell you all these things now," Scott sidestepped again. "God, I know I hurt you."

"Why should I not go to the police with this?" Amber demanded.

"It's your decision," Scott replied.

"Really?"

"Of course."

"And at that point . . . I go to the police . . . with this, what do you see happening?" Amber let out a sigh.

"Obviously they would question you; they would want to know everything. I mean, it is your decision, of course. Um . . . I . . . I wanted to tell you what has happened and I wanted to tell you that I lied to you," Scott insisted.

"And what stopped you from this?"

"Previous to now?"

"Yes," Amber demanded.

"I could make excuses how to justify it to myself," Scott began.

"You're not doing great right now," Amber stated.

"Well, I know I'm trying. I justify it to myself by saying, 'No, she just had a fight with her sister, don't tell her.' No, no, it was probably just weakness and hoping that I could hold onto you."

As Amber continued to press Scott, the cell phone connection was lost. Scott dialed Amber back, and she picked up the call.

"Did you hear me?" Amber demanded. "Are you driving? Hello?"

"Amber?"

"I'm here, I can hear you just fine."

"Okay, thank you for answering."

"So, where are you right now?" Amber inquired.

"I'm in Modesto," Scott replied.

"Doing what?"

"I'm helping in the search," Scott didn't know that Amber could verify his story by simply calling the cops.

"Really?"

"Yeah. I've been putting out flyers, helping in the search."

"Why did you follow through and meet me and have this date and do all these things with me and tell me all these things, why? What purpose did I serve in your life during this last month?"

"Amber, you are . . . you changed me this last month. You are so special, you're amazing. And I just . . . ." Scott stopped himself mid-sentence.

"And so what are you telling me, your wife was not?" Amber pressed.

"I, I can not explain it all now," he said.

"Yeah, there's a lot of things you're not wanting to explain to me right now, Scott," Amber barked.

"Too many people would be hurt."

For a man who thought he was smart, Scott was really tripping over his excuses during this conversation. In the end, 116 days of anguish would pass before Sharon Rocha would learn the fate of her daughter and grandson. If a stranger spirited Laci away in a robbery or baby-napping, how would that revelation hurt any more than not knowing? That was all Amber wanted to know.

"So, how is that . . . how is that gonna put any more hurt than what's already out there now?" Amber asked furiously. "How would you think this wouldn't just break my heart to meet someone and, I even tell you where I'm at in my life and, you know, I'm starting my own business. I just moved out, you know . . . what I've been through in my life already to this day. You're very well aware of it, we've spent many times on the phone or even together and me talking about these things. How could you possibly not think you being married would affect me? How?"

"I don't know how to answer that right," Scott said. "God, I don't want to say it again, but I mean you obviously don't deserve this. I had no idea this was going to happen," Scott insisted.

"Sounded like you did," Amber asserted. "I should believe you that no, you couldn't have anything to do . . ."

"No, no, no, that's not what I'm saying. . . ." Scott insisted.

". . . with her disappearance? Is that what you're telling me?"

"I had nothing to do. My God, Amber, I had nothing to do with her disappearance."

"Then who did?" Amber demanded.

"We don't have any idea," Scott responded.

"Really?" Amber replied.

"There was a robbery here . . ." Scott offered again weakly.

Amber interrupted. "You think a robber had something to do with her disappearance? . . . Well, robbers don't kill people, pregnant people, for that."

"I just, I can't ask you to trust me, I can't ask you to believe me," Scott rambled. "I just . . . I can't tell you and I . . . I will be able to in the future if you'll listen to me, but then I don't know if you will. I can't ask you to do that."

"You know, the only thing that would ever make me or change my mind, is that she is found alive or comes forward or whatever . . ." Amber stated.

"God, I hope she is found alive. We all hope she's found alive. We're all working for that."

"Really? And you think that's gonna happen?" Amber inquired.

"I hope so," Scott responded.

"Do you feel that she's honestly going to be found alive?"

"I've been losing hope."

"You've been losing hope?"

"For the last couple of days," Scott explained.

"Life does not lose hope," Amber declared. "That hope never dies until she is found. And how can you call me and talk to me at night and sound so joyous and everything else while you're going . . . that is just beyond me, Scott."

"I know you won't believe me, but I, at night . . . I haven't slept in weeks," Scott said.

"Really?"

"And yes, I have put on a face to talk to you until I could tell you," Scott insisted.

"And when were you gonna tell me? When you got back from Europe?" Amber asked in a derisive tone. "So why is it you have such a hard time with the truth?"

"I don't think I do. But I lied to you and I hate myself for that," Scott explained.

"You didn't think you knew you lied to me?"

"No, no, no, I have always told the truth."

"Oh, really?" Amber was flabbergasted.

"Let me . . . well, no, with exceptions obviously."

"Oh, truth with exceptions, huh? That's a new one for my book." Amber had him cornered. Apparently, Scott was unable to make the distinction. When I first read this transcript, I thought again about the definition of a sociopath. Where most people have some reaction to the act of telling a lie, such as feelings of guilt or shame, Scott appeared to face no such moral quandary. For him, the issue was simple: *Will this benefit me or not?*

"I wish I could tell you everything," Scott began to sob. His behavior was an anomaly: During the search for Laci, Scott would shed few tears. Witnesses who had known Scott for years consistently described his calm, quiet demeanor; he never got upset or angry. That may explain why many of these observers didn't find it suspicious that Scott never grieved in public.

If Scott's apparent indifference was merely a matter of his even-tempered nature, however, why was he crying on a regular basis with Amber?

Amber had little patience for his outburst. "Oh, save your tears," she told him now.

"This situation has . . . is so unbelievably painful," Scott said.

"That you didn't expect this to be so big? Is that what you just thought—Oh, well, no big deal, just another lost woman and it would disappear and then you would return from Europe and you and I . . ." Amber was right on target. How could this young fertilizer salesman from Modesto ever have imagined the national outpouring of interest and support when Laci went missing?

"Amber, never," Scott implored.

"Oh, you didn't . . . you didn't plan on wanting to move away with me?" Amber ranted. "Isn't that what you were leading up to? And when you returned . . . you just hoped I would put my trust in you and that you would . . . whatever decisions that you were gonna make for Ayiana and I, . . . that I could say yes without question. Do you remember that conversation? Because I remember it very clearly. That was just after I confronted you about Shawn's knowing of your wife."

"Yeah," Scott acknowledged.

"Where was that leading to?"

"I can't tell you everything now. I'm sorry." With each utterance, Scott's excuses sounded weaker.

During the ninety-minute call, Scott continued to evade Amber's questions.

"So, should I be afraid of you?" Amber asked at one point.

"No." Scott replied.

"So where do you think you're going to find Laci?" Amber asked later.

"Our hope, and it's a sad hope, is that . . . well, I mean, we need [a] tip. That's why we have such a big reward. And we just hope that someone's holding her for her child and that we can, you know, get her back with a tip," Scott responded.

"So, what, you're not elated that you're having a baby?"

"Sweetie, we can't talk about it," Scott insisted.

"Really? Now at this point, if she's found and she's dead, can we still [not] talk about it?" Amber inquired.

"My God, don't say that."

"Isn't that reality? Isn't that the reality of a missing person?"

"Yeah, I guess," Scott replied.

"So, tell me then, if she's found . . ."

"Don't. Yeah."

"You have to look at both sides, right? The other scenario, she may not be found alive and then what?"

"Don't know that," Scott stated. When he was pressed to respond, Scott admitted that if his wife was found dead, he would tell Amber the truth.

"Okay, so now tell me the scenario when she's found alive," Amber asked next.

"Then I could tell you everything," Scott responded.

"So either scenario at this point, whichever comes first at any point, then you could tell me everything?" Amber reiterated.

"Yes," Scott responded.

"When's your baby due?" Amber asked.

"Um, February sixteenth is the last date," Scott said. In fact, Laci's due date was February 10—Amber's birthday.

"So, [you say] you only want to have one child—in which case, assuming we're together, it would be Ayiana—when you had a child on the way? How can you say that?"

"Baby, you don't know everything," Scott assured her.

"Scott, is this baby yours?"

"I can't . . . I can not tell you everything." Again, whether he was actually denying that Conner was his own son—or merely attempting to throw up a smokescreen—Scott's craven responses would elicit revulsion from the jury when they heard the conversation replayed months later.

"You can tell me everything. That's a simple yes or no."

"Amber, honestly, to protect everyone, I can't tell you everything," Scott insisted.

"That only leads me to believe that it's not."

"Amber . . ."

"Because if it was, you'd say of course it's my baby, that's my wife," Amber continued.

Scott declined to answer.

Amber pressed on. "Who else knows about me, Scott?"

"That you and I have a relationship?"

"Do your parents know about me?"

"No," Scott replied.

"Well, I thought that was [the] topic of conversation. 'Oh, I talked my parents' ear off about you over the holidays.'" Amber's voice was growing angry.

"Well, that trip didn't happen," Scott said matter-of-factly.

"Oh, that trip didn't happen. You know, I'm led to question other things that happened, Scott," Amber snapped.

Amber next confronted Scott about his role in searching for his wife.

"You're doing everything you can, you're putting up flyers . . . that's it, putting up flyers?"

"No, I've been going door to door," Scott explained.

"What do you expect to find from knocking on doors?"

"I don't know where else to go . . ." Scott said.

"You're having conversations with me when all this happening?" Amber asked.

"Yeah," Scott said.

"Really? Isn't that a little . . . isn't that a little twisted, Scott?"

"It is," Scott agreed.

"Well, at least you agree with me there," Amber said.

"Well, that's the truth, isn't it?"

"You have a missing pregnant wife and you're talking to your girlfriend. Hum! Did you think about that one?"

"It sounds terrible," Scott said.

The conversation returned to the search.

"I think that we will find her with her child," Scott predicted. Only rarely did Scott speak of Conner in a personal fashion. He was "Laci's" child, "her" baby, "the" baby.

"I know you've never said this but you've indicated so many other things that I could assume possibly that she's missing because you love me. Right?"

"Amber, she's missing because someone abducted her," Scott responded without hesitation.

"This has to be the biggest coincidence I have ever heard of," Amber said near the end of the call. "I mean, are you psychic? I mean, you predicted your wife would be missing!"

"No," Scott replied.

"How can you not expect me to even think or ever to . . . to let this pass that you possibly planned this?"

"I did nothing like that," Scott insisted.

"Oh, well, then, again, this is the biggest coincidence ever."

# CHAPTER ELEVEN

# JANUARY 7, 2003

Early on January 7, Scott dialed the Enterprise rental office in Modesto and reserved a truck for the following afternoon. The Enterprise staffers alerted the Modesto police, and a court order to place a GPS tracking system on the rental was quickly obtained.

Scott then called Amber. He lied about his whereabouts, telling her he would be out posting flyers and was on his way to the Volunteer Center. In fact, police records showed that Scott was actually in Fresno when he placed the call. During this lengthy conversation, which has never been made public, Scott tried to convince Amber of another lie: that he had taken a polygraph test.

Amber told Scott that she had been researching the case online. "Scott, you really haven't done everything you can yet. You don't speak in public with your family, you . . . you know, there's rumors that you won't take a polygraph test."

"Yeah, there's a lot of rumors," Scott agreed.

"Have you taken a polygraph, uh . . . the polygraph test?"

"Yes, I have," Scott replied.

"You have?" Amber asked, surprised.

"Yes," Scott repeated.

"And what happened?" Amber inquired. "What . . . how did that go?"

"Fine. I mean, I have nothing to hide," Scott stated.

"You have nothing to hide?" Amber asked.

"No," Scott declared.

"And so it went fine?"

"Yes," Scott insisted.

"And so then wouldn't I read somewhere that you're . . . that . . . that there's no possible way that you're [*sic*] suspect? At this point, they haven't ruled that out, Scott."

"Yeah, well, as you read it, of course, everyone's the suspect, I'm the prime suspect um . . . you know, and all they say is they haven't ruled me out, they haven't ruled me in," Scott explained. "Um, and they can't talk about the case and they can't tell anyone about the polygraph test."

"You know they've searched your house and warehouse and everything else . . . Have they found anything?" Amber inquired.

"No," Scott said. "Otherwise, I wouldn't be, you know, free. They just . . . they have so little to go on and yes, I have not spoken to the press because I am not the focus of this, it's finding Laci, that's the focus of this."

"I know, but you're the husband," Amber stated.

"Yes, I am," Scott agreed.

"Okay, so one thing I want you to do . . . I want you to prove to me you took a polygraph test."

"Okay, I will," Scott agreed.

"Okay, I want that tomorrow," Amber instructed. "I will give you a time . . ."

"I'll try," Scott interrupted her.

"No, no 'try.' You will make it possible," Amber insisted. "I will ask you to go in front of the press and I want you to talk about your polygraph and that you've taken it and completed it and . . ."

"I think I can do that," Scott said.

"You think?" Amber questioned.

"I have to . . . I mean I have to ask my attorney, obviously, and I have to ask the police," Scott explained.

"I don't see where an attorney would disagree for . . . for a plea of innocence?"

"That's true," Scott agreed.

"I want to see . . . I want to see this tomorrow," Amber demanded.

"Amber," Scott said.

"You taking your polygraph test. I want to see you speak in public," Amber commanded. "It could be one minute, five minutes, whatever. It could be very short and brief, I want it from you, if you want my respect and my trust and everything else, then you will do this for me, Scott, for us."

"I need to check with the police and my attorney," Scott said again.

"You need to check with the police and your attorney?" Amber asked. "You know, it's not like this is some huge thing for you to do. It's quite small, it's . . ."

"I don't know what's huge and what's small now," Scott replied.

"I could tell you the disappearance of Laci is huge."

"Oh, I know that," Scott confirmed. "I took the polygraph test," Scott said.

"I need to check with them if I can say that I have or not [taken the test]."

"Why? Why couldn't you?"

"Because right now the police have not released that I have to the press. They say we can not comment," Scott insisted.

"Who runs your life, Scott? You're a thirty-year-old man," Amber declared. "Who runs your life, you or the media or the . . . ?"

"In this kind of situation, the police and my attorney," Scott replied.

"I have faith that you'll make this possible and that you will take that polygraph test and you speak in front of . . ."

Scott interrupted. "I took the polygraph test."

"Okay," Amber said. "Then that's no problem. Nobody's telling you not to get up in front of the public."

"Yes, they are," Scott declared. "The police, the families, and my attorney." The lies were spilling from his mouth with abandon. I find it hard to believe that Scott ever thought he could get away with the deception. In fact, he told Amber he would try to give her answers within twenty-four hours. He simply didn't care about repercussions; his only concern was extricating himself from whatever challenge was right in front of him.

Later in the conversation, the topic turned to Scott's attorney, Kirk McAllister. Without identifying him by name, Scott said that his lawyer had been a district attorney for seventeen years.

"He knows the cops can make bad cases," Scott commented. "They can interpret things wrong. He said this is a game of life and death," Scott stated, referring to McAllister's remarks about the "deadly game" his client was playing—a remark he would later gleefully relay to his parents. Scott Peterson was fairly insightful about other people, but not about himself. He was obviously excited about the attorney's description, but he failed to realize that McAllister wasn't delivering a compliment. Scott's attorney was trying to shut him down, to keep him quiet, but Scott wasn't interested in taking his advice. He truly believed he could take on law enforcement and win.

"This is a capital case," Scott told Amber. "If they interpret something wrong, and they were to arrest me, there's no bail for me. I would have to wait until the trial cleared me, which could be months."

"So does he think that I'm involved?" Amber asked.

"No," Scott replied.

"No? Are you sure he knows about me, Scott?"

"He does," Scott assured Amber.

"And what's his name?"

"The first day we sat down," Scott replied, apparently responding to Amber's first question.

"What's his name?" Amber again demanded.

"His name is um . . ." Scott paused.

"He's your attorney and you don't know his name?" Amber shot back.

"Amber, hold on, Kirk McAllister," Scott finally divulged.

Amber laughed, then took down the spelling of McAllister's name.

Scott told Amber that McAllister would be angry if he learned that he was speaking to her. After additional prodding, however, he finally provided Amber with McAllister's phone number.

"Okay. I still expect you to talk to him. So would you rather me just be a call of surprise, or do you want to fill him in first?" Amber asked.

"Well, I told him about you," Scott said. In frustration, Scott blurted out, "Give me something that is in my control."

"So, is the polygraph admissible in court?" Amber asked.

"No," Scott replied.

"No? Then what do you have to lose?" Amber asked, sounding puzzled.

"I already took it, Amber," Scott insisted.

"Okay, I want to believe that you have," Amber said.

Scott told Amber that he was meeting with the chief of the Modesto Police Department, Roy Wasden, later that afternoon; from there he was going to Laci's parents' house, where he'd been invited for dinner.

"How are her parents doing?" Amber asked.

"It's awful, it's awful for everyone."

"You didn't answer my question, Scott," Amber stated.

"I mean, her mom is taking drugs," Scott revealed.

"What kind of drugs?" Amber asked.

"You know, like Xanax and stuff," Scott explained. "And that's the way she's functioning . . . She looks like she has no emotion, so I'm worried about her." Was Scott truly incapable of seeing what the entire world could—that Sharon Rocha's heart was being ripped from her body? Or was he merely projecting his own coldhearted behavior onto his wife's grieving mother?

As the call ended, Amber was still insisting that either Scott or his attorney telephone her by noon the following day with proof that he had submitted to a polygraph.

Early on January 8, police tracked Scott to the Red Lion. Just after one o'clock in the afternoon, Scott left the volunteer center and headed to his attorney's office, then to Home Depot. The police watched as he talked on the cell phone from the car.

As he pulled out into traffic, Scott dialed into his voice mail and retrieved a message from Amber.

"Hi, Scott, this is Amber. I was calling, uh, to say, obviously, at this point . . . you have no desire in attempting to prove your innocence to me, so at this time, I'm driving to Modesto to the Modesto Police Department and I'm going to wipe my hands clean of all this."

Scott, who had allowed Amber's noon deadline to pass without any response, returned her call immediately.

"Hello," Amber answered.

"Hey, Amber, it's Scott," he began, his manner cool. "Did you not receive my call? I tried to call at eleven-thirty, 'cause I just got your message?"

"You didn't try calling me at eleven-thirty!" Amber shot back.

"Yes, I did," Scott claimed. More and more, Scott's behavior was calling to mind Hitler's theory reminiscent of the big lie: If you say something completely outrageous, but repeat it often enough, many will finally believe you. Over the years, Scott had evidently learned simply to bulldoze his way through such confrontations. More often than not, he would succeed.

"No, you did not. My phone was sitting right by me. My phone never rang."

The two went back and forth, with Amber finally demanding to know what he was calling about.

"Well, I wasn't sure, you said yesterday that you'd expect a call by noon," Scott began.

"Yes, by either you or your attorney, yes," Amber stated flatly.

Scott insisted that he *had* taken the polygraph, at a place called Priority Investigations.

"And the police were there with you?" Amber asked.

"Yes," Scott affirmed.

"What were the names of the police people?" Amber demanded.

"Al Brocchini, who is a detective," Scott said.

"Okay."

"Well, no, I'm sorry I think it was Craig who was there," Scott confirmed.

"No, Craig what?"

"Grogan," Scott replied.

"He was there when you took the polygraph test?" Amber inquired. "Yeah."

"So, I could call . . . contact them, and they could give me proof that you took this, correct?"

"Sure," Scott agreed.

"True, or yes?" Amber asked.

"Yeah, yes," Scott said.

"Interesting. Okay, that's something I will do then," Amber threatened. "You know, Scott, when people find out, and they will, no one will think your behavior is innocent. Do you understand that?"

"Yeah, I know that, but I had nothing to do with this. So, you know, once we find her . . . you know, everyone will know that I was not involved in this. And I just, you know, I hope that you, uh . . . are not, um . . . involved in any degree, and . . ."

Amber fumed. "How . . . *buck up!* Back up to th[at] statement."

"Yeah. Well, I was trying to explain it to you. But, you know, what I mean by that is obviously you're not involved in . . . but I mean I don't want, um . . . to have any repercussions from people, you know," Scott insinuated.

"What repercussions? My hands are clean of this, Scott!" Amber railed.

"Oh, I know, and I'm the one that . . . that lied to you."

"Exactly," Amber said.

"And put you in the position."

"Exactly," Amber shot back. "So where do you think that behav—. . . they are not going to think your behavior is innocent."

"No, of course not," Scott backed down. "No, they won't. You're right. Of course they won't."

Next, Amber demanded that Scott walk her through the details of Christmas Eve day.

As Scott steered Laci's SUV through the streets of Modesto, he told Amber that Laci had awoke first and had cereal for breakfast. Laci's favorite show, *Martha Stewart Living,* was on TV, he explained, and she was mopping the floor while watching it. He left home around 9:30 or so, stopping by his warehouse and then heading for the Berkeley Marina for an afternoon of fishing.

"So you're telling me that she . . . she . . . at this point, she was still feeling great in the morning? After, I mean, you told me that she was aware of me, right?" Amber asked.

"Yes," Scott affirmed.

"And she was still doing great in the morning with that? She wasn't emotionally distraught about . . ."

Scott interjected. "No."

". . . you not being with her, and faithful to her, and having someone else? Because that . . . that's just really hard for me to believe," Amber insisted.

Amber next launched into a tirade about a former boyfriend of hers who was married when they first began their relationship. She explained that he'd tied the knot in a quickie wedding at a Vegas drive-through chapel, and the evening had resulted in a "wedding night" pregnancy.

"I was with him, and she was pregnant and had to deal with that," Amber explained. "I said, you know, are you sure you want to be with me? I mean, you have a pregnant woman here with your child. That was hell for me."

Amber went on to explain that the woman hadn't taken the news of her husband's infidelity well. "She was a complete crazy woman," Amber explained. "She wanted to fight me. Every time [he] would speak to her on the phone, his wife would ask, 'Are you still with that bitch?'

"Are you telling me Laci was okay with me?" Amber insisted.

"Well, when you get all the facts, it will make sense to you," Scott contended.

"So, I'm still having a very hard time thinking in Laci's shoes: *My husband has a girlfriend and I'm pregnant with his child.*" Amber paused, as if taking a moment to envision how she would feel in that situation. "So when did . . . when did she first learn of me?"

"After our first date," Scott responded coolly.

"After our first date?" Amber angrily repeated.

"Yeah," Scott affirmed, as he drove the streets of Modesto.

"So why did you carry the charade of lying to me if she already knew and you had the opportunity to come clean with me, especially knowing how I feel about truth?"

"I don't know," Scott said.

"Was there . . . what reason, what purpose would that serve?" Amber demanded. "If Laci already knows about me and the situation had come up for you to have that opportunity to be honest with me, why did you keep up the deception?"

"Just so I wouldn't, you know, hurt other people and make a . . ."

"Who are you gonna hurt?" Amber quizzed.

"Well, her family and . . ." Scott stated.

"The truth . . . truth is so much easier to handle than a lie, Scott!"

"I know, and I'm so weak in that regard," Scott admitted. "I was so weak in that regard. This has made me so much stronger in that respect."

"Really? But look at where you're at now, Scott, with this in your life."

"I know. I know."

"Is it that . . . is it that lying is so fun for you?" Amber asked.

"No. Lying is terrible."

"It seems to come to you so easily," Amber said.

"It doesn't, and it's a terrible thing, and I've done it. And I know that it's wrong and, I'm just . . . I have no . . . I'm stronger . . . stronger now."

"Or you could just add it to your collection of hobbies now, can't you—pathological liar?" Amber shot back. "You can add that to your resume with all your, uh . . . *degrees.*"

"I will never lie again. I know you can't believe that."

"No, I can't," Amber agreed.

The conversation moved on to Scott's reluctance to appear on television. Scott defended his decision, telling Amber that he didn't agree with the angle the media was taking.

"Now, when you watch, like, Fox News and they give, you know, twenty minutes to it, right? Fifteen of those minutes is asking the family, you know, Sharon, Laci's mom, how do you feel? Laci's brother, how do you feel? What has it done to you? When they should spend twenty minutes on the disappearance showing, you know, those things you just talked about and trying to develop those leads. The family should only appear in order to help. Should only appear and say, 'You know what, she's gone from here . . . ' "

"But you haven't [appeared]," Amber said.

"They have not shown my appearances because when they do, I hold up the flier, and say this is what's important," Scott explained. "They want some kind of drama beyond that."

"Of course, you're gonna want to direct them away," Amber chided. "In the back of your mind, you're thinking, There's Amber, of course I can't show my face in front of the camera left and right, because in the back of my mind Amber's out there somewhere. There's Amber, you know, somebody I've been telling I'm in Europe. Of course that's in the back of your mind, of course. If I were in your shoes, I wouldn't want my face to be shown, either. Because there's Amber, right?"

Ignoring Amber's theory, Scott insisted that he had been on camera.

"So did you love Laci and *your* baby?" Amber probed.

"I love Laci. I loved Laci, no question," Scott insisted. "And she doesn't . . . She doesn't deserve to be missing."

"So you loved her, but there's me. How can I make sense of that, Scott?"

"Honey, I'm sorry, Amber, I can't tell you all the details."

Amber next asked Scott if he had told his attorney about her.

Scott said he had, although his attorney had advised that speaking with Amber was "not a good idea."

"He said 'You should not be talking to her,' " Scott continued. "He said, 'The police had a hard-on to make a case against you, Scott.' And he repeated that three times."

I find it telling that Scott acknowledged that his lawyer had admonished him not to speak with Amber—yet he chose to ignore that advice. Once again, Scott just didn't seem to think the rules applied to him. Only in hindsight, while he was in jail awaiting trial, would he admit that his decision had cost him dearly.

"It's not going to get to trial because it's not a case, but he said this is a capital case, and they can make anything enough to arrest you. You will not be allowed bail. You will be in jail for months until we can get you released."

The conversation ended with Amber threatening to go to police with the details of their sexual affair.

"Well, yeah, if you think that's the right thing to do, do it." Scott told her.

It was just before 4:00 P.M. when surveillance teams observed that Scott was heading toward police headquarters on Tenth Street. Using the tracking device on the Land Rover, the team trailed behind him as he slowly circled the building. It appeared that he might be looking for a parking space, but he didn't stop. Instead, he drove toward the Investigative Services building that housed the Detective Division, a few blocks away. Cops followed behind him as he crept along F Street to Thirteenth Street, then turned south on E Street, lapping the department's satellite office at a slow crawl.

Using their cell phones, the surveillance officers alerted detectives inside the building. Rushing to the window, Detectives Buehler and Owen and Sergeant Alan Carter gazed out at the street in time to see the green Land Rover motoring eastbound on F Street.

Scott never did park the Land Rover and go inside either police building that afternoon. Grogan later theorized that his suspect was doing some surveillance work of his own—checking to see if Amber Frey was making good on her threat. I wonder what Scott might have done if her car was in the parking lot. He was obviously suspicious about her police connections by this time, and further conversations should be reviewed with this in mind.

Scott may have been concerned about Amber's actions, but clearly that wasn't the only thing on his mind. Later that day, he called the Dish Network to request that the Playboy Channel be added to his programming package.

At 4:00 P.M., police watched from a distance as Scott pulled into the parking lot of the Enterprise car rental office on Seventh and G Streets. Noting that he was wearing the symbolic yellow and blue ribbon on his shirt, they watched as he loaded several items from Laci's Land Rover into a white Chevy rental truck, left the parking lot, and returned home.

That same day, police divers were examining the waters beneath the Berkeley Marina with a sonar device. Search teams focused on the waters off the Cesar Chavez Park, where earlier cadaver dogs had picked up a scent. Detectives had been advised that a blue tarp had been recovered from the bay earlier in the month, near the corner of the Cesar Chavez Park.

Interestingly, an officer from a neighboring police department reported that she had seen a blue tarp on Brooks Island on December 28. That site was directly in line with the area in the park where the tarp was recovered, and where search teams were now poised to begin their sweep. Investigators wondered whether the tarp, which was similar in color to the one Scott had used to wrap his umbrellas, was linked to Laci's disappearance. Authorities forwarded it to the Department of Justice's crime lab, where an examination revealed the presence of cat and dog hairs. The hairs were submitted for comparison against those of Scott's pets.

When the searchers had no luck in the Cesar Chavez section, they shifted to the water near the Old Pier. There, one of the officers noted an object on the screen. It appeared to be the silhouette of a human body floating off the marina, about three miles from the shore.

# CHAPTER TWELVE

# JANUARY 9, 2003

At sunrise on January 9, police dispatched divers to the Berkeley Marina to take a closer look at what they believed to be the silhouette of a human body.

As Grogan waited for word from the dive teams, he was advised that Scott had taken the white Chevy rental truck and was on Highway 132 heading in the direction of the marina. Scott had loaded a black suitcase into the rental's cab and a white one into the bed of the truck. By 10:30 A.M., he was pulling into the marina's yacht club. "He drove to the end of the road, where the road circled around. Peterson slowly drove around the circle as he looked at the water," the surveillance report read. "Once around the circle, Peterson turned into a parking lot [and] drove around the parking lot twice."

At 10:44, officers reported that Scott exited the marina and drove to the San Luis Reservoir, where he entered the parking lot for O'Neil Forebay. He circled the lot for several minutes, then left the parking area, traveling east on Interstate 580.

"Peterson was utilizing counter surveillance driving when he left the San Luis Reservoir area," the surveillance report stated. "Since Peterson's vehicle was equipped with a tracking device, surveillance units backed way off, allowing Peterson to drive into parking lots, make U-turns for no reason, stop on the side of the road and eventually end up at the Double Tree in Bakersfield. All of Peterson's erratic driving was captured and stored in the tracking device."

The surveillance officer reported that he next trailed Peterson to the South Central Valley, near Fresno. The officer verified that

Amber Frey was not at her massage therapy center nearby. Scott returned to Bakersfield, where he checked into a Double Tree Motel and stayed the night. "Cell records indicated he was at a motel," profiler Sharon Hagan wrote in a Criminal Investigative Analysis. "He didn't answer incoming calls and let them be transferred to his voice mail. This behavior was inconsistent with his habit of frequent cell phone use."

That evening, Grogan telephoned Sharon Rocha and Lee Peterson to advise them that search teams "had viewed an image that appeared consistent with a human body" in the San Francisco Bay. He told both sets of parents that a team of divers would conduct a search on Saturday, January 11. A dive team had attempted to view the object earlier that morning, but weather conditions had prohibited the underwater search, he said.

Grogan also explained that if the object did turn out to be a body, it might not be Laci. He warned them against believing any news reports they heard, advising them to wait until police contacted them. The detective later reported that neither Lee nor Sharon believed the discovery was Laci.

"Have you informed Scott?" Lee Peterson asked Grogan.

The detective replied that he hadn't, but said he would call Scott to let him know.

According to friends and family, Scott had hoped that going out into the world and "doing something" would "make it easier" to deal with Laci's disappearance.

By the morning on January 10, TV trucks encircled the area of the bay where police teams were working. As officers worked an underwater grid with sonar devices, Scott was at the Enterprise rental office in Modesto exchanging the white truck he had been driving for a silver Saturn.

Police weren't prepared for this latest change; Scott's new car had no tracking device.

Scott was still driving the silver car when he left home on the morning of January 11. He checked the undercarriage of Laci's Land Rover before leaving his house, apparently looking for a tracking device. Police observed that Scott was carrying a duffel bag and had stopped at the bank, possibly withdrawing money. From there he drove to the Red Lion and remained there for about thirty minutes. Once he emerged, he began using counter surveillance tactics on members of the team.

One of his maneuvers was to come to a sudden halt on the freeway, forcing officers in pursuit to pass him. At one point, after leaving the highway, he approached a member of the team who had turned off on a cul-de-sac in Modesto. When Scott got out of his car and began walking toward her, the officer reported, she quickly drove off.

Based on Scott's behavior, Grogan ordered the supervisor of the visual surveillance to cease the covert operation. From that point on, police kept tabs on him by monitoring the wiretap on both his cell phones.

The police had since obtained a new warrant, expanding their wiretap beyond Amber's calls to include sixty-five other individuals. Most were family and friends, but the list also included a number of high-profile members of the media, including Greta Van Susteren, Diane Sawyer, Matt Lauer, John Walsh, Gloria Gomez, Dan Abrams, Larry King, and Rita Cosby. Had any of these figures known they were being recorded, of course, they would have been furious. I am surprised that not one of them raised any objections when they found out. I know for a fact that some of them tried to get copies of the transcripts of their calls, but they were never turned over by police. Ultimately, however, the officers had the courts' authority to do so, and the media was fair game.

"Throughout the day, officers who were monitoring the wire on Scott's cellular phone updated me," Grogan wrote in his report. "Scott told his friends that he was in Bakersfield, to verify that he was not at or near Bakersfield at that time based on his cell site."

Even as he was stringing the cops along, Scott was apparently still up to his old manipulative tricks with his family and friends. "Scott acted as though he was crying in one telephone conversation and then in the next behaved completely normally when the telephone calls were separated only by a few moments," the detective noted.

"Later in the afternoon," Grogan reported, "we were informed that the dive team in the San Francisco Bay had identified the object on the sonar and a dive team determined it was a boat anchor." The news traveled fast: "Within a few moments, we were informed that Scott received a phone call from a cellular phone number associated with Laci's mother, Sharon Rocha, where a female voice informed Scott that officers in that area had found a boat anchor rather than a body."

"Hi Scott, this is Mom," Sharon's message began. "It's about quarter to one, just wanted you to know, I just got a call from Ron Cloward, who is at the boat marina, and it was a boat anchor. Of course, we knew it wasn't Laci. But I just wanted you to know." Listening to the message, Scott broke in with a loud whistle. To the agent listening in, the whistle sounded like "a sigh of relief."

That afternoon Scott spoke to his father, telling him that he was in Bakersfield when in fact he was in Gilroy, some two hundred miles away. He also spoke with Guy Miligi, telling him that he'd gone back to work, believing that "going and doing something" would make it easier to cope.

"God, yeah, I couldn't imagine," Miligi concurred.

"And then, now all the suspicion, man, did you see all the people at the marina?" Scott asked.

Miligi said he'd heard about the crowd. Scott said he'd received a call from the Modesto police chief informing him that the object in the bay turned out to be a boat anchor.

Scott laughed. "They had eighty-eight people out there, you know, and they came up with an anchor. Maybe they will send the eighty-eight people somewhere else and start working, I don't know." Scott was campaigning among his friends, but to what effect? Did he hope they would relay his reservations to law enforcement? If the community thought the cops were on the wrong track, would the police really change their tactics? It was wishful thinking.

Scott ended the conversation abruptly. "All right, man, I gotta go, or I'm going to have to pull over here," he told Miligi, suggesting he might be about to cry.

Scott's display of emotion didn't last long. Within four minutes he was back on the phone, leaving a message for his friend Mike. His tone was upbeat; the officers listening in detected no signs of sadness in his voice.

Sunday was a quiet day for investigators but Monday, January 13, brought a twist in the case that forced investigators to become more circumspect in their dealings with Amber Frey.

When Detective Buehler reported for duty on Monday, he learned that the tap on Scott's cell phone revealed that he and Amber had had a thirty-minute phone conversation on Sunday evening. The records also indicated that Amber had received a two-minute call from Scott earlier that day. But Amber had not recorded these calls. For reasons police could only speculate on, Amber mentioned neither conversation when Buehler reached her that afternoon.

Since she'd first called the police on December 30, Amber had been staying with Doug Sibley, her friend Shawn's uncle. Now, she told Buehler, she wanted to move back to her own house in Madera.

Buehler interpreted Amber's request as an attempt to maintain her privacy, and to ensure that Doug would not overhear her phone conversations with Scott. Buehler noted that "it also matched up with her apparent lack of concern of a violent attack as she continued to stay at her residence through Tuesday night, 1/13."

"It appeared possible that Frey is attempting to maintain contact with Peterson in the event he is not involved in the disappearance of his wife," Buehler wrote. "At this time, it is unknown if she is making more contact with Peterson or if she is not cooperating with this investigation and possibly giving him information."

That same day, Grogan was advised that the *National Enquirer* intended to run a story in the upcoming issue, scheduled to hit the newsstands on Thursday, January 16, that could blow Amber's cover.

The police didn't know how much information the paper had. They knew that the article was likely to include "unspecified details about a girlfriend, quite possibly from the Fresno area, along with some restricted information about evidence that would appear in print." The physical evidence "included but was not limited to concrete anchors that were made and had been discovered during the investigation."

Detectives discussed the "positives and negatives" of releasing information about the affair "to the family of suspected murder victim Laci Peterson."

During the meeting, Grogan received a call from Scott's lawyer. McAllister was angry that the detective had been speaking with his client knowing that Scott had secured counsel. Grogan informed McAllister that he was not in violation of any law. Scott was not in custody, nor had he filed any complaints.

The lawyer said his concerns were ethical ones.

Grogan said his concern was for Amber Frey's safety, and he wanted Scott to know that police now knew about her.

Still unaware of either her son-in-law's relationship with Amber Frey or the impending *Enquirer* article, Sharon Rocha appeared on live television that evening, telling viewers that she stood firmly behind Scott. Sharon Rocha, Ron Grantski, Lee Peterson, Amy Rocha, and Modesto Police Chief Roy Wasden were all Larry King's guests that night. Also appearing as a commentator was defense lawyer Mark Geragos, who was not yet representing Scott.

When King asked how Scott was holding up, Lee said that his son was "devastated," that he was "just terribly distraught. He's lost a lot of weight. I've never seen him so sad. He's just what you'd expect from someone who is missing their wife and baby." He told the audience that "Scott and Laci were a wonderful couple, just very devoted and did everything together. They had such a marvelous life. They had a home they bought two years ago, [that] they were remodeling. And, well, the baby was coming, and they gardened. They just did everything together."

Laci's mother seconded Lee's portrait of Scott and Laci's happy marriage. "They just are really truly in love with each other. They're partners. They're a team. They love each other. They planned together. They play together. They're always smiling. They're just a very happy, well-adjusted couple. Never been any indication, I never heard Laci say she was even angry with Scott for any reason at all."

"We have no question in our mind about Scott. He's part of our family," Amy Rocha added.

"One of the things that does come up, Lee, [is] why Scott doesn't appear for interviews," King asked. "Do you know why?"

"Yes," Lee began. "Well, he's very emotional. He would . . . he would break down. He wouldn't be able to finish an interview. And he doesn't want the media focus on him, he wants it on having Laci's picture in front of the nation so that someone may report something and we can get her back in our family."

Then King asked Chief Wasden to comment on why Scott was still under suspicion "while the family on both sides stands by him?"

"We won't speculate in public, and we won't speculate in the media. We will follow through on that," Wasden replied. "At this point in time, Scott has not been eliminated from the investigation."

When Detective Grogan reported for work on Wednesday, January 14, he was alerted to yet another unreported phone call between Scott and Amber that was picked up the night before.

Unbeknownst to Amber, police were now tapping her phone as well as Scott's.

"It was apparent by listening to this recording of their conversation that Amber may not have told Scott Peterson she had made contact with detectives from the Modesto Police Department," Grogan wrote in his report. "Amber and Scott had also communicated by telephone on Sunday, 1/12/2003, and due to technical problems with the wire, we were not aware of what was said."

Investigators met to continue the discussion about Amber, the wiretaps, as well as concerns about the upcoming article in the *Enquirer.*

"Because . . . the information that was coming out in the *National Enquirer* quite possibly would include Amber Frey's name, and possibly other details about her (that we could not possibly know at this time), it was believed necessary to inform the family of her identity," Buehler wrote in his report. "There are computer generated reprints of one of the photographs of Amber and Scott together on 12/14/2002, during the evening of the formal gala they had attended, that we could not be certain were retrieved from family, friends, and clients of Amber Frey."

"For this reason, along with not wanting the family to be caught without this knowledge, it was agreed to inform them of this information," Buehler noted.

That afternoon, Grogan contacted Scott on the cell phone he used to talk with Amber Frey. Scott picked up right away.

Grogan could hear voices in the background. "Are you by yourself?" he asked.

"Yeah, what's up?" Scott asked.

"That photograph I showed you of the girl."

"Okay. Should we be having a discussion or is Kirk gonna call me up again and say that it's inappropriate?"

"Well, I guess that's up to you to make the decision," Grogan advised.

"He told me it's a dictatorship. Not to—not to talk to anyone, unfortunately."

"Okay, I just want you to know that I know who that is." Grogan was referring to the woman in the picture. "I know it's Amber, and I wanted to give you an opportunity, maybe, to talk to me about that."

"Okay, well, appreciate the call. I'm glad I have—have listened to Kirk, though. But, yeah, we can't," Scott sighed loudly, "have any discussions."

"I just want you to know—that I'm not going to the media about this or anything. That's not happenin'. But I wanted you to know that I know that she's out there, and I wanted to see if you could explain it."

Scott interrupted the detective mid-sentence. "Yeah, I just, you know, really shouldn't talk so . . ."

"Well, then that's fine, but you're not gonna see me on Larry King talkin' about it, okay?"

"All right."

"I mean, is there going to be other Ambers out there, Scott?"

"What's that?" Scott acted as though he could not hear the detective, just as he did whenever Amber asked him a difficult question.

"Are there other people out there, Scott? Other Ambers?" Grogan repeated.

"Other press people, or . . . ?" Scott asked at the same time.

"Well, I'm talkin' about other gals," Grogan clarified.

"Maybe we shouldn't talk about . . ." Scott started.

Grogan asked Scott if his low-key attitude with the press, and his hesitancy to become involved in interviews, had something to do with the fact there were females like Amber who may have seen him. Instead of answering, Scott told Grogan that he'd discuss the matter with his attorney, and if McAllister agreed, he would set up a meeting.

The phone call ended.

Scott also spoke with his dad that day. His mom had already left him a message telling him that she was putting "a check in the mail" for his expenses. "I got an envelope all ready, and we're gonna be here," Jackie Peterson said in the message. "So the mailman hasn't come yet. Give me a call. Love you. Bye."

When Scott returned her call, he got Lee on the line. "Okay, how much do you need?" his dad asked.

"I don't know, not much," Scott told him.

"A couple of grand?"

"Yeah, that would be fine," Scott said.

"We'll put five in just for the hell of it," Lee Peterson said.

"Oh, great, yeah, pay some bills," Scott stated.

"Where are you?"

"I'm going to workout for a few minutes here at the club," Scott said.

"Good, good," his dad responded. "I told Mom how great your club was."

"Relax a little bit," Scott said. "I don't know if I'm pulling an O. J. by being at the club or not, but . . ." Scott was referring to O. J. Simpson's claims that he was searching for his wife's "real" killer when he was actually playing golf.

"I wouldn't worry about that," Lee Peterson said. Once again, Scott's parents were reinforcing the kind of anything-goes behavior Scott showed throughout his adult life. *Go ahead, hang out at the country club while your wife is missing. You had an affair? Don't worry about it. You can do no wrong. And, by the way, we'll take care of your bills.*

In fact, to the police it didn't look like Scott was worrying about much of anything. Just days after he'd called to get the Playboy Channel added to his cable system, he had called to replace it with a seriously hard-core porn package, including the Ten and Ecstasy sex channels.

Interestingly, Scott's half sister, Anne Bird, learned that Scott ordered the "upgrade" on January 12, 2003, the very day he'd attended her son's christening. When the subject came up later with the priest, he couldn't resist a moment of dark humor.

"Must have been some service, huh?"

Officers monitoring Scott's calls made some notes of their own in January. During one call, a college buddy told Scott that the newspapers had been "brutal" to him. The reporters were "not his friends," Scott replied. "They can make me the biggest villain in the world if they keep covering it." As the monitoring officer noted, Scott's comment seemed like one you'd expect from a criminal, not a husband concerned about the desperate search for his missing wife.

In this period, Scott also called Sergeant Ron Cloward to ask if the officer had "any" directions for him. Cloward responded that there would be times when police "did things that people did not agree with." In some instances, he explained, they might even make Scott or his parents angry.

"Right," Scott replied. During the call, he did not appear to be affected by the comment, but later conversations would reveal a different attitude.

Scott ended the dialogue by asking the sergeant to call him if there were "anywhere else" he could look for Laci. It was as if Scott had suddenly grown anxious to convince the police that he was interested in helping in his wife's case.

In stark contrast was another call Scott placed to his parents' home. This time, Scott's brother Joe answered the phone. The media "is trying to make me feel bad," Scott told him. Of course, it's clear why the prospect of all this attention was such a burden for Scott. He couldn't appear before the media because he knew the scrutiny could only do him harm. Scott's obsession with the media may seem to have bordered on the histrionic, but in hindsight it's clear that it was just another of his self-preservation instincts.

Scott told his brother that he'd just received a call from Craig Grogan. "He knows that I don't take his calls because his caller ID is blocked, but he calls me from a different phone line. I don't know where he's calling from, but I can hear cars in the background, so I answer it. He's just throwing out all this shit, just for me to talk."

"What is he talking about?"

"They are just so searching for something, they are trying so hard. My attorney said yesterday, 'They have such a hard-on for pinning the case on you.'"

Joe missed the allusion. "He feels they have a hard case on you?"

"No, no, his expression was that they have a hard-on to make a case against [me], but these cocksuckers . . ." Scott continued. Grogan had tried to "throw some bait out" by getting him to talk about the headliner in his car, which needed to be fixed. "So he throws that out there and says, 'You know, I need to clear up a few things.'"

Less than eight hours before this call, Scott was asking Sergeant Cloward what more he could do to help in the investigation. I find it revealing that he would make such overtures to people at the top—including the mayor—but when it came to Brocchini and Grogan, Scott's true feelings were revealed by the choice words he had for them in private.

As Officer Jacobson would ask in one report, "Exactly what is Scott Peterson so worried about?"

# CHAPTER THIRTEEN

# JANUARY 15, 2003

At headquarters on Wednesday, January 15, 2002, Detectives Brocchini and Buehler were attending a briefing with Department of Justice Criminal Profiler Sharon Hagan. The topic: The explosive story about to run in the *National Enquirer* detailing Scott's relationship with an as-yet unnamed woman. Police knew that woman to be Amber Frey.

The group decided to inform Scott and Laci's families simultaneously about the story, which was due to run the following day. Lead Detective Craig Grogan and Detective Phil Owen would travel to San Diego to tell Lee and Jackie Peterson in person. Brocchini and Buehler would meet with Sharon and Ron Grantski in Modesto.

That afternoon, Buehler placed a call to Grantski and arranged a meeting at the Detective Division on F Street, the details of which have never before been reported. Upon their arrival, Sharon and Ron were escorted to a lunchroom on the first floor of the detective offices.

Buehler began by giving Sharon and Ron a very general overview of the case. He hesitated before disclosing the substance of the *National Enquirer* story, but when he did, Laci's parents were stunned. Buehler explained that the story was also expected to contain important information relating to physical evidence in the case. He didn't know how the tabloid had obtained the details, and cautioned them that the article might include some information the police were not aware of.

The press has always been both a help and hindrance to law enforcement. Publicity about an investigation can bring witnesses forward. Nosy reporters can uncover problems with a case, or even pressure a suspect to make a misstep that might ensure a conviction. The limits placed on the police do not bind the media, so we journalists often push microphones into a suspect's face and "offer" the chance to give a different take on the story. As in the Peterson case, these interviews can become critical evidence at trial. Sometimes, however, this power can cause problems for investigators. Evidence they would prefer be kept under wraps is sometimes exposed, and suddenly they have to respond to our timetable, not their own. Obviously, Buehler was not prepared to break Amber's story to the families, but now he had no choice.

Buehler admitted to Sharon and Ron that his team had known about Scott's relationship for about two weeks. He told them that Scott and Amber began dating in November, and continued to see each other after Laci's disappearance. Even now Scott was still in touch with Frey, and the two had spoken of a future together. When she had confronted him about his marital status, Scott had told her that he had "lost his wife" and that the matter was too difficult to speak about.

"Why did he have to kill her?" Sharon Rocha moaned, breaking down in tears.

Buehler sat motionless, eyeing Brocchini. No one uttered a word. Sharon Rocha's desperate sobs filled the room.

After what seemed like an eternity, Sharon managed to compose herself. The detective filled her in on additional details concerning the affair. Buehler pulled out three photos and slid them across the table. Two of them were taken in Amber's kitchen. One showed Scott and Amber side by side, the other captured Amber looking at Scott lovingly. The third was a photo of Amber in the red dress, posing next to a tuxedoed Scott in front of a Christmas tree.

As Sharon stared at the photos, Brocchini requested that she and Ron not tell anyone about Scott's claim that he had "lost" his wife. They could discuss other information they had learned with family and friends, to help everyone prepare for the media onslaught to come.

The detectives knew they were walking a tightrope with the Rochas. While they needed to be truthful with Laci's parents, Brocchini and Buehler didn't want to destroy any hope that their daughter might still be found alive. They assured them that the investigation would continue as a missing persons case—not a homicide.

Sharon confided that she was immediately suspicious when Scott first told her that Laci was "missing." Scott had yet to tell her exactly what happened that day.

"She said he deflected, gave her only brief information about leaving the house shortly after 9:00 A.M., returned home, noticed Laci had not prepared any food nor was she baking," Buehler later noted in his report.

Sharon then tearfully told the detectives about something that occurred just the night before. Scott had come over to her house, she explained. He was talking on the cell phone about Laci's due date, and she overheard him state that the expected date for Conner's birth was February 16. The conversation completely surprised Sharon, who knew the correct date was February 10. When she tried to confront Scott about the error, he brushed her off and walked away.

In San Diego, Grogan dialed the Petersons.

"Lee, I caught a flight today, and I'm down here in San Diego," Grogan told Scott's father. "There's something I want to talk to you about, I think it might be upsetting to Jackie. I didn't want to just drop by. We haven't found Laci or anything like that, but I was hoping that maybe I could meet with you for a few minutes, and then you could decide on how best to handle it with Jackie. Do you think that would work?"

"Um, yeah, I suppose, can you tell me about it?" Lee inquired.

The men arranged to meet at Einstein Bros. Bagels at Lomas and Santa Fe by the freeway.

"What is this all about?" Lee Peterson asked the two detectives seated at the table in the bagel shop.

"When Scott came in with you a while back, I showed him a photo that was sent to us, and it's a photograph of him and another girl," Grogan started.

"What?" Lee exclaimed. "And what circumstances?"

"Well," Grogan said, pushing the photos across the table to Scott's father.

"Well, how old are these? Who is this?"

"We've talked to her. Those photographs were taken this Christmas. So it was taken on December . . ."

Stunned, Lee interrupted. "This Christmas?"

"It was taken December 14 of this year," Grogan explained.

"Where are they taken?"

"She lives in the Fresno area, and it was on the day when Scott said he was meeting his boss in San Francisco," Grogan said.

"How did you get these?" Lee asked.

"Well, we talked to the girl, and she gave us this photo," Grogan said. "This is a function that they went to together. She sent out this photograph of her and Scott in some Christmas cards to other people. I don't know how many photos are out there, but my concern is that you and Jackie were going to see one of these in the paper. Now I know you're probably thinking, can you believe me or not, and am I trying to put something over on you or something like that. All I can tell you, sir, is that I give you my word that those are the circumstances."

Again Lee Peterson interrupted. "Did she volunteer these or . . . ?"

"Yeah, she had the photographs."

"[Does] she know him as someone else?" Lee asked.

"Scott was telling her that he was not married to start with. They had been set up by a friend, a mutual friend. They carried on a relationship from about mid-November and they haven't actually seen each other since Laci's disappearance, but they have continued to talk over the phone."

"Since Laci's disappearance?" Lee repeated.

"Yeah," Grogan replied.

"I'm shocked," Lee told the detectives.

"There's something very disturbing. . . . It's one thing if it's just some relationship that, I mean people have affairs," Grogan said. "That doesn't necessarily mean anything, but . . ."

"That's true," Lee interjected. "You know, I don't know if I should talk to you fellows anymore without talking to Kirk. You know, I'm a babe in the woods here. I don't know law enforcement or, you know, lawyers or whatever. And I don't want to say something that could be taken out of context later, or whatever. So, I don't think I can talk to you anymore."

"All right," Grogan agreed.

"Well, just wanted you to understand before this hit the press," Detective Owen added.

"This is gonna hit the press?" Lee shot back.

"I don't know if these photos are going to be in there or not. My problem is she sent out photos to a lot of people," Grogan said.

"These photos?" Lee asked again.

"It's a photograph similar to that, that she sent out in her Christmas cards," Grogan replied. "And I don't want you to see Scott in this photo [for the first time] in print."

"Well, you wouldn't release that to the press, would you?" Lee questioned.

"She was under the impression that her and Scott had a relationship and she was proud of him, so she was sending out Christmas cards to her friends," Detective Owen explained. "She came to us with the pictures."

"She came to you?" Lee asked, still stunned. "Since Laci's disappearance? Why in the hell would she do that?"

"She says that at first, Scott said that he was not married. And then the friend that set them up to start with made some inquiries and found out that he was married, and told this girl. The girl then asked Scott about it on December 9. Scott told her that he had lost his wife." Grogan paused and looked at Lee Peterson. "That concerns me."

"I don't know, what can I tell ya?" Lee stated, clearly confused.

"She felt a little lied to because she found out Scott was married," Owen clarified.

"Well, what do you want from me?" Lee asked the detectives. "Why are you . . . except to protect my wife and I and so we'll have prior knowledge of it."

"I understand that your job as Scott's father is to try to protect him," Grogan comforted.

"Sure," Lee agreed.

"And I'm not trying to dissuade you from that. But I wanted you to know that these exist, that we didn't release them. This information is very concerning. If Scott told this girl that he lost his wife before, weeks before Laci disappeared . . ."

"That sure isn't proof that my son was involved in this thing," Lee said, defending Scott. "And I'll stake my life that my son was not involved in his wife's disappearance. I'm behind him. And I can understand someone having an affair, I mean, it's not a good thing, but I can understand. . . ."

"It seems to me that you weren't aware of this girl," Grogan stated. "Are you aware of any others?"

"No. Maybe this was at a party. Maybe Laci was in attendance and they were taking funny pictures because I have pictures of them in Hawaii with mutual friends . . ."

"No," Detective Owen interrupted.

"Why not?" Lee asked.

"Couple of reasons," Owen began. "One is [that] the photographs kind of speak for themselves, but the other thing too is, the gal that's in the photo talked to us."

"I'm shocked, but I still don't think my son is involved in his wife's disappearance," Lee said. "He may have had an affair, but the kid couldn't hurt a flea. I mean, he feels bad when he hurts your feelings."

It's hard to interpret Lee's reactions in this conversation. He is certainly showing the protective instincts of a parent. Yet his denial seems so strong that I'm not sure he knew exactly what he was protecting. Did Lee Peterson ever really know his son?

"If we could clear out Scott, that would be fine with me," Grogan explained. "But we're weeks into this, and we're not able to do that."

"How about the forensics from the boat and the car?" Lee asked. "I will bet you that there's nothing there."

The detectives explained that some items had been sent out for testing but the results were still pending.

"You guys have gotta believe me, he's the least likely person to harm anybody," Lee repeated.

"He hasn't been real truthful with us, though," Owen told him.

"You mean about this?" Lee asked. "Oh, he's probably not going to volunteer something . . ."

"But in a case like this, it would be better that he tells us up front," Owen told Lee. "There are other things he hasn't been truthful about, so you kinda have to think . . ."

"Can you tell me what those are?" Lee asked. "If I was under investigation, and my wife disappeared, I don't think I'd be talking about an affair I had with some other woman. I doubt either of you fellows would either. If you knew that you were innocent, and all you had to do was wait things out and be, you know, be exonerated, I doubt you'd be volunteering anything either."

"I understand that you had concerns right from the beginning," Grogan said. "But, I mean, if Scott wanted to be out from under the microscope on this thing, there's a lot of other things that he could have done. I mean, we're in an adversarial position right now, where I can't talk to him without his attorney. . . . He's refused to take the polygraph test. Everybody else in this investigation that we've asked has taken one.

"The key thing that bothers me, and I want you to think about, is him telling this girl that his wife was lost and he's crying and upset in that conversation with this girl," Grogan advised. "She had the impression that he was saying his wife had died. That is several days before, that's December 9, before Laci disappears. And that concerns [me]."

Lee grew defensive. "I don't know, maybe he was drinking or something. I don't understand that either. But my son did not hurt anybody."

"The other thing you need to know is that we felt an obligation to also notify Laci's family about this," Grogan said.

For the rest of the conversation, Lee Peterson struggled to come up with an explanation for the photos. He seemed unwilling to believe that his son was actually involved in an affair—never mind in Laci's disappearance.

"I want the truth, and I know the truth. Scott's not involved," Lee insisted.

"Well, if you know the truth, you just found out that you didn't know all the truth," Owen pointed out.

Later that evening, Detective Buehler received phone calls from Laci's father, Dennis Rocha, and her brother, Brent. Both men expressed concerns about the safety of their family, and asked whether Scott was going to be arrested, and what actions they should be taking.

Buehler advised them both that there was no arrest pending. "The mere fact that Scott was involved in a relationship outside of his marriage was not enough to arrest him for the suspected violent crime," the detective noted. The investigation would continue, "slowly and cautiously," he said.

As Buehler was ending the conversation with Brent, a call came in from Amber Frey. She had just received a letter from Scott in which he returned a picture of her—the first one she'd ever given him. In the accompanying note, Scott told Amber that he didn't deserve to have the picture. The letter was handwritten on Double Tree Hotel stationery from Bakersfield, but was postmarked from Modesto. She was unsure what it all meant.

Buehler received one other important call before ending his shift—this one from Kim Peterson, who'd been running the volunteer search center. After hearing the news about Scott's affair, the family had decided to close down the center.

"Peterson advised it would be difficult for them to have this volunteer center continue to run with Scott being there in view of the circumstances and knowledge that had come up," Buehler entered in his report. "The family members were all of the belief that Scott had killed Laci and now they only hoped to recover her body and locate it."

Kim also told Buehler that the volunteer fund account contained some $20,000. Sharon Rocha was concerned that Scott might try to access the money for his own use. Indeed, the police later learned that—despite his parents' contributions to his upkeep, Scott did inquire about using the center's funds to pay for his personal expenses.

On January 16, the long-awaited *National Enquirer* story hit the newsstands. Though the article did not identify Scott's girlfriend by name, it was accompanied by photos of the two of them together. It also contained information about other potentially incriminating evidence that police had gathered in the course on of their investigation.

Detective Craig Grogan's first order of business that morning was to call Sharon Rocha at her home on Marklee Way. As he had anticipated, she was distraught. Grogan asked Sharon if he could come over that morning with a recording device for her phone, to capture any calls from Scott. Sharon agreed, and they arranged to meet at 10:30 A.M.

As he pulled up in front of Sharon Rocha's house, Grogan got a call alerting him that Lee Peterson hadn't spoken with his son since police had shown him the photos the previous day. This was puzzling: What father wouldn't call his son immediately under such circumstances? Was Lee afraid that Scott would just lie to him as he had everyone else? Like Jackie, Lee showed a consistent attitude throughout the investigation: Their son could do no wrong, but they would never confront him about the truth.

The police concluded that the Petersons, on some level, must have suspected Scott was complicit in his wife's disappearance.

Grogan related the information to Buehler, then stepped out of the vehicle into the cool January air. Sharon Rocha answered the door, looking exhausted. Brent and Amy Rocha were in the living room, along with Ron Grantski, Sharon's friend Sandy Pickard, and another unidentified woman.

While Buehler remained in the living room, Grogan followed Sharon and Ron to a back bedroom. Laci's parents outlined the reservations they'd been having about Scott. Sharon said she was particularly troubled by Scott's "nonchalant attitude" about her daughter's disappearance. She was also bothered by the fact that it had taken more than a week before Scott actually sat down and answered her questions about the events of December 24. Even then he was "hesitant," and she learned little from their discussion.

Ron also admitted having concerns about his son-in-law. His normally bright eyes were bloodshot and drawn; beneath his bristly white beard he wore a frown. He told Grogan that he was suspicious of Scott early on, but didn't want to believe he was involved. He felt the family should stand behind him until they had evidence to the contrary. Yet he admitted that Scott had been distant with him since Laci disappeared, and wouldn't make eye contact.

Grogan noted the couple's observations, but his main priority was installing the recording equipment on the home phones before Scott's next call. As he was setting up the wiring in the bedroom, the phone rang. It was Scott, calling to speak with Sharon. One of Sharon's friends had answered the cordless phone in the living room and brought it to the rear bedroom for Sharon.

Grogan quickly activated the recorder and handed Sharon the headset to the standard phone.

"Hi Mom. Scott."

"Hi, Scott," Sharon replied, keeping her eyes fixed on the detective.

"Why are there signs at the center that we're supposed to close today?"

"I don't know, is it closed?" Sharon asked, holding back her emotions.

"You don't know why?" Scott asked.

"No. I haven't talked . . . nobody's called me. I haven't heard anything."

"Huh," Scott sighed. "How are you doing?"

"Not very good today. Not having a good day."

"Well," Scott began.

"No, it's been a real rough day today," Sharon continued. "Scott, we've seen some photos of you with another girl. Is there somebody you've been seeing?"

"No," Scott replied. "Yeah, the police have a very . . ."

Before he could finish, Sharon interrupted. "Well, we've seen the photos and it's you with this other girl."

"Uh, huh," Scott said noncommittally.

"So what's that all about?"

"Well, I'll sit down with you and talk to you about it."

"Well, are you seeing somebody else or not?" Sharon asked. "Is that why you're not coming forward or . . ."

"No." Scott insisted.

"You're not seeing anybody?" Sharon probed.

"No." Scott lied again. "Is that why Brent called me this morning?"

"In the photos you're by a Christmas tree, Scott, and . . ."

"Yeah." Scott offered no explanation.

"You guys are kissing and you're trying to tell me that you're not seeing somebody else?"

"We'll, we'll sit down, okay Mom?"

Scott tried to tell his mother-in-law that the alleged affair was just a theory originating with police. Even as Sharon described the photos, Scott continued to deny the obvious.

"When are we gonna sit down and talk?" Sharon demanded.

"Well, I'll see ya definitely today," Scott told her.

"Are you coming over here?"

"Yeah," Scott agreed.

"No," Sharon shot back. "And don't come over here because that's not a good idea to come over here."

When I first learned about this conversation, I wondered why Sharon did not corner Scott at the house and, figuratively, pummel him for information. On reflection, however, it's clear how useless that would have been. Scott was a consummate liar; nothing Sharon might have done would change that.

When Grogan emerged from the rear bedroom, he saw that Buehler was in the living room showing photographs of Scott and Amber to the group gathered there.

As Laci's family grappled with the devastating news, Scott was in his car, dialing Stacey Boyers's mother, Terry Western, who helped run the volunteer center.

"Why is the center closed today, Terry?" Scott asked when she answered the call.

Terry said that Kim Peterson had told her about the article in the *National Enquirer* claiming that Scott had a girlfriend. She said they were all "devastated."

"I know the police have this theory, and they have asked me a bunch of . . ." Scott asked.

"I hope to God it isn't true," Terry replied.

Scott let out a sigh, then thanked Terry for being straight with him. "I wish that people would tell me about the fucking *National Enquirer* thing," he fumed. It was ironic; Scott was thanking Terry for her honesty, even as he lied to everyone else.

In a later conversation with another friend from the volunteer center, Scott again denied the affair. When the woman told him that she believed him, Scott didn't correct her. Concerned only about his image, he allowed her to end the conversation by writing off the allegation as a "*National Enquirer* article."

A little while later, Scott checked his voice mail. Jackie Peterson had phoned to suggest that Scott highlight Laci's pregnancy on the missing persons posters and on the Laci Peterson website. Scott deleted the message before it was over, a gesture that wasn't lost on the officers. He then listened to a second message from an NBC reporter calling with questions about "reports of a girlfriend."

"Yeah, right, bitch!" Scott said before deleting that message, too.

The third message on Scott's voice mail was from Brent Rocha. He'd finally gotten his hands on the *Enquirer* article, and advised

Scott they needed to talk about "why these things were coming out in the press."

Scott deleted this one, too.

As Scott erased his brother-in-law's message, Brent was calling again. This time Scott answered.

"Do you have a minute?" Brent asked.

"What's up with the article?" Scott inquired.

Brent described the *Enquirer* article, confirming that it included pictures of Scott with a woman. He mentioned the article's contention that Scott had taken out a hefty life insurance policy on Laci, and insinuated that this was a motive for murder. "Is it true?" Brent asked in a controlled voice.

"No," Scott replied.

"No life insurance policy?" Brent questioned.

"I mean, we have one of those whole life policies, you know that is a retirement fund as well," Scott stated. "But the FBI has . . ."

The call was lost.

Brent tried back several more times, reaching Scott's voice mail each time. A few minutes later, Scott phoned him back. He told Brent that he had been trying to find the article but had been unsuccessful.

"Well apparently there are pictures of you and the girl together. So we know that's true, right?"

"Yeah, there was an encounter," Scott admitted.

"Knowing that, what can you tell me about my sister to make me understand that you are telling the truth and that I can still support you?" Brent queried.

"You know how happy we were together and that never changed or wavered," Scott replied. He insisted he had nothing to do with Laci's disappearance.

Brent asked if Scott thought that "that girl" had anything to do with Laci going missing?

"She didn't," he defended her. "She couldn't have. She didn't know about Laci."

Scott's certainty on this score raises an interesting question. In truth, he barely knew Amber—yet after only four dates and a number of phone calls, he was sure that she had nothing to do with Laci's disappearance. How could he be certain that his mistress had nothing to do with his wife's fate—unless he knew the real story?

Brent asked if Scott was happy about the baby coming.

"Absolutely," Scott assured him.

"They are out to nail you right now," Brent commented.

"Of course they are."

Despite public suspicions to the contrary, police detectives aren't usually interested in arresting the wrong man. Yet today police conspiracies are a common defense. O. J. Simpson's claim that the LAPD wanted to frame him was ludicrous, but it succeeded at trial. Maybe Scott thought the tactic would work for him, too.

Brent told Scott that the family had been standing behind him, but now they were unsure what to believe. He said the article also mentioned spots of blood found on Scott's kitchen floor and in his truck, as well as cement in his shop that he used for "anchors or something."

Scott acknowledged that he'd made a boat anchor with the cement, and that he put some of the material on the driveway. He said police asked him a lot of questions about the cement.

"The police already questioned you?" Brent asked.

"Yes," Scott replied, though he added that he'd never heard about the blood spots. He told Brent he could look at the warrant that police served on his house, which itemized everything that was taken. Police took a sample of one suspected spot from an exterior door that tested negative for the presence of blood.

"Okay," Brent said.

"If that helps you to know how unfactual this article is in lots of respects," Scott added.

"Hey, it's coming from the *Enquirer*, so who knows what this is saying," Brent said.

Scott pointed to a prior *Enquirer* article that featured an interview with an eyewitness who claimed he saw Scott putting a body in the back of his truck. Brent admitted that he'd read that, too.

Scott said it was embarrassing and wrong that the paper talked about an encounter with "this girl."

"So, that part is true, huh?" Brent asked.

"Yeah, yeah," Scott admitted.

"So, you don't think she had anything to do with it?" Brent asked a second time.

"You know Laci and I are happy together," Scott said.

"You know every time I saw you together . . . I told you, Scott, the day after she left, she loved you so much, she totally adored you. . . . Is there anything else like this person, this woman, that might throw us off or catch us off guard?"

"You know, this was the only thing like that," Scott said.

"What do you think happened to her?" Brent asked.

Scott told his brother in law he believed that someone who knew Laci's routine "pulled over and grabbed her," or "it could have happened down in the park."

If Brent Rocha had been relatively even-tempered with Scott, Sharon Rocha was far more confrontational.

"Scott, this is Sharon, are you there?" Sharon said, adjusting the police department's headset. "Scott, pick up the phone if you're there. I need to talk to you . . ."

"Yeah," Scott replied.

"Where are you?" Sharon inquired.

Scott started to answer, but Sharon interrupted him. "Well, since you've managed to lose all of my confidence in you, what I want to know is, where is my daughter at, Scott?"

"I wish I knew, Mom. I wish I knew where she is."

"You do know," Sharon snapped. "You do know where she is and I want you to tell me. Where is Laci and her baby? Where did you put them?"

"Where is my wife and our child? I don't know," Scott replied.

"You killed my daughter, didn't you?"

"No, I didn't, Mom," Scott said.

"Yes, you did, Scott. And I want to know, just let me bring my daughter home, okay? That's all I want. I don't want anything else from you. I want you to tell me where my daughter is. I want to bury my daughter. Now would you tell me where she is, Scott?"

Scott spoke over his mother-in-law. "Don't know where she is. I want my wife . . ."

"Stop lying," Sharon insisted. "I'm tired of your lies. You have looked me in the eye . . . for weeks and been lying to me. You have looked me in the eye for years and been lying to me. Now where is she?"

"I wish I knew," Scott said.

"You do know," Sharon shot back. "Stop lying. For once in your life take some responsibility and tell the goddamn truth. Where is my daughter?"

"I want her home, Mom and . . ."

"Shut up," Sharon commanded. "Don't tell me such stupid things. You tell me where she is. Where did you put her?" Sharon paused to catch her breath. "Scott, tell me where she is."

"I'm sorry . . ." Scott interrupted, but Sharon continued to rail.

"And you can run away . . . you can go do whatever the fuck you want, but tell me where my daughter is."

"I'm sorry," Scott started again.

"I have every right to know where you put Laci," Sharon insisted.

"We all have a right to know where Laci is . . ."

"Quit lying to me," Sharon yelled into the receiver. "Don't bull-shit me. You tell me where she is."

"We all want her home."

"Shut up," Sharon demanded. "You are such a fucking liar. You make me sick, Scott. Where is Laci? I want to be able to bury my daughter. Now, tell me what you did with her."

"I want her and our child home . . ."

"Oh shut up. You're disgusting. Do you know there's not a person in this town who wants to see your face? Now you tell me where she is and then you can get the hell out of here. Tell me where she is. I want my daughter, Scott. That's all I want from you. I don't care what happens to you."

Scott tried to say something, but his mother-in-law continued to rage. "Mom, we all want her back."

"Oh God, you are disgusting," Sharon retorted, then turned to Ron. "Do you have anything to say to him?" She handed Ron the phone.

"If you've got anything left in you, Scott, you better tell us where she is," Ron commanded.

"I wish I knew, Ron. We all want her back," Scott repeated.

"No," Ron fumed. "The police have . . . the police are gonna be seeing you before long, Scott. And your world is crumbling."

"My world is done without Laci and my child," Scott said. "We all want her back. And I'm sorry that you guys feel I had something to do with this. But the only important thing is getting her back."

"Scott, I don't know how you can just . . . I don't know how you can do this, just keep saying . . . we've seen pictures," Ron said. "We've seen other things, so, you're in trouble. We want her back."

"We all want her back," Scott said again. "There's no question to that. We're, we need to find her and Conner."

Sharon shouted in the background: "I know, well same thing, I want her back, too. I want her back, too."

"I've had enough of this," Grantski fumed. "I don't want to talk to you any more. You tell us where Laci is." Ron angrily hung up.

Consider this—how would you, an innocent person, react to such a hysterical accusation from the parents of your wife? Would you quietly protest your innocence, or join Sharon in tears? Would you remain calm and deliberative, as Scott did? Whenever a guest on my program tried to argue that everyone reacts differently to grief and loss, I wondered, then shall we eliminate all the great works of literature that illuminate the contours of universal human behavior? If we give up a belief in basic shared characteristics, motives, and behavior, psychology itself becomes a worthless field of study. I believe that Scott Peterson did consistently exhibit conduct of a classic sociopath. I was not surprised that he proved unable to feel Sharon's grief, for he had none of his own.

At 4:05, Scott dialed Brent. "I don't know why I called you," he said, "but I just got off the phone with Mom and Ron."

"Yeah," Brent replied.

"I can't lose any more of my family here, you know," Scott told his brother-in-law.

"Hey man, you know what? They think you did it, bud. They think, ya, ya know, the police are tellin' 'em it's you and they're upset . . ."

"Yeah, I . . ." Scott agreed.

". . . and ya know, I'm trying to hang in there with ya but, uh, I mean their evidence is piling up on ya Scott, and you know what, they think they got ya, they really do," Brent said.

"I didn't do anything, man," Scott insisted.

"To be honest with ya . . ." Brent said before being interrupted a second time.

"Again, I don't know why I'm calling ya right now, but . . ." Scott explained.

"I don't have anything to hide from you," Brent said. "Whatever happened, happened for a reason, but I want my sister back, ya know?"

"I do, too. I want Laci back and my baby, Conner," Scott said.

"It's going to be over, they got a lot of things and they don't even tell us half of what they got," Brent said.

"I . . ."

"Ninety-nine point nine percent, they think it's you. That's my guess, you know what I mean?" Brent asked.

"What's that?"

"That's my guess and I think, ah, I'm not much in contact like my mom is in contact, so she might know different things," Brent explained.

"I mean, there's nothin' to know. That's uh—*God,*" Scott said. "All right, again, I don't know why I'm callin'. I'm just so upset by it."

"But, I definitely want to keep in touch with you so, you know," Brent said. "I'm not being judgmental. I don't know anything right now. Ya know? I'm lost. I don't know what the hell happened and I'm not going to judge you for doing it until you know, they can say anything they want to try to talk me into it, but I'm keeping an open mind," Brent paused. "I don't know what my mom said. She still pissed?"

"It's so hard to talk to her. She thinks I did something to Laci . . . it's . . ." Scott laughed nervously as he spoke.

"Ya, she thinks you did, Scott."

"I know," Scott agreed.

"She didn't think you did until a couple of days ago, til this article came out and she met with police," Brent said.

"Gosh, I can't . . ."

"She was standing by you, you heard her in the media," Brent continued. "She was supportin' ya one hundred percent. Then, all of a sudden, she took a ninety-degree turn, cause they got some stuff on ya man, let me tell ya. . . .

"They got a lot of forensic stuff, so I don't know," Brent said. "I don't know the details on it, but . . ."

"There's nothing to have," Scott said again. "Okay, again, I don't know why I called, I just, uh . . ."

"Hang in there, ya know, let's get through it. Let's get my sister home, okay?"

I doubt that Brent was being truly candid with Scott. His suspicions, like Sharon's, were mounting rapidly. Yet, he seemed determined to keep the lines of communication open, hoping that Scott might slip up and reveal something to him about Laci.

Scott's next call was from Kim McGregor, who lived three houses away from the Petersons on Covena Avenue. The thirty-year-old woman became friendly with Scott through her volunteer efforts at the Command Center at the Red Lion. Since Laci's disappearance, she had been taking care of the Petersons' dog.

"Is everything okay?" Kim asked.

"Na, nothing, nothin's right," Scott said. "But thank you for taking care of McKenzie."

Kim agreed to keep McKenzie while Scott headed to the Bay area to distribute fliers, and then down to L.A. to open a volunteer center there. He told her he would probably be gone about a week.

When the two hung up, Kim dialed the Modesto police. Her call was transferred to Detective Buehler. The two had met earlier that year, when Buehler had worked on a stalking threat leveled against Kim. Now she alerted Buehler that Scott was preparing to leave town. She also reported that Scott didn't sound "like he normally did," that he sounded slightly depressed, and Kim wasn't sure if his change in demeanor was significant.

Sharon Rocha also called the police to alert them to a conversation she had with her friend Terri Western, the real estate agent. Scott, she said, had approached Western at the Red Lion Hotel on January 14 and asked about selling his house.

When the police followed up, they learned that Scott had broached the subject when he and Western were alone at the command center. She saw that Scott appeared to be crying, so she walked over to give him a hug. Scott told Western that he needed to sell the Covena Avenue house, explaining that he didn't want Laci to come home to the same environment and "this house." Western admitted the statement was strange, but she paid little attention until she learned about the girl from Fresno the following day.

Western said that another friend, Judy McKinney, had a similar encounter. McKinney recounted that several days earlier she had brought in an article from the *San Jose Mercury News* that quoted one of Scott's former college professors as calling Scott "kind of smart." McKinney showed the article to Scott, in Terri Western's presence.

"Kind of smart?" Scott reportedly commented as he skimmed the article. "I'm *real* smart."

Many sociopaths have above-average intelligence, and they often expect to be recognized for it. Their belief in their own "special" status helps feed their conviction that normal social mores do not apply to them. Such individuals can be relatively insightful about others. They are generally adept at reading what their targets "need," and then morphing into a personality they feel will generate the best results.

Scott Peterson was skilled at projecting myriad personalities. With Laci, he was steadfast, gentle, and hardworking; with Amber he was successful, worldly, and romantic. He seemed to be particularly anxious that people should perceive him as bright—asking Shawn Sibley whether Amber was intelligent, and buying phony diplomas to showcase on his wall. But the height of arrogance was reached when he took on California law enforcement.

Scott had fooled so many people for so long; he was convinced he could win this game as well.

# CHAPTER FOURTEEN

# JANUARY 21, 2003

As the press worked feverishly to identify the "woman from Fresno," police pressed forward. Detective Al Brocchini again reviewed tapes of the *Martha Stewart Living* shows that aired in Modesto on December 23 and 24.

Scott had told Brocchini that he took a shower on Christmas Eve morning, poured himself a bowl of cereal, and then joined Laci to watch her "favorite show." Scott recalled that Martha was baking something using meringue. Brocchini wanted to see for himself at what time, if at all, Martha had referred to meringue. Having seen plenty of cases in which a suspect drew events from a previous day to create an alibi, he was eager to view the December 23 show first. Sure enough, forty minutes into the hour-long program, Martha and a guest, Bill Yasis, whipped up chocolate pastry layered in meringue.

Brocchini replaced the cassette with Stewart's Christmas Eve broadcast. This time, Martha spent the first segment baking lemon butter cookies, and during the second half-hour prepared cioppino, a kind of fish stew. The detective did not catch any mention of meringue during the Christmas Eve show, and stated as much in his report.

Martha had, in fact, mentioned meringue during the Christmas Eve show—at 9:48 A.M. Pacific Standard Time. For Brocchini and the district attorney alike, this would prove an embarrassing oversight.

Ironically, the discovery eventually led the prosecution to determine that Scott did not leave the house at 9:30, as he had claimed, but rather after 9:48—thus narrowing the window of time when Laci disappeared.

Detective Grogan was sitting in the Rochas' living room, speaking with Sharon and Ron about a statement the family was preparing in response to the *Enquirer* article, when Scott Peterson's face popped up on the TV screen. Amazed, the group watched Scott's first television interview since his wife's disappearance. During the segment, on the local station KTVU, Scott called the *Modesto Bee's* story about his alleged affair and a recent life insurance policy on Laci "a bunch of lies."

However, Scott did not deny his involvement in Laci's disappearance.

That afternoon, Laci's family members held a press conference. A tearful Sharon Rocha called on Scott to "tell everything he knows." Her statement prompted a flurry of calls to Scott's cell phone, mostly from reporters looking for his response.

Scott just erased the messages.

Under Grogan's direction, search teams kept exploring the various bodies of water in the region. After probing nearby reservoirs, they were left with a list that included the Delta Mendota Canal, the San Lois Reservoir and O'Neil Forebay, and the San Francisco Bay.

Police also searched the Squaw Leap/Millerton Lake area, where Scott and Amber had picnicked with Ayiana in December. The rugged terrain and steep inclines led officers to conclude that it would have been too difficult to dispose of a body in Squaw Leap, but Millerton Lake was a more plausible locale, and they made a note to check it at a later time.

Brocchini and Buehler toured the area with Amber. They were curious to see whether she would reveal any additional calls from Scott since the one in early January. But Amber didn't mention any of the recent unrecorded conversations, and the detectives never revealed that they had intercepted them. Her failure to report the calls had detectives concerned, and internal police reports indicate that they had not ruled her out as a suspect or accomplice in Laci's disappearance.

"Although Amber Frey is taking steps to cooperate with authorities, she remains secretive with previous conversations she has had with Scott Peterson," Jacobson, the officer in charge of the wiretaps, wrote in a report. "She informed us early on that she wanted to cooperate in this investigation, even stating she was tape recording her calls with Peterson. Yet, the evidence based on the intercepts has led us to believe that Amber Frey still has a desire to have Scott Peterson in her life and that she may even lie or conspire with him to withhold evidence."

Unsure of her allegiances, police scheduled Amber for a polygraph on January 21. They also decided to examine her alibi closely. She had told police that she worked with a client at American Body Works on the morning of December 23, then spent the rest of the day and following morning with her daughter. When a neighbor had stopped by her home around 2:30 P.M. on Christmas Eve and asked why she was still wearing pajamas, Amber responded that she was off that day. Later that afternoon, Amber took her daughter to visit with her mother, and that evening she accompanied her friend Richard Byrd, the Fresno police officer, to a holiday party.

In the days that followed, police carefully investigated Amber's story and concluded that she wasn't involved in the suspected homicide. Still, they insisted that she take a polygraph.

During this same period, Amber told police about a conversation she had with Scott in early December.

"Scott told Amber that his friend Jeff was attempting to change his employment situation so he could travel less and have a relationship with a girl he met," Buehler wrote. Scott said he was concerned about the same thing. He was working too much, he told Amber, and wanted to do something about it.

By the end of January, he promised, he'd be able to spend more time with her.

"Scott asked Amber if she would trust in his abilities to make decisions and if he contacted her regarding a big decision (to possibly relocate) if she would trust in his judgment," the detective continued. "He told her he felt her style, along with her daughter, would fit in well with his life, and they could explore this in more detail near the end of January, as things would settle down for him at that time."

In a later phone conversation, Scott told Amber that Laci's entire family believed he had killed Laci. Amber responded that his refusal to tell the truth about other things—such as their affair—had only hurt his case. He'd done nothing to prove his innocence, she told him.

"There's nothing I can do," Scott countered.

Amber replied that he could start by "cooperating with authorities," that he should "take the polygraph."

Scott insisted he'd been the only one telling the truth.

"You're lying again."

Scott then agreed to a polygraph, on the condition that Amber accompany him. When she told him she'd meet him the following day, although Scott immediately backed off, telling her that he would take it in a few weeks.


The wiretaps on the suspect's cell phones continued to offer insights into Scott's situation. According to a transcript of one voice mail, Jackie Peterson offered some motherly advice.

"I wanted to talk to you about something," Jackie said, "I would [think] that you should deny, deny, deny. I was told that years ago by an attorney, and I think you should talk to Kirk and do that . . . I had to do that at the time. I'm sorry, but that's what I had to do and I really feel that that's right. Um, that you must deny these things, not to the press, not to anybody, but to your family. Because . . . it will be talked about and it could leak and it's not good if there is any truth to your [unintelligible]. I'm not saying there is . . ."

It is not known whether any attorney actually said that to Jackie Peterson, but as investigator Steven Jacobson commented about this transcript, "It appears by this message and by his very own words

[that] Scott Peterson is following these instructions." To Jacobson, the message also reflected badly on Jackie: "I also believe by his mother not being specific by mentioning the affair alone, but by using the term 'deny anything,' his mother and father know more about what really happened to Laci."

Jackie's instructions would never be played for the jury, but I discussed them several times on my program. While in public Jackie always insisted on Scott's innocence, behind the scenes she was desperate to keep him quiet. From the second day of the investigation, Scott's parents were advising him not to take a polygraph. In all the recorded conversations among the three, Lee and Jackie were never heard to encourage him to participate in press conferences; nor did they ever ask him if he had anything to do with Laci's disappearance. To the contrary, the three were more likely to denigrate the cops, or debate whether Scott was in "good shape" legally. Only when the Amber story broke did Jackie agree that it was time for Scott to make a media push. In hindsight, this seemed more for her son's benefit than that of his missing wife.

Scott didn't return his mother's call right away, but he did respond to a message left by Sharon.

"Hello," Sharon said.

"Hi Mom, it's Scott."

"Where are you?"

"Trying to get this volunteer center to happen in Los Angeles," her son-in-law told her. "Can't believe they cancelled it."

"What do you mean you can't believe they cancelled it?" Sharon snapped.

"Why can't we have it? We need to keep her picture out there and the Volunteer Center in Modesto," Scott replied.

"When are you gonna give up the charade, Scott? When are you gonna call it quits and admit what you've done?"

"When I find my wife and child," Scott responded flatly.

"Well, you're the only one who knows where they are, so why don't you fill the rest of us in so we can go get them?"

"Mom, I didn't call you to . . ." Scott said.

"Well, that's the reason I called you," Sharon retorted.

"Oh well . . ." Scott said.

"I want you to tell me where Laci is," Sharon spoke over Scott. "I'm tired of your lies. . . . I'm tired of your conniving, I'm tired of your manipulation. You know damn well they're not opening a stupid center down there, because you've embarrassed your family and everyone else. You have shamed this world, Scott. You have had people out looking for Laci and somebody else when you've known all along where she's been, so tell me where she is. I want her back."

"I know you won't believe that I want her back also . . . that's all I . . ."

"Oh, I'm sure you want her back too, yes, you're broken-hearted," Sharon continued. "I know that, Scott. So now, just be honest with me and tell me where she is."

"I can't listen to you tell me . . ."

"And I can't listen to your fucking lies anymore . . . now get to the truth."

The connection went dead.

Sharon Rocha was already reeling from news of her son-in-law's dual life when Detective Grogan learned that Modesto's mayor, Carmen Sabatino, had told reporters that the Modesto Police Department did not believe Laci's body would be found. He then declared that the searches were being discontinued.

None of it was true, of course, and Grogan knew the mayor's comments would be upsetting to Laci's family. Anxious to set the record straight, the detective placed a call to the Rocha residence. When he didn't reach anyone, he paged Kim Peterson.

Detective Buehler was at headquarters when Kim phoned back. She told the investigator that she was at the Rochas' home, and asked him to come and assist her. Grogan and Buehler arrived to find a house full of people.

The detectives spoke with Sharon and Kim in a back bedroom.

Chief Wasden had already assured the Rochas that the mayor's announcement was incorrect, but Sharon had spent much of the day distraught over how Laci may have died.

"I explained to Sharon that based on Detective Buehler's experience and mine, coupled with the opinion of Sharon Hagan . . . and evidence obtained during the search warrant, it did not appear there was a violent or bloody crime scene in the home," Grogan wrote in his report. "I told Sharon that it was our opinion that Laci likely died after she went to bed that night and may not have awakened or been aware of what was occurring.

"Sharon's concern was that her daughter was placed in water alive with cement attached to her based on the story she had read in the *National Enquirer*. I told her that was a very unlikely scenario." Grogan noted. "Sharon Rocha seemed to find some comfort in the release of the information."

Later that evening, in a brainstorming session, Buehler and Grogan drafted two lists—one cataloging reasons Scott may have elected to dump Laci's body in a body of freshwater, the other noting reasons he might have chosen the San Francisco Bay. They hoped the exercise would help them determine where they should focus their efforts.

By night's end, the freshwater list was ten entries long. The number of reasons Scott may have chosen the San Francisco Bay had reached forty-one. Among them:

- Peterson's statement to police that he was at the Berkeley Marina on Christmas Eve.
- The pay stub from the marina stamped with a time consistent with his statement.
- The cell site records showed Scott's location at the marina.
- The bloodhounds who tracked Laci's scent at the marina.
- Scott's two-day fishing license purchased on December 20 for December 23–24.
- Scott's "whistle" on the wiretap on January 11 as he listened to Sharon Rocha's voice mail that the object in the bay was anchor, not a body.

- Peterson's trips to the marina since December 24.
- Scott's research of the San Francisco Bay, including one map that showed how deep the currents are.
- Salt water in the boat; not fresh water.
- Scott calls home and leaves Laci messages as he's leaving the bay, saying he's going to be late.
- Purchased just $13 of gas in Livermore—not a significant amount for a truck but enough to establish his whereabouts.

O ver the weekend, Scott reached out again to Brent. He told his brother-in-law that he was still out of town, but he wanted to let him know that the volunteer center in Los Angeles was poised to open. His statement was met with silence.

After a few seconds, Brent asked Scott if he'd ever read the definition of a sociopath.

A sociopath, he explained, is someone with mental illness who thinks they can get away with things. "It's you," Brent declared. "I think you need to come clean. You are not going to get away with it."

Scott laughed. "Brent, I didn't do it, man."

"You messed up, man, everything is leading to you. What did you do with my sister?"

"I didn't do anything."

"Tell us where she is at so we can bring her back," Brent begged.

Scott threatened to hang up, but Brent pressed on, accusing his brother-in-law of avoiding the family. He pointedly asked Scott why he wasn't cooperating with the investigation.

"I have," Scott said.

"So many things don't add up," Brent said. "Why didn't you take the lie detector test?"

Scott told Brent he only telephoned to tell him about the center opening up. "If you want to call me up to accuse me of these things, I'll take your calls, but hopefully you will find out these things are not true."

"It's gone too far," Brent said, telling Scott it was time to "clean it up."

Scott maintained that he was following the advice of his attorney.

"Since when did you start talking to attorneys?" Brent asked.

"You hire them because they know the right thing to do."

"If you loved Laci, you'd be out there talking for her, trying to get her back. Not looking for some damn attorney that's going to try and get you off," Brent snapped.

"I hope you see by my actions that I am trying to get her back. The media is against me."

But Brent had had enough. He was no longer looking for Laci, he said, because he believed that Scott "did it."

"That's a shame," Scott responded. "There will be people that will help me and we will be working toward that goal."

In their analysis of Scott's sentiments, though, the police agreed with Brent that Scott was just "hiding behind his attorney." As Steve Jacobson wrote, "Hiring a criminal defense attorney would perhaps be the last thing I would consider if my pregnant wife came up missing." He then set out the real reason that everything seemed to be going against Scott: "Like the police, the media is suspicious of Scott Peterson because of his alibi story and the amount of lies he tells.

"Scott has access to many other attorneys who are working out other matters with Laci and her immediate family (will and probate). Why Scott hired a criminal defense attorney, early on this investigation to 'defend' him has and will remain interesting."

S cott returned from his weekend in Southern California to find that his home had been burglarized. Dialing headquarters, he reported that he'd arrived home at 7:45 P.M. on Sunday, January 19, to find that some clothing and other personal items were missing. Although nothing of value had been taken, some food and alcohol had also been consumed.

Scott had not set the house alarm because of the way he'd secured the front gate. He had received a call from Kim McGregor about an hour before he arrived home that evening, advising him that she'd just been to the house to feed McKenzie. When she went into the backyard, she found the side door open. Nobody was home, so she closed it and left.

The police later determined that the entry had occurred through an unlocked gate. A small window was broken in the rear dining room door, and one or more individuals then reached inside, unlocked the door, and entered the house.

Police found the scene inside curious indeed. The thief or thieves had emptied a bottle of Jack Daniel's and opened some Christmas presents, along with stealing some property.

Police found the empty whiskey bottle on the floor near the bar in the dining room. According to Scott, it had been one-third full when he left for southern California. Several Christmas gifts were lying on the floor near the empty bottle, their wrapping paper ripped open. One of the gifts, a sweatshirt from Carmel intended for Ron Grantski, was gone. Another was left unwrapped on the dining room table, its colorful paper dumped in the kitchen garbage pail. Police noted that two of Scott's jackets had been taken from a coat rack near the door. It was clear that the suspect had spent some time in the couple's kitchen, drinking a Pepsi and eating a pear. Both items were left on the kitchen counter. Police found a used glass in the sink.

A search of the bedrooms was inconclusive; Scott couldn't be sure if anything had been taken from the closets, but it appeared that all Laci's jewelry was still there.

Later that week, Grogan learned that Scott's neighbor, Kim McGregor, had been identified as the person responsible for the burglary. Another neighbor on Covena, Amie Krigbaum, dialed 911 to report seeing a white female leaving the Peterson home with a handful of items around the time the burglary occurred. She told police she saw the woman place the objects in the trunk of a white Honda and drive off.

During an interview with McGregor at headquarters, she confessed to the burglary and told police she didn't know why she did it. Based on this, the police spent some time trying to identify or eliminate her as a suspect in Laci's disappearance. They found no indication that she even knew the Petersons before Laci vanished.

After it was clear that McGregor was cooperating with the investigation, the police asked her to phone Scott and speak with him about the burglary. During the conversation, Scott told her not to worry about what she had done. He then advised her "not to tell anyone about it."

The detectives asked that she call Scott right back to tell him that she'd already gone to the police with her story. Scott said he already knew that, even though the confession had only just taken place, and then admonished her "not to talk about it ever again."

The police later reported that they found it "interesting" that Scott advised McGregor "not to tell anyone." In one of the recorded calls with his sister, Scott had referred to McGregor as "psycho girl." Maybe he expected such behavior from her. Then again, "this may have been a hidden defense strategy to deflect attention from himself to an unknown, mysterious burglar who may have had something to do with Laci's disappearance," Jacobson wrote. "Perhaps Scott realized with her confession to the police, she could not remain the mysterious burglar he had hoped." Or, he conceded, it could have been a simple "act of leniency" on Scott's part.

When the police formally notified Scott of McGregor's involvement, he declined to press charges. However, a few days later, police recovered a video camera behind a store not far from the Peterson's house. It had been thrown into a fifty-five-gallon drum used by local restaurants to dump their grease. Inside the camera was a video of Laci Peterson, including footage of her at a July 4 gathering that would later hold jurors spellbound as Laci came to life in the courtroom.

In the short term, however, the camera revealed to the police that Kim McGregor hadn't been truthful with them. They ordered her back to headquarters for a second interview and warned her to come clean—or else. Faced with the threat of prosecution, McGregor admitted to stealing the video camera and Laci's Social Security card.

She said she had taken the camera from the dining room and the Social Security card from Scott's dresser. She could not explain why, but admitted that when she awoke the following morning and realized what she had done, she decided to dispose of the evidence as quickly as she could. She'd forgotten about the Social Security card, but later found it and turned it over to police.

McGregor told police she was fascinated by the case and wanted to learn more about Scott and Laci. After leaving headquarters, the police wiretaps captured Kim calling Scott again to alert him that Detective Brocchini had asked her to take a polygraph. Kim felt Brocchini was trying to use her to get information from him, and she didn't know what to do.

"Taking the polygraph shouldn't be a problem for you," Scott said.

McGregor was scared and wanted to refuse the test. Scott said she could, but explained that police "will think something is up and they start to look you know, looking at you harder, you might as well do it. I think they will be fair to you." To the police, the implication was clear. Scott, too, was avoiding the polygraph not because he thought the police would entrap him, but because he knew he would fail the exam.

The wiretap also captured another telling moment. On January 20, Scott played back the voice mail message he'd left for Laci on her cell phone on Christmas Eve, alerting her that he would be arriving home late from the marina. He listened to it twice, then saved it again. "Perhaps Scott is keeping his recollection fresh by reviewing his messages," Investigator Jacobson wrote in his report.

That weekend, Scott learned that the police had contacted Amber and were requesting that she submit to a polygraph.

"When do you plan to take a polygraph with me?" Amber asked Scott during a phone conversation.

Scott said he still intended to take the test, but it would be a "clean" test from a private company because police polygraphs are "dirty."

In a subsequent conversation, Scott told Amber that he'd been sick to his stomach after this call. She shouldn't have to do anything for Al Brocchini, he raged; "he's disgusting, and he shouldn't even set eyes on you." Scott was also upset because he felt that Amber didn't trust him, and that she believed he was involved in Laci's disappearance.

Amber said she'd heard things on the news.

"What, all of the other people I've killed?" Scott groused.

Interestingly, during the investigation, the Modesto police were contacted by detectives in San Luis Obispo investigating the disappearance of one of Scott's fellow Cal Poly students, a woman named Kristen Smart. A six-foot-one blond, Smart was last seen on May 24, 1996, in the company of a male student at the college. When they realized that Scott had been attending Cal Poly at that time, the police investigated the possibility that Scott might be linked to the nineteen-year-old's disappearance. Speculation about a possible connection was also being discussed in the media. I was surprised to learn later that members of Scott's own family were privately wondering the same thing.

Amber said she didn't believe those stories, but she did find it interesting that Scott had a life insurance policy on Laci. She also asked him why Scott's dad was still denying their affair and telling the press that the pictures of Amber and Scott did not prove anything.

Scott said he didn't know, but he advised Amber that he was just down the street from her, and that he shouldn't be driving much further that evening.

Amber invited Scott to her home.

"What was that?" Scott asked.

Amber didn't repeat the offer. Scott sounded as though he was crying; to the police, the emotion seemed to be forced.

"Is it just because of me that you are crying?" Amber asked.

"It's just because of what's happening to you," Scott told her.

"In a very obvious manner, Scott wants Amber to invite him over to her place," Jacobson wrote in his summary of the conversation. "A very unorthodox move for a grieving husband who has been denying having a girlfriend. Not hearing the offer, Scott begins to act as if he's choked up and won't be able to drive much further. Amber asks Scott to call her when he finds a place to sleep. It's not what Scott wants so he begins to cry a little louder, telling her how much he cares for her and that he won't be able to think about her once he finds a motel. Amber doesn't offer her place a second time, and Scott terminates the call. Immediately after hanging up, Scott checks his voice mail. While listening to his voice mail message, lasting fifty-two seconds, Scott is never once choked-up, blowing his nose, coughing, crying, or making any other sound effect that would indicate that he was so severely upset that he couldn't continue to drive home."

To Jacobson, this was "yet another obvious deception . . . an attempt I believe was geared at getting Amber to let him come over." He noted, "This once again goes to show the character of Scott Peterson and the real reason he chooses not to take the polygraph test or cooperate with law enforcement."

When Scott called Amber the following day, January 20, she told him that the *National Enquirer* had been asking questions.

"God dammit!" Scott replied. "It's my fault. I'm sorry, baby."

Amber admitted that she'd given police the photos of the two of them together. Scott told her that the *Enquirer* hired a private investigator because they tried to hire his own private investigator.

"I see you're back to wearing your wedding ring," Amber noted.

After a long pause, Scott agreed.

When Amber told him she understood because he was in the "public eye," Scott changed the subject, stating that he "feels sick."

Amber pressed Scott about the promise he'd made to her several days after Christmas—that the two of them could soon start planning a future together.

"Okay," Scott said, pausing for what seemed like a long time. He then added that they couldn't talk with each other until the case with Laci was resolved. He also told her that he'd spent the night at a motel in Merced, where he learned that his home had been burglarized. In fact, he had driven home that evening and discovered it on his own.

Another telling call came from Kim McGregor, who phoned Scott after taking a polygraph to tell him "it was easy." The polygrapher had asked her to find out why Scott hasn't taken one, she said.

"Well good, you sound relieved," he replied. He then told McGregor that he hadn't actually been asked to take the test.

Kim said she was asked whether she'd known the Petersons before Laci's disappearance. She was surprised that her denial registered as inconclusive, since she really didn't know them before that time. The police noted, Scott didn't sound at all concerned when McGregor told him her test had come back inconclusive; it was obvious he didn't suspect her.

That evening, about 11:00 P.M., Scott called his parents in San Diego. His father answered the phone. After some talk about Scott's lawyer, Kirk McAllister, their conversation moved on to the break-in at Scott's house.

"They smashed up my French doors pretty good," Scott said. "I had to get them repaired." Even though Kim McGregor had already confessed to him, Scott told Lee he thought Laci's father, Dennis Rocha, might have done it while on a "drunken binge." He also speculated that Brent may have helped.

When Scott wondered if Ron Grantski could be involved behind it, Lee said he was betting on it. He asked if Scott had given the police the three men's names. Scott said he had. "I gave Dennis's name as the number one suspect," he added.

At one point, Jackie Peterson joined the conversation.

"I know it was one of those guys, Ron, Brent, or Dennis," Scott told his mother. "It was probably Dennis."

Jackie said she didn't think Ron was involved. He had called Lee that afternoon to express the hope that the two men could still go fishing together.

"This guy is a snake," Scott replied, adding that Ron didn't have a "good past."

"Oh, I love it when the pot calls the kettle black," Jackie said ruefully.

There were more enlightening interviews in the days to come. Detective Buehler tracked down David Fernandez, who had dined with Scott and Shawn Sibley at the conference in Anaheim that past October. David had originally intended to introduce his friend Eric to Shawn, but he soon learned that Shawn was engaged.

David said that Scott Peterson didn't seem to be deterred by Shawn's engagement. He assumed Scott wasn't married because of the way he was "hitting on Shawn." According to him, Scott made suggestive comments throughout the evening, and at one point asked Shawn about her "favorite sexual position." Scott pressed her about why she hadn't picked a wedding date, and asked whether she was really happy in the relationship.

David said that Eric Olsen was turned off by the conversation and left right after the meal. Scott boasted during the dinner about having a lot of money and a high salary. He told the group that he owned two homes, one in Modesto and the other in Southern California. These stories, also used with Amber, suggested Scott's clear need to elevate himself in the eyes of others—particularly women.

The investigators were also asking friends and family to review the events since December 24 with fresh eyes. Were there any incidents or conversations that may have seemed unimportant, but might have a different significance now that they knew about Amber Frey?

Sharon Rocha described a conversation she had with Scott about a week after Laci went missing. Although her son-in-law was "vague" about details, when he left home on Christmas Eve morning he told Sharon that Laci was sitting in a "little chair," combing her hair in a style that her sister Amy had taught her on the previous evening. Scott had never mentioned this detail to the police.

Sharon also told police that she was taken aback when she learned that Scott continued working out and golfing at the Del Rio Country Club after Laci went missing. She was having trouble eating and sleeping and could barely imagine a moment of relaxation or leisure while her daughter's fate remained uncertain.

In mid-January, Sharon and Ron had invited Scott over for dinner. Although he arrived late, he seemed to be "in a good mood." Scott told the group that someone had asked him earlier that day how he was doing and he had said "fine."

"That's the first time I've said that," he added.

During the meal, Scott prattled on about computer problems he was having, but he barely mentioned Laci. At one point, Sharon told him she'd been watching coverage of the case on the Fox News Channel. A fisherman being interviewed about Scott's alibi mentioned that shrimp was the appropriate bait for sturgeon fishing in the bay. Scott just shrugged his shoulders and grinned.

Sharon told Grogan that she had tried to dismiss Scott's behavior because she realized that if Scott was responsible, Laci would not likely be coming home.

Brent Rocha and his wife, Rose, recalled that several years earlier, after the funeral for Laci's grandmother, the family gathered to talk. At one point, Rose, Scott, and Laci began discussing their childhood. Rose was taken aback when Scott suddenly burst out crying. From his outburst, she assumed that his childhood had been an unhappy one. She later told Brent that she found Scott's display of emotion out of character, considering his usually reserved, calm demeanor. Scott's flowing tears suggested to Rose that Scott had not come from a "loving family."

Brent also described an early visit with Scott on December 25, 2002. He arrived at the house at about 7:00 A.M. to find Scott still wet from a shower and wrapped in a towel. While Brent waited, Scott went into the bedroom to dress. When he emerged, he told Brent that "he had a bad night."

"I was very angry, but anger came out." Scott did not elaborate, and Brent didn't press him further.

Brent was frustrated when Scott ignored his repeated requests to check Laci's clothing. Brent wanted to see if any items were missing. "I kept asking him, and he wouldn't do it," Brent told Grogan. "Scott seemed uninterested in doing what he could to assist."

Sharon showed up at the house soon after Brent. Scott and Sharon spoke briefly with a neighbor, and then Scott announced that he was going to the warehouse to retrieve some tape so that he could start hanging missing persons flyers. He left around 8:45 A.M., and for the next several hours, his whereabouts were unknown.

I believe that Scott must have used this time to move things around from the night before. We know he returned to the warehouse at some time that morning because the jacket and the lures turned up in the boat. We know the tarp and umbrellas were moved into the backyard. We may never know whether he used this time to dispose of other incriminating items.

Detective Grogan also reached out to Scott's half brother, Mark Peterson. He learned that the Peterson clan wasn't as close-knit as Jackie and Lee had claimed. This was no Brady Bunch story, as the Petersons had been telling reporters.

A sales representative for a packaging company, Mark Peterson had been estranged from the family for nearly thirteen years. A disagreement with his father and his brother, Joe, over the family business had placed an untenable strain on the father/son relationship. Mark said that he and his father had barely spoken since the falling out—that is, until Laci went missing.

Mark had met Laci only three times—once before her marriage to Scott, again at their wedding, and then once more at Thanksgiving dinner that past November. His sister, Susan Caudillo, had hosted that gathering, and Mark and his family had attended. It was the first time in years that everyone was together for the holidays. Mark acknowledged that he and Lee were still on the outs when he accepted the invitation. However, Susan was anxious to show off her new house, and his wife wanted to maintain a relationship with his children's grandfather, so Mark agreed to go.

He was also excited by the news that Scott and Laci were expecting a baby.

"The only thing I really remember is that Laci was pregnant . . . just kind of tired and a little bit uncomfortable," Mark recalled. "I remember her being a little bit on the quiet side that evening. But, there was, you know, a house full of people, so I didn't really . . . I don't even think I had much of a conversation with her that night."

The next contact Mark had with his family was on Christmas morning, when he was advised that Laci was missing.

"Well, I'm obviously, I'm a little curious about the family dynamics, and I know that Scott was obviously the youngest child," Grogan said. "Jackie had children from another relationship, right?"

"Through my sister, I did hear that a man and a woman approached Jackie and said, 'We're your children that you, that you adopted out,'" Mark said, referring to Don Chapman and Anne Bird. "Since then, I think that Jackie has tried to kind of stay in touch with them. I don't know any specifics about her past," he explained.

In response to questions, Mark admitted that he actually knew very little about Scott, or about the Peterson family dynamics. He and his siblings, Joe and Susan, lived with their mother growing up, and only visited their dad on weekends. There was a ten-year age difference between Mark and Scott, and the two spent very little time together as kids.

"We always lived in the same town, we all lived in San Diego and we would probably see Scott ah, on the weekends, you know, that kind of thing," Mark explained.

"As a child, what was Scott like?" Grogan asked.

"Well, I was a child when Scott was a child so," Mark chuckled, "I don't know what he was like. I mean he was just a normal kid."

"Lee and Jackie seem kind of protective of him," Grogan said. "Do you know why that is?"

"I think my dad does because essentially Scott . . . I think he raised him pretty much like an only child, really. You know they did everything together. Scott came along at a time in my dad's life . . . when Scott was probably, oh . . . when he got to that kind of really fun age of, like, eight and ten years old, you know, my dad was . . . he was doing okay financially then. And I think he was able to kind of spend a lot of time with Scott. I mean, if they traveled, they took Scott with 'em, that kind of thing."

During the conversation, Grogan tried to establish who in the family had been closest to Scott. Jackie's third child, John, had come to live with the family when Lee and Jackie married, and he and Scott had grown up together. John went by the last name Peterson, yet Mark wasn't sure whether Lee had actually adopted him.

Mark believed that John was about five years older than Scott, but had no information about how to reach him.

Grogan was particularly curious about Lee and Jackie's overprotective ways with Scott. The detective explained how they had tried to stop him from questioning Scott at headquarters on Christmas Day. "They came over to the station here when I was talkin' to Scott, and, you know, wanted to pull him out of an interview and didn't want him talkin' to me without an attorney, and didn't want him to take a polygraph test. And it just seemed unusual the amount of concern there. Do you have any idea why that is?" Grogan inquired.

"Well, I can't get into my dad's head," Mark responded, "but we had this case a few years ago . . ." He described the murder of Stephanie Crowe, which occurred just inside of San Diego. "The case was thrown out because the judge in fact said you guys [the police] coerced this child, basically, to confessing," Mark said, "and there was a TV movie about it and I'm sure Dad watched it. . . . You watch that a week before your own son is being interrogated, I think there's a tendency there."

The TV movie Mark was referring to was *The Interrogation of Michael Crowe*, a special presentation on my network, Court TV. Court TV was instrumental in obtaining and airing the interrogation video, which led to the suppression of Michael's confession. Some years later, a drifter, Richard Tuite, was tried and convicted of Stephanie's murder.

"Okay, so you don't think there's anything different there?" Grogan pressed. "I mean, what I am struck by is, I don't know the theories." He changed course. "Not too long ago, they gave him twenty thousand dollars for a membership to a golf club."

"Lee and Jackie did?"

"Well it just seems to me that they're very protective of him," Grogan said, "like he's able to get whatever he needs from them." Grogan thought that the Petersons seemed to do "a little bit more in helping him along than, you know, a normal thirty-year-old guy" might expect from his parents. "So I was just kind of curious if there was, you know, something that happened to Scott previously, or if there was some reason that that's going on?"

"Yeah, I don't know, I couldn't help you with that," Mark advised. "I don't think there was anything where they feel like they owe him anything. . . . I mean, he grew up in more of a privileged background, you know, upbringing than, than my other siblings did. He grew up in basically the nicest neighborhood in San Diego County, and you know it's probably one of the nicer neighborhoods in the whole country. I think he was just kind of their little, you know, baby and they . . .

"Like I said, he was kind of raised as an only child. But I'll tell ya, I'm really surprised that they would give him that amount of money for a country club membership. . . . I never really thought that they gave him anything.

"I always thought they were very proud of the way Scott went out and worked while he was going to school at Cal Poly, and was able to start a restaurant on his own, and was able to get an education and find a job in Modesto," Mark continued. "They thought of their son as someone who just went out and made his own life. I was under the impression that they were extremely proud of the way Scott was able to get these things done on his own, so when you say they gave him money for a golf club membership, I'm kinda really surprised at that."

"As far as any violence with Scott," Grogan asked, "any violent acts that you're aware of as a juvenile or anything?"

"No, absolutely not. I mean, not even as a, not even as a five-year-old or ten-year-old, I never saw him lose his temper," Mark said.

"Never, even as a child?"

"No."

As the conversation drew to a close, Grogan asked Mark if he had any questions for the police.

"Well I'm curious about reports of Scott's finances. I hear reports of bankruptcy and heavy debt. . . ."

"Right now it looks like he is having some financial problems," Grogan said.

"And it doesn't look like the business was doing very well. . . . And then personal debt . . . what we do have shows that he is quite a bit in debt."

"Yeah." Mark seemed to be digesting the information he was now gleaning from the detective. The picture the officer was painting was quite different from what he'd been led to believe by family members. "I guess our concern, the Peterson family concern, is that with all this heavy focus on Scott, that other leads might be put on the back burner?"

Grogan explained that police were working all leads, but had been unable to eliminate Scott as a suspect.

"Would the simple fact of Scott taking a lie detector test and passing—would that be enough to, I don't wanna say clear because I know there's some margin of error, but . . . is there too much evidence for even a lie detector test passing on Scott's part to clear his name?" Mark asked.

"Right." Grogan replied.

"Scott has chosen his path and declined to take it. I guess I've been wondering if Scott would have just taken this test and passed it, you know, it wouldn't have . . . 'cause I'm real troubled by this, you know. I just don't see his personality as the one that could perpetrate this kind of thing, planned it, you know, especially for monetary gain. . . ."

"Yeah," Grogan commented.

"I guess I was looking for a little bit of ammunition to go to my family and say you know what? If he would just do this, it might help things along. But I'm not so sure that's what would happen anyway . . ."

"Well, ah, it certainly would not hurt his position," Grogan said.

In late January, an agent from the FBI interviewed Timothy Caulkey, a childhood neighbor of Scott and the Peterson family. From the time he was about five years old until they moved away four years later, Caulkey had lived across the street from the Petersons. He told the investigator that he remembered Scott's older brother John as a troubled child, and recounted several minor incidents of violence and mischief that he believed may have involved John. But there was no proof linking John to these events. More to the point, as the FBI noted, Caulkey "couldn't provide any information on Scott," because "Scott was three years old at the time and Caulkey couldn't remember much about him."


In the coming days, police learned that Scott was meeting with friends to discuss the sale of his home and was looking to purchase a new vehicle. From the wiretap on his phones, police found out about a meeting between Scott and two real estate agents, Brian Ullrich and Brian Argain.

"I want to keep this quiet, obviously," Scott told Argain on one call. "Even if Laci comes back we will not wanna stay there, either way, however this comes out."

"How soon do you wanna look at doing it?"

"I'd like to put it on the market right now," Scott said. "Make sure you keep it quiet. . . . Can I sell it furnished?"

"Yeah, you can."

The police dispatched an officer wearing a wire to the Appetez Restaurant to record the conversation, but very little of it was caught on tape. Police also learned that Scott had been phoning around to local car dealerships, wanting to sell Laci's Land Rover and buy a new truck. Investigators also learned that Scott was planning to travel to southern California to appear on *Good Morning America*. The show's producers offered to pick him up by limousine, transport him to the airport, and return him home the following day.

Phone records also showed that Scott was planning to spend some time at his half sister's house in Berkeley, California. Anne Bird called Scott early in the evening on January 22, to talk about Scott's upcoming stay. She and her husband, Tim, were departing for Puerto Vallarta, Mexico, on a pleasure trip, and offered Scott the use of their home while they were away.

"I'll leave the key under the mat," Anne said, then gave Scott the address. "The house is very distinctive; we just removed a shrub from the front yard."

Investigators listening in on the call observed that Scott was giggling and sounded very upbeat while speaking to his sister. "I will leave Tim's golf club for your protection," Anne joked.

"Ha, ha, ha," Scott replied.

"I just hope that . . . everything just somehow has some miracle ending."

"Yeah, I know it will."

"I mean everything so shitty has happened that something really good must be around the corner."

"That's what I'm figuring."

Anne told Scott that she and Tim would be returning on February 2, and he was welcome to stay as long as he'd like. "Have you been sleeping okay?" she asked.

"I am up to about three hours right now, midnight to 3:00 A.M.," Scott replied. "That's better!"

"*Murder She Wrote* is on at 3:00 A.M."

Scott laughed, "Ah, not a choice for me."

"I know that is probably not good for you to watch her." Anne told Scott that she would love to take her brother to Puerto Vallarta with them someday. "Hopefully, we will be going with Laci and your new little guy. I am really hopeful and feel strongly that she is being held somewhere."

"Yeah, she'll be back," Scott said.
"Keep your chin up."

The police used their wiretaps to keep tabs on Scott while they continued to search for Laci's body. They found a tidal expert to review the Internet sites Scott had visited on his computer, which mapped an area near the Berkeley Marina. Grogan also ordered a sonar scan of portions of the San Francisco Bay. The detective believed there was a "very strong likelihood" that Laci's body was in the bay. After a careful study of the computer sites, the expert advised Grogan that, depending on the amount of weight and the water current situation, it was possible that Laci's body had been swept out of the bay, where it might never be retrieved.

# CHAPTER FIFTEEN

# JANUARY 24, 2003

In late January, an unexpected turn of events abruptly changed both the tone and the focus of the investigation. Amber Frey was thrust into the spotlight when her name became public knowledge.

The identity of Scott Peterson's girlfriend had been a mystery until a friend of Amber's called into a radio show with the intention of defending her. Instead, the information she gave out—the fact that Amber was a massage therapist, and the location of the party she had attended with Scott on December 14—was all the press needed to identify the unknown woman.

By 10:30 that morning, reporters and photographers were surrounding the office building where Amber worked, trying to contact her. Panicked, she dialed Detective Buehler. By 12:30, the situation had escalated, and Amber placed a second call to headquarters. This time she suggested making a public statement that might appease them and make them go away. Buehler agreed that such a briefing, where she could address members of the press all at once, might be a good idea. With the help of the police, Amber prepared a statement for the press conference scheduled for 7:30 that evening.

In Amber's brief remarks she admitted to a romantic affair with Scott Peterson, and stated that he had told her he was "unmarried."

After the event, Amber was escorted into a rear training office, where several of Laci's close friends were waiting for her. The police arranged for a meal to be brought in to headquarters so that the women could speak in private. One of them, Lori Ellsworth, had invited her to stay at her home that evening. It proved difficult for

Amber to leave headquarters, since members of the press had staked out the exits. So the police had to escort her to Ellsworth's home for the night.

The next morning, Amber met Sharon Rocha. During that meeting, Sharon would attempt to make sense of Scott's affair, asking Amber to identify specific dates she had spent with her daughter's husband. Sharon seemed anxious to understand these events, glancing at a calendar from time to time as if trying to recall Laci's movements on those days.

Moments after the press conference, Craig Grogan made a series of phone calls. First he called Scott Peterson, alerting him that Amber had just gone before reporters. Scott had listened to the statement on the radio and simply expressed concern for her.

Grogan next dialed Scott's mother. Jackie Peterson was angry, and berated the police for informing the media and the Rochas about Scott's affair while deflecting any blame away from her son. She accused the department of embarrassing and humiliating Amber Frey.

"I think it's very sad," Jackie said during the call. "She's only twenty-eight years old, and the whole world knows that she made a mistake a month ago. . . . You knew way beforehand this girl had nothing to do this . . . and you let her go through this, you let Sharon's mother go through that, and then you hold a press conference to put her out there like a dog . . . doing it for a show. For what? For nothing. She had nothing to do with it. I was . . . I . . . I'm shocked if that's police work. You should be looking at the people that take pregnant women that want babies that . . . criminals, parolees in your neighborhood, you should be looking at those kind of people."

Once again Jackie was happy to disparage the police, yet she couldn't bring herself to acknowledge her son's wrongdoing, or place any responsibility with him. "I think from the very beginning you guys got some bug" about Scott, she told Grogan. "And I'm not saying you but your partner, he didn't like Scott, he's dead set Scott did it, and he's gonna build a case against him. And that's where the concentration's gone. You don't have a ton of people over there doing work."

Jackie didn't reveal that she'd already learned about the news conference from Scott, who had phoned her shortly after five o'clock. He told her he found it "bizarre" that the police department was playing a role in Amber's statement to the press. Jackie Peterson had responded by telling her son that all of America was going to be "laughing their heads off, wondering what kind of city Modesto was."

"It's a witch hunt for an affair or a one-night stand," Jackie stated. She then asked Scott to clarify which it was, an affair or a one-night stand.

Scott said he didn't want to talk about it.

"Okay, I'll have to watch it," Jackie said, and warned her son not to have any more contact with Amber.

"Of course not," Scott agreed.

Earlier, Jackie had instructed Scott to start "shredding" all of his paperwork before throwing it in the trash. Scott told her he'd never done it in the past, but agreed it was a good idea.

Later that day, Scott spoke to his father. He told Lee that he was upset about the media frenzy over his affair with Amber, but Lee advised him not to worry. "Everybody, I won't say everybody, but two-thirds of the people in this country have affairs."

Scott confided that he felt "dirty" for doing it, and told his dad it was "wrong."

"A lot of people have them," Lee sympathized.

"I did such a bad thing cheating on Laci," Scott replied.

"Having an affair is not that bad, believe me it isn't, it was just the timing. It happens to more people than you can imagine." Lee instructed his son to "stay the course" and advised him it was time to call his attorney and start a "media blitz."

Jacobson was intrigued by this advice. "I, too, was waiting for Scott to come forward and accept responsibility for having an affair and to field questions relating to how this shouldn't be viewed as a motive for foul play in her disappearance," he recorded. "But such comments made by his mother and earlier comments he himself made about the Modesto Police Department indicate to me that Scott Peterson may not have been raised to accept responsibility, but to deflect it on to others."

Grogan recognized that while Scott was apologizing to all the right people, he was showing no remorse or guilt for his behavior. He was behaving in a textbook fashion—promiscuous, manipulative, impulsive, irresponsible—and now he was exhibiting the callous lack of conscience that is a shared trait among sociopaths. His father's willingness to dismiss the affair must have bolstered his confidence.

The day after Amber's announcement hit the airwaves, Detective Grogan sprang into action. Wanting a reaction from Scott, he dialed his cell number, wanting to leave a message that the police were continuing their search of the San Francisco Bay. When Scott answered the call, though, Grogan had to think on his feet.

"Um, I just wondered if you wanted to talk about Amber at all," he asked Scott. "Now that all that stuff is out there?"

"No, I don't see what there is, I mean you know, I'm . . . like I said, I'm glad she did it. Ah, I hope they leave her alone," Scott replied.

"So, you have, you don't want to make any kind of statement about that?"

"Oh, I don't think there's anything more to be said, I mean, well, you guys talked to her so you know about us and . . . that's pretty much it."

Later that afternoon, Scott called Grogan back to apologize for not coming clean to them about Amber Frey. But his momentary expression of regret for this lie wouldn't stop him from lying again—this time in front of television cameras.

In the days ahead, the media reported that Scott Peterson had attended Super Bowl Sunday in San Diego on January 26. The Oakland Raiders were pitted against the Tampa Bay Buccaneers. Interestingly, the police had tracked Scott to the Berkeley Marina

Laci Rocha and Scott Peterson at Scott's graduation from California Polytechnic Institute, 1998.

Scott *(right)* as a young man with his father, Lee *(far left)*

The Shack, the restaurant Scott owned before moving to Modesto with Laci

Scott and Laci in happier times; as Laci's friend Terry Western put it, the couple "always appeared to be on their honeymoon."

Scott with Amber Frey; their relationship began a month and four days before Laci disappeared.

Evidence photos from the Petersons' home on Covena Avenue: Conner's nursery, which Scott later used as a junk storage room, and the couple's bed, showing the suspicious indentation that piqued Detective Al Brocchini's interest.

Suspicious signs at the Petersons' home: dirty white towels atop the washer, Scott's newly washed jeans, the mop and bucket by the side door. Bottom: Crime scene investigators examine the French doors for evidence.

On New Year's Eve, shortly after making his infamous "call from Paris" to Amber, Scott attended a candlelight vigil for Laci. Photos of him grinning would later make a strong impression on the jury.

The tarp police found in the Petersons' backyard that reeked of gasoline fumes; police speculated that Scott may have used the tarp to wrap Laci's body, and then placed it under a leaking gas motor to throw off the scent dogs.

Scott's dog, McKenzie, with one of the umbrellas found in Scott's truck on December 24, 2002. As Detective Grogan would point out on the stand, "those umbrellas are approximately the same height as Laci Peterson." (The man at left is unidentified.)

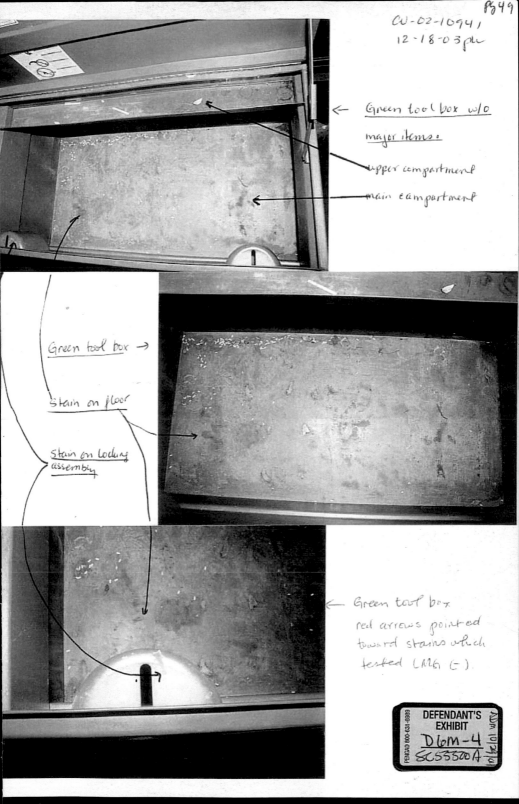

CU-02-1094,
12-18-03 pm

← Green tool box w/o
major items.

upper compartment
main compartment

Green tool box →

Stain on floor

Stain on locking
assembly

← Green tool box
red arrows pointed
toward stains which
tested LMG (−).

DEFENDANT'S
EXHIBIT
D6M-4
SC53500A

A forensic examiner's write-up on the green toolbox from Scott's truck

Scott's warehouse, with his Gamefisher boat at left

The worktable where police believed Scott made the homemade anchors he used to weigh down

Coast guard divers searching the San Francisco Bay for Laci's body. By the summer of 2004, after she was found, mourners had turned the Covena Avenue home into a makeshift memorial *(below)*.

Investigators on the rocky northern shore of the San Francisco Bay, where Laci's body was found on April 13, 2003; a yellow tarp covers the body *(below)*. Inset: Laci's Bali bra.

The red Mercedes-Benz Scott was driving when he was arrested on April 18, 2003.

DEFENDANT'S
EXHIBIT
D8G-1
SC55B2007

Scott's booking photo, showing his new blond hair and goatee.

Sharon Rocha and Ron Grantski arriving at the courthouse.

Jackie Peterson is followed into the courtroom by Scott's brother John and his sister-in-law Janey Peterson; the woman on the left is unidentified.

The boat Mark Geragos parked near the courthouse—to demonstrate that Scott's boat was too small for the crime—was a stunt that backfired, as onlookers covered it with flowers and angry signs.

Modesto Detectives Craig Grogan *(left)* and Alan Brocchini *(center)* arriving at the courthouse. Although Brocchini would sometimes be thrown by defense questioning, Grogan proved an effective foil for Mark Geragos.

Scott with his attorney, Mark Geragos. "Mr. Geragos needs to stop joking so much," Sharon Rocha complained during the trial. "There is nothing humorous about the fact that my daughter was murdered."

EWS EYEWITNESS
PETERSON VERDICT
LIVE AUDIO FEED San Mateo County Co
TITLED CAUSE FIND THE
DEFENDANT SCOTT PETERSON
ILTY OF THE
JVC

that very morning before he headed to the airport and boarded a plane for San Diego. Later Scott called his mother, telling her that Grogan had let him know that all the evidence leads to the San Francisco Bay, and that police intended to resume their search there.

Scott's mother asked if Grogan was "crazy," and wanted to know why he was calling her son. Scott replied that he believed the detective was looking to get a "reaction" out of him.

"I can't imagine anyone being stupid enough to say they went fishing in the Berkeley Bay after having committed a crime there," Jackie replied. "I mean, not even you, Scott."

During the call, Scott told his mother that he wanted to talk with *Good Morning America*'s Diane Sawyer, and also to appear on *60 Minutes*. He was ready to speak with select members of the press— on his terms. Jackie agreed that Scott should tell his side of the story, but she cautioned him to speak with his attorney first. She also said she wanted to travel to Modesto to be with him, so that he could show the media that he came from a good family.

The police grew concerned, however, when they overheard Scott's father ask him about a trip to Mexico he was planning for the following weekend. Scott said would fly down, possibly from Fresno, and that he'd pass through San Diego some time during the week to drop off McKenzie. In recent days, the investigators had learned that he was looking to sell his house "as is," had been cleaning out the warehouse, and intended to drop his dog off with friends or family. Now, with the news that he was planning a secret trip to Mexico, they worried that he was trying to flee the jurisdiction.

Scott's passport had been confiscated, of course, but passports and travel documents were not required for a trip to Mexico. Fugitives from justice often cross the border and then flee to European countries where the United States does not have extradition treaties. Scott had plenty of friends and business associates overseas.

Another alarming thought was that Scott had not discussed the trip with anyone other than his parents. Was it a coincidence that

Scott started planning the trip after Grogan told him that the investigation would now be focusing on the bay?

By now Scott had made at least five trips to the marina. Surveillance units had observed him sitting in his vehicle near the boat ramp, gazing out at the water.

"Scott may be curious as to where investigators are searching, what they may find, or what they might have found that they are not telling reporters," Jacobson wrote.

As Scott prepared to brave the public eye, his forlorn lover went into seclusion. After the press conference, Amber Frey sequestered herself in an undisclosed location in Modesto. Journalists began calling her father, Ron Frey, and asking him to pass their interview requests along to his daughter.

Later, Ron Frey told Grogan that his daughter was being besieged with offers for interviews from media outlets including CNN, *The O'Reilly Factor,* and *Larry King Live.* Connie Chung had extended an offer to fly his daughter to New York, where she would "be treated special." Some media groups were making monetary offers.

Amber was anxious, and unsure about how to proceed. On one hand, she was concerned about her finances, fearing that the hordes of journalists would prevent her from returning to work. And while she told her father she could certainly use the money, she didn't want to make that a basis for her decision to appear in the media. She also wanted to protect the integrity of the police investigation and her daughter's safety. In the end, Amber opted "not to get involved in any more media attention."

Yet, with the affair now public knowledge, Scott Peterson suddenly became very available to the press. His first engagement would be with *Good Morning America* cohost Diane Sawyer.

Ironically, Scott's mother-in-law and sister-in-law had appeared on the very same program with Charles Gibson the previous day—speaking out about Scott's affair. During that interview, the women told Gibson that their view of Scott had changed since learning about Amber.

Gibson asked what Scott had told them about the affair.

"Absolutely nothing," Sharon answered. "He was asked by one of our family members, about day three after Laci went missing, if he was having an affair. And he told us no at that time. And, since this has come forward, he's denied it. And he finally did admit it to Brent, my son . . ."

"Does this change your support of Scott?"

"It makes us, it gives a lot of doubt. There are other questions we have that if he wasn't truthful about that, that makes us wonder if he's been truthful about everything else."

Sharon and Amy also brought their message to viewers of the *CBS Early Show* and Fox's *On the Record* that day, unaware that Scott intended to appear before the cameras the following morning.

Dressed in slacks and a blazer, Scott sat one-on-one in the Los Angeles studio with Diane Sawyer. "As you know, he has said in the past that he was off fishing Christmas Eve, the day she disappeared," Sawyer opened the piece by saying. "But now a girlfriend has gone public and his wife's family has accused him of not telling all. I spent more than an hour and a half talking to him and his family about the police investigation and the girlfriend, and as you'll see he was alternately composed and then, at times, in tears.

"But Peterson knows at this moment police have focused their investigation on him. And when he arrived for the interview, before any tears, he said he wanted to address the questions about the girlfriend and himself first."

Sawyer's first question to Scott was direct: "I think everybody sitting at home wants the answer to the same question: Did you murder your wife?"

"No, no ah, I did not," Scott said. "And I had absolutely nothing to do with her disappearance. And you use the word murder, um, and right now everyone's looking for a body and that's the hardest thing because that is not a possible resolution for us. And you use the word murder and yeah, that is a, a possibility. Um, it's not one we're

ready to accept and it creeps in my mind late at night and early in the
morning and during the day all we can think about is the right resolution is to find her, well."

"Did you ever hit her?" asked Sawyer. "Did you ever injure her?"

"No, no, oh God no. Um, violence towards women is unap-
proachable. It is the most disgusting act, to me. I know that suspicion
has turned [to] me, one, because I'm her husband and that's a natural thing, and, um, I, I answered your question because of suspicion
it, it's been turned to me of the inappropriate romantic, um, that I
had with Amber Frey then."

Sawyer asked Scott about the affair with Amber. "Why were
you doing it?"

"I, I can't answer that. I don't know. That's a, a, question you
should have an answer to. Definitely, and I don't know."

"Were you in love with her?"

"No, I'd have to say that I respect her as, as I imagine everyone
does after seeing her come out and do the press conference and
[what an] amazing character she has," Scott said.

"Was this the first time? Are there others out there?"

"No," Scott replied. "Our romantic relationship and that is ah,
it's inappropriate and it was inappropriate and I owe a tremendous
apology to, to everyone. Obviously, including Amber and her family and her friends and our families. Ah, it should have been, it
should have been brought forth by me, immediately, the romantic
relationship."

"Had you told anyone? Did you tell police?"

"I told the police immediately."

"When?"

"That was ah, the first night we were together with the police, I
spent ah, with the police," Scott said. It was another amazing example of Scott's willingness to lie at a moment's notice—even when he
knew the lie would be exposed immediately. Did he truly believe he
could con the world, or was it simply that he didn't care about long-
term consequences?

"You told them about her?"

"Yeah, from December twenty-fourth on."

"Did your wife find out?"

"I told my wife."

"When?"

"In um, early December."

"Did it cause a rupture in the marriage?"

"It was not um, a positive, obviously. It's ah, inappropriate, but, it was not something that we weren't um dealing with."

"A lot of arguing?"

"No, no, um, I, I ya know, I can't say that, that even, ya know, she was okay with the idea, but it wasn't anything that would break us apart."

"There wasn't a lot of anger?"

"No."

Sawyer was dubious. "Do you really expect people to believe that an eight-and-a-half-month pregnant woman learns her husband has had an affair and . . . [is] casual about it? Accommodating? Makes a peace with it?"

"Well, I, yeah, you don't know, no one knows our relationship but us. Um, and that's at peace with it, not happy about it."

"Why did you tell her?"

"It was the right thing. There's no other reason than that."

"And did you see her again after you told Laci?"

"Yes."

"You saw Amber again?"

"I did."

"But didn't tell her?" Sawyer asked.

"Didn't tell Laci?"

"Didn't tell Amber."

"No, no, no, yeah, that was definitely not the right thing."

"Because again you know that people sitting at home have imagined that either you were in love with someone else, therefore you decided to get rid of this entanglement, namely your wife and your child, or, there was just an angry confrontation."

"Neither of those was the case. It is, it's that simple."

"What about Laci's family?" Sawyer asked.

"They're wonderful people. They're obviously um, upset with me about the romantic relationship with Amber. Um, and they have little trust as they've expressed in the media to date. Um, but I believe that they're still looking for Laci and I would like to work with them and I think it, we'll be together on this effort . . . continue to look for Laci."

The investigators were astounded by Scott's performance—from his claim that he immediately told the police about the affair, to the ridiculous assertion that he'd told Laci about Amber in early December, yet it caused "no real conflict" between the two of them. "Based on my knowledge of Laci through other family members and individuals close to her," Grogan deadpanned in his report, "I found this to be very unlikely."

After the segment aired, Scott received a call from Amber, who confronted him about his claim on the show that he didn't love her. Scott explained that the media had cut out the part about him caring for her. "Obviously, I care about you," he said.

Amber brought up the polygraph exam he had promised to take. Scott told her that he intended to find an examiner near her home. Amber asked about the cost of the test. Scott said about $750.

"The police do it for free," she replied.

Scott chuckled, then told her that his phone was cutting out.

Next Scott called a company called Expert Polygraph Services of Fresno, and spoke to a polygrapher named Melvin King. Without identifying himself, he questioned King about the testing process.

"Primarily of interest to me, currently, is confidentiality," Scott told him.

King assured him that everything was done in the strictest confidence. The polygrapher asked Scott why he was calling, and what he was looking to accomplish.

Scott told him it was personal.

"I'm gonna guess it has something to do with infidelity," King said.

"You're probably right on there," Scott replied.

That day, Scott scheduled a meeting with his friend Brian Argain about selling his home. He also set up an interview with *America's Most Wanted* for later that evening. Next, he rang his parents. Jackie answered the phone.

Scott told her that his lawyer, Kirk McAllister, and the Stanislaus County district attorney had met for dinner earlier in the week. During the meal, he said, the district attorney told McAllister that they were going to make Scott an offer. "The DA said 'If Scott tells us where the body is, we won't kill him,'" Scott added.

"Oh, my God," Jackie Peterson replied.

"Yeah, the DA thinks I'm guilty, too."

Lee Peterson grabbed the receiver. "What were you saying about the DA?"

"Oh, he made me an offer. If I tell him where the body is, they won't put me to death."

"Oh geesh," Lee responded.

Scott told his father that Kirk had to relay the offer because it is was part of his legal responsibility.

"He said they're just struggling to find anything, you know that's why they [the police] call me and all that weird stuff they've done, like go down and meet with you. They call me and say, 'We're searching the Bay again, Scott.' They're just trying to, you know, crack people. He [Kirk McAllister] said that if they had the stuff that they say they have, I would be hooked up right now."

"Kirk is pretty confident you're in good shape, though?"

"Yeah, I mean, Kirk tells me I'm playing a deadly game here. But he is pretty confident."

"Kirk says you're playing a deadly game?" Jackie Peterson repeated.

"Yup."

"Geez," Jackie sighed.

"Kirk knows if the DA thinks they have enough to arrest me and they arrest me, there's no bail, it's a capital case," Scott said.

"Can you handle that with no bail?" Jackie asked.

"God, I can't imagine being in prison, you know, for who knows how long. . . . But they have to have something credible to go on,"

Scott said. "They won't and they can't, so I'm not really worried about it."

"I don't think they have anything, they couldn't have," Lee Peterson said.

"No, there's nothing to have," Scott replied.

"No, that's what I mean," Lee said.

"Yeah, okay, there's hair and, you know, skin in our cars," Scott chuckled. "You know, but if that's what they think they have . . ."

"I just wonder if Brocchini wouldn't plant something because he's so intent about solving this," Jackie Peterson chimed in.

"There's a possibility . . . there's no question," Scott said.

"What could he plant? He doesn't have anything." Lee Peterson asked.

"Oh, that's true," Scott agreed.

Then Scott started talking about arrangements for his dog, McKenzie. To them, it sounded as though Scott intended to give the golden retriever away. When Jackie Peterson asked her son if he would miss McKenzie, Scott choked up and said he was going to cry.

In a prior conversation, Jackie Peterson indicated that she had deposited $50,000 into her son's bank account. The two had also talked about a trip to Mexico. During that same call, Scott had also told his mother that he had spoken to the producer of *America's Most Wanted* and had "kicked the guy's ass around." He wished he'd dealt with this producer before he'd appeared on the show with Diane Sawyer. The two agreed that Scott would become more skilled doing TV interviews as he gained more experience on camera.

"Why would a grieving husband be so proud of kicking a producer's ass?" police wondered. "For a grieving husband who should be showing appreciation for such a show that has the desire to keep his wife's face fresh in the minds of millions of viewers," Investigator Jacobson noted, this was odd behavior indeed.

Jackie asked Scott if "this guy from *America's Most Wanted* was going to help with the search." Scott said he thought the upcoming show would generate more tips on the case, and said his interview went well.

"People are more likely to call in tips to the show than to the police," Jackie said, adding that the host said he passes on the tips to police. But Jackie said she was not sure she wanted to do that because "you'll never hear them again."

Scott told his mother that when the program aired an earlier story about Laci, Brocchini went to the studio to help take calls himself.

"Huh, then what did he do with them?" Jackie asked.

"I don't know," Scott chuckled. "He probably threw out the ones he didn't like."

"Yeah, that's what I feel about him. I wish he didn't have such an agenda."

As their conversation continued, Jackie and Scott lashed out at Kim Peterson, referring to her as that "little witch" and insinuating that she had discouraged the family from appearing on the show for a long time.

As part of the investigation, Detective Brocchini had contacted the producer of *America's Most Wanted*. The producer told him that Scott had refused to answer a number of his questions, and had wanted a chance to edit the interview. When the program aired later in the week, it was highly critical of Scott.

The police also contacted District Attorney James Brazelton about the alleged offer to McAllister. Again, Scott was lying. There was never an "offer." Instead, Brazelton recalled that he'd run into Kirk McAllister in the parking lot of the courthouse several days prior, and in what he recalled as a fifteen-second conversation he told McAllister "his boy might be able to avoid having the needle in his arm if he tells us where the body is so the family can have a decent burial."

McAllister replied, "That's an attractive offer, but Scott doesn't know where she's at." Brazelton said he'd never discussed the case with Scott's lawyer over dinner. In fact, he had never formally met with McAllister to discuss the case.

As the police noted, Scott reacted to all this talk of the death penalty with a startling lack of emotion.

The police were also puzzled by Lee Peterson's question to his son about whether his attorney thought he was in "good shape." "Apparently, there is more to know about Scott Peterson's involvement with Laci's disappearance, which would have prompted that question," Steve Jacobson wrote. "Scott responded back that his attorney told him he's 'playing a deadly game here.'

"I know that Kirk McAllister is a very respected, seasoned criminal defense attorney. If, in fact, he made this comment to Scott, it indicates the seriousness of what he knows Scott's involvement to be and the consequences of playing such a game with law enforcement," Jacobson continued. "In an effort to have his client stop 'playing the game' or to show him the seriousness of the 'game,' Kirk tells him it will have the ultimate consequence, that being death."

As Jacobson noted, McAllister's remarks elicited a series of "self-serving" statements from Scott. "Not once do you hear Scott becoming upset, or adamantly proclaiming his innocence," Jacobson wrote in the report. "Instead, what is heard is his concern for being in prison 'for who knows how long.' Scott even has to be reminded by his dad that the police would not plant any evidence because there is none. And Lee Peterson is right, the police would be unable to plant a body because one can't be found, and chances are, it never will be."

Scott's comments about McKenzie "indicated that Scott and his dog would be parting ways." "There appeared to be a strong bond between Scott and his dog, one in which Scott says brings tears to his eyes as he watches him at the sliding glass door," Jacobson also noted. "Yet, while grieving from the loss of his wife, he will now be separated from his dog for an undetermined amount of time but will be afforded the opportunity later in life to get the dog back. I ask the question, where is Scott going?"

Based on everything they had heard so far, Jacobson noted, "Scott may be contemplating two things: (1) being arrested and jailed for a 'long time' or (2) fleeing the United States of America in an attempt to avoid prosecution. Scott has shown more genuine emotion from the separation of his dog than the loss of his wife, Laci Peterson."

Faced with no other choice, the police decided to meet with the district attorney and try to persuade him to file a case—or, at the very least, to stop Scott Peterson from leaving the country.

Early on January 29, the police recorded a call between Scott and his Tradecorp supervisor abroad. When his boss asked whether he would be attending a Tradecorp meeting in Mexico in the coming days, Scott said he would be there.

The call indicated that Scott might not be attempting to flee the jurisdiction, but was simply attending a conference south of the border. Still, detectives contacted Scott's boss and asked that he cancel any future trips for his employee.

That same morning, the second half of Scott's taped *Good Morning America* interview was broadcast. This time, Scott was shown seated with members of his immediate family. After viewing the program, Scott called his brother Mark.

"I think I may have, and it's entirely possible I told them wrong about the girlfriend on air." He was acknowledging that he had lied in saying that he'd told the police about Amber. Scott believed that Sawyer picked up on the discrepancy because she announced after the interview that police sources were disputing the statement.

"So, I screwed up," Scott said.

"Did you correct it today?" Mark asked.

"No, no I didn't."

"So, you misanswered [*sic*]. Is that what you are saying?"

"I must have. I did not tell the police about her that night."

That day, with no attorney present, Scott sat down at his home for a series of additional media interviews. During the tapings, he addressed the $250,000 life insurance policies he said that he and Laci had taken out on each other when they purchased their home two years earlier. He reiterated that this was done long before Laci disappeared.

Real estate was also on Scott's mind. Later that day, he also spoke to his friend Brian Argain for a second time about the sale of 523 Covena. Brian suggested that Scott speak with his attorney to find out if he and Laci were both on the title. If so, he might have to get the court's approval before selling the house.

By day's end, Scott was on the phone to the Modesto PD complaining that members of the press were banging on his door. When the cops arrived, there was no one in the area. The police learned that a radio shock jock had been outside Scott's home earlier, with a bullhorn, screaming out an offer of $64,000 to Scott if he would take a polygraph. Other reporters had also been on his property, rattling his gate in attempts to speak to him. By the time cops arrived, they had all dispersed. Detective Grogan was alerted to the situation, but his attempts to reach Scott by phone failed.

When Scott finally returned Grogan's call, the detective let it be known that he'd seen his interview with Diane Sawyer.

"You'll probably see it um . . . they caught me answering a question about that I told you about a girlfriend, but it's not true, we both know that," Scott said.

"Okay," Grogan responded. "Well, I understand there was a circus of media over there at the house too, and bullhorns . . ."

"Yeah, we had a couple of shock jocks here screaming with the bullhorn."

"All right. Well how are you doing?"

"I'm losing it. I miss her . . ." Scott choked up. "I got so much to say that I haven't been able to function at all, haven't called adult friends, just . . . I can't even talk but I'm trying. But I'm just a mess without her."

"Well, there is a lot of stuff going on right now," the detective sighed. "With the press and ah, I mean it looks like most of that stuff is kinda turning the wrong direction on ya."

"I know it, you know I did the press and every question I answered today I gave the website, the phone number, I didn't see any of it, but I'm guessing they didn't put a damn thing in there. It's just unbelievable. They're not helping me find my wife. And I know the dogs you brought out, they're looking for her right now. Yeah, they need to be, I need them so bad to be looking for her. Ah . . . I need her back. Tell me there's some leads, tell me something there, to look for."

"Well, I'm not telling ya that there's anything that's pointing any direction . . . right now, that is, somewhere other than you."

"No."

"I mean . . . you and I both know what happened to Laci."

"Do you know what happened to her?"

"We both do."

"Craig, I need to know what happened to her. Are you telling me you know what happened to her?"

"Scott, I mean let's be serious with one another."

"Well I know where we're looking for her. And I think we're probably gonna find her over there in the bay."

"Oh."

"It's a matter of time."

"Craig, I had nothing to do with Laci's disappearance. Hey, ah, I'm gonna go."

"Scott, what I'm offerin' ya is an opportunity here to end all of this nonsense."

"I'm gonna go find her, Craig."

"Why don't you come back here and sit down with me and tell me what happened."

"I'm not involved in my wife's disappearance. We're gonna find her. And I need your help doing that and I just hope your department's following leads. I want to find her, that's all there is to it. Yeah, I'm going now. Bye."

As January came to a close, the police were forging ahead with a renewed focus on Scott. By now, they had received 5,800 tips on the case. Scott, meanwhile, had sold Laci's Land Rover to Robert's Auto World for $7,500, and purchased a 2002 white Dodge truck.

Two women also came forward claiming affairs with Scott Peterson while he was married. Police found both Janet Ilse and Katy Hansen's claims credible. In addition, a third woman calling from the Las Vegas area was also claiming an affair with Peterson. While researching this book, I have heard references to other women—including a few members of the "mile-high club" who became intimately acquainted with Scott while flying overseas—but to date the reports have never been confirmed.

As Brocchini sought more information on the alleged affairs, Grogan sat down with Sharon and Amy Rocha to look through Laci's jewelry once again. The detective wanted to learn if either woman noticed any items absent from the collection. Both agreed that the only piece that appeared to be missing was a pair of one-carat diamond stud earrings Laci typically wore. Their claim was in stark contrast to Scott's statement that his wife had been wearing several valuable pieces when he last saw her on Christmas Eve.

Interestingly, Anne Bird told me that she'd been at the Harvey Clars Auction Gallery in Oakland when a pair of one-carat screw-back earrings, eerily similar to the ones that Laci had been wearing, was being offered for sale. Screw-back earrings are not very common these days, so Anne asked where the seller had obtained them.

"A reliable source," she was told.

"Would you speak to police?" she asked, suspicious that the earrings might have been Laci's.

"Yes," she was told.

Anne grabbed a brochure, then called Jackie to tell her about the earrings. Jackie contacted Sharon Rocha. As far as Anne knew, nothing ever came of the tip, and she learned later that the police never checked out the lead.

Now that Scott's infidelity was widely known, and allegiances within Scott's circles were being tested, Buehler set about re-interviewing Laci's friends in search of new insights. In late January he met again with Renee Tomlinson, Stacey Boyers, Lori Ellsworth, and Kim McNeely.

The women all recalled being troubled by Scott's healthy appetite on Christmas Day. They felt it "strange" that Scott began eating almost immediately upon returning from police headquarters that day. They were also troubled by his directive that no photographs of him be used at the volunteer center, released to the media, or used in any fashion during the investigation. He also prohibited any wedding pictures or video from being distributed and did not want any photos of him involved in the search. Scott was often the first to arrive at the volunteer center in the morning, but he refused to permit the media to enter until 9:30 A.M. He made it a habit to leave by 9:20. One day, when a reporter came in early, Scott demanded that he leave.

As the days progressed, friends reported that Scott remained "nonemotional," organized, and very much in control. He was able to recall different ideas and suggestions that were made, as well as the assignments that were handed out at the volunteer center. When one of the women asked Scott to supply photos of Laci's jewelry so that volunteers could show them to pawnshop owners around town, Scott simply ignored her repeated requests. Such controlled behavior clashed with Scott's claims that he was so distraught over Laci's disappearance that he was losing paperwork and unable to supply things to police.

During the long meeting at headquarters, all four women reported that until recently they had viewed Scott as a "good, attentive" husband. They based their impressions on his willingness to endure some of the "small irritations" that Laci thrust upon him. The consensus was that Laci was an incessant talker, and that her ceaseless chatter sometimes irritated those around her.

The women recalled that once, at a party, Scott had told a friend that Laci's talking was so constant that he sought refuge in the bathroom—only to have Laci follow him to the door and just keep chatting. The women agreed that Laci's constant jabbering didn't dull their affection for her, but they admired Scott for his patience.

Over the past few months, though, the women's opinion of Scott had changed. Conduct they once dismissed as "isolated" incidents of rude behavior had now taken on a new significance.

One friend recalled that Scott grabbed her buttocks at a party in November 2000. At the time she'd chalked it up to an accidental brush, but now she believed it may have been intentional. Scott also disturbed another of Laci's friends when he told her he didn't like her young nephew. Embarrassed by Scott's rude comment, Laci apologized, telling her friend that Scott was not accustomed to being around children. Scott reportedly told his wife that he saw nothing wrong with his comment. After all, the boy wasn't her friend's child. Besides, he claimed, it was nothing against kids in general, he just couldn't stand this particular tot.

And there was more. Renee remembered that the previous summer, when Scott was out of town, she was at the house when he called to speak with Laci. Renee overheard Laci asking him about the status of their health insurance, since she was in the first stages of her pregnancy. When Laci learned that the insurance wasn't active, she accused Scott of not caring about her and the baby. For weeks after the phone confrontation, Laci had expressed frustration over her husband's failure to take care of the insurance issue. It was the only time that Renee recalled her being truly upset with her husband.

The women also agreed, however, that Laci regularly ordered her husband around in front of her friends, telling him to take out the garbage, change a CD on the stereo, and perform other jobs around the house. At the time, the women all thought it was "so cool" that Laci was able to give Scott directions without him getting angry. Now, they wondered what resentment may have been building up within Scott.

Renee also reported that Laci complained about Scott's recent traveling, as well as his upcoming trip to Europe in late January. At a party the two of them attended on December 7, 2002, Laci had been upset over the prospect of Scott traveling to Brussels so close to the baby's due date. She said she had even asked her husband to cancel the trip.

On another mid-December visit, Laci had complained again about Scott's increasingly busy work schedule. She explained to Renee that she was looking forward to a trip to Carmel she and Scott had planned for later in the month. Even though Scott's family would be there, Laci was eager for the time to spend with her husband. She hoped he would stay home more once the baby arrived.

Another friend, Heather Richardson, told Renee that she believed Scott never wanted children. Laci had mentioned having a three-way sonogram performed on the baby to appease Scott's concern about possible birth defects, and told Heather that abortion would likely be an option if any were detected. Laci's friends believed that Scott was pressuring her to have the test performed, and that the possibility of an abortion was his idea, not hers.

During the conversation, the women recalled that on December 25, while everyone was congregated at police headquarters for a press conference, Scott told friends and family that he would not be taking a polygraph. He said he had spoken with his father, who instructed him to speak to an attorney. Lee also advised him that he was too emotionally distraught to do well on the test.

After Scott's pronouncement, Renee walked over to give him a hug. "Laci loved you so much," she told him.

"You make me feel so bad," Scott responded—a strange reaction, which Renee now took as a sign that he had something to do with her friend's disappearance.

Another friend, Kim McNeely, recalled that Laci had learned she was pregnant soon after Renee's baby shower. However, when she approached Scott excitedly about her home pregnancy test, he brushed her off, saying he was hung over from a party the night before.

Kim also recalled Scott asking her then-boyfriend whether a father could expect to have sex again after a child is born. The boyfriend said that it wouldn't be the same. Scott seemed concerned about how the arrival of the baby would change his sex life, in terms of frequency and quality.

At one point, Kim asked Laci if she and her husband were still having sex. Laci told her "no," but confided that she still "pleasured" her husband.

As the interview drew to a close, Buehler asked the women if they'd ever seen Laci react under stress. They recalled Laci's relationship with her longtime boyfriend Kent Gain. They knew the relationship had an element of "domestic violence" to it, they said, because Laci spoke freely about the situation. Stacey Boyers told Buehler that when she found out that her own boyfriend, Brian Argain, was cheating on her, both Scott and Laci were very supportive throughout their breakup. From things Laci told her, Stacey believed that Laci wouldn't have tolerated Scott cheating on her.

In the end, Laci's friends agreed that she would have told at least one of them if Scott had confessed to his relationship with Amber Frey—even though she hadn't done so with Janet Ilse.

In the days that followed, Buehler met with two female employees of the real estate firm where Scott's friend, Brian Argain, was employed. The women told police that when they mentioned Scott, Argain made it clear that he was standing by his friend. According to the employees, Argain had said something to the effect that "Even if he did it, he's still my friend."

For Grogan, a second interview with Laci's aunt Robin "Marie" Rocha reinforced Scott's discomfort around children. She recalled an incident at a birthday party with Scott and Laci in September 2001. At one point, she needed to put her infant daughter down so she could use the restroom. Marie approached Scott and asked if he would hold the child for just a moment. As she recalled, he leaned back in his chair, held his hands up in the air, and said "no." She came away from the incident convinced that Scott never wanted a child.

Marie also told the detective that her niece could be headstrong at times. Laci often talked about babies, and "If Laci wanted to have a baby, she would have a baby whether Scott wanted one or not," she said. Marie described Laci as a loving and kind person, but also stubborn and accustomed to getting her way. Yet she was "totally in love with Scott" and never said a derogatory word about her husband.


On January 30, Scott received a phone call from the Fox News Channel's Rita Cosby, asking if he had heard about a possible Laci sighting in Washington State. Scott said he had but didn't sound very optimistic about it. Excitedly, Cosby recited the details, explaining that a woman who appeared to be pregnant had come into a convenience store with no jacket on. When the clerk asked her why she wasn't wearing one, the woman allegedly told her she'd been kidnapped and the guy had a gun. The clerk did not call police immediately.

"Police are now looking at the video," Cosby said.

"Definitely, when did she see them?" Scott asked.

"Apparently last week."

"Wow, okay. Do you know who is looking at it [the video]?"

"It's the local police there in Longview, Washington State."

The call ended abruptly.

A little while later, Scott's friend Heidi Fritz called about the same sighting. Scott confirmed what Cosby had said.

"Oh my God, that's great!" Heidi exclaimed. "Where is it?"

"I don't know," Scott said flatly. He explained that he'd called the Longview Police and they were getting the tapes together to view.

Heidi asked Scott if he could drive up there. "Oh definitely, yeah, if it's even close I'll get up there. . . . We're hoping it's her." Scott said he'd phoned the Longview Police and was waiting for a call back.

Heidi said she was so excited because Scott had said all along that he knew in his heart that Laci was still alive and now this woman [the clerk] was reporting that she saw her.

For a moment, Scott didn't respond. Then he said he was hopeful. "We're praying it's her."

Heidi's husband Aaron picked up the line and asked Scott how he was feeling.

Scott hesitated, then remarked, "Um, I'm hopeful on this, I am feeling really good right now. I just want to know." He promised to let the couple know as soon he heard back from the Longview Police.

"Hey, stop cutting your hands, all right?" Aaron said.

"I'll try."

The following morning, Scott's friend Mike Reed called about the incident in Washington. Scott told him he hoped it was true, so he'd know where to look. While the two were speaking, Scott's mother was leaving a message on Scott's voice mail, excitedly asking her son if he wanted to hop on a plane and go to Washington. She indicated that she was ready, and mentioned a friend named Rachel who lived nearby so they would have a place to stay. Jackie said that she'd called the Modesto PD, but the chief was in a meeting. She choked up and began to cry, saying that she hoped the sighting would come to something.

Hanging up with Reed, Scott checked his voice mail. He laughed when he heard his mother describing Rachel putting up fliers, and he did not return her call. It was another telling moment that would be played for the jury at trial.

About thirty minutes passed before Jackie called her son again and asked if he'd heard about the Longview report.

"Yeah," he said. "is there any more news?"

"According to today's paper, they are going to view the video," Jackie replied. "I [asked] Dad, are they capable of viewing the video?"

"Yeah, I know, I want to see the damn thing. How can they ID her?"

"Why don't you hop on a plane?"

"Well, I'll definitely [go], you know, I called up there and talked to one of them."

"Oh, good for you."

"Hopefully we'll see what's . . ."

"God, at least that's a lead," Jackie said.

"Yeah."

"I didn't take much credence in it until I heard [the clerk] was forty-five, but she is still a ditz if she didn't remember" the incident earlier.

"Yeah, when was it she last saw her?" Scott said, laughing.

"The end of December, which is [enough] time to get there, you know," Jackie said. "And then I hope they have video on the border," she added, referring to the Canadian border.

"Yeah, it's the end of January."

"Yeah, I know, sweetie."

"The report said she waited a week or something, but now [they're saying] she waited a month."

"Chief said, yeah, it's a month." (Jackie and Scott often called Lee Peterson "Chief.")

"The woman only saw the pictures of Laci on CNN recently," Jackie added.

"Hmm," Scott sighed.

Before he hung up, Scott asked about McKenzie. "When I come down there, I'm going to give the dog a bath," he said.

"The gardeners are afraid to come in," said Jackie, as McKenzie barked in the backyard.

Scott dialed the Longview Police Department—having told his mother and friends he'd already done so. "I think you are the police department that's looking at tapes of her [Laci] at a grocery store," Scott told the officer who took the call. He asked to speak to a detective or whoever was helping in the investigation. There was no indication that Scott had ever spoken with the department before.

"What's your name again?" the officer asked.

"Scott Peterson."

Scott was placed on hold. While he waited, a call was coming in to his line and the call to Longview police was lost. It was Scott's mom again.

Scott claimed he'd just spoken to the Longview police "again," and they had fifty or sixty hours of tape to view. "They seem really nice up there," he said.

"Well, you know, you're the only one who can truly identify her," Jackie said.

"Yeah, I know, that's what I told them. That I would be up there in a minute if there was even a possibility."

"Maybe she is in Canada by now," Jackie said. "You might ask if the Canadians have tapes at their borders."

"Yeah."

Jackie said she was going to ask Rachel to "plaster the place with posters," and suggested that Scott should give her a call.

"Definitely," Scott replied. He mentioned that he intended to pick up some "peanut butter slices" for the dog. Jackie told him he was welcome to come home anytime.

While Scott and his mother talked, Rita Cosby was leaving him a message saying that it was important to get word of that sighting out to people. Scott deleted the call before it was finished. He also had a message from his former employee, Eric Olsen, and this call he returned. After some business talk, the conversation turned to the Washington sighting. Scott told Olsen he intended to "hang around the airport" in case he had to go up there.

Just before noon, Jackie phoned back to ask Scott where he was. He said he was in San Juan Bautista—not waiting at the airport, as he had told Eric Olsen. Jackie asked her son if he'd read the local paper. He said he hadn't.

Jackie then mentioned Mark Geragos, "the high-priced lawyer, the one you pay a fortune to have him." She'd apparently seen Geragos quoted in an article in the local press, and his words were directed at Scott: "He would tell you that you have been caught up in something larger than you ever thought of and you have to weather the storm."

Scott chuckled.

Jackie then admonished him not to talk to anyone.

At four o'clock that afternoon, Jackie called her son once more. She had just heard on *The Abrams Report* that Laci wasn't the one on the video. She was sorry.

Scott erased her call, along with several others from the media, including one from a representative for *Larry King Live*.

As January came to a close, investigators were focused on a single individual. "This is an ongoing investigation with only one known suspect at this time, that being Scott Peterson," they concluded in an ongoing report filed at the end of the month.

By this point, Detective Craig Grogan was in an odd and somewhat uncomfortable position. The Rocha family was asking him to act as a go-between in the battle between them and Scott. Sharon was worried that Scott was going to throw away or sell items of sentimental value to the family, and she implored him to contact Scott and ask him to return her daughter's belongings to her family.

Grogan reported that Scott had already sold Laci's Land Rover, but the news didn't upset her. (Later, the dealer who purchased the car would return it to the family for the token sum of one dollar, to ensure that the donation could be listed as a gift on the family's tax return.) Sharon wanted personal items, things that had a direct link to Laci. She was unwilling to speak with Scott directly, and wanted Grogan to mediate.

"Hi Scott, it's Craig Grogan," the detective said in a phone message he left on January 31. "I'm calling at the request of the Rocha family. Sharon would like to see if you have any photographs of Laci when she was a child or photos of her that you would part with. Ah, she's also asking about some Tiffany lamps which apparently were Laci's grandmother's. I'm just asking for them and we're not trying to make you do anything but if you'd be willing to do that, I'd be willing to be an intermediary for you guys." Sharon had also asked for some other items from the nursery.

As the detective prepared to leave the office that day, he was told that Amber and Scott were speaking on the phone. Scott was telling Amber to let her know that he had scheduled a polygraph exam. He wanted her to meet him at the polygrapher's office at eleven o'clock the following morning. Replaying Scott's calls, Grogan learned that Scott had actually made the appointment for nine o'clock. Yet Amber believed that she was going to accompany Scott to the test, and called police to ask if an undercover officer could escort her there.

The police later instructed Amber not to meet him at the office. No undercover operation was planned.

In a follow-up call, Scott asked Amber if she believed their relationship would continue. He saw no reason to take the polygraph if she saw no possibility of the two of them going forward together. He explained that he was taking a risk by agreeing to the test because if the media learned of his intent to take one, it would be "bad."

The two got into an argument when Amber asked Scott to use her name during the examination. He insisted on replacing it with another name. He was worried that the polygrapher would go to the media with the results of the test if he realized who his client was.

Scott next advised Amber to take precautions so that she wasn't followed to the office the next day. He also told her that he'd been thinking about her, and that he was nervous about their meeting.

The following morning was February 1. Just before nine o'clock, Scott dialed Amber and asked her to meet him in thirty minutes.

"Are you kidding?" Amber asked.

"It's real close to you," Scott her.

Amber asked if Scott was just now contacting the polygrapher. He said yes, then gave her directions to Expert Polygraph Services, on the corner of Palm and Browning Streets, and told her the examiner would meet them in the lobby. When Scott declined to reveal the polygrapher's name, the two started arguing again.

Amber asked if he would be there whether or not she came.

"I will be waiting there at nine thirty. I hope to see you there," he told her.

It's unclear whether Detective Brocchini acted on his own when he decided to stake out the location that morning. What is clear is that he parked a discreet distance away from the polygrapher's office, in a school parking lot about two hundred yards away. He was hidden among eight other cars.

Yet just after 9:30, Scott came up to his unmarked car and startled him. "While watching the intersection, I saw someone walking up toward the back of my vehicle," Brocchini wrote in a report. "I looked in my mirror and noticed it was Scott Peterson. Peterson was wearing blue sweatpants and a blue sweatshirt, and he was holding a spiral notebook. I immediately exited my vehicle and walked towards Peterson."

"I wanted to thank you for going to *America's Most Wanted* and answering the phones," Scott said.

Brocchini thought it odd that Scott did not ask how he found out about the test. "It's too bad you want to take a polygraph in private," the detective replied.

Scott told him that it was "not appropriate" for him to take one with the police, then turned and walked away. He entered the office complex and then emerged ten minutes later. As he was walking back toward his truck, Brocchini drove over to him and parked behind his vehicle.

"Scott," the detective yelled. "Is it true that Kirk McAllister fired you as a client?"

"That's news to me."

Brocchini told him that Gloria Gomez, a local reporter, had reported from outside McAllister's office last night that he had been fired.

"You mean the news reported it?" Scott replied.

"Yes."

Scott was silent.

Brocchini told Scott he had a lot of "explaining to do."

"You don't know, I just stop on the side of the road and break down for no apparent reason," Scott said. "I just really miss Laci."

Brocchini told Scott he "did not act like someone who missed his pregnant wife." As Scott walked away, he yelled after him that he had some explaining to do about "the other girlfriends I identified."

"Right, other girlfriends," Scott mumbled.

Brocchini said that he had a photo of Scott with another woman, but Scott ignored the statement. Instead he climbed into his truck and got on his cell phone. According to Brocchini, Scott remained "calm and emotionless" throughout the confrontation.

As he pulled out of the parking lot, Scott was dialing Amber Frey's number, ready to accuse her of telling police about the polygraph.

Amber didn't pick up his call, but a few minutes later she called him back. When he told her he'd found Detective Brocchini in the parking lot, she was nonplussed. "What are you talking about?" she asked.

Scott said he was heartbroken. He had "totally" trusted her, but now she couldn't be trusted. He'd given her the name and the place, and Brocchini showed up. "What does that say?" he demanded.

Amber insisted she hadn't spoken to Brocchini in weeks.

"Well, then how did he end up there?" Scott broke down in tears.

Amber said she'd nothing to do with it.

Scott admitted that he had done a terrible thing by lying to her, and now he knew how it must have felt.

Amber asked Scott if he intended to follow through with a test.

Scott said he'd still take one, as long as she met him there, and insisted that he had taken a "big risk" in going to the polygrapher's office.

Amber said she would feel safest with Scott taking the polygraph at the police department.

"That's not even an option," he told her.

"What did you tell the polygrapher?"

Scott said he paid him three hundred dollars and explained the situation.

"Can I call him?"

Scott gave her Melvin King's telephone number.

As the two argued, Jackie Peterson was anxiously leaving a message asking Scott if Kirk McAllister had really dropped him as a client.

A short time after the parking lot encounter, Detective Brocchini arrived at Amber's home to find her in her pajamas chatting on the phone with him. Once the two hung up, he discouraged her from having any further contact with Scott, explaining that it could be "detrimental" to the case.

Amber handed over more audiotapes to Brocchini, along with the recording of their conversation just after Scott discovered Brocchini in the parking lot. Brocchini reported that the tape captured

Scott "acting" like he was crying. "Peterson encouraged Amber to meet him 'anywhere, anytime, in any public place as long as the police were not involved,'" Brocchini wrote. "Frey asked Peterson why he did not want to be with law enforcement and Peterson said law enforcement had 'systematically lied to his family and Laci's family' and we were trying to say he was involved in the case."

Later that day, without immediately identifying himself as a police officer, Brocchini contacted Melvin King. Through a series of questions, he learned that the polygraphs King performs are completely confidential.

"When I asked if he was served with an FBI subpoena would he turn over records of polygraphs, . . . King said there is no requirement for him to keep records and it is not unusual for his polygraph records to be destroyed," Brocchini wrote. "King's answers indicated he was willing to work with someone regarding a confidential polygraph."

Once Brocchini identified himself as a police officer, King revealed that he was a retired lieutenant for the Fresno Police Department. A thirty-five year law enforcement veteran, King had been conducting polygraphs for twenty-eight years.

In response to questions, King said that he didn't know the identity of the man who was scheduled to take a polygraph that morning, and that the man had canceled the exam after his girlfriend refused to go with him. King said that Scott had been told that he needed to bring someone with him to the polygraph, and that otherwise the test would be of little value, "as the result had to matter to someone in order to add pressure to the exam."

King also said that he'd received two calls from a woman asking whether the person who had an appointment that morning had completed the test. Citing confidentiality, King had declined to answer her questions. This contradicts the account Amber recalls in her recent book. According to her, she asked King, "Is Scott Peterson scheduled to come in for a polygraph?" and King answered, "Yes. He said he was just waiting to hear from the person who would be coming with him."

In any event, King told Brocchini that he would not polygraph Scott Peterson. He later advised Scott to take the test with law enforcement. He told Scott how Congressman Gary Condit had taken a private polygraph test after the disappearance of Chandra Levy in 2001, and how useless the test had been in proving his innocence.

"Peterson never told King why he didn't want to take a police polygraph," Brocchini wrote.

# CHAPTER SIXTEEN

# FEBRUARY 2003

In Modesto, detectives continued refining their profile of Scott. After profiler Sharon Hagan identified Scott as a "narcissist," police psychiatrist Phil Trumpeter met with investigators at police headquarters to offer guidance on how best to interview Scott and the people close to him.

At no time did the members of law enforcement officially label Scott a sociopath. But narcissism is a major trait of sociopathy; such individuals care for no one but themselves, tending to their personal needs and desires to the exclusion of all else. Egocentric and selfish, the sociopath exhibits an absence of conscience, an ability to lie at will with no guilt or remorse. The sociopath often has a flat affect, displaying none of the emotions a normal human being would in the same circumstances—for the sociopath simply doesn't feel the same things others do.

Though it would still be several weeks before the case was publicly classified as a homicide, after hearing Sharon Hagan's interpretation of the evidence, the Modesto police were confirmed in their conviction that Scott was the leading suspect in the murder of his wife. The investigators believed that the motive might have stemmed from one or more factors that were converging in Scott's life: his failing business; the pressure of becoming a parent when he did not really want a child; his wife's "expensive" tastes and high expectations, including her desire for a new car and a new home; and, of course, Scott's relationship with Amber Frey.

The absence of evidence at the Peterson house suggested that Laci was the victim of what is termed a "soft kill," a death from strangulation, poisoning, or suffocation, which might not leave behind a great deal of blood or other forensic material. The two drops of blood present on the couple's duvet cover suggested that Laci might have been killed on the bed; the fact that Scott had no significant injuries, aside from a scuffed knuckle, led police to suspect that Laci did little to defend herself. She "may have been drugged prior to suffocation or poisoning or otherwise incapacitated without a struggle," officials speculated in one internal report.

The detectives believed that after killing Laci in the bedroom, Scott had wrapped her body in a tarp inside the house, then dragged her out through the back door, wadding up the throw rug in the process. It was likely Scott—not Laci, as he later claimed—who had mopped the floor on the day of her disappearance. Scott was later observed vacuuming around the couch, coffee table, and washer and dryer, possibly attempting to rid the home of potential evidence. Scott admitted to placing umbrellas wrapped in a tarp in the back of his truck at 9:30 on Christmas Eve morning. They theorized that he loaded Laci's tarp-encased body into the truck and then transported it to the warehouse after releasing McKenzie with his leash attached.

Once he reached the warehouse, police believed that Scott had attached homemade anchors to Laci's body, and that he may also have wrapped her body in chicken wire and plastic wrap—both of which were found in the warehouse during the search. He may have replaced the boat cover on the Gamefisher after putting Laci's body inside. Police believed he then drove to the San Francisco Bay, where he dumped her weighted body.

Scott told police that several people had observed him attempting to back the boat down the ramp at the marina. While no such witnesses were ever located, the fear that he'd been sighted may have explained why Scott had changed his alibi from golfing to fishing near Brooks Island.

It seemed apparent that Scott didn't want anyone to know about his boat. In another change from his normal behavior, he also stopped using his cell phone after 10:06 A.M., including the entire time he was at the bay. He did not make a single call until after he was convinced witnesses saw him around the marina. When Scott learned of a planned bloodhound search, he moved the boat cover to a shed in the rear of his home. There he placed a leaking, gasoline-powered leaf blower on top of the tarp, which would obliterate any other odors. As police noted, there was no sign that Scott was otherwise careless with his equipment. This looked like a deliberate act.

With their working theory in place, detectives on F Street began preparing a case for the district attorney. By mid-month, however, it became clear that they needed more evidence. The police did not have a body; nor was there sufficient physical evidence to link Scott to the crime. DNA evidence collected during the search warrant had not yet returned any results. The case, thus far, was entirely circumstantial.

At headquarters, Grogan was investigating the possibility that Scott had intended to flee the country. On February 1, Scott's employee Rob Weaver alerted investigators that his boss had just advised him to "pack his bags," telling him that they were flying to Guadalajara in two days.

A surveillance team had followed Scott (with McKenzie in tow) to his parents' home in San Diego. During the surveillance operation, police again planted a tracking device on Scott's vehicle. They learned that he was scheduled to depart from LAX International Airport on February 3, on a United Airlines flight to Guadalajara, and Weaver was expected to meet him at the airport and join him on the flight. Weaver promised to contact police if it became apparent that Scott didn't intend to return to the States.

Before Scott was scheduled to depart, he called polygrapher Melvin King to ask if anyone had inquired about the February 1 appointment he had cancelled. King advised Scott that a woman had phoned but did not identify herself. In a second call to King, Scott explained that he had encountered an undesirable third party in the parking lot just before the meeting. King, in turn, informed Scott that a detective from the Modesto Police Department had phoned and wanted to know what was going on. The rest of the call was lost.

Later that day, Scott spoke with Amber. After speaking with King, she said, she would be willing to reschedule the examination for another day. She also told Scott about a surprise phone call she'd received from Al Brocchini, offering to accompany her to the appointment with Scott.

"It's not a possibility," Scott replied. "I will meet you anywhere [but not] with the police, especially Al Brocchini."

Amber said she wanted to do the polygraph where she felt protected and safe because he had been so dishonest with her.

"Then there is no future between us," Scott said. "That kills me, but that is a decision you will have to make."

By now, accusations of bad faith were volleying back and forth between Scott and Amber on a regular basis. In a later conversation, Scott complained to Amber that the cops had lied to his family, friends, and "everyone else."

"It's not like you've been honest," Amber retorted.

As if to defend himself, Scott insisted she was the only person he'd ever lied to.

There was one thing he wasn't lying about, though. Though the agents had been deeply suspicious of Scott's plans to travel to Mexico—watching as he boarded the plane and monitoring his calls while he was in Mexico—once he arrived they may have been surprised to discover that he was, in fact, conducting business there.

Scott Peterson, it seemed, would be returning to Modesto after all.

Deputy District Attorney Rick DiStaso met Amber Frey for the first time at the Modesto police headquarters in mid-February, where they spent much of the time discussing Scott. Amber also expressed an interest in being interviewed by TV news personality

Connie Chung, saying that she was upset at the way she was being portrayed in the media. She was told that no one could prevent her from giving an interview, but she was cautioned not to release any information about the case when speaking to reporters. Amber later phoned Sharon Rocha to get her feedback; ultimately, she would decide against granting an interview to Chung or anyone else until the case was resolved.

Throughout the month, Detective Grogan found Sharon Rocha a consistent source of important information. At one meeting, while the two were watching a crime scene video from December 26, Grogan asked Sharon to look for anything that appeared to be misplaced, reorganized, or missing. She pointed to a pair of men's tennis shoes near the French doors, the usual entrance to the home from the back yard. The sneakers, she assumed, belonged to Scott; normally, she said, Laci kept a pair of shoes there, too. Sharon also noticed that her daughter's pocketbook, which had been hanging in the closet, was now hanging on a hat rack in the dining room area.

Sharon also reviewed the events of Christmas Eve with Detective Grogan. In hindsight, she found it telling that Scott wasn't alarmed when he first returned home to find McKenzie still wearing his leash and Laci's car parked in the driveway. Scott's claim that he didn't grow worried until after he showered and dressed for dinner made no sense to her. Her daughter was a "communicator," she said; Laci would have left a message on Scott's cell phone, or a note for him at home, if she'd gone out for some reason.

Laci's mother also told Grogan that Scott had left it up to her and Ron to call the police that night. Indeed, Scott never once suggested that the police should get involved. He didn't even know that Grantski had called the police until the officers arrived in the park that evening.

Grogan asked Sharon if Scott ever mentioned that he missed Laci. Sitting back in her chair, Sharon was thoughtful. "No," she replied. Scott never appeared genuinely upset. For the most part he appeared "nonchalant," unflappable. He answered most questions with a simple yes or no. He never elaborated when asked directly about events leading up to Laci's disappearance. When speaking about Laci, Scott had stock responses—insisting that they had to make sure Laci's picture was "out there," for instance, on the argument that someone was bound to call with information that would help locate Laci.

Sharon told Grogan that recently she'd received several messages from Scott's mother, Jackie. At first she had been reluctant to return the calls, worried that the conversation wouldn't go well if Jackie wanted her to support Scott. Eventually, though, Sharon had chosen to speak with her. Jackie told Sharon that Scott's family was praying for Laci's safe return. She offered her assistance, saying she thought it was "horrible" that police had shown Sharon the photos of Scott with another woman. Sharon believed that what police had done was appropriate, but said nothing.

When Jackie tried to excuse her son's affair, blaming it on a one-night stand or the fact that Scott had been "drunk or something," Sharon pointed to the fact that Scott had kept in touch with Amber after Laci disappeared. Jackie insisted that everything seemed normal between Scott and Laci at a baby shower everyone attended around Thanksgiving. At the shower Laci said that she was having trouble sleeping, and suggested that she and Scott get separate beds. Still, Laci didn't seem angry at Scott when she made the comment, Jackie recalled.

Jackie's remark didn't seem particularly significant to Sharon. She had heard Laci complain about difficulty sleeping because of the pregnancy, and heard her worry that she was keeping Scott awake at night. Laci told her mom that she'd offered to sleep on the couch, but Scott would not allow it.

Later in the week, Sharon contacted Grogan to alert him to an e-mail she had received from Scott in response to her request that he return Laci's belongings.

Mom,
I have never taken the opportunity to apologize to either Ron or yourself for lying to you about my infidelity to Laci. I am truly

sorry that I was not forthcoming with you immediately. I know that both our goals is to find Laci and Conner, I am hoping together we can do more than separate.

I understand you are organizing a search this coming weekend, and you know that we are trying to put together a national search day this Sunday (I have attached a rough draft of the press release). I am wondering if you want to keep the two separate or try to combine them? . . . I am hoping that any search is one that directs people's efforts towards finding her safely, targeting medical institutions, houses and the like, the only possible end to this is them back in our arms. . . .

For all of us, and more important for Laci we need to find her and bring her back where she belongs, among us, we can do this if we can communicate and work together.

Scott

Attached to the e-mail was a flyer promoting a "National Search for Laci Day, Sunday, February 9, 2:00 P.M." It listed two phone numbers, one for the Modesto Police Department and a second for a "non-police tip line." This was the first Sharon heard about the private number, and she worried that calls might bypass police and go directly to Scott.

Grogan also met with Amy Rocha at headquarters to try to settle the question of Laci's jewelry. The detective was still trying to determine if any pieces were missing. Scott had initially told police that Laci was wearing a necklace, a wristwatch, earrings, and possibly a blue sapphire and diamond ring when he left her on Christmas Eve morning. In a follow-up conversation with Grogan on December 30, Scott described the items as diamond earrings, a diamond solitaire necklace, and one of two diamond-encrusted watches that Laci owned.

After meeting with members of Laci's family and a jewelry sales consultant, however, the police concluded that the gold-and-diamond watch and necklace Laci typically wore were the same items they had found in Laci's jewelry box. The only items that remained unaccounted for were the diamond earrings and one diamond-and-gold Croton watch that no one had seen her wear.

Amy told Grogan that Laci had recently tried using eBay to sell a Mickey Mouse watch with diamonds encircling the face. While the missing Croton watch had been videotaped for the eBay ad, the watch hadn't been sold there. Moreover, the videotape revealed that the watch was not running at the time, and there was no evidence that Laci had replaced the battery. Why would she be wearing a watch that wasn't working? Amy had no idea where the Croton watch might be.

At Grogan's request, Amy once again described Scott and Laci's visit to Salon Salon on December 23. The detective was especially interested in Laci's attire. Amy recalled that Laci was dressed in a cream-colored scarf with tassels and a black pea coat. Beneath the coat, she wore an off-white blouse with black flowers and a pair of beige slacks. Her shoes were black slip-on Mary Janes from Nine West. Other salon employees remembered the details of Laci's clothing differently, but as anyone who's examined many witnesses knows, this is not unusual. As much credence as eyewitness testimony is usually given, studies have demonstrated that it is not always reliable. If you place one person on each of four corners at an intersection and ask each of them to describe the same accident, you're likely to get four distinctly different stories. Recollection is not always reliable and police must account for this in any investigation.

Grogan also contacted local TV reporter Gloria Gomez of Channel 13 News, asking to view the raw footage of her interview with Scott at his home on January 29. Gomez agreed on the condition that they let her cameraman film them watching the video—allowing her to get her own news story out of the event.

Gomez told police that she conducted the twenty-five-minute interview with Scott in his living room. His only stipulation was that the program not air before six o'clock that evening, but he gave no reason for the request. Reporters from several other media outlets also sat down with Scott that day and they all had had to agree to the same stipulation.

In addition, Scott advised Gomez that the network could run no "teases" or "promos" before the interview. The reporter was surprised that Scott knew so much TV lingo. A final condition was that Gomez and the cameraman remove their shoes before entering Scott's house—yet another instance of Scott's inappropriate concern for his possessions, like his reaction to a possible scratch on his truck or his dining room table, when police searched the premises weeks before.

Once the two of them were inside the living room, Scott asked for a preview of every question Gomez would ask on-camera. She told him some of them, but not all.

At headquarters, police reviewed the raw video. While talking about his unborn son, they noticed, Scott simply referred to Conner simply as "baby," never referring to him as "his" or "ours." He declined to elaborate, saying only that "it was entirely too difficult to speak about."

"Do you go into the baby's room?" Gomez asked.

"No, that door's closed," Scott replied.

"How long will it remain closed?"

"Until there's a little guy in there . . ." Scott's voice broke and he seemed to choke back tears as he spoke.

In his amazing performances, for Sawyer, Gomez, and others, Scott repeatedly demonstrated his belief that the public and press could be duped. Scott's cracking voice and ability to cry on cue became more apparent once the police wiretaps revealed how swiftly he was able to turn them on and off.

Gomez called Scott the following day to clarify some issues. Scott refused to expand on his answers, and simply said "no comment" when asked if he had put his house up for sale or had traded in the Land Rover.

Later, I rebroadcast portions of Gomez's interview with Scott on *Catherine Crier Live*. The footage showed Scott's cell phone ringing during the taping. Instead of answering the call—which could have been someone with information about Laci—he jumped up, turned it off, and then told Gomez "they could pick up" where they left off. That was an ah-hah moment for me—an unconscious signal that Scott knew Laci was not coming home. This observation was picked up quickly by other talk shows, and Scott's reaction became an element of the prosecution's trial presentation.

Meanwhile, officers continued their search efforts in the San Francisco Bay. Investigators had discovered what appeared to be a red paint transfer on the right, or starboard, side of Scott's boat. Red paint was also found on a black plastic fishing pole holder on the same side, as well as on bolts that protruded through the outside of the boat. Samples were collected to compare with red navigational buoys in the bay, which "would provide an area for both cover and to tie off the boat and avoid flipping it when putting the body over the side." However, a match was never made.

Search teams used cadaver dogs to identify which areas of the bay to scan with sonar devices, but investigators worried that the grid searches would prove fruitless if the current were moving the body along the bottom of the bay. Police contacted Dr. Ralph Cheng from the U.S. Geological Survey for help in determining whether and where currents would carry weighted objects, such as a body, in San Francisco Bay. Dr. Cheng, a hydrologist with the U.S. Geological Survey, met with Detective Phil Owen in mid-February. Owen gave Dr. Cheng the necessary details: Laci weighed 153 pounds at the time of her disappearance, and had possibly been weighted by four anchors totaling thirty-two pounds. She may also have been wrapped in chicken wire and some type of plastic wrap. Dr. Cheng concluded that Laci's body could be somewhere in the waters off the southern or eastern areas of Angel Island.

Laci's family also organized searches that month. Although more than 350 people turned out to assist the family in their search of the San Joaquin Valley that first Saturday, the numbers diminished in the two subsequent searches.

Still desperate to locate her daughter, Sharon Rocha phoned Scott several days before Laci's expected due date of February 10 and left the following message:

"Scott, this is Sharon. I'm calling you to ask you to please either call Ron and I or call Brent or call the police department anonymously, disguise your voice, whatever you have to do, but please call and let us know where Laci is," Sharon said in the voice mail. "We need her home immediately, Scott. Please, I know you loved her once, please don't leave her out there. The baby's due date is Monday, we want to have her home, Scott. You loved her once. I think you still do. So please don't leave her out there all alone. Call us and let us know where she is, please."

Scott phoned her back.

"I lied to you about having an affair," Scott told Sharon. "That's right. But I don't know anything."

"I think you do. I think you're still lying. We need to have her home, Scott. Like I said, you loved her once."

"I loved her. I love my son. I love her. I want them home."

"I'm having a hard time believing any of that 'cause you're not showing it."

"She is my joy and my happiness."

"Then why did you kill her?" Sharon asked.

"I did not hurt her."

"Maybe you didn't hurt her, but you did kill her."

"I did not," Scott insisted.

"Well, you know what? You're the one that's gonna live with this. You're the one who's gonna burn in hell for doing this and lying to everybody. So, if you have any compassion, any soul at all, for any redemption at all, Scott, you've got to tell us where she is. Don't leave her out there all by herself."

On February 10, Laci's family and friends held a sunset candlelight vigil at East La Loma Park to mark her due date with remembrance and prayer. Three days later, Scott's family held a press conference in San Diego to announce that they were contacting hospitals and clinics around the country in the hope that Laci might arrive to give birth. Once again, Scott was conspicuously absent from both events.

On February 18, police served a second search warrant covering Scott's home and vehicle, along with a storage locker he had rented in the Fresno area since vacating the warehouse on Emerald Avenue. In the warrant applications police cited a number of reasons for the additional searches, and described at length Scott's "suspicious" behavior:

- Scott's response to being shown a faxed copy of a photo of him and Amber in early January, "Is that supposed to be me?"
- Scott's claim that he had purchased one ninety-pound bag of cement from Home Depot to make one anchor and had thrown the rest away in a garbage pail at his home. A subsequent examination of that trash pail failed to produce any evidence of loose cement. (He told Brent Rocha that the balance of the concrete was used in his driveway but told Brocchini it was used in the backyard.)
- Scott's five trips to the Berkeley Marina in rented or borrowed vehicles, including one right after police left a message indicating they knew Laci's body was in the bay.
- The whistle police believe he emitted upon learning in a voice mail from Sharon Rocha that the police had recovered an anchor—and not a body—during a search of the bay.
- Scott's claim that he had used the gun police recovered from the glove box in his pickup on a hunting trip he took with his dad in November 2002. Police learned that the gun was registered to Lee Peterson, but Lee was not aware that Scott was in possession of the weapon, nor did he see Scott carrying it during their hunting trip.
- Lee told police he had spoken to his son on Christmas Eve during the time period that Scott was driving from the Berkeley Marina to his residence, yet Scott did not mention that he owned a boat or that he had been fishing.

The affidavit also listed a number of the suspicious items police had collected during prior searches: the master bedroom duvet cover, with its apparent blood spots; the blood spots in Scott's truck; the blue tarp, umbrellas, and chicken wire from Scott's truck; Laci's jewelry; the vacuum cleaner and bag; the boat cover; and a pair of white tennis shoes from Laci's closet. Tests determined that the blood in the truck and on the duvet cover was human. Later in the month, forensic analysis would confirm that it was Scott's.

The twenty-page document also chronicled the contradictory statements Scott made in the early stages of the investigation—in particular, his claim to Detective Grogan on December 25 that he returned home at around 4:45 P.M. the day before, dumped the wash water from the blue bucket, took a shower, and washed his clothes before he noticed McKenzie in the backyard with his leash on. Yet in an earlier interview with Brocchini he had said that he noticed the dog immediately, and that McKenzie and their cat had run ahead of him into the house. He then quickly dumped the bucket before they tipped it over or drank from it.

The document also cited what appeared to be circular cement rings that corresponded in circumference to a plastic form containing water and cement residue found at the warehouse. It contained the conclusions from the bloodhound searches—that Laci had been transported by vehicle from her home, and then from Scott's warehouse along the route he had taken toward the Berkeley Marina. Details of Scott's statements to Amber Frey, and his attempts to conceal that relationship, were also noted.

On February 18, the detectives met Scott Peterson on his driveway. Scott wanted to know how long the searches were going to take. "At least one day," Grogan told him. Scott led the police through the back gate and into the home via the French doors. Pointing to two packed duffel bags on the floor, he explained that he needed several articles of clothing contained inside, and asked if he could take the bags with him. The police would have to search them first, he was told. Inside one, officers found a bottle of wine and a prescription bottle of Viagra, purchased from an Internet site called First Online Pharmacy. The label on the bottle indicated that the prescription was originally filled in July 2002, and had since been refilled several times.

Later, during a phone call, Grogan asked Scott about the Viagra.

"The prescription you had. Do you wanna tell me what that's all about?"

"Ah, what prescription?" Scott asked.

"The Viagra?"

"No. Personal deal," Scott replied.

Grogan apologized that the discovery of Viagra was leaked to the press.

"That doesn't bother me, don't worry about it," Scott replied. "Pretty small shit compared to where my family is, so I don't care."

Detectives also searched Scott's wallet. They found assorted credit cards and five-hundred-dollar bills. In one of the duffel bags, they discovered a white envelope containing $1,081 in cash. Another clear plastic sandwich bag was stuffed with $1,000 in cash.

"I looked at Scott's left and right hands," Grogan noted. "I saw he was not wearing a wedding band, but he had one ring in his property [in a duffel bag] that looked like a man's wedding band."

During the search, Grogan took the opportunity to quiz Scott about a variety of matters. Was Scott still operating out of the warehouse on Emerald Avenue? Scott said he still had two crates of product, a forklift, and a fax machine there, but the rest of his things were in his new warehouse facility in Fresno.

"Where's McKenzie?"

Scott told him the dog was in San Diego with his brother Joe and Joe's wife, Janey, who had been serving as Scott's public relations counselor in recent weeks.

"Do you have a storage locker?" Grogan asked.

He said he did and described its location to the detective. It was only then that Grogan revealed that the search warrant covered the locker, too.

"If the storage locker is in the warrant, then why did you ask me?" Scott asked.

"To see if you would tell me the truth," Grogan replied calmly.

Grogan then inquired about the 1-866-LACI-INFO line Scott had set up. He wanted access to the tips coming in on that line. Scott told him he had received very few calls, and forwarded only one to a lieutenant regarding a sighting in Fresno.

Grogan said that police had already received more than seven thousand tips. He was surprised that Scott had received only one. Scott told him there were others, but he had deemed them unimportant and had discarded them.

"Have you or your mother received the faxes coming in to the tip line?" Grogan asked.

"I'm not comfortable answering your questions," Scott replied.

Scott then told Grogan that the Laci info line was primarily for the press, but it was also designed to help him find out what was going on, since he wasn't being kept apprised of leads the police were following. Scott admitted that his mother had received one tip, but he declined to answer when Grogan asked if his mother had a fax machine.

"Is Kirk McAllister still your attorney?" Grogan asked.

"I don't want to answer that question," Scott replied.

Grogan asked Scott if he would come to headquarters for an interview.

"Why?" Scott asked, claiming that police had not been treating him "fairly." He argued that police were wasting valuable time investigating him rather than following up on serious leads in the case.

Detective Brocchini would later place a pretext phone call to the family's private tip line. Using details from one of the actual police tips received on January 5, he identified himself as Henry Lopez, and claimed he was a truck driver who had seen Scott's truck on Highway 580 at around 3:30 P.M. on Christmas Eve. He observed a bundle in the back of the boat wrapped in a blue blanket and thought it might have been a Christmas present.

Acting as Lopez, Brocchini stated that he would speak to police and left the Department's "cold line" as his contact number. The detective also asked an agent from the DOJ to place another call to the tip line, leaving the first name "Denise" and a phone number to see if the tip was forwarded.

Jackie Peterson did follow up on the agent's call. In a voice mail message, she requested that the woman call back to identify herself and provide more information. Brocchini's tip, however, received no return call. Later, Jackie would agree to fax Grogan any leads she received on the 1-866-LACI-INFO line, but she didn't get around to this for another ten days.

When Grogan finally received Jackie's "tips" on February 28, the information was not in any order. Of the thirty pages, ten were duplicates of a single page. The tips began on February 17 and ended on February 20. One tip that apparently came in on February 18 between 2:38 and 3:26 P.M. was missing. The pretext message from Al Brocchini was not among them, nor was the tip from the agent at the Department of Justice.

Stacey Boyers, the manager of the Laci Peterson Fund, later received two invoices from Jackie Peterson for the "1-866-LACI-INFO" tip line. Sharon Rocha denied payment, stating that the expenditure had not been approved. In addition, she said, there appeared to be no legitimate purpose for the line.

As they executed their search, investigators observed that the Petersons' Christmas tree had been taken down, but several wrapped gifts for grandparents and a child still lay on the floor. A mattress and box spring from a guest bedroom were propped against the window in the dining room area. The set had been replaced by a futon couch from Scott's warehouse. Although the Petersons' neighbor Karen Servas had said that Laci always opened those dining room curtains, Scott would later tell people that she left them closed in the winter to keep out any draft. Of course, most people like a bit of sunshine coming in on a chilly day, and it seemed that Scott was no different. He was using the mattress to block the view from the street while still allowing light to enter the room.

In a dresser in the master bedroom, police found what looked like dirty garments mixed in with Laci's clean clothes—as though they had been "removed from a hamper or worn and placed into dresser drawers." In one corner of the room, detective Rick House spotted a large brown paper grocery bag. Inside was a blue-green basket-weave handbag containing a beige shirt and a paperback romance novel. House recognized the purse and its contents from his search of Laci's Land Rover on December 26. Also inside the grocery bag was a white striped shirt, a pair of men's blue pajamas, a pair of women's blue and white Jockey panties, and two pairs of white ankle socks. House had seen none of these garments in the vehicle that day.

When Grogan reviewed the information, he developed a new theory that was never publicized. On Christmas morning, when Scott left for the warehouse, he may have cleaned out Laci's dirty clothing from the laundry hamper and taken the items with him. "Laci had likely changed into nightclothes on December 23, possibly the blue pajamas belonging to Scott Peterson, which may explain why those items were packaged separately in a paper bag," Grogan wrote in his report. "The pajamas may have been removed from Laci Peterson at the warehouse."

During a meeting with investigators the following month, the first-response team couldn't remember if any of that particular clothing had been in the washing machine or in the laundry basket next to the machine, and no one recalled seeing a paper bag in the area. Although police would continue to speculate about these items, Laci's body was ultimately discovered still clad in a bra, partial beige pants, and jockey underwear. It made no sense that Scott would redress his wife after killing her in her pajamas.

During the search, investigators also observed that the couple's cat, a gray-and-white Siamese, kept checking its bowl for food. An examination of the kitchen revealed that there seemed to be no food for the animal, which appeared to be very hungry. Scott told officers that he was going to the store to get cat food, but returned to the house several times empty-handed.

Concerned about the cat, officers searched inside the kitchen until they found a can of salmon in the kitchen, which the animal devoured. Grogan observed that the cat regularly went outside, rose on its hind legs, and scratched at one of the small trees in the rear yard. Grogan remembered Scott saying he'd bought the chicken wire to wrap around the trees to stop the cat from doing just that. Grogan inspected the trees and bushes in the rear yard; several showed evidence of scratches at the base, but none had been protected with the wire.

Inside the home, police noticed that several chairs, cushions, and other miscellaneous items had been piled into Conner's room, making it impossible to walk through the once-tidy space. Despite what he'd told Gloria Gomez—that he couldn't bring himself to go into the nursery until "a little guy" was sleeping in there—Scott had clearly turned the nursery into a storage space. The photographs of this room, juxtaposed with Scott's tearful lament, would provide powerful moments during his murder trial almost two years later.

On an upper shelf of the hallway closet, officers found three of the framed college diplomas in Scott's name that they'd seen displayed on the living room wall during the December search. Police also found a poster with a note from "Laci's husband" to volunteers that had been pinned to the door of the Red Lion Hotel, a photo of Laci, and a teddy bear in a box on the patio. The letter to volunteers read:

AS I SEE EVERY PERSON COMING THROUGH THIS DOOR, OR OUT SEARCHING, I TELL LACI ABOUT THEM, LOOKING FOR HER. EARLY THIS MORNING, I FELT SHE COULD HEAR ME. SHE THANKS YOU. LACI'S HUSBAND.

Throughout this case, I found so many moments like this that telegraphed what chumps Scott thought the rest of the world must be. He truly believed he could act his way out of suspicion.

Police also confiscated a bottle of prescription medication, as well as some Benadryl capsules and a sample of Robitussin cough syrup. Detectives were still looking at the possibility that Scott had poisoned Laci or immobilized her with drugs before killing her. (A thorough toxicology examination on Laci's remains would ultimately turn up no evidence of any such substances.)

At one point during the search, Grogan invited Laci's sister, Amy, into the house, asking if she could identify the garments Laci wore on December 23. Grogan showed her a pair of white size 7M slip-on shoes near the French doors leading out to the backyard and sunroom. Amy said she hadn't seen Laci wearing those shoes—her sister normally wore a size 6—but said that Laci might have worn that type of shoe while working in the yard.

In a later interview with Laci's mother, Sharon Rocha said that her daughter wore a "light boat shoe" around the house, but that she wore lace-up tennis shoes—not slip-ons—when she went walking in the mornings.

Checking the rest of the house, Amy made an unusual find in the bedroom. While going through Laci's dresser, she came upon a sheer black maternity blouse with a tan-colored square pattern and a black lining. It was the one Amy had described Laci wearing on December 23. Oddly, the blouse's sleeves were pulled inside out. Amy remarked that her sister wasn't one to remove and wad up a nice blouse, then put it in her underwear drawer. Bunched in the same drawer were several other items that appeared to have been worn, including a maternity skirt, maternity jeans, and a tan sweater.

Amy said that her sister would never have put dirty clothing on top of clean underwear. And, indeed, when Grogan later reviewed photos of the drawers taken during the initial search on December 26, none of the items Amy found was present.

Checking Laci's closet, Amy pointed out a pair of cream-colored pants clipped at the cuffs and hanging upside down on a hanger. The slacks looked wrinkled, suggesting that they'd been worn at least once after ironing. Amy also pointed out a scarf she believed Laci was wearing in Salon Salon the night before she disappeared. Sorting through Laci's shoes, though, she couldn't find the black Mary Janes her sister had on that evening.

The officers did allow themselves one light moment in the Petersons' home. As they were searching, one of the investigators spotted a crown that must have belonged to a party costume of Scott's. The officer put it on, and one of the crime scene photographers chuckled and snapped a picture. It was an innocent moment, under emotionally trying circumstances, but the incident would come back to haunt them later when defense lawyer Mark Geragos would use the photo at trial in a bid to paint the officers as callous clowns.

In a search of Scott's white Dodge, the original bill of sale for the Gamefisher boat was found in a brown duffel bag. Also in the bag was a receipt for $27.01 from a Borders' bookstore in Emeryville, California. Police speculated that the purchase might have included the books Scott sent to Amber Frey. Also in the duffel bag were three collection notices from the company that had installed the Peterson's swimming pool, and a notice of resignation from the Del Rio Country Club. The resignation form confirmed that Scott was attempting to sell his new country club membership. There was also a check made out to the Del Rio for $750.

Perhaps the strangest find, which police came across in a black plastic case on the passenger floorboard, was a typed short story, a single page long, concerning how a person of "low" character could be attracted to a person of "high" character. The story also dealt with "weak" souls and "strong" souls. "It is unknown if this was written by Scott Peterson to be delivered to Amber Frey or anyone else," Brocchini wrote in a report.

A day planner seized from the truck outlined Scott's activities between January 6 and February 23, 2003. In the date box for March 28 was written "Important Date for A." It was the only entry for the month. In a blue notebook also found in the truck was a second note, "3/28/03 important date for Amber."

A sealed envelope addressed to Kirk McAllister using Amber's home address was also confiscated from the Dodge but was later ruled as a privileged communication by the court. The police were never allowed to read the enclosed letter.

During the search of the storage locker that Scott had quietly rented at Security Public Storage on Woodland Avenue in Fresno, police found Scott and Laci's wedding album. It had been dumped into a metal wastebasket with some bills. Mark Geragos would later protest that Scott had simply used the trash can as a storage container for the album as he was moving into his new space, but the choice of containers was not lost on members of the jury. Police also confiscated a buck knife with an "unknown" stain on the handle and blade, two sets of boat wheels with reddish brown stains, and miscellaneous papers and other items.

As police searched, Scott got on the phone with the Dish Network. A clerk for the company later told police that at 2:03 P.M. she received a call from a man identifying himself as "Mr. Peterson." Laci Peterson was a Dish Network subscriber.

"I have an account in my wife's name," Scott had said. As the clerk told police, "He wanted to disconnect their account because he was moving. I offered him a Dish moving option to have the service continued at his new residence. He said he didn't want to do that because he was moving overseas." Police would eventually conclude that Scott pulled the plug on his satellite TV to prevent detectives from finding the two explicit pornography channels.

This information would produce heated debate at trial. The defense objected strenuously to its admission. The issue also generated some serious argument on my program. Many pundits pointed out that it isn't illegal to watch this garbage, and that there's nothing about the act of watching an X-rated film that constitutes evidence of guilt in a murder case. Allowing the jury to consider it, they said, would be highly prejudicial. However, I agreed with Judge Delucchi's ruling to admit the information. It wasn't the fact that Scott was watching porn, but the idea that he was behaving as if Laci wasn't coming home, that qualified this testimony as evidence of his state of mind. Certainly no one was ever outrageous enough to suggest that his wife would have approved of his new subscription, had she come home with Conner to find him watching these channels.

The twenty investigating officers, under the direction of Crime Scene Manager Rudy Skultety, spent about ten hours inside Scott's house on February 18, along with Detective Grogan and profiler Sharon Hagan. Reporters were stationed outside the home throughout the day, and many remained overnight and into the next day, when investigators returned to continue their work. Journalists watched as detectives took measurements of the perimeter, driveway, and other sections of the property. Ultimately, police confiscated nearly one hundred items, including fur samples from McKenzie for comparison with hairs found on a blue tarp that washed up in mid-January. Those tests did not produce a match.

During the afternoon, Grogan received a call from Scott saying that he didn't want police to allow anyone to enter his house while the search was being carried out.

"Are you specifically speaking about Sharon Rocha?" Grogan asked.

"Yes," Scott replied. He told Grogan that he might meet with Sharon later to give her some of Laci's things, but he was not yet granting her permission to remove any items.

While the search continued, Scott stayed with his sister, Anne Bird, in Berkeley. Grogan later talked with Bird about the family's recent trip to Disneyland with Scott and Laci in late November 2002. The thirty-seven-year-old mother of two told him that she and her family had joined her brother John and his wife, Scott and Laci, and Jackie Peterson for a two-day visit to the theme park. Anne had visited with the Petersons several times after learning that Jackie was her birth mother, but she always considered her adoptive parents to be her "true parents."

Anne recalled that Scott and Laci seemed "very happy" during the family's Thanksgiving trip. Scott had even rented Laci a wheelchair so that he could wheel his pregnant wife around Disney's California Adventure Park and "pamper her."

Anne didn't think Laci needed the wheelchair, but she went along with it to humor Scott. Scott told police he had rented it "to cut down on the amount of walking" she had to do. The young couple appeared to get along well, and Scott seemed excited over his impending fatherhood. During the trip, he carried Anne's six-month-old son in a car seat. He even comforted him one night at dinner and managed to stop his crying, Anne recalled.

While Scott was staying with Anne during the search, they talked about Laci's disappearance. Anne wondered what he thought had happened to her. He described the suspicious purple car with Confederate flags that had supposedly been spotted parked near his home on the morning of Christmas Eve. Kim McGregor's mother had reported hearing screams coming from the park at about 10:15 that morning, Scott told her. He theorized that his wife's disappearance could be tied to some "psycho" who abducted her that morning—or, he added, by Kim McGregor's boyfriend. Having done some research, Scott said that Laci was the fifth pregnant woman in the state of California to disappear in recent years. He also speculated that Laci's body was in an area known as Mapes Ranch because, he told Anne, the bloodhounds had led officers to that area.

During the conversation, Scott admitted to Anne that he had an affair while living in San Luis Obispo when he and Laci were first married.

When I interviewed Anne Bird, she told me something that I never heard elsewhere throughout this investigation. Before the November trip to Disneyland, Jackie confided to her that "Scott and Laci were having trouble *again*." This comment made Anne watch the couple carefully. She noticed that Scott seemed to be going through all the motions, wheeling Laci around and catering to her needs, but upon reflection she thought that he seemed distant throughout the trip.

Anne recalled that after Laci's disappearance, Jackie's attitude about Laci's mother changed dramatically. Beforehand, Jackie had referred to Sharon as "cool." By late January, she would be calling her "that bitch with all those 'catty' friends."

Anne also observed that Scott was a heavy drinker, and that his excessive use of alcohol continued during future visits to her home. On one occasion, he called her house and found that an attractive babysitter he had met before was there. He stopped off and bought the ingredients for a special kind of martini popularized by the TV show *Sex and the City*. Once home, he mixed the drinks and tried to get the young woman to "party" with him. Anne was surprised at his behavior; his wife and baby were still missing.

In mid-February, police received a strange tip from an American Airlines employee claiming that Laci Peterson had called the reservation line almost two months earlier, on December 22 or 23, to book tickets to San Diego for Christmas Day. The agent, who wanted to remain anonymous, told police that Scott could be heard yelling in the background. Apparently, he wanted to use frequent flyer miles rather than pay for the $98 round trip tickets.

It's unclear what finally prompted the ticket agent to call in February after being silent for so long. However, one thing is certain—the agent provided plenty of detail. "Susan said I could use her miles," Scott reportedly shouted when Laci tried to explain to him that it would be better to save the free miles for a more expensive ticket.

Laci had booked two seats for a flight from San Francisco to Orange County, returning the following day. The reservation was such that she and Scott could pay at the counter on the day of departure. The agent remembered that Scott wanted to fly to San Diego, but settled on Orange County because the fare was lower. The agent couldn't understand why Scott would want his pregnant wife to ride in a car for three hours after a one-hour flight, just to save a few dollars. Laci also asked about flights to Mexico in early February, but the agent advised that she would need her doctor's permission to fly that late in her pregnancy. Scott sounded relieved when it became apparent that Laci wouldn't be able to accompany him, indicating that it would save him money, the agent recalled. Laci explained that Scott's company was paying for his ticket.

Police subsequently subpoenaed the American Airlines accounts for Scott, Laci, and Scott's sister, Susan Caudillo. What those subpoenas produced, if anything, is not known. The conversation would have been inadmissible in court in any event because there was no real proof that the caller was actually Laci or that it was indeed Scott yelling in the background. Even if this was established, the exchange only demonstrates that Scott could lose his temper. Nothing about the call incriminated him in the murder of his family, but it certainly suggested that there may have been much more going on in those closing hours before Christmas Eve than has yet been established.

A number of these intriguing ancillary stories developed as February drew to a close. Several checks addressed to Laci and Scott Peterson were discovered in the possession of a convicted forger named Sarah Taberna. The checks were cash advance drafts from a credit card company. When first questioned, Scott explained that he hadn't been regularly checking the mail delivered to his warehouse, and perhaps the material was stolen from there. Then Scott said that he often took his mail home, and thought that the checks could have been stolen from there. He suggested that whoever had taken the checks could be linked to Laci's disappearance, and that the person might have stolen the checks during her abduction. Grogan noted Scott's concerns, and promised to follow up. Scott insisted that he wanted the thief prosecuted. Taberna, who had brought the checks to the police in the first place and admitted that she'd stolen them, was cleared of any connection with Laci's murder.

Another story involving a check arose from a search of Scott's truck. Police found a draft for $450 made out to a Gainesville, Florida, psychic named Noreen Renier and signed by Jackie Peterson. There was a note attached, requesting that Scott mail it to Renier. Apparently Scott stuck it in the glove compartment and forgot about it.

In a phone conversation with Renier, Grogan learned that Jackie had hired the psychic to assist in the search for Laci. Jackie sent her one of Laci's T-shirts, but Renier claimed that the garment was of no value to her, and asked for something more personal, such as a toothbrush, hairbrush, or a shoe, to complete a psychic connection. When Craig Grogan contacted her, Renier asked him to mail her a shoe or something else she could use in trying to help find Laci. Grogan said he would consider her request and call her back.

In early March, the detective received a second call from Renier. She had performed her first session, she reported, and determined that Laci was the victim of an assault and was most likely deceased. Renier said she had not yet established Laci's whereabouts and could not point to an exact location where a search should be conducted.

Grogan later received a report on Renier's psychic session in which she claimed to be speaking to Laci. She claimed that Laci had been struck in the head with a baseball bat or some similar object as she was walking through a doorway. Renier reported experiencing the trip to the San Francisco Bay, and described the scenery and railroad tracks she passed before ending at a large body of water. Renier also talked about cement weights being tied around the body. Police read the report, but determined that it contained no new information.

Police also recovered from Scott's Dodge truck a bag full of Laci Peterson missing person posters with the original reward of $25,000, rather than the half million dollars now offered, along with a second sack of Laci Peterson buttons. Volunteers had run short of these materials. Now they would learn why.

Another interesting storyline revolved around a man from a small town in Missouri. In mid-February, the man left four messages on Sharon Rocha's answering machine. "Just give me the word, and I'll take care of Scott," the messages said. The caller left a return phone number.

Believing that the caller might be a hit man, Sharon notified Detective Grogan. He learned that the man lived at home with his mother, and had a criminal record for theft by use of a computer. During their conversation, the man told Grogan he had been following the Laci Peterson case. When Amber emerged, he became convinced that Scott was involved in Laci's disappearance. In an attempt to assist police, the caller had located Scott's phone number and in late January left him a message, saying, "I'm your girlfriend's psychiatrist, she told me everything. I'm going to turn you in."

The man from Missouri believed the message would "put pressure" on Scott and "force" him to confess. He told Grogan the key to the case was in the child's nursery. He suggested police locate a teddy bear in the room and check it for dust. If it were dusty, it would mean that Scott did kill Laci. Any person who is actually grieving for the loss of their wife and unborn child would go into the nursery and hold the child's toys, he said.

When asked about the messages he left for Laci's mother, the man said he was simply trying to offer his assistance in the investigation. After a subsequent background check on the man, police decided he was harmless.

By early March, forensic testing produced some meaningful new information. The single hair recovered from a pair of pliers found in Scott's boat at the warehouse was consistent with a hair from Laci's hairbrush. Because there was no root affixed to the recovered piece, only mitochondrial comparisons could be made. Statistically, the hair might belong to roughly one in six hundred women in the Modesto area.

Unwittingly, the officer who retrieved the hair, Dodge Hendee, became the center of a major controversy that played out over several days during Scott's preliminary hearing. When the evidence envelope was opened for testing, the single hair had become two. Mark Geragos insinuated that the hairs might have been planted, recalling allegations about O. J. Simpson's glove. But the judge refused to suppress the evidence, finding it more likely that the hair found clamped between the serrated pliers was broken and simply came apart in the bag. Ultimately, the report concluded that "the ends of those hairs looked like they had been mashed and torn between two hard objects, not inconsistent with needle nose pliers." Some plant material, fibers, and a substance with adhesive qualities had adhered to one of the hairs, but an attempt to match the adhesive to Scott's duct tape was unsuccessful. When compared with Laci's known hair, however, the evidence "appeared to be in the same range of variation."

In March, the police publicly reclassified the Laci Peterson case as a homicide.

"As the investigation has progressed, we have increasingly come to believe that Laci Peterson is the victim of a violent crime," detectives announced at a press conference. "This investigation began as a missing persons case, and we all were hopeful that Laci would return safely. However, we have come to consider this a homicide case."

Police also announced a change in the criteria for the $500,000 reward being offered for information leading to Laci's safe return. "Based on this belief, an additional reward is now being offered for information that leads to her location and recovery," investigators said.

Police also delivered two binders with information related to the investigation to the Stanislaus district attorney's office, officially involving them in the case for the first time.

At headquarters, Grogan continued to work the evidence. In early March, he reviewed a report from John Yarborough of the Institute of Analytical Interview in Parker, Arizona. Police had mailed Yarborough several videotaped interviews of Scott Peterson for micro-expression analysis. A micro-expression is a very short facial expression of an intense, concealed emotion. Yarborough and his colleagues at the Institute were trained to read and interpret those involuntary messages for emotion.

Yarborough pointed to two occasions where he saw "significant micro expressions." The first was when Scott was asked about blood in the truck during an interview with KTBU Channel 2. He said Scott "micro-expressed" fear when asked a follow-up question if Laci's blood was in the truck. The second "micro-expression," this one of anger, came when Scott was questioned about the shades being closed at his home on December 24, during a time when Laci would normally have opened them.

Yarborough indicated these two occasions were "hot spots," though he did concede that he didn't know exactly what Scott had been thinking at the time he made those expressions. However, he did note that Scott referred to Laci in the past tense on more than one occasion.

Grogan also reviewed a Voice Stress Analysis that had been commissioned by a local television station. Expert Al Starewich had performed the test, using videotape interviews of Scott Peterson with members of the media.

Starewich found that Scott was lying when he said he had nothing to do with Laci's disappearance. He was telling the truth about some other matters—injuring his knuckle, for example—but he was nervous another blood stain was found in his truck. He showed abnormal stress when speaking about saltwater on his clothing, Starewich added, and he lied about telling Laci about Amber. The report concluded that, "Scott knows that Laci is never coming home." None of this information would ever be made public, but it may have helped officers tailor their future interactions with Scott.

At headquarters, police took a closer look at the phone book found on Scott's kitchen counter on Christmas Eve. It had been open to an advertisement for a criminal defense attorney when police entered the kitchen. While examining the directory, detectives noticed that the page with the attorney's ad was thicker than others in the book, and that the book naturally opened to that ad. The discovery left police uncertain whether Scott opened the book to that page on purpose or the already open book flipped to the advertisement on its own. Police later learned that the attorney, Richmond Herman, paid extra for the special feature.

Police also spoke with the criminologist who examined the needle-nosed pliers and a pair of wire cutters that had been found in Scott's warehouse to determine if either had been used to cut chicken wire found in the back of Scott's truck. Dean De Young of the California Department of Justice determined that neither pair had been used to cut the wire. He saw that the needle nosed pliers were rusted, and asked police if they had been in contact with water or salt water. Police confirmed that they had been in salt water when found in the bottom of Scott's boat.

Grogan continued his search for Laci's gold-and-diamond Croton watch. He learned that on December 31, 2002, a woman named

Deanna Marie Renfro had pawned a gold Croton watch for twenty dollars. The name Renfro was familiar to police. In late December, police had interviewed Marie and Donnie Renfro about a woman who claimed to be the victim of a rape followed by a satanic ritual perpetrated by several people traveling in a brown van. The victim claimed that after the assault she heard the group discuss a Christmas Day death, which they promised she would read about in the newspapers. The police were interested in the Renfros because they had been traveling in a brown Chevrolet van and were camping in the park. Yet detectives ultimately decided the cases were not linked. Although Mark Geragos would introduce the pawn slip at trial, implying that it was evidence that someone had robbed Laci for the watch, the description of the pawned item didn't reference the diamond bezel on Laci's watch, and it seemed unlikely that they were one and the same pieces. The police and jury never bought the argument by defense counsel, and Laci's Croton watch was never recovered.

Most of the other information police gathered through the eight thousand tips that were received led nowhere. The recovery of Elizabeth Smart in mid-March prompted a number of calls about whether the course of the investigation would change. Several tipsters claimed that Laci was having an affair with a trainer at her gym, but they could find no proof of such a relationship.

Other tips were a bit far-fetched. A woman named Penny Gagnon called to report that she'd been propositioned by Scott Peterson in a California bar in October 2002. Gagnon claimed she had been fighting with her husband of three years and had gone to a bar one afternoon to cool off. During her alleged encounter with Scott, Gagnon claimed that he spoke of killing his wife and disposing of her body by weighting it down and sinking it in a body of water.

"He came straight out and said, 'You wanna have an affair?' And I said, 'You're a very good looking guy, but I'm married,'" Gagnon told Detective Brocchini during a phone interview. "He said, 'Well, so am I.' I said 'Well, I'm a Christian, that's not my thing.' He said, 'Well, my wife's pregnant and I wanna kill her.' And . . . and it's like so, so off the wall that it didn't even sink in what he was saying. I didn't even question it really. Well, I did question him, I said, 'Why do you wanna kill her?' But not thinking he was serious, I guess is what I'm trying to say."

"He tell ya how far along she was?" Brocchini asked.

"He said about six months, and I said 'You don't wanna kill her, you guys have a new life ahead of you."

"So then what?"

"Then I remember him saying, 'If you were to kill somebody, and didn't wanna get caught, how would you do it?' If I had thought he was serious, there's no way I woulda given him any ideas, but I just said I would kill 'em and tie a weight around their ankles and throw 'em in the ocean."

Brocchini subsequently interviewed Gagnon's husband, who said his wife had no reason to lie. He supported her story, saying that she'd told him the same story right after seeing Scott on the news when Laci went missing. Of course, she waited months to come forward to the police. Yet when she was asked where the encounter had taken place, and whether she could provide any proof that she'd actually been there at the time—such as a credit card receipt—Gagnon was unable to comply. Investigators remained skeptical, and never followed up on her story. That is hardly unusual. Reports of this nature always emerge during high-profile cases. Important leads can fall by the wayside as the police try to perform triage on the constant flow of information, but most investigators work diligently to separate the serious from the merely sensational.

Even family members offered leads that were dead ends. Lee Peterson dredged up other cases that bore no resemblance to Laci's disappearance, sending the police copies of articles he felt might lead them in new directions—and, no doubt, away from Scott.

Despite Scott's continuing pleas of innocence, his life was being severely affected. He told Heather and Mike Richardson that 60 to 70 percent of his clients at Tradecorp refused to see him. His employer had agreed to keep him on, but he had given Scott thirty days to hire someone as a figurehead so he could continue working behind the scenes.

When police interviewed Mike Richardson, he said it seemed odd that Scott had chosen him to be best man at his wedding. The men had only been friends a short time, and Scott had several brothers— none of whom were in the wedding party. Scott's friend Aaron Fritz was a groomsman, along with another friend named Eric. Mike could not recall Eric's last name.

Another friend, Brian Argain, told police that he was no longer comfortable associating with Scott. Scott had left him several messages asking him to get together for a round of golf, but he repeatedly declined. Argain also noted that while Scott was usually direct with him, he no longer looked him in the eye when talking about his wife's disappearance. He said many of Scott's friends felt the same way, claiming that they'd become suspicious of him in recent weeks. As the receipt found in his belongings confirmed, things were so tense for Scott that the country club was refunding his $23,000 membership fee.

He was still a free man, but his world was rapidly shrinking.

# CHAPTER SEVENTEEN

# APRIL 2003

On April 13, around 4:15 P.M., Cerrito residents Michael Looby and Nicole Belanger were walking their dog beneath a cloudy, threatening sky. They had strolled about a quarter mile off a popular bike path near the Richmond Inner Harbor on the northern shore of San Francisco Bay. It was low tide, and their dog stopped in a grassy area amidst the marshland and began sniffing something furiously. When Looby walked over to investigate, he discovered what looked like the decomposed body of a baby.

Looby and Belanger hurried to a nearby housing development, where they asked a resident, Keith Woodall, to call the police. The Richmond fire and police departments wasted no time responding. Lying among the leaves and other debris, near a rocky area called "the breakers," they found the fetus. It was lying on its back with its head tilted upward. Although all four limbs were attached, the right arm was almost severed. At 4:53, the town's fire captain, Erik Newman, officially recorded that the infant was dead.

None of the investigators at the scene was able to determine the fetus's gender or race. Its genitals were not intact, and its intestines were exposed. A piece of nylon twine was entangled in the remains and appeared to be looped and tied or tangled around the neck. Coroner's Investigator Chris Martinez, a deputy with the Contra Costa Sheriff's Office, took several photographs of the scene and of the fetus, then gently wrapped it in a towel and placed it in doubled plastic bags for transport to the Contra Costa Coroner's Office.

The police ruled it an unexplained death. A preliminary police report stated that the infant, which weighed three and a half pounds, was full-term and appeared to be only a few days old. It was ashen gray and appeared to be essentially disemboweled. There was no obvious cause of death, as the external trauma had most likely occurred post-mortem.

In the wake of the discovery, a missing persons teletype was sent out to agencies across California. At eight o'clock the following morning, a clerk with the Modesto Police Department notified Detective Grogan about the gruesome discovery. The Richmond Police Department was investigating.

Although he was due in court to testify in a kidnapping case, Grogan immediately called Contra Costa County Detective David Villalobos, leaving him a voice mail before he turned off his cell phone and entered the courtroom.

During the lunch recess, Grogan received a call about another body.

This time it was an adult female, just found off Point Isabel in Richmond. Contacting Lieutenant Pete Small with the East Bay Regional Park Police, Grogan learned that park visitors had reported finding the remains shortly before noon. The responding officers had located the body of a woman washed ashore directly east of Brooks Island—the very spot where Scott said he was fishing on Christmas Eve.

Lying prone on the rocks, the body was clad in a bra and what appeared to be remnants of pants. The park police had not located a skull, and both legs were missing below the knee. Smalley knew about the fetus that had been recovered from the same general vicinity; the recent stormy weather must have moved the bodies onto shore, he thought.

Small suggested that the Modesto police hasten to the scene. The press was already arriving, and, more important, it was still low tide. Soon the body would have to be moved, and any evidence might be washed away. Grogan instructed Small to photograph, videotape, and recover the body as soon as possible, whether Modesto police had arrived or not. He also requested that no details about the clothing or condition of the body be released.

Sergeant Carter and Detectives Hendee and Owen helicoptered to Point Isabel Park. As they landed, the officers could see reporters already camped out in the parking lot just east of the shoreline. From that vantage point, it wasn't possible to see the body, which was concealed beneath a yellow tarp, but two news helicopters had already taken footage, and one of the choppers was still circling.

Sergeant Dave Dubowy of the Park Police greeted the Modesto investigators and led them down to the cordoned site. This area of the beach was frequented by joggers and dog-walkers, he told them, given the traffic, he didn't believe the body had been there long.

The badly decomposed body had no head, hands, or feet. There was nothing below the right knee and only the tibia and fibula bones remained beneath the left. A good portion of the woman's buttocks, hips, and lower abdomen were intact, but they had undergone extensive decomposition. The rib cage and part of the spine were exposed, and the stomach and most internal organs appeared to be missing.

While the officers would have to wait for DNA testing before a positive ID could be made, there was some very telling evidence still clinging to the body. The bra that was fastened around the woman's chest was virtually intact, and bore a Bali label. Her pants were so decomposed that most of the fabric was mere fuzz, but the waistband revealed a Motherhood maternity label, and the color of the trousers, off-white or cream, could still be determined. The last article was a pair of Jockey brand underwear, also severely degraded.

One other item that was carefully retrieved was a strip of gray duct tape, about twelve to fourteen inches long, that had been affixed vertically down the front of the woman's pants.

Police on the scene interviewed A. Gonzalez, the woman who had reported finding the body. "Around 11:45 A.M., I was walking down the shoreline and just kept looking over the rocks, watching some dogs. And I was curious what they were looking at and I looked . . . and it was a body, face-down, and I saw the body and went and called authorities." When asked how she knew it was a body, she admitted that the decomposition had made it difficult. What she saw "had the shape of a body, but it looked like someone had wrapped it like a mummy." Gonzalez, who had a bachelor's degree in gerontology, was studying to be a physical therapist. Having taken a number of anatomy and physiology courses, she said, she had worked with a lot of cadavers.

Gonzalez also said that the body had been "pretty tangled in the rocks," and that she hadn't seen a head. The body was half in the water and half out, and from the lower thighs down, she couldn't see the legs. Gonzalez reported that there were a few additional people walking around, including one other woman who had spotted the body, but had already left the scene.

The interviewing officer asked if there was anything else they should know. Gonzalez said, "After the body gets investigated, they have to know there were dogs eating it."

The officer repeated, "There were some dogs eating it?"

Yes, she confirmed. "So all the markings aren't going to be true to the crime scene."

"Okay, could you say how many dogs there were?"

Gonzalez said there was definitely "one big black dog" that they'd spotted near the body. "It left a while ago. I think the owner was concerned about it getting sick."

Dodge Hendee reboarded the helicopter and took digital videotape and photographs of the recovery sites for both bodies. He also recorded their relationship to Brooks Island and the Berkeley Marina.

Officers from the Contra Costa Coroner's Office rolled the female body into a sheet and placed it inside a body bag. Police then ordered that cadaver dogs be brought to the scene to search for additional body parts.

Brian Peterson of the Contra Costa Coroner's Facility (no relation to Scott) performed the autopsy on the fetus, now referred to as "Baby Doe." He determined that it was a full-term male infant in an advanced stage of decomposition. The skin was discolored but well-preserved. He estimated the gestational age of the fetus at between thirty-three and thirty-eight weeks.

Dr. Peterson was unable to determine whether the umbilical cord, only half a centimeter long and ragged at one end, had been tied or if it had simply detached in the water. The decomposition also prevented him from concluding whether the fetus had actually gone through the birthing process. He did, however, find evidence of meconium in the body, indicating that the baby had most likely not been born alive.

Meconium is a substance that accumulates in a fetus's lower intestine in utero. In 95 percent of live births, a baby expels the meconium within twenty-four hours after he or she is born. The fact that meconium was protruding from Baby Doe's anus indicated that if he was born alive, he probably did not survive for more than twenty-four hours. Dr. Peterson found no deformities or abnormalities that could have prevented the baby from surviving outside the womb if properly cared for.

The lungs were found to be small and wet, and Dr. Peterson could not say whether the baby had ever taken a breath. The stomach was empty, and there was no animal or fish activity. This was quite unusual given the advanced state of decomposition and suggested that the baby had been in utero until very recently. The body's condition also made it impossible to use its weight to reach an accurate estimate about age. Yet the height indicated that the child was close to full term. An estimated gestational age of nine months was based on its crown-heel length, although it could have been a large seven-and-a-half-month-old infant, since such measurement standards are merely averages.

Whether Conner was born alive became a critical issue at trial. Defense counsel Mark Geragos would tell the jury in his opening statement that Conner was carried almost to full term and was born alive. Since his client had been under police scrutiny from the moment Laci was reported missing, there was no way Scott could have removed and later disposed of Conner's body. Someone else must be responsible. The debate over Conner's life would become critical in the battle for Scott's as well.

None of the coroner's observations eliminated the possibility that this was Scott and Laci Peterson's child.

The coroner noted that a piece of fiberglass-type tape was loosely wrapped around the fetus's neck and left shoulder when the body was recovered. The tape appeared to be knotted at the point of the shoulder. Speculation would abound as to whether the loop and knot were man-made or simply the result of churning waters entangling the body in floating debris. There was only a two-centimeter gap between the material and the neck, which meant that the circumference of the loop was smaller than the baby's head. This could support the notion that the noose was affixed by someone after the baby was born, but the prosecution experts had other theories. The baby's brain had liquefied, allowing for the possibility that the loop could have slipped over the collapsed head. Furthermore, if the tape had been tied around the neck, the state would argue that there should have been a residual mark on the skin at the throat. There was none.

The coroner ruled that the autopsy could not reveal a cause of death.

Detective Grogan was left with the grim task of informing Laci's family of the discoveries. On the afternoon of Monday, April 14, Grogan left messages for Sharon Rocha, Ron Grantski, and Brent Rocha, requesting that they contact him.

About four o'clock he spoke to Sharon Rocha, informing her that the bodies of an adult female and an infant had been recovered from the San Francisco Bay. They had not yet been identified, but he promised to keep her updated. A little later, he relayed the same message to Laci's brother.

Around ten o'clock that evening, Grogan contacted the family again to prepare them for breaking news reports that the female's body had no head, hands, or legs. Both Sharon and Brent asked Grogan where Scott was. He did not know. Sharon told Grogan that she'd left a message for Scott the previous day, but her call went un-returned.

She then checked with Jackie Peterson, who had been trying to reach him since the previous evening and was beginning to worry. Sharon told Jackie that she thought Scott might want to be with family because of the news about the bodies. The press reports alone, however, weren't enough to convince Jackie that these were the bodies of Laci and Conner. She told Sharon about another female body, similarly mutilated, that had washed up in January.

That same evening, an autopsy was performed on the Jane Doe. It was in an advanced state of decomposition, missing not only its head, and portions of the lower legs, but all internal organs from the ab-dominal cavity except the uterus. Since no evidence of tool marks was found at the bone joints of the missing appendages, the medical ex-aminer performing the autopsy concluded that either someone with great surgical skill had removed them, or the victim had been weighted in those areas, and then the water's currents and decompo-sition had caused the limbs to pull apart at the joints. The bones bore no sign of injuries that occurred before death, such as resorption lines, callous formation, or rounding of fracture margins. However, Dr. Peterson found that the woman's fifth, sixth, and ninth ribs were broken; the fracturing appeared to have occurred shortly before her death.

Jane Doe's missing limbs suggested that the body had been in the water a long time. The corpse also showed signs of extensive fish ac-tivity. In foraging on human remains, fish start by eating exposed areas of soft tissue that are unprotected by clothing. Once the exte-rior flesh has been eaten away they will swim up sleeves or through other gaps in clothing, and often find their way into the chest cavity and consume the internal organs.

In a subsequent review of the autopsy at my request, San Anto-nio's chief coroner, Dr. Vincent DiMaio, confirmed the Contra Costa coroner's findings, and theorized that the fractures were most likely sustained around the time the woman died. It appeared they were the result of one violent blow, such as a kick, to the left side of the rib cage. The injuries could have been the result of similar violence to the body shortly after death, but simply dropping the body in transit would not likely result in such breaks.

While the body could have been identified as Laci Peterson by the tattoo on her left ankle, a missing ovary removed when she was a child, or the abdominal scar from the surgery, the state of decomposition eliminated these possibilities. Dental records were useless because the head was absent. The body did have an enlarged uterus, which signaled her pregnancy, but there was no physical evidence of a vaginal delivery. The fact that the woman had been wearing underpants supported this theory, he noted. The cervix and area below the belly button were intact, and there was no sign of a man-made incision to remove the baby. Yet a tear in the body's abdominal wall was large enough to permit the fetus to exit the womb through it, as interior pressure from bacteria and gases built up inside the mother—a sad phenomenon known as a "coffin birth."

In his confidential report, Dr. Peterson noted that the condition of the female's body was consistent with an exposure of three to six months in "a marine environment." There were barnacles adhering to the exposed skeleton. Some of the deep muscle tissue was still red, indicating that decomposition had not progressed completely through the remains. The cold temperature of the San Francisco Bay had slowed the decomposition process.

A toxicology examination of the woman's tissue revealed no illicit drugs or poison, only elevated levels of caffeine and PEA (a product of decomposition). As with Baby Doe, the autopsy alone could not determine the cause of death.

A large plastic bag bearing the logo of a company called Target Products, Ltd. also washed up in the area where the two bodies came ashore. It had a piece of silver duct tape wrapped around it. The police recovered the bag and used the Internet to identify Target Products as a Canadian company. The owner said that the bag sounded like what they used to cover pallets of their product, concrete grout used in bridge construction. They were currently shipping material to the San Francisco Bay area for projects, including the Richmond Bridge.

After the bodies were found, the detectives also began recovering fliers that had been posted by Scott Peterson. They wanted to know if he had used duct tape to affix them, if the brand matched the strip on the woman's body, and if the adhesive on the tape could be linked to a substance on the hairs found in Scott's boat.

A t 5:50 that evening, police received a call from a woman reporting a suspicious incident. While she and her husband were dining at a restaurant called Skates over the weekend, the couple noticed something unusual in the bay through the restaurant's window. It looked like dark brown or black hair bobbing up and down with the waves about 150 feet from the water's edge. She said "the hair" did not appear to be attached to a person, which was the reason she didn't report it. It wasn't until hearing the news that police had recovered a headless body at Point Isabel, about three miles north of the restaurant, that she realized the incident might be significant.

Kristine Crawford and her certified cadaver dog, Dakota, arrived at the scene at 6:30 in the evening. Dakota, a six-year-old pit bull terrier, was a seasoned investigator who had taken part in sixty searches since being certified. A second dog, Merlin, and her handler, Eloise Anderson, were also called in to search the southern portion of the beach. When Dakota and Kristine Crawford started traveling north along the shoreline, Dakota hit on a piece of fabric tightly wedged between two boulders. In almost the same area, she showed interest in the breeze, which was blowing onto the shore in an easterly direction. Dakota walked into the water, but was forced to stop when it reached her shoulders. Investigators flagged the spot for future reference.

As they were wrapping up the search, an unidentified woman told the officers that she had spotted a tarp in another area of the beach. However, follow-up using the cadaver dog indicated no ties to the body.

The police also found pieces of duct tape stuck to some of the rocks in the area, and one officer located a dense metal rod that was wrapped in duct tape. Although the rod broke into pieces when he attempted to dislodge it from the rocks, he kept it as evidence.

As Grogan was overseeing police activity on the shoreline, Detective Brocchini was searching for Scott. It was likely he had quit driving his white 2002 Dodge Dakota truck, with its GPS tracking system because he suspected that he was being followed. Scott had apparently traded vehicles with his brother, John. Agents were watching his parents' house, his father's business, and an address in San Diego where the Dodge truck was parked. At one point in the evening, Lee and Jackie Peterson left their residence in Jackie's 1998 Jaguar. Scott was not with them.

On Wednesday, April 16, around 9:00 A.M., Brocchini finally located Scott through wiretaps on his cell phone. Peterson was checking his voice mail from 3949 Le Cresta Avenue in San Diego.

Surveillance units were immediately dispatched to the location, which was a house belonging to his sister Anne Bird's adoptive parents. Scott was staying there with Anne's permission, and using their Lexus instead of his Mercedes-Benz. Forty-five minutes later, Brocchini got word that Scott was walking around the neighborhood. An agent reported that his appearance had changed considerably since she'd last seen him in February 2003. He had grown a thick goatee and bleached his hair, eyebrows, and beard blond, with an orange tint. The female agent noted that "he appeared to be walking in the surrounding areas through alleys with no apparent place to go."

About eleven o'clock, the agent called back and reported that Scott knew he was being watched. At one point, he disappeared into an alley. As she pulled away from the curb in an attempt to locate him, she saw him at the corner, watching her. As she drove by, he smiled at her and shook his head. He also went up to a surveillance vehicle, asking the driver, "What agency are you with? Are you state or local?" He was obviously writing down the vehicle license plate numbers as well. Eventually Scott returned to the residence, but agents discontinued their surveillance around 5:30 when they realized that he'd slipped away again, this time possibly by motorcycle.

Meanwhile, police learned that usable DNA samples had been extracted from the bone and tissue recovered from both bodies, and results could be expected the following day. Based on that information, Detective Grogan was finally able to obtain an arrest warrant for Scott Peterson.

Now, all he needed was his suspect.

During my interview with Anne Bird, she revealed that she was the one who alerted Scott to the discovery of the bodies. She was en route to the Round Table pizza parlor in San Pablo with her kids when her husband, Tim, called with the news. Anne immediately dialed Scott to see if he knew. When she told him that the body of a woman had washed up, he reacted coolly. "They'll find it's not Laci and keep looking," she said. Later, when she told him about the baby, though, he grew very angry. "How could anyone do this?" he asked. Later, when prosecutors asked Anne to characterize Scott's reaction—did his anger seem to come from pain, frustration, pure rage?—she responded without hesitation that his anger seemed a result of being "discovered."

Interestingly, Scott had stayed with Anne for about ten days before the bodies washed up. She also supplied him with a key to her parents' house in San Diego, and to their three-story "cabin" in Lake Arrowhead. Anne found out later that Scott was using both places regularly without asking. Sometimes he let her know where he was by speaking in code. "I'm at Uncle Jim's cabin," he would say, or "it's busy," meaning that someone else was there with him.

Unbeknownst to the media, prosecutors intended to call Anne to testify, among other things, about Scott's visits and his revelation that he had "borrowed a shovel" from the cabin that he never returned. He never explained to Anne why he needed the shovel. But she knows that he also had access to a "secret room" in the basement of the Lake Arrowhead house, where a hidden door set flush with the wall led to a storage space and woodpile. Anne, who alerted Scott to the room when he needed to build a fire in the cabin, told me that she never looked in the "secret space" after Scott stayed there, but thought it a good spot to bury something, like jewelry.

During our interview, Anne also detailed her brother's stay with her family. When he first arrived, she was convinced of his innocence and was angry with police and Sharon Rocha for insinuating otherwise. She told me he started out as a great houseguest. One night, Scott insisted on making homemade spaghetti sauce after she pulled out a canned version. "Why are you using that?" he said. "I know how to make homemade sauce. It's easy, you just crush tomatoes." With that, he grabbed the car keys and headed to the store for fresh ingredients. Though Anne was pleased at his helpfulness, she was also curious about his high spirits during such a tragic time. Her story recalled Scott's odd behavior on Christmas Day, when he invited his neighbor Karen Servas to dinner, offering to prepare her a separate meal of tortellini less than twenty-four hours after Laci went missing.

During the visit, however, Anne grew increasingly uncomfortable with her brother's behavior and began keeping notes. While searching for Laci, Anne and two male friends took Scott to a local bar called the Ballast Pub. When one of the men asked Scott if he killed his wife, he responded, "No, I loved my wife," speaking of Laci in the past tense. When Anne and Scott paired up for a game of pool, she said, he remembered him getting angry when they lost the game.

Later that night, after speaking with Scott at their house, one of Anne's friends decided he was guilty. Scott had made a big fuss over one of the men's cars, a Ferrari, and was drinking heavily—mixed drinks, wine, and fancy concoctions in a martini glass. Another time, Anne and Scott were at the local yacht club. Anne's mother was babysitting and had insisted that she be home by 9:30 P.M. She kept trying to get Scott to leave, but he ignored her pleas and continued to order drinks. "He was being totally inconsiderate," she recalled.

All those subtle signs of trouble were eclipsed, however, when those bodies washed up close to her Berkeley home.

The following day, April 18, Sergeant Carter and Detectives Buehler, Grogan, and Brocchini drove to San Diego in unmarked vehicles to assist in Scott's arrest. Arriving at 4:00 A.M., they checked into the Best Western Escondido Motel. Even though they had a signed warrant, they wanted to wait for the DNA results before attempting an arrest. Once Scott was located, he would simply be watched pending those results, unless he headed for the Mexican border.

Brocchini remained in contact with surveillance agents, as well as the "wire room," where calls were tracked. Ernie Limon of the Department of Justice had picked up their suspect early that morning leaving 377 Lytham Glen in Escondido in a dark red 1984 Mercedes-Benz. He lost him briefly, but with air support had him back in sight. Scott seemed to know he was being trailed, and was driving in a manner commonly referred to as *counter-surveillance*. He got onto the freeway, immediately got off, then abruptly reentered once again. Agents noted he was talking on his cell phone at the time.

While driving in the high-speed lane of the freeway, Scott suddenly pulled over to the shoulder lane and stopped momentarily, almost causing a collision with members of the DOJ team. Scott then continued northbound into the city of Solano Beach, where his parents lived. He continued driving erratically through the residential area of Rancho Santa Fe, traveling on roads that were lined with leafy trees that created a canopy and shielded the Mercedes-Benz from the air. He drove near his parents' residence but never turned on their street. He made sudden stops and U-turns, and drove at a high rate of speed through the hills. At one point, agents saw him display his middle finger as he drove by.

As he raced along, Scott called his brother, Joe. He said he couldn't join Joe at the golf course that morning because he was being followed by "private investigators." He explained that he'd lost them and then "another set got him."

"Where are you at? Are you—well, I don't want to ask you that, I guess." Joe said.

"I'm on Genessee. These guys, they know I'm on to them," Scott said. He told Joe he'd stopped on the highway and they'd stopped behind him. "I think I'd better skip it because I don't think I want a picture of me in the press playing golf."

"I saw the picture where everybody is leaving flowers and stuffed animals and everything in front of your house," Joe said.

"Oh yeah?"

"Yeah," Joe confirmed. "Any indication when they may identify these bodies?"

"No."

"There is so much hype out there it's just insane."

"Yeah, it's bad."

"I have also heard that they can identify them pretty darn quick, two to three days, you know," Joe said.

"Yeah, they know it's not her," Scott replied.

"Yeah, that's what I think. I think they know already or they are telling them to retest them, I don't know."

"Oh, I think they're just holding off because they don't know anymore," Scott replied.

"Who it is—yeah, that could be, that could be."

"Have fun, guys," Scott said.

"Sorry, bro."

"It's not your fault. Thanks for the thought, though."

Just before 8:00 A.M., agents chased Scott back onto the I-5 Freeway northbound. Suddenly, he cut across four lanes of traffic and abruptly left the highway. The agents followed him off, then kept up with him when he reentered unexpectedly. They saw him clap his hands, apparently applauding them for their efforts.

Scott's game continued.

Just after eleven o'clock, the media was reporting that DNA results would soon confirm the bodies as those of Laci and Conner Peterson and that Scott Peterson's arrest was imminent. Detectives now feared that these reports might cause Scott to attempt an escape. Furthermore, his continued erratic driving could endanger members of the DOJ team or the public.

"Stop and arrest him," Grogan instructed Limon.

Limon and his team followed Scott west on Carmel Mountain Road and then south on South Camino del Mar, which becomes Torrey Pines Road. As they approached the Torrey Pines Golf Club, Limon switched on his flashing blue and red police lights. Scott immediately pulled over to the right. Officers wearing dark jackets with yellow letters identifying them as police jumped out of their vehicles and ordered Scott to turn off the ignition and get out of the car.

Scott was dressed in a blue sweater worn over a white polo shirt, white shorts, ankle high socks, and Nike tennis shoes. Dark sunglasses shaded his eyes. He wore no jewelry, not even a wedding ring. His hair, eyebrows, and beard were all dyed an orangey-blond color.

Scott offered no resistance as police handcuffed him. After asking what agency they were with, he followed with a second question: "Have they found my wife and son?"

One officer said someone would talk to him about that shortly and directed him to sit on the curb, away from public view.

"Do you know why you're being detained and arrested?" Agent Limon asked.

Peterson replied, "Because of my erratic driving?"

That wasn't the reason, he was told. Did he know of any other?

"Well, Modesto wants me about a murder."

At 11:15, the Modesto investigators arrived at the scene. Scott was placed in the rear of a Ford Taurus station wagon that police had parked a short distance away. Detective Grogan placed a tape recorder on the seat, stating the date and time: April 18, 2003, 1135–1136 hours. He formally notified Scott that, pursuant to a warrant, he was under arrest for the crime of murder. He asked Scott if he had any questions. Scott said no.

As Scott and Grogan were transported to a DOJ office, a tape recorder captured their conversation. Grogan asked who should be notified about picking up the Mercedes-Benz after it was searched. While there was a certificate of title and other documentation in the car, it had not been registered in anyone's name. This prevented police from simply checking the license plate to locate the owner. A double-edged knife in a case was found along the left side of the driver's seat, along with a driver's license issued to Scott's brother John. Scott's newly lightened hair was a close match to John's photo on his license.

During a more thorough search of the Mercedes-Benz over a three-day period, police found the following: U.S. currency totaling $14,932, with $14,000 in $100 bills still wrapped in paper bands from the bank; three credit cards, two in Scott's name, and one in the name of his half sister, Anne Bird; a Columbia foul-weather jacket; a hand shovel; a backpack containing a water purifier, water bottle, climbing rope, filet knife, roll of duct tape, cooking grill, rain pants, Ziploc bags, extra socks, fire starters, camp kit with cooking utensils, leather gloves, two folding knives, a folding saw one pair of scissors, two packs of razor blades, and a waterproofing spray; a camp axe, hammock, binoculars, mask and snorkel, fishing rod and reel, and a Leatherman tool. Twelve pairs of shoes ranging from flip-flops to waterproof boots to dress shoes, and an entire wardrobe including numerous pants, shirts, jackets, underwear, socks, neckties and sweaters, and a cowboy hat were all packed into the car. Sixteen music CDs and two California guidebooks, twenty-four blister packs of sleeping pills, twelve tablets of Viagra, four cell phones, a gas credit card in his mother's name, and a quantity of Mexican currency were also found.

As many observed after the arrest, it was evident that Scott was going somewhere for quite a while. One destination might have been the nearby Mexican border, and he was familiar with that country. His supporters would argue he was simply trying to hide out from the press for a while, but as I pointed out at the time, Scott's friends and relatives had kept him concealed from the cameras in their homes for some time. The items in the car indicated to me that Scott had packed for more than a camping trip.

At 12:05, Scott was brought into a large training room in the DOJ office. He complained that his shoulders ached from having his hands cuffed behind him and asked if they could be loosened. Grogan left the room and returned with a waist chain and cuffs. He read Scott his constitutional rights. Scott nodded his head, affirming that he understood, but said nothing.

Grogan then told Scott that he could be booked into San Diego County or, if he waived the right, in Stanislaus County. Scott said he wanted to speak with his attorney before answering. He also wanted to use the telephone. Grogan informed him that he could make three calls, but first he had to be photographed.

When Scott was given a phone, he immediately dialed his attorney but was only able to leave a voice mail message. Next he called his mother and told her he had been arrested. His third call, bizarrely, was to Heather and Mike Richardson. "Hey, this is Scott, I just wanted to make sure I returned your call," Scott reportedly said. "I made you some lavender cookies, that is what I was going to send, but I got arrested a couple of hours ago so I have to go."

Heather later reported that Scott had called the day before to get her mailing address so he could send the cookies. Laci used to bake them regularly, using dried lavender flower petals. She also recounted her call to Scott on April 16 to see "how he was doing." The bodies had been recovered by that time, and she wanted to hear what Scott might say about the discovery. But she didn't ask about the bodies, and, amazingly, Scott didn't mention them either. Instead, he talked of traveling to Arizona and New Mexico to post fliers about Laci's disappearance.

By this time, there were more signs that Scott Peterson was experiencing serious psychological dysfunction. Scott would not be examined, and psychiatric testimony would not be permitted during the trial, but there was increasing public conversation about Scott's flat affect and arguably inappropriate responses to unfolding events. Months after Laci's brother had actually confronted

Scott about his behavior calling him a sociopath, that description would resonate publicly as people learned more about the seemingly charming young man's psyche.

Scott asked police if he could make "one more call." When Grogan asked who he wanted to contact, he said, "his work," to tell them he wouldn't be coming in. Grogan told him he would have the opportunity to make that call later.

Detective Grogan left the room for a few minutes. DOJ Agent Charles Willkomm remained with their charge. Suddenly Scott, who was still wearing sunglasses, turned to him and said, "I want to apologize for the way I was driving this morning. I didn't know who you guys were."

"Thank you . . . but I wasn't with the team that followed you," Willkomm replied.

"Oh," Scott said. "Okay. I just wanted to apologize."

The conversation rambled for a while. Then, looking at his watch, Scott noted, "I was supposed to take my niece to the movies in a couple of hours today." He paused, then added, "Well, maybe in a couple of weeks I'll be able to do that."

Willkomm would record that Scott "did not seem worried or overly concerned that he had been arrested. . . . Peterson's demeanor was calm, devoid of grief, concern, or anger. Most of the time, Peterson displayed a distant stare toward the wall across from where he sat and occasionally smiled while talking to me."

Late that afternoon, Scott was placed in leg irons and waist chains in addition to the handcuffs. Detectives Grogan and Buehler then put him in a car for the ride to the Stanislaus County Jail. The vehicle was wired with transmitters in the trunk to record any conversation. Brocchini and Carter followed in a separate car, monitoring those transmissions.

At 5:20, as they were driving back to Modesto, Grogan received a call informing him that the DNA results were complete. Jane Doe had been identified as Laci Peterson, and Baby Doe was indeed Scott's biological child. Investigators had compared DNA from the muscle and bone samples from the autopsy to DNA from Laci's mother and father, Sharon and Dennis Rocha. They had also taken eight hairs from a brush that had belonged to Laci, as well as a pap smear they obtained from her gynecologist. They also had a blood sample from Scott Peterson, which they used to identify the fetus. The law required that the next of kin be notified. Scott Peterson was that person.

Because of the highway noise and the concern that it would mask any response Scott made upon hearing the news, Grogan opted to postpone the notification. At 6:50 P.M., the detective told Scott that the bodies found in the San Francisco Bay had been identified as Laci and Conner through a DNA match. Pulling the sunglasses from his eyes, he bowed his head. Grogan saw a tear run down the side of his face. Scott wiped it away, and closed his eyes. He put his sunglasses back on, his eyes still shut. He did not utter a sound, but Grogan saw no more tears. Fifteen minutes later, Buehler asked Scott if he wanted any water or food. He declined.

At eight o'clock, the officers stopped at In & Out Burger in Bakersfield. By then, Scott was ready for a "double-double" cheeseburger, fries, and a vanilla shake. While seated in the car with Grogan, waiting for Brocchini and Carter to return with food, Scott commented on a woman carrying a small child wrapped in a blanket to the car parked in front of them. Scott remarked that the baby appeared to be only about a month old. After making the observation, he fell silent again.

Grogan had requested that Scott be booked in an undisclosed location to thwart media coverage, but en route to Modesto he learned that arrangements had been made for a single "pool camera" to be set up inside the gate at the jail. Scott would be booked there.

Just before midnight, the group pulled into the facility. Scott was escorted into the jail in full view of the camera. On the second floor, he was booked according to standard procedure and charged with two counts of 187 P.C.—murder in the first degree.

With the incredible publicity surrounding Scott's arrest, new tips began coming into police headquarters. One such call came from Miguel Espidia of Redwood City, who said that he'd been a classmate of Scott and Laci at Cal Poly. Upon reading a newspaper article that mentioned Laci's headless body, he recalled a conversation he said he had with Scott back in 1995.

Espidia couldn't remember how the conversation started, but he and Scott were driving in a car when Scott began describing how he might kill someone. He said he would wrap the head in a plastic bag, then weight it down. He would throw the body into saltwater, so that the salt and the fish would eat away at the fingers, destroying the fingerprints. If you weighted the head, he said, the body would float upward. The fish and salt would eat away at the neck, eventually separating the head from the body. If a body were found without fingerprints or a head, Scott thought it could not be identified. Scott assured him that he would never do such a thing, Espidia said; these were just his thoughts.

Detective Brocchini would later testify about this call at trial. As he described the tip, he mentioned wrapping the head with duct tape as one of the things Scott described to Espidia. Since the report had actually said nothing about duct tape, Mark Geragos climbed all over the detective, accusing him of embellishing the story to make it an exact fit with the Peterson facts. Brocchini would later say he hadn't refreshed his memory about the tip before testifying and was simply confused, but Geragos scored points with trial watchers. Although it was a minor infraction, this was one of several embarrassing mistakes that would damage Brocchini's credibility during the trial.

While going through the property seized after Scott's arrest, Detective Buehler came across a tiny scrap of paper with a woman's name and phone number. The name, Natalie Mangura, matched that of a woman who had phoned the tip line the previous night. The twenty-eight-year-old Mangura told Buehler that she'd been housesitting at the home of Anne Bird's parents in San Diego, and she knew that Scott was there on April 18, just hours before his arrest.

She first encountered Peterson on Monday evening, April 14, at about 11:00 P.M. when she arrived to find a two-door reddish Mercedes-Benz parked in front of the house. As she entered the house, she yelled, "Is anybody home?" Scott Peterson answered. Natalie had been advised that Scott might be staying at the residence temporarily, but she hadn't expected him until the following week. He quickly told her he could sleep downstairs and she could stay upstairs. Uncomfortable when he insisted, Natalie told Scott that she didn't need to stay overnight since the family cat had died. "Did you kill the cat?" Scott smiled. "No," she explained, the cat had died of natural causes. Before leaving, she gave Scott her cell phone number and asked that he contact her when he was leaving so she could resume her duties.

Natalie reported that Scott had been preparing his taxes when she arrived that night. She later learned from Anne that he used one of the homeowner's cars, a Lexus, to mail his taxes so that he wouldn't be recognized by the media or investigators.

Several days later, police received additional information about the Mercedes-Benz Scott was driving when he was arrested. Michael Griffin, a substitute teacher, had advertised a 1984 Mercedes-Benz in *Auto Trader* magazine, asking $5,000 for the car. On April 12, Scott Peterson responded to the ad and showed up to test drive the automobile. He then offered $3,600 cash and Griffin agreed. Scott left, returning just ten minutes later with thirty-six $100 bills. Scott produced the necessary DMV forms downloaded from the Internet. When Griffin examined them, he noticed that they'd been filled out in the name of "Jacqueline Peterson." He questioned this, yet Scott insisted it was correct. "It was kind of a 'Boy Named Sue' type name," Scott claimed. "That's what my parents stuck me with." He added that he went by the name "Jack."

Griffin told police that Scott appeared to be in a hurry. He couldn't produce any ID, but did recite what he claimed was a Florida driver's license number.

At trial, Griffin told the court that the double-edged dagger found in the car when Scott was arrested actually belonged to him.

He had forgotten to remove it when Scott took the car. But the balance of the very long list of recovered items belonged to Scott.

Police interviewed a second man, mechanic Mario Ruvalcaba, who said that a man named Scott had called him from a cell phone with an 858 area code about his car ad in the *Auto Trader*. The two arranged a meeting at Ruvalcaba's place of business.

"Scott was a tall white guy, about thirty years old, with blond hair and a goatee," Ruvalcaba recalled. "After the test drive, Scott said, 'Fine, I'll take it right now.' He seemed anxious to get the car and said he would pay cash.

"We filled out all the paperwork," Ruvalcaba continued. "I noticed that he put 'Jacqueline Peterson' on everything. I didn't see the name 'Scott' anywhere. I thought maybe he was gay, or a transsexual, and that Jacqueline was his female name."

There was one problem. Ruvalcaba needed to get Scott a copy of the "smog certificate" for the vehicle, and postponed the deal until eight o'clock the following morning. In the meantime, Ruvalcaba called another prospective buyer to let her know the car might be sold. The woman cried and carried on so much that Ruvalcaba agreed to sell it to her instead. "I phoned Scott to tell him that the deal was off, and he was really angry. He accused me of wasting his time."

Later that day, Scott returned to Ruvalcaba's shop.

"I have the cash. I'll take the car right now," Scott announced.

Ruvalcaba told him no, but Scott continued to push. After leaving, he phoned the shop again and said, "Are we dealing or not?"

Very firmly, Ruvalcaba again said no.


On April 21, District Attorney Jim Brazelton, members of his staff, and investigators from the Modesto Police Department met with the Rocha family prior to Scott's arraignment. The district attorney informed them what to expect going forward. He could never have imagined the media firestorm that would rage throughout the proceedings.

At 1:30 that afternoon, Scott stood impassively before the Honorable Judge Nancy Ashley of the Stanislaus County Superior Court.

He was clean-shaven, yet his thick hair was still a strawberry blond. His face revealed nothing as the charges were read: "On or about and between December 23, 2002 and December 24, 2002, defendant did commit a felony, murder, violation of Section 187 of the California Penal Code, in that the defendant did willfully, unlawfully, and feloniously and with malice aforethought murder Laci Denise Peterson, a human being. It is further alleged as to Count I Murder, that the defendant acted intentionally, deliberately and with premeditation." He was also charged with a second count of murder for the death of the unborn Conner Peterson.

Scott responded with four words: "I am not guilty."

The charge carried a special "enhancement" under California law alleging that he deliberately killed Laci and her unborn child with premeditation. The combination of charges meant that Scott was not eligible for bail, and if found guilty, he could face the death penalty.

During the proceeding Scott was assigned a public defender, even though McAllister had accompanied him to court. It would be another month before Mark Geragos took the case. Outside the courtroom, McAllister would not discuss why he was no longer representing Scott. Some pundits speculated that the reason was financial.

Following the arraignment, the Rocha family held an emotional press conference. With tears streaming down her face, Sharon praised the Modesto police. She recalled that from the moment she received Scott's Christmas Eve phone call, "I knew in my heart something terrible had happened to Laci and her son. My world collapsed around me." She said that Laci's killer "should be held accountable and punished for the tragedy and devastation forced upon so many of us. I can only hope that the sound of Laci's voice begging for her life, begging for the life of her unborn child, is heard over and over and over again in the mind of that person every day for the rest of his life." Ron Granski added, "I feel sorry for Jackie and Lee. They don't deserve this, but our family didn't either."

As Scott was led back to jail, police continued their interviews. Mike Richardson had been seen on television discussing Scott's new hair color, so he got another call. Mike explained that he had invited

Scott to his ranch in Fillmore about three weeks earlier. When Scott arrived, Mike immediately noticed the color change. Scott said that he'd been swimming in his friend Aaron's pool in Mountain View and the chlorine had bleached his hair. Mike didn't ask any more questions, but was skeptical. This information prompted police to obtain a search warrant for hair samples and full body photographs and to test whether hair dye or pool chemicals lightened Scott's hair.

Additionally, Heather Richardson told detectives that during her conversation with Scott, he admitted to an affair with a woman in San Luis Obispo while Laci was living in Prunedale. Although he did not name her, it was probably Janet Ilse, the woman who'd walked in on Scott and Laci in bed those many years ago. However, it might have been Katy Hansen, who was sitting next to Scott at graduation when a pretty brunette walked over and presented him with that flowered lei and a big kiss. Whichever girl it was, Scott seemed surprised that Laci hadn't told her.

Heather also recalled an argument between Scott and Laci after Scott's graduation from Cal Poly. She and Mike had attended a celebratory dinner with the couple afterward. Heather could tell that Laci was upset. When they left the restaurant, everyone drove to the house Scott was sharing with his three roommates. Laci and Scott went into the bathroom. Heather overheard her yelling at him. Scott did not respond.

"It sounded like he was just taking it," Heather said.

Laci never explained why the two had been arguing, but at the graduation ceremony she commented that Scott had been living with the guys and "acting single."

Still, even if Laci knew about that affair, Heather did not believe she was told about Amber Frey.

Police also interviewed Jim Allen, the manager of the Torrey Pines Golf Club, where Scott had told police he was heading when he was arrested. Although Scott did not have a tee time reserved, said Allen, Lee Peterson was in the book on April 18 for a foursome at eight o'clock that morning. Only three golfers showed up that day, and Allen added another lone golfer to round out the group.

Detective Grogan also spoke to a technician, Denise Ducot, who said she worked with Kim McGregor at Valley Oak Pediatrics Center. According to Ducot, another coworker told her that McGregor was claiming a sexual interlude with Scott Peterson after Laci disappeared. The police found no further evidence of such a liaison.

In a similar vein, police also learned of a stripper at a club in San Diego who claimed to have had a short affair with Scott. The day before his arrest, she said, he asked her to run off to Mexico with him. Police thought the information was credible, but the woman was fearful of recrimination at work if she came forward. Such leads appeared to corroborate the detectives' suspicion that Scott was planning to leaving the country. Scott simply may have waited too long to get away because he did not expect the DNA identification of the bodies to occur so quickly.

On Friday, April 25, Deputy District Attorney Dave Harris and Detective Grogan met with members of Laci's family at Sharon Rocha's home to discuss the death penalty. Dennis, Sharon, Brent, and Amy Rocha, Ron Grantski, and family representative Kim Peterson all supported the death penalty as punishment if Scott was found guilty.

During the meeting, Sharon mentioned Heather Richardson's recollection that Scott had once expressed that he didn't want to have children. Days later she heard Heather tell a TV reporter that Scott was looking forward to being a father, then read the same comment in the *Modesto Bee*.

Sharon told Grogan that the family was planning to hold a memorial service for Laci and Conner on Laci's birthday, May 4, at 3:00 P.M. at the First Baptist Church in Modesto. Ron Grantski later contacted the detective saying the family had learned that Amber's sister, Ava, and her mother, Brenda McGhee, intended to show up. The family didn't want them there, and Ron asked Grogan to relay the information. While the family was very appreciative of the way Amber had handled her involvement, they feared her presence would sensationalize the solemn occasion. He also asked that Amber not attend.

After the family meeting, District Attorney James Brazelton called a press conference to announce that "A decision has been made to seek the death penalty in the case of the people of California versus Scott Peterson."

Publicly, Laci's family had no comment.

On April 29, Grogan received a call from Rick DiStaso. The Public Defender's Officer had just informed DiStaso that defense attorney Mark Geragos had agreed to take Scott Peterson's case, pro bono. Geragos would be arriving on May 2, and all legal issues, upcoming motions, and the sealing of search warrants were on hold until then.

While there was no question that Geragos was taking the case, it was unclear whether he had agreed to represent Scott free of charge. It has never been entirely clear what the financial arrangements were. Geragos repeatedly declined to disclose how much he was charging the family, but later told colleagues that he took the case for a "flat fee." The figure that circulated was $1 million, but that amount has never been confirmed.

On *Larry King Live* the following evening, the flashy defense counselor was a call-in guest. Although he declined to reveal whether he had agreed to take the case, he indicated that he'd met the players and was seriously considering it. "I can tell you that Scott's mother, especially, is a very compelling advocate for her son," Geragos told King. "And I've met with Scott, and I've talked with the public defenders. I was up in Modesto yesterday. And I'm going to sleep on it and make a decision."

"Mark, can you give us the balancing points? What's for and what's against?" King asked.

For one thing, Geragos conceded, "I think he's already universally convicted in the court of public opinion. I don't think there's anybody that you can talk to that doesn't just assume his guilt." But the attorney noted that "part of why people go into criminal defense is to defend the underdog and to try to make it a truly adversarial system. And that is definitely intriguing in this case."

"So what's the downside?" King asked.

"Well, the downside is that it's a monumental undertaking, in terms of time, number one, and effort, and I suppose, as well, the other clients and the impact of the other lawyers in my practice. . . . And there's a whole lot of other factors, others that I won't even get into on the air."

When pressed, Geragos did claim that he was "tremendously impressed" by Scott. "And obviously, that's something that leans towards me taking the case as well."

At one point in the program, the show was opened up to callers. To the surprise of many, Lee Peterson phoned in to confront legal analyst Nancy Grace, a passionate believer in Scott's guilt. The exchange was heated, with a lot of cross talk.

"Nancy Grace," he said, "I've watched many programs. I don't like to watch them, but it kind of keeps me informed, and I can feel the public sentiment. And I just have to say, for some reason you seem to have a personal stake in this, a personal vendetta against my son and I do not understand it. . . . It is so obvious that you are just caught up in this thing and there's no room for, you know, innocence until proven guilty. And I'm just appalled by that. I don't think that's your place, to be a spokesman for . . . the district attorney . . ."

"I know he may not believe it," Grace responded, "but my heart goes out to [Lee] and the pain his family's having. But I am speaking on behalf of what I believe to be true, on behalf of Laci Peterson, neither against Scott, for Scott, for the state, against the state, but what I believe to be true regarding her murder."

"You are speculating on these facts as much as I am," Lee Peterson argued.

"And you are believing what your son is telling you."

As Peterson began to respond, Grace interjected.

"Please don't interrupt me," Peterson asked. "You've had your say here for months, and you've crucified my son on national media. And he's a wonderful man. You have no idea of his background and what a wonderful son and wonderful man he is. You have no knowledge of that and you sit there as a judge and jury, I guess, and you're convincing him on the national media, and you should be absolutely ashamed of yourself."

"Sir, I think he should be ashamed of himself, as whoever is responsible for the death of Laci Peterson," Grace responded. "I am simply stating [what] has been leaked or what has been put in formal documents, and if you find them disturbing, I suggest you ask your son about some of them, sir."

"There you go, Nancy. Look at this look on Nancy's face. You absolutely hate my son. I don't know what it is."

"No, I don't hate your son. I don't know your son."

The argument went on for a while, but Lee continued to defend his son. "You don't have any facts," he told Grace at one point. "All you have is your anger and your speculation. I think you hate men."

On May 2, Deputy District Attorney Rick DiStaso asked Investigator Kevin Bertalotto to contact Kirk McAllister and ask if he had any information that might clear Scott of the murder charges. Three days later, Bertalotto encountered McAllister in the hallway of Stanislaus County Court Building. He knew McAllister from past cases, and approached him with an extended hand.

"Good morning," Bertalotto said, shaking the lawyer's hand. He then asked McAllister if he "wanted to share any information" that could clear Scott to the district attorney's office.

"Go fuck yourself," McAllister responded.

"Don't shoot the messenger," Bertalotto replied. "We've always got along good."

"Yeah, I know," McAllister shot back, patting the investigator on the arm. "Well take this message to whoever—*Go fuck yourselves.*"

The battle was on.

# CHAPTER EIGHTEEN

# SUMMER 2003

On May 4, 2003, thousands of friends and family members packed into the First Baptist Church in Modesto to bid farewell to Laci and Conner. Everyone in attendance was fully aware that it would have been Laci's twenty-eighth birthday. Scott had requested permission to attend. Not surprisingly, he was turned down. The jail arranged to beam the services into his cell.

As the ceremony proceeded, it was reported that Laci's accused killer was meeting with his attorney instead of watching the services, although defense sources tried to dismiss this as just another attempt to portray Scott as a heartless killer. In fact, they said, he and his family had their own quiet service inside the jail.

Scott's brother, Mark, expressed a desire to attend Laci's funeral, but was angrily admonished by his father. "We'll disown you if you do," Lee Peterson reportedly warned his son.

Scott was under high security and in isolation because of rumored death threats. Stanislaus County Sheriff's Department spokesperson Kelly Huston confirmed this on April 21. "Some of the inmates in our facility that have nothing to lose with [the] three strikes [law] in California have made some mention of 'taking care of him,'" Huston said, venturing that some inmates "would love the notoriety of having done something or have some attachment to this case." The fact that Scott also was charged as a "baby-killer" increased the chances that he would be the target of violence. In the prison hierarchy, those charged with crimes against children were on the lowest rung. His six-by-nine foot maximum-security cell, outfitted with nothing but a metal bed with a three-inch mattress and a stainless steel sink and toilet, would be his home for many months.

In June 2003, Amber Frey, her lawyer, Gloria Allred, and Detective Buehler went to the Stanislaus County District Attorney's office to meet with Deputy District Attorney Dave Harris for the first time. Harris, serving with Rick DiStaso as the trial prosecutors in the Peterson case, first showed Amber a courtroom so that it would seem familiar if she was called to testify at the upcoming preliminary hearing.

Later in the meeting, Amber gave Buehler a photocopy of a two-page penciled letter from Scott dated April 25, in which he wrote that he would be acquitted of the charges, and that while in custody he would use the time to "do the work of the Lord." He thanked Amber for leading him to God, and apologized for the fact that she'd become embroiled in such media frenzy. He said that he was looking forward to getting the preliminary "trial" over with, as if he believed that the proceeding would end any suspicion that he'd been involved in Laci's death. May 4 was Laci's birthday, and he was asking friends to fly a kite in her memory. He ended the letter by saying that children are "miracles and gifts."

Only a few months earlier, Scott had told his devout girlfriend that his failure to attend church could jeopardize their relationship. During their affair, however, Scott had realized how effective a dose of religion could be in manipulating Amber—and he continued to do so from his jail cell.

Amber also gave Buehler two e-mails from Scott, whose address was now purposelife2003@yahoo.com. She'd received both of them before his arrest, but in hindsight it seems that Scott was trying to lay some "good character" groundwork. In the first, dated April 3, Scott said that he'd just flown a kite with his two nephews. In the second, received five days later, Scott explained that he was helping to rebuild a deck at a home for battered women. While there, he said, he noticed a young man staring at him, and recognized him as someone he had tutored at the St. Vincent de Paul Center for Homeless Children while he was in high school.

On June 4, the district attorney announced that the brown van rumored to belong to the "real killers" was not connected to the Peterson murders. Several days later, a judge issued a gag order to all parties in the case, but he also unsealed the search warrants as the press had requested.

In mid-June, district attorney investigator Kevin Bertalotto arranged to meet a man named Harvey Kemple at a McDonald's in Modesto. Related by marriage to the Rocha family, "Uncle Harvey" was the second person who heard Scott claim he was golfing, not fishing, on Christmas Eve.

Kemple remembered remarking to his wife, "What was Scott doing golfing on Christmas Eve?" His wife, Gwen replied, "Scott told me he went fishing." Later, the couple's daughter overheard them discussing the discrepancy, and mentioned that Scott told her he'd been *at work* that day.

A colorful character, Kemple became one of the better-known witnesses during the trial when he related a story about Scott burning the chicken he was barbecuing at a July 4 pool party. "Scott was more upset over burning the damn chicken than finding Laci," Kemple griped.

On June 26, 2003, Judge Girolami ordered that 176 recently discovered wire taps of Scott Peterson's phone calls be handed over to the defense as part of discovery. The recordings turned up on a computer hard drive on June 13, 2003. Five days later, prosecutors revealed their existence when they asked the court to review them for relevance. Prosecutors maintained that no one—not even the investigator in charge of the wiretaps—had listened to the recordings. Ultimately, the judge denied the defense's request to throw out those and nearly three thousand other secretly recorded conversations. On March 3, 2004, Delucchi ruled that the tapes would be admissible at trial. That same day, Delucchi also ruled to exclude the dog-tracking evidence gathered around the couple's home and inside Scott's warehouse, striking a partial blow to the prosecution's case. Despite calling it "at best iffy," the judge did allow the trailing dog evidence from the Berkeley Marina search.

The ruling was a partial victory for Geragos, who had argued that the dog-gathering evidence was "complete voodoo" and "utter nonsense."

In late September, investigators returned to the San Francisco Bay to continue their search for additional evidence. In particular, they were looking for other body parts and concrete anchors.

After countless delays, the preliminary hearing in the Stanislaus County Courthouse got underway on October 29, 2003.

As expected, it was a huge media event. It was the first time the public and the press got a firsthand look at many of the people they had been hearing about for months: Scott and Laci's friends and family members, detectives, forensics experts, even the couple's housekeeper.

Among those who garnered extraordinary attention was Scott's high-profile trial lawyer, Mark Geragos. Known as Susan McDougal's attorney during President Clinton's travails, he also handled Winona Ryder's shoplifting case. Ironically, Geragos represented Gary Condit during the investigation into Modesto resident Chandra Levy's disappearance and murder in Washington, D.C. Perhaps his most notorious client was pop star Michael Jackson. Geragos had been the first attorney to represent the singer in his 2003 child abuse investigation, although Jackson would soon dismiss him, reportedly because of the attention he was giving the Peterson case.

Before Scott hired Geragos, the attorney had appeared regularly on *Larry King Live* to talk about the case. While he now took the role of defense attorney on the shows, Geragos still made note of critical evidence such as the computer tidal charts, the cell phone records, and, of course, what he called the "enormous coincidence" that "the very place that he put himself, the very alibi, if you will, turns out to be the exact place where the body is recovered. That is either an incredible coincidence or damning piece of evidence."

"Is it a slam dunk?" King asked his guest Mark Geragos.

Geragos didn't sound terribly bullish. "Even though it's a circumstantial evidence case, the most damning piece of circumstantial evidence comes out of his own mouth and his own hands, when he hands the police that receipt from the very location where, two miles away, she's found," Geragos said. "I mean, that is just a devastating thing. . . .

"If Scott Peterson did this crime," he went on, "and everybody's, you know, innocent until proven guilty, and as I've said, it's a damning, circumstantial case—the man is a sociopath if he did this crime. I mean, there's no other way to put it," Geragos told King. "This is his wife, his unborn baby boy. If he's the one who took the two of them up there and put concrete around them and threw them into the ocean and concocted this story and went out onto Diane Sawyer and gave that impassioned plea with the tears—I mean, that's not somebody that generally you're going to want to give a manslaughter [conviction] to."


Even though the case had first broken nearly a year earlier, public interest was escalating rather than fading. The initial fascination was understandable. The Christmas Eve disappearance of a beautiful young mother-to-be, the family's heartbreaking pleas for help, and the reticent husband with a dubious alibi all made good copy for the press. While most were skeptical of Scott's story, he was still a good-looking, white, middle-class suburban husband who'd seemed to have a wonderful marriage and a happy life.

Interest surged when the affair with Amber Frey was revealed, and again when the breaking news reports announced that two bodies had washed up along the shoreline. When Laci and Conner were identified, rumors began to circulate that Scott had slipped away from the police; his dramatic pursuit and arrest on April 18, 2003, closed one phase of the case and opened another.

Despite what even Geragos acknowledged—that Scott had all but hanged himself in the court of public opinion—the State was nevertheless saddled with an almost purely circumstantial case.

Many observers still asserted that the evidence was insufficient to produce a conviction. The prosecution had no DNA, no confession, and precious little crime scene forensics to work with. The preliminary hearing would be the first chance for the prosecuters to lay out their findings. It would also be the first time Mark Geragos could ask the judge to dismiss the case for lack of evidence.

The hearing lasted eleven days. Prosecutors announced that they would not introduce GPS or wire tap evidence during the preliminary hearing, but did not exclude the possibility that they would offer this at trial. Nor, at this stage, did they intend to call Amber Frey.

Geragos wanted Amber's attorney, Gloria Allred, barred from the proceedings. Nothing if not feisty, Allred was not about to be removed without a fight. Judge Girolami overruled Geragos's motion, but instructed Allred not to discuss any testimony with her client. Geragos also attempted to have Allred placed under the same gag order that applied to the principal attorneys and witnesses, but to his dismay the judge refused. On television and in print, Allred would lash out at Geragos and his client throughout the trial proceedings.

The prosecutors' first witness was a DNA expert. Dr. Constance Fisher, an FBI forensic analyst, testified about the hair clasped in a pair of pliers in Scott's boat. Speaking in broad terms, Fisher explained that the DNA recovered from a hair with no root attached was mitochondrial, meaning that the information from this analysis would not as precise as if it had been obtained from nuclear DNA. Yet important findings would still emerge from the genetic material. Comparing it with hairs from Laci's brush and DNA from her mother, the experts established probability about the source of the hair—roughly one in 112 individuals in the Modesto area would have possessed the DNA profile of the hair in question and Laci could not be excluded as a contributor. One person who was clearly eliminated as a match was Scott.

Before she could testify about those findings, the defense team challenged the science in a three-pronged attack. Geragos attacked first the validity of the testing and then the database from which the information was drawn. Finally, he asserted that the sample was contaminated. Fisher insisted there had been no contamination during her tests and maintained that her conclusions were accurate. The judge finally ruled that the expert's testimony was admissible and permitted her to state her conclusions.

The defense called its own DNA expert to rebut Dr. Fisher's findings. Dr. William Shields, a professor at the State University of New York's College of Environmental Forestry, testified that one in every thirty-three samples of DNA could give a false exclusion or match. According to the current FBI database of 5,071 samples, this shared genetic sequence is found in less than 1 percent of Caucasians. While Fisher concluded that the DNA from the hair sample could be found in 1 out of 112 Caucasians, Shields estimated the sequence could be found in as many as 1 in 9. Detectives Buehler, Owen, Hendee, and Evers were the police witnesses. Hendee testified about collecting the hair from the pliers, but on cross-examination Geragos tore into him, suggesting that sloppy police work or something more insidious had conspired to create "additional" evidence in the form of a "second" piece of hair. Yet it was again established to the court's satisfaction that the hair may have simply broken in two after it was removed from the pliers and placed in the evidence bag.

At one point during the cross examination, when Harris objected to a question from Geragos as "double speculation," Geragos retorted, "Like this entire case."

The primary detective on the case, Al Brocchini, spent the better part of three days on the stand. After outlining the investigation time line from December 24 forward, he responded to a line of accusatory questions posed by defense lawyer Kirk McAllister, who had not yet left Scott's defense team. Trying to establish that Brocchini had rushed to judgment about Scott, he argued that Brocchini and other police officers didn't pursue leads that might have exonerated the defendant.

Outside the courtroom, Lee and Jackie Peterson expressed their feelings about the police—in particular, their distaste for Detective Brocchini.

"You should be ashamed," Jackie shouted when the detective passed.

"I've seen bums before," Lee Peterson chimed in.

The couple's aggression toward officers wasn't limited to the preliminary hearing. Even before Scott's arrest, police overheard Jackie Peterson making derogatory remarks about Al Brocchini in taped phone conversations with her son. In one conversation, she got very personal, impugning Brocchini's family, even his mother, in her comments.

In court, Dr. Brian Peterson, the coroner who performed both autopsies, delivered his findings. Laci's family chose to leave the courtroom during his testimony, fearing that it would be too difficult to hear. Through co-prosecutor Dave Harris's questioning, Dr. Peterson argued that Conner had not been born alive, as the defense would argue. He testified that Laci's uterus had been intact when her body was submerged in the bay, and that the condition of the two bodies was dramatically different, leading Peterson to conclude that Conner had been sheltered in her womb until just before he was found.

Under cross-examination, Geragos tried to elicit testimony that Conner was born alive and had taken a breath. Dr. Peterson responded that he could not rule out that possibility, but said it was unlikely based on his findings.

While being held in jail, Scott was reportedly shown the autopsy photos of Laci and Conner. "She's got no fucking head!" he reportedly cried out, breaking down in sobs.

The revelation that Laci's body had trace amounts of caffeine also upset Scott, prompting him to exclaim, "They tortured her!"

On November 18, Judge Girolami ruled that there was enough evidence to bind Scott over for trial. He was formally arraigned on December 3, 2003. His plea of not guilty came as no surprise, but Geragos's request for a trial date of January 26, 2004, less than two months away, came as a shock.

On December 12, 2003, the defense filed a motion for a change of venue. Scott could not receive a fair trial in his wife's hometown of Modesto, they contended, because of all the pretrial publicity—including eight thousand articles published worldwide and about one hundred and fifty stories in the local papers. On January 8, the change of venue was granted.

Girolami ruled that a jury could be found in one of fifteen adjacent larger counties. While Geragos fought hard to move the trial to his home turf in Los Angeles, the case was finally sent to Redwood City in neighboring San Mateo County.

In the weeks before the preliminary hearing, Geragos nearly lost control of the case. Scott was reportedly dissatisfied with his high-priced defense attorney, expressing frustration that Geragos wasn't visiting him in jail, and claiming that his questions weren't being addressed. Scott's parents had reportedly forked over the hefty $1 million retainer, and Scott wanted some pampering. In mid-to-late September, Scott went to the extent of signing a substitution agreement with another firm. The firm reportedly agreed to take Scott's case because the partners believed there was a viable defense—and because "it was winnable."

When Geragos learned of the agreement, a member of the inner circle later revealed, he went to the jail to confront Scott in person. He reportedly told Scott he would "fry" if he made the switch. He also guaranteed Scott a victory—and according to sources, got Scott to sign another retainer agreement.

In the months ahead, Lee and Jackie Peterson solicited funds from friends and family to help offset the cost of Scott's defense. The million-dollar retainer had wiped them out, and Geragos would come back to them mid-trial asking for more money. While several of Scott's siblings reached into their pockets to help, reportedly there was one family member who did not participate. While Scott's half sister, Susan Caudillo, regularly went before the cameras defending her brother, she reportedly did not contribute to his defense fund. In another of the odd coincidences surrounding this case, I later learned that Caudillo was constructing an in-ground "infinity pool" in the backyard of her new home. Like Scott himself, she had failed to give to others while quietly arranging to sink her money into a lavish swimming pool—dumping tens of thousands of dollars into its construction. As Scott sat in jail, Susan threw a big party to unveil her brand new pool.

# CHAPTER NINETEEN

# THE TRIAL

"Scott thought he was smart enough to fool us, but there were many crucial little clues he left," said Juror Number 7, Richelle Nice. "One turning point for me was the photo of the bed in Laci's room. It shows that the comforter was just thrown on the bed. That's the way Scott told cops Laci left the room before she vanished.

"But anyone who knows Laci knows she wouldn't have sloppily tossed the comforter. Then there were the statements Scott made about what his wife was wearing when he last saw her, which turned out to be different from what was on her corpse. Kidnappers would not have taken her home to change her clothes. Also, consider that Scott ordered hardcore-porn channels on his TV after Laci disappeared. That was a big sign to us that he knew his wife wasn't coming home.

"For me, Scott convicted himself with his lies. The case did not have much to do with the prosecution or Amber."

— as told to *New York Post* correspondent Howard Brewer

The trial started amid a swarm of media attention that recalled the Simpson trial. In the four-month period that began when this attractive young expectant mother disappeared, and ended when her good-looking, seemingly All-American, middle-class white husband was arrested for her murder, people had become vested in the story's outcome. They grieved with Sharon Rocha as she pleaded for Laci's safe return. And they became fascinated with Scott's quixotic behavior—his infidelity with a likeable young woman, his improbable fishing trip taken within a mile of where the bodies were found, and the break for the border he may have been planning before his arrest.

In our television age, the real-life drama we can watch on camera in the courtroom, or through real-time updates from just outside, rivals any soap opera. And the juxtaposition of personalities in the Peterson case was perfect: the staid, bookish prosecutor, Rick DiStaso, and his government team, versus the flashy defense attorney "Hollywood" Mark Geragos. Geragos was already well known to court watchers through his representation of celebrity clients—including Congressman Gary Condit, who along with murdered Washington intern Chandra Levy, also hailed from Modesto.

Less familiar to the public was the judge selected to preside over the Peterson case. When the trial was moved, Geragos wanted to keep Stanislaus County Superior Court Judge Al Girolami on the case, but Girolami made it clear he would not follow the case to Redwood. The first choice to replace him was retired Contra Costa County Superior Court Judge Richard Arnason, but when Geragos objected, the trial stalled for a week while the search continued. Ultimately the job went to another respected retiree—Alameda County Judge Alfred Delucchi.

Delucchi had been in retirement since 1998 when he was tapped by California Chief Justice Ronald George to take charge of the Peterson trial. During his tenure the seventy-two-year-old jurist had presided over a number of high-profile cases, most notably the 1991 trial of Huey Newton, who murdered Black Panther co-founder Tyrone Robinson. Even in retirement Delucchi continued to hear East Bay murder cases, sentencing Giles Albert Nadey Jr. to death in 2000 for the sexually motivated murder of a minister's wife. When Delucchi's name was suggested, both the prosecutors and the defense attorneys hailed him as an "ideal fit" for the case.

Delucchi had rejected Court TV's request to televise the trial of Newton, and he did the same in the Peterson case, much to the disappointment of the press. The decision pleased Sharon Rocha, who felt that what went on inside the courtroom was "personal." With a gag order imposed on attorneys and witnesses alike, it was the marvel of electronic messaging from our reporters, such as Beth Karas, that kept Court TV and the public informed of the day's events.

With the judge in place, jury selection began in San Mateo County Superior Court on March 4. One woman who was not chosen on the panel stopped on the courthouse steps and told reporters that she had no idea that Scott would be "so charismatic." Nearly three months later, on May 27, a jury of twelve citizens and six alternates was sworn in. The makeup was split evenly along gender lines. The majority of the twelve-person panel was Caucasian. One African American woman had been selected, along with two men in their forties—a retired police officer and a high school sports coach. Other panelists included a male firefighter and paramedic, a union worker who had once been charged with violating a restraining order, and a woman whose husband was killed while serving a prison term for murder. Another man, a devout Christian in his mid-sixties, asked permission to consult with his priest before taking a place on the jury of the capital murder case. The six alternates were also divided evenly between men and women. Three of the alternates later joined the panel.

The trial began on Tuesday, June 1 in Superior Courtroom 2M of the Redwood City Courthouse. Stanislaus County Prosecutors Rick DiStaso and Dave Harris appeared for the prosecution. At the defense table were Mark Geragos and his co-counsel Pat Harris, who was sitting second chair. Scott's attorney, Kirk McAllister, had faded into the background.

The court case was expected to last at least four or five months, and from the start pundits were asking whether DiStaso and Harris were up to the task. DiStaso, the small-town Modesto district attorney, had relatively little experience in capital cases. His profile contrasted sharply with the big-gun lead defense counsel, who swaggered into court behind sunglasses even on cloudy days, telephone always at ear, surrounded by his personal fan club. As the case began to unfold, onlookers wondered whether the two dedicated civil servants could hold their own against the showy, seasoned Geragos.

Seated on opposing sides of the brightly lit courtroom, its walls papered to look like wood, were the families of Laci and Scott. Journalists crowded the middle rows of the gallery, and the back was filled with trial watchers who lined up each day for the remaining seats.

DiStaso delivered his opening remarks in a low-key, nontheatrical style. As sunlight streamed through the bank of windows just beside the jury box, the slender, boyish prosecutor outlined his case over the clicking of reporters typing into their laptop computers. He spent his time covering the details of that December 24, laying out the elements of Scott's early behavior that had raised the suspicions of the police. He told jurors that he would prove the defendant did not leave for the Berkeley Marina at 9:30 A.M. because Scott's cell phone records would show he was close to home at 10:08. He also accused Scott of lying about watching Martha Stewart with Laci on the morning she vanished—a declaration that would be viewed as a monumental blunder the next day, when Geragos delivered his opening statement to the jury.

Commenting on the case that first afternoon, one onlooker, local defense attorney Jeffery Boyarski, warned that Geragos better be able to back up any claims he makes to jurors in the opening statement. "The first rule is, if you're not sure you can prove something you better not even say it," he said.

Yet the next morning, with dramatic flourish, Geragos aimed for the bleachers. He promised not only that he would refute the State's case, but that he would prove his client was "stone cold innocent." He conceded that Scott *was* guilty of exceptionally bad behavior— freely referring to him as a cad—but he insisted that this bad behavior did not make him a murderer.

"You want to say his behavior is boorish, we are not going to dispute that," the defense lawyer told jurors. "But the fact is, this is a murder case and there has to be evidence in a murder case."

Geragos insisted that Scott Peterson loved Laci, and that he'd been anxiously anticipating fatherhood when his wife disappeared. Despite Scott's infidelity, he told jurors that his client was not about "to chuck this entire life he had" for a woman he had dated just four times.

Geragos controlled the courtroom as he delivered an overview of the evidence he said would exonerate his client. There were witnesses who saw Laci walking her dog after the time police believed she was killed, and a defense expert to testify that Laci had carried her fetus to term, all disputing the prosecution's time line. He also insisted that the hair that police recovered from Scott's boat had been left there when Laci visited the warehouse with her husband on December 20, not after Laci's death.

At the close of his statement, Geragos swooped in for the kill. Standing with a wide grin in front of two large flat screen monitors located directly across from the jury box, the lawyer aired the Martha Stewart tape from December 24, 2002. There it was—footage of Stewart discussing meringue cookies with a guest on her Christmas Eve show. Either Brocchini had missed the reference when he reviewed the tape at headquarters that previous spring, or he had misrepresented the evidence during his investigation. Geragos's decision to play the tape was the opening volley in an aggressive play to paint the investigation as sloppy and improper. And Geragos delighted in turning the knife, by rolling the tape a second time.

"I played it twice, just in case the Modesto PD couldn't hear it," he remarked sarcastically as the courtroom erupted in laughter.

Ultimately, however, Geragos's bold move would be transformed into a stunning coup for the State. The mention of meringue occurred at 9:48 A.M.—at least eighteen minutes after Scott claimed he had left the residence. This narrowed the window of time during which Laci went missing. Rather than leaving her at 9:30, Scott must have been in the house until at least 9:50. Since McKenzie was found dragging his leash at 10:18, the time that elapsed while she was alone had now shrunk to only twenty-eight minutes. It is hard to imagine how the defense team could have missed the significance of the timing. Perhaps their arrogance blinded them to how this new timeline would help the prosecution.

In my years as a trial lawyer, I followed many long-standing techniques of presenting a case to a jury. One such tactic, known formally as "primacy and recency," is more popularly called "start strong and end strong." Jurors tend to remember best what they hear first and last in a presentation. Material in the middle, consequently, can get lost. It's in the litigator's best interest to grab the jury's attention early, to get them vested in the story.

Prosecutor Rick DiStaso went in a very different direction. Rather than beginning with a dramatic witness, such as Amber Frey, the medical examiner, or one of the lead investigators, the State called the Petersons' housekeeper, Margarita Nava.

With a thick Spanish accent, Nava testified that she had cleaned the Petersons' house on December 23. She left a single mop outside and dirty rags inside a bucket atop the washing machine. When they conducted the preliminary search that first evening, however, the police had discovered two mops and an empty pail outside. Nava's testimony was the first step in what would become a painstaking recitation of each fact in the case. The prosecutors were not sensational, but they were certainly meticulous. Their strategy was to cover all the bases, leaving Geragos little room to poke holes in their arguments.

Geragos had quite a talent for cross-examination. From the very beginning, he used the State's witnesses to make his own case. Laci's own sister, Amy Rocha, admitted to him that she had vehemently insisted that Scott "was the last person who would hurt anyone." He got Sharon Rocha to say that if Laci knew that Scott was having an affair with Amber, she would have told her mother—but then forced her to concede that Laci hadn't told her about Scott's 1998 affair with Janet Ilse. More important, Sharon admitted she hadn't told police that Scott had used the phrase "Laci's missing" in his initial call on Christmas Eve until Amber Frey went public. She testified that the significance of those words had not been clear until she learned about Scott's infidelity.

The cross-examination of Ron Grantski was another coup for Geragos. When Grantski referred to Scott's "fishy story," claiming that the mysterious trip occurred too late in the day, Geragos elicited that Grantski himself had gone fishing in the late morning that very day. And, like Scott, he hadn't mentioned the trip to any family members.

Brent Rocha's wife, Rosemarie, also fell victim to Geragos's skill. In her testimony, she mentioned that Scott had once commented that he "was kind of hoping for infertility." Under cross-examination, though, she admitted that she did not tell police about the incriminating remark until Amber Frey surfaced.

As each new State witness was damaged by the defense team, many trial watchers were highly critical of the prosecution, wondering aloud when—or even if—the case would begin to take shape. Many people voiced concern about the prosecution's slow pace and lackluster presentation. Yet the parade of witnesses continued.

Peterson family friend "Uncle" Harvey Kemple provided some levity with his animated delivery on the stand. First, he established that Scott had claimed to be golfing on Christmas Eve. Then he recalled a family barbeque where Scott had burned the chicken he was cooking and told the jury that Scott showed more emotion then than at any time during the search for Laci. Kemple also revealed that in early January he followed Scott from the Command Center at the Red Lion to a local mall, where Scott said he planned to hang flyers. Instead Scott sat idly in his car for nearly an hour, never hanging a single poster. On another morning he followed Scott from the Command Center to the Del Rio Country Club, where Scott allegedly played golf.

On cross-examination, Geragos's cocounsel, Pat Harris, questioned Kemple's spy tactics, implying that tailing someone without their knowledge seemed an immature action for an adult male. Jurors chuckled aloud. At one point the judge sarcastically joined in, asking the defense counselor if he had any more questions about "the chicken."

The next group of witnesses testified about Scott's activities on the morning that Laci disappeared. They included neighbors Amie Krigbaum, Tara Venable, and Karen Servas, who had discovered McKenzie dragging a dirty leash at 10:18 A.M. that day.

When Servas explained how she'd retraced her steps to the store and bank to arrive at the exact time she discovered McKenzie, Geragos challenged the accuracy of the timestamp on her store receipt. He later showed that the store's cash register was off by ten minutes when his team checked it in 2004.

After Servas, a litany of witnesses, including nine police officers, testified about their involvement in the case. Among them were responding officers Derrick Letsinger, Matt Spurlock, and Jon Evers.

As he had before, Geragos elicited responses from the witnesses that further diluted the case against Scott. In my opinion, Judge Delucchi gave the defense counselor enormous latitude with his questioning. He permitted a lot of hearsay evidence—statements the cops heard from third parties—under the "state of mind" exception. What the officers heard from others, in other words, was allowed because it might have shaped their attitudes, or state of mind, about Scott early in the investigation.

As the prosecution laid out its case, word began to surface that some jurors seemed bored; there was even some yawning reported during the testimony. All that changed on day eleven, however, when a pool cameraman videotaped Juror #5 conversing with Laci's brother, Brent, as the two walked through the courthouse metal detector. The juror was heard on the tape saying ". . . lose today . . ." before both men parted, smiling.

The media exploded. TV commentators spent endless airtime analyzing what the two men had been saying, and what impact it would have on the trial. The judge and attorneys were all made aware of the situation, yet the uproar failed to derail the trial.

That afternoon jurors heard from Laci's gynecologist, Dr. Tina Endraki. One of the key issues in the case was Laci's due date and the gestational age of the fetus. Endraki's testimony helped the prosecution establish that Laci's February 10 due date was accurate. Her testimony was bolstered by Laci's medical records, which noted the baby's gestational age at thirty-two weeks on December 23, Laci's last office visit.

Other witnesses were called to testify about the jewelry Laci had been wearing when she disappeared. Among them was a pawn-broker, who recounted Scott and Laci's two visits to his shop. He reported that the couple sold him several pieces, including gold chains, rings, and a charm.

Geragos used this occasion to create doubt in the jurors' mind by discussing one of Laci's watches, a Croton timepiece that had been missing since she disappeared. She had never been seen wearing the watch, and a videotape made to accompany its listing on eBay showed that its battery was dead. However, Geragos produced a receipt for a Croton watch similar in description that was pawned in Modesto on December 31. Could Laci have been wearing this watch when she was abducted by strangers? Is that why it had never been located? The prosecutor objected, the judge sustained the objection, and no further discussion ensued.

The next day, Juror #5 was in the news again. The judge cleared both Brent and the juror of any misconduct and stated that the media had misinterpreted what transpired at the metal detector. But he also implemented a new arrival procedure to prevent jurors and witnesses from interacting. Geragos's response was to demand tighter controls on the press.

When court resumed on Day 11, jurors heard from Laci's yoga instructor, Debra, who recalled that Laci was in pain and needed help to her car after her December 20 yoga session. She also recalled a statement that Laci reportedly made to her: "The dog probably thinks I'm mad at him, because I never walk him anymore."

The statement brought Geragos to his feet. No such comment was ever reported to the police, he argued, and he wanted the testimony stricken from the record. Wolski then denied telling police that Laci's only exercise was walking the dog, even though police recorded the comment in her official statement. She also denied telling officers that Scott was "excited" about the baby.

Laci's three best friends, Stacey Boyers, Renee Tomlinson, and Lori Ellsworth also took the witness stand that day. Jurors heard them express doubts that a fatigued Laci would have walked McKenzie that morning. While they believed the Peterson marriage was good, all three women had grown suspicious of Scott as the search dragged on. Stacey described Scott vacuuming around the washer/dryer area in the den on Christmas Day. (An expert later testified that no DNA evidence linking Scott to Laci's murder was recovered from the vacuum.)

It was not until Day 13, when Detective Allen Brocchini took the stand, that real sparks began to fly. Brocchini testified about his Christmas morning interview with Scott, and the jury listened as portions of their interchange were played in open court. This was the first time they heard Scott in conversation, and the first time the jury got a thorough overview of the police investigation. Brocchini discussed the evidence collected during searches of Scott's home, vehicle, and warehouse. But his testimony—and, more important, his videotaped interview with Scott—were all but lost on the jury. Ironically, jurors would later report that it was Brocchini's taped interview with Scott Peterson at headquarters that first night that was the first topic that came up when they kicked off their deliberations. While the jurors didn't understand its significance when it was played in court, that interview became key evidence during deliberations, as the panelists were able to see Scott's early lies for themselves.

"We were looking for inconsistencies," Juror Steve Cardosi later reported. And there were plenty. During his testimony, Brocchini explained that the lures Scott claimed to have used on his fishing trip were still in their package, unopened, and the tan-colored tarp found rolled up in the rear of his pickup had been moved to a shed behind the Peterson house. Saturated with gasoline, the tarp had to be aired out for several days before it was logged into evidence lest the overwhelming fumes mask or destroy forensic evidence.

Brocchini went on to detail his first meeting with Amber Frey, during which she agreed to record her telephone conversations with Scott to assist the investigation. He also testified that in an attempt to corroborate Scott's story about watching Martha Stewart with Laci, he reviewed tapes of the shows that aired on December 23 and 24. Brocchini initially contended that while the December 23 show discussed the subject, he thought the December 24 show had no reference to meringue. Perhaps because of Geragos's opening statement to the contrary, Brocchini admitted that he later watched the show a second time and discovered that the word "meringue" was mentioned at 9:48.

If Scott actually saw this segment, as he'd told the detectives, then under the defense's abduction theory Laci had only twenty minutes to finish mopping the floor, load the breakfast dishes, make the bed, use her curling iron, change clothes, don her sneakers, take the dog to the park, and be abducted. Suddenly, Scott's story was looking less plausible.

The next morning, "Juror 5-Gate," as it was dubbed in the press, erupted when the heavyset airport security screener, whose name was Justin Falconer, was ousted from the jury. Minutes later, Falconer stood before a bank of microphones. "I'm a distraction to the jury," he conceded, admitting that he'd listened to friends discussing the press coverage of his interaction with Brent Rocha, which led to his dismissal.

Falconer said that he agreed with the judge's decision to remove him from the panel. But then he launched into a tirade, attacking the prosecution's case as thin and boring, "It was driving me nuts," he railed from behind dark sunglasses. "He's innocent." Falconer, who was on disability leave from his job, told the crush of journalists that he had not heard any evidence that would prove Scott guilty of murder. He excused Scott's affair, calling it "his little side thing," and sneered at the prosecution's claim that Amber was the motive for the double murders. "If they try to say that Amber is a motive for this after four dates, then . . ." he paused, shaking his head from side to side in disgust.

"Honestly, guys say pretty stupid stuff to get a girl," he said about Scott's remarks to Frey that he "lost" his wife. Acknowledging that he was a father himself, he stated that "pregnant women are crazy," complaining of exhaustion one day and "running a marathon" the next. He also balked at yoga instructor Debra Wolski's testimony that Laci was "too exhausted" to walk McKenzie on Christmas Eve.

"I didn't believe two words of that woman," he sneered.

When reporters asked about Scott's cool demeanor, Falconer said, "I can kinda understand where he's coming from," and admitted, "I'm not a very emotional person, either."

Falconer's remarks sparked a flurry of speculation and additional criticism about the State's case. If this was the best the district attorney had, many critics sniped, Peterson would walk.

Falconer maintained that several jury members felt the way he did. He implied that he was a good friend of Juror #6, the firefighting paramedic, who eventually became the foreman. Other jurors later bolstered Falconer's claim by revealing that in the first weeks, they too thought the case was flimsy—nothing more than a botched police investigation.

However, there were several jurors who did not seem the type to fold easily. The union worker, Juror #8, was not responding to Geragos's theories. Juror #11, the African American woman, had a close relative in the Sheriff's Department. She was pegged as pro-prosecution as well. Television panelists thought the State's best-case scenario was not a conviction, but a hung jury, and the opportunity to try Scott a second time. One local paper came out with a painful headline, misspelling Rick DiStaso's name so that it read "Disasto."

At the time, I couldn't help agreeing with the pundits. While I thought the prosecution had a strong circumstantial case, the many delays, the disorganized presentation of witnesses, and Geragos's dominance in the courtroom seemed to spell trouble. Additionally, Judge Delucchi had taken to chastising the prosecutors in open court. The jury had to think DiStaso and Harris were engaged in stalling tactics—or, worse yet, were trying to hide things from the defense.

When court finally reconvened, Judge Delucchi addressed the jury. "You have all been questioned individually by the Court, and I want to reaffirm, and to strike home, or emphasize as much as I can, that you are not to listen to, read, or watch any media reports of this trial, nor discuss it with any representatives of the media or their agents."

"So what we're going to do now, we're going to seat the first alternate as Juror Number 5." That first alternate was both a doctor and a lawyer. Those of us covering the case were stunned that this man had not been struck by either side during jury selection. It is very rare that a legal professional becomes a juror in a case of this sort. This man was not a criminal attorney, but his specialized knowledge in the fields of law and medicine could have posed a problem. How could he ignore his own technical experience as he evaluated the witnesses? Could he keep this information to himself or would he inject what was essentially new evidence by sharing his professional opinions in the jury room?

The defense saw its opening.

"I would like to move for a mistrial," Geragos barked. Furious, he argued that the media attention had resulted in the "choosing off of jurors." He insisted the press "had insinuated itself in the case in a way that is unprecedented."

"I think this is an outrage," Geragos roared as he paced the courtroom. Referring to nicknames certain jurors were given by a TV commentator, Geragos said, "I do not believe that the jurors should be called names on TV. I don't believe that the jurors should be interrogated and cross-examined. . . . I have a client who is on trial for his life. But these people have given up their life. They shouldn't have to be subjected to this . . ."

"All right. The motion for mistrial is denied," Delucchi ruled. "We have to live with the media. They do what they do. We have to do what we have to do. So that's the way it is." And with that he called Detective Brocchini back to the stand for cross-examination.

From the outset, Brocchini and Geragos were posturing, verbally circling one another as questions and answers volleyed back and forth. Some trial watchers speculated that Geragos was purposely exhibiting disdain for the police, to reinforce his theory of their rush to judgment.

At one point, Geragos sarcastically asked the detective if he'd used his professional training to determine whether or not Scott's clothes had been run through the washing machine.

Sensing that tempers were hot, the judge called for an early recess.

That afternoon, Geragos was back on the offensive. Again, he pointed to Brocchini's conclusion in regard to the Martha Stewart tapes.

"Well, let's take a look at your report . . . on the twenty-first [of January]. Specifically you say you reviewed the 12/24/2002 from the beginning including commercials; is that correct?"

"Yes."

"There was no mention of meringue during any of this show, correct?"

"That's what I wrote."

"Okay, then several times during the show, Martha Stewart commented on it being Christmas Eve, right?"

"Yes."

"Okay. Now, that information, yeah, that information was known to you, or you thought it was very significant, correct? That's why you wrote it in the report, right?"

"It was an important piece of the puzzle."

"Okay. Also on that date there was, you had already interviewed, or somebody from the Modesto PD had interviewed a witness at Scott's warehouse; isn't that correct?" Geragos was referring to Scott's warehouse neighbor, Ron Prater. "Didn't that witness tell you that Scott was at the warehouse on the twenty-third?"

"Yeah, but he wasn't positive it was the twenty-third or the twenty-fourth."

"And did you see a TV when you were in the warehouse?"

"No, I didn't."

"Okay. So you were aware on the twenty-third, or by the time you wrote this report, that Scott was apparently not at home, according to Margarita Nava, on the twenty-third? All right, so [on] 12/28, within three days of you being assigned to this case, you had a statement from Prater who said that he saw Scott and his truck was parked out front, and he was already there by eight-thirty or nine o'clock, correct?"

"Not correct. He wasn't sure if it was the twenty-third or the twenty-fourth."

". . . Now, after you prepared this report here on January twenty-first, you then wrote in the same report: I find it highly suspicious that Scott Peterson would claim to be watching Martha Stewart with Laci on 12/24 while Martha was baking with meringue."

"And then your conclusion is there is no meringue mentioned on the show on 12/24, correct?"

"That's what I wrote. But I was wrong." Brocchini conceded.

Adding to the tension, Geragos then played the December 24 Martha Stewart show on the courtroom's large video screen for a third time—just to force the issue regarding Brocchini's negligence. "Now, apparently when you watched this video, you missed that?" Geragos asked.

"I missed it."

"Okay. . . . The absence of that was something you thought was suspicious, and part of the . . . the 'puzzle' is the way you said it?"

"Objection, your Honor," Prosecutor DiStaso said, rising from his chair.

"No, overruled," Delucchi ordered. "He can answer that. You can answer that, detective."

"Well, I thought it was suspicious that it wasn't in there, but I also think it's better that it is," Brocchini replied, keeping an even tone.

"Now, I'm still on the same interview, the one that we played for the jury yesterday, the next portion of that, you have that in front of you?"

"I have it here. I don't know what the next portion is that you're going to talk about."

"I just want to make sure you've got it there to refresh your recollection."

"I do."

"Okay. Then you asked him, 'When did you realize you were going to go fishing?' Is that correct?"

"Yes."

"And he said. 'Well, that was a morning decision.' It's either—and then going on to the next page—That's a morning decision is what you said, correct?"

"Yes."

"Go play golf at the club or go fishing, right?"

"Right."

"Now, at any point did you know that Ron Grantski had gone fishing that same day?"

"Objection, your Honor. Relevance?" DiStaso said, jumping up for a second time.

"Overruled," the judge declared.

"Maybe I'll ask it better," Geragos began again. "I assume you know now Ron Grantski went fishing virtually the exact same time."

"I do know now."

"Okay. When did you learn that?"

"After this trial started."

The barrage of questions continued, as Geragos hammered away at the obvious discrepancies between Brocchini's testimony and actual police reports. The defense attorney cited Brocchini's earlier testimony that he had not seen a pair of white sneakers Scott claimed he'd pulled from a duffel bag and placed on the dining room wet bar the day Laci went missing. Waving a police photograph, Geragos pointed out that members of the Modesto Crime Scene unit had in fact, captured the tennis shoes on film.

Geragos effectively demonstrated the detective had made numerous errors in his investigation. As Brocchini's second day of cross-examination progressed, Geragos interrogated him about a witness statement that had been expunged from his police report. Brocchini had to admit that he had removed a statement by a woman named Peggy O'Donnell, whose company, Adventures in Advertising, was located near Scott's in the same industrial park.

"Did you go out and interview Peggy O'Donnell?"

"No. Somebody else did, though."

"Did you follow-up to see what the information was?"

"No, but I . . . it was done."

"Okay. Now, specifically one of the things that you thought—I think you told the jury yesterday it was an exciting moment for you, if I'm not mistaken—is when you found the hair in the pliers; is that correct?"

"Yes."

"Okay, did you think it was significant or would be important information to your report to have people know that Peggy O'Donnell saw Laci at the warehouse on 12/23? Did you think that's something that would be significant since there was a hair that got you excited on a pliers at the warehouse on 12 . . . what was the date that the pliers was recovered?"

"12/27. The date I saw it was February 11. . . . And that was important information. I didn't know it was Peggy McDonald [sic] but I did know we had to send somebody out there to interview Peggy, and it was done."

"Oh, so after you got this information you sent somebody to interview Peggy?"

"No, I don't know when. I just know she was interviewed."

"You don't know when it was done because, until I brought it up, you didn't realize that you had excised it and somebody would catch it; isn't that correct?" Geragos asked accusingly.

"I don't know."

"Can you tell me how that particular piece of information got excised out of your police report?"

"I excised it."

"You did it?"

"Yes, I did, if it's not in there . . ."

In the report, O'Donnell claimed that Laci visited the warehouse complex on either December 20 or December 23, and asked to use her bathroom. O'Donnell's testimony was important to the defense because it was evidence that Laci had been to Scott's office after he bought the boat. This visit might account for the hair found inside the craft.

Brocchini did not think much of O'Donnell's report. He had been inside the warehouse on December 24, and again on December 27, and was certain that a woman in Laci's condition could not have climbed over the pallets stacked floor to ceiling to get to the bathroom in the rear of the storage space. In fact, based on the cluttered condition of the warehouse, he was confident that Laci had not gone inside that day. She might never have seen the boat.

Brocchini knew that O'Donnell never saw Laci inside Scott's warehouse. He also knew that another officer had followed up on the tip and logged the interview with O'Donnell into his report. Yet Geragos was insinuating that the detective had done something sinister. Brocchini did not interview the woman, so he did not leave the information in his own report, but the other officer's report was always available.

I later learned that Detective Brocchini was quite concerned about the way he was portrayed in the press. He feared for his job— as did his mother, who became the target of nasty comments by friends at the beauty parlor and her bingo game.

Before convening court the next day, Judge Delucchi angrily reprimanded the Modesto Police Department for violating his gag order. A department spokesman had commented on the Peggy O'Donnell controversy, apparently telling an AP reporter that the report was not hidden or expunged, but was available in another officer's report. The judge was furious.

Later that morning, Brocchini again fell under attack. Geragos began by quizzing the detective about Scott's neighbor Kim McGregor and her role in the burglary of the Peterson home. He pressed for details about McGregor's alibi for December 23 and 24, and then waited to pounce as the detective explained that she had visited an ex-boyfriend and his two Hawaiian roommates on the twenty-third. Producing a flier about the burglary across the street at the Medina residence, Geragos noted that police were looking for three dark-skinned, non-African American men. The lawyer drove the point home when he got Brocchini to confirm that he had not investigated McGregor's Hawaiian friends. Brocchini insisted that McGregor was investigated, and that police had eliminated her as a suspect. Nevertheless, the attack continued.

Geragos finally wrapped up his cross-examination by criticizing the detective for not following up on three witness accounts that might have placed Laci in the park on the morning of December 24.

He referred to a woman named Victoria Pouches, who claimed to have seen a woman walking a dog that was barking furiously, and a man named Chris Van Zandt, who also claimed to have seen a pregnant woman walking one of the park trails.

Geragos pointed out that the detective never brought Van Zandt to the park to show officers where he made the sighting. "Wouldn't it have been the prudent thing to do, when you got forty or fifty officers out there looking in the park, to have actually driven to the guy's house and shown him a picture of Laci, shown him a picture of McKenzie and say, 'Hey, is that the dog?' So you can eliminate that lead?"

"No."

"No? Okay. Now?"

"Prudent thing to do is, as soon as we got the information, we went there, we did a search of that area, a thorough search. We contacted people. We searched the bushes. Went to the area he described. . . . He said he couldn't ID her. He said he couldn't tell us if it was Laci or not. He saw a pregnant lady walking with a golden retriever. So going to where he was and showing him a picture would not—that would not have been prudent at the time."

After three days of cross-examination Geragos finally passed the witness, and on June 30 DiStaso began his redirect. Brocchini was again caught in a snafu when he was asked about the tip he received from Miguel Espidia, Scott's former college classmate. According to Brocchini, Espidia had told police about a 1995 conversation in which Scott observed that if he wanted to "get rid of a body" he would bag the head, wrap it with duct tape, and then dump it in the bay. When Geragos got Brocchini to concede that Espidia had never actually mentioned duct tape, the detective was left looking like he'd intentionally embellished the story. Later he would explain that he had not reviewed the tip information in a long time when asked about it in court and was simply mistaken about the duct tape.

After concluding his testimony, the detective made himself scarce throughout the remainder of the trial. Some reporters tried to suggest that Brocchini had lied about evidence to claim credit for solving the notorious murder. Every story needs a villain, and for a time this hard-working detective was unfairly cast in the role. A few ardent commentators even labeled him the "Mark Fuhrman of the case." Yes, he made some mistakes along the way, errors in judgment and even questionable omissions in his reporting. But there was no falsification or suspected planting of evidence. Nothing he did wrong would have changed the outcome of the case. Nevertheless, the media portrayed him as a zealot focused entirely on one person, Scott Peterson.

It wasn't until Amber Frey took the stand on Day 34 of the trial that the pundits changed their tune about the progress of the trial. During six days of testimony, which included the recorded phone conversations, Amber introduced a very different Scott Peterson to the jury. Those conversations didn't prove that he was a killer, but they offered motive, innumerable lies, and plenty of incriminating statements.

To the surprise of many, Amber came across not as a wicked home-wrecker but as a naive, honest young woman who was truly in love with Scott Peterson. She was entirely credible. Critically, in the time she was working with the police she'd managed to get Scott to repeat several damning statements he first made long before the recordings began. In early December he told Amber that he had "lost" his wife and this would be his first holiday without her. Several times before Laci disappeared, he talked of a future with Amber and her daughter. He told her there would be a window of time when he would be absent, but that by the end of January he would be home and free to expand their relationship. He told her on several occasions that he did not want his own children. In fact, Scott wanted a vasectomy and told Amber that her daughter Ayiana would be the only child he needed. Amazingly, Amber was able to get Scott to repeat all of this information after she began taping him on December 31. It would have taken an ogre to shrug off the story of Scott attending the emotional candlelight vigil for his missing wife just after he'd been concocting stories about wild Parisian parties for his lover's amusement.

Later, it emerged that the jurors were particularly repulsed by this behavior. "That spoke [volumes]," juror Greg Beratlis later told journalists. "You know, here's a guy [whose] wife was abducted . . . yet he's romancing his lover or girlfriend, for lack of a better term, at her vigil," jury foreman Steve Cardosi agreed. "You know, when you think about that his wife, pregnant with his baby, you know, he at some point in there had to have loved her, and for him to be romancing another woman while she's missing was a pretty big topic for us."

"That's part of the twisted mind of Scott Peterson," added juror Mike Belmessieri, a former police officer. "His wife is missing and he's on a love affair in Paris and Luxembourg or wherever . . . and the whole time he's talking from Modesto, USA."

Testimony from Shawn Sibley and Scott's employees Eric Olsen and David Fernandez had set the stage for Amber. Visibly nervous, Olsen told jurors about "inappropriate" conversations he'd witnessed between Sibley and Scott at a business dinner they attended in October 2002. David Fernandez, a fertilizer salesman, followed with more details, including Scott's questions about "favorite sexual positions."

Sibley testified that Scott described himself as a "horny bastard" that night. He also told her he had "lost" his soul mate, and feared that he was destined to spend the rest of his life alone.

Amber's testimony began on August 10, 2004. Dressed in a dark suit, her long blond hair falling around her face, Amber rode the escalator to the second floor courtroom. Surprisingly, her own testimony was very brief. It was Scott's own words on tape that had the real impact. Because she was one of the few people left who was still listening to Scott by mid-January, he couldn't stop talking to her. Even though much of what she told him was accusatory and berating, he often stayed on the line for hours at a time. While he never confessed, he made countless remarks that would sound particularly incriminating at trial.

During Amber's three days under direct examination, the jurors heard hours of recorded conversations while Amber sat in the gallery with her attorney, Gloria Allred. Amber's long-awaited appearance had been hyped in the press as the linchpin of the prosecution's case, yet jurors later reported that her testimony, and the hours of recorded phone conversations, constituted only a small piece of the whole. "It was all too clear that Scott had been planning Laci's murder even before he met Amber Frey," as juror Richelle Nice later reported.

After several days' worth of scheduling delays Amber's cross-examination began on August 23, 2004.

"Go ahead, Mr. Geragos," Delucchi instructed.

"No questions, your Honor," Geragos responded.

The courtroom gasped. "What?" a juror exclaimed.

"Just kidding," Geragos said with a smile. The room burst into laughter. "Trying to lighten it up a little."

Geragos may have gotten the laughs he was after, but Sharon Rocha later made it clear outside the courthouse that she found nothing amusing about the lawyer's habitual, often joking asides. There was nothing funny about the murder of her daughter, she told reporters.

Geragos began his questioning by asking about Amber's first meeting with Scott, but his examination was interrupted by the lunch break. That afternoon, Geragos picked up where he had left off.

"Prior to that [first meeting]," he asked, "you indicated to the jury that you had talked with Shawn Sibley, right?"

"Yes."

"Okay. As you sit here today, do you remember if . . . before you met him the first time, if you knew whether he was e-mailing back and forth with your best friend, that he was labeling himself as 'Horny Bastard'?"

"I don't recall exact conversations or I don't know that."

"Okay. What about . . . did she tell you when she was down in Orange County, that they had a conversation about, how do you pick up girls, or something along those lines, or what should I write on my name tag to pick up girls?"

"I don't recall that."

"Shawn ever tell you that she suggested writing, 'I'm rich'?"

"I don't recall that."

"But do you remember saying to Shawn, 'Why do you want me to meet this guy if he calls himself "Horny Bastard"? Or why do you want me to meet this guy if he is trying to pick up girls?' Do you remember ever expressing that kind of concern to her?"

"No. Because our conversations, or the conversation I had with Shawn, didn't really entail those details that you are speaking of."

"So Shawn did or didn't tell you about this stuff?"

"I vaguely recall her talking about it. But as far as the content in the conversation, I'm sorry, I don't."

"Well, when you say the content, you know the 'H. B.' rings a bell, right?"

"Yes."

"The name tag with 'I'm rich' rings a bell, right?"

"Vaguely, but . . ."

"Did you ever ask her . . . I mean, Shawn is protective of you?"

"Yes, uh-huh."

"She is protective of you because she knows you have been hurt in the past, correct?"

"I would agree, yes," Amber replied.

"So she's looking out for you, right?"

"Yes."

"Okay, did you ever go back to her, whether it was before you met Scott or after, and say, Why didn't you tell me about this? or Why would you fix him up with me if this guy is using 'H. B.,' or How do I pick up girls, or anything like that?"

"Because other conversations that they had one-on-one, [there] was something that stood out to her—that he was looking for a soul mate. And she said that in their conversation . . . again, I don't know the great depth of their conversation. But to her it was very significant that she felt that this was somebody that she would like to introduce to me, and that I was looking for somebody to be with."

"Now, when you say in looking for a soul mate, and you . . . that didn't cause you any pause, that here is a guy looking for a soul mate;

but, did you say to yourself, Wait a second here, this guy doesn't make a whole lot of sense?"

"No, I didn't."

The "H. B." or "Horny Bastard" comment really resonated with juror Richelle Nice. "Trying to nail down a motive was one of our toughest issues," Nice later said of the jury deliberations. "In the end, I guess Scott just wanted to be free. He wanted to be that 'H. B.' that Amber's friend Shawn Sibley called him."

Geragos next established that the two drank heavily on their first date.

"So you have been drinking . . . basically within forty-five minutes of seeing . . . meeting this guy, and straight through at the restaurant, at the bar, then when you finish and leave the bar . . . close to closing, when you can't buy alcohol any more?"

"Correct."

"Okay. So you stop, you buy what a bottle of gin at the store with the . . . Food Maxx, whatever it was?"

"I believe that's what it was. Bombay Sapphire."

"Bombay gin and tonic. You back to the hotel . . . two of you start drinking some more?"

Geragos continued to hammer Amber on the number of drinks she consumed that night on her first blind date with Scott. As he roamed the courtroom, his client, attired in a suit and tie, stared at the witness with no expression. The lawyer also got Amber to concede that within the first hour of the date, Scott disclosed his upcoming travel plans, explaining that he'd be away for much of the time. He was trying to paint a picture of Amber making more of the relationship than Scott did. After all, they had only a handful of dates; the rest of the relationship was on the phone.

Amber also fielded questions about meeting Buehler and Brocchini at her home on December 30, 2002.

"Do they tell you . . . how they believe he's a big suspect in the case, right?"

"They said at that point yes, and that there was—they were looking to eliminate as well."

"Okay. And they talked to you about the fact that they asked for,

for instance, receipts or pictures, and you gave them the condoms, you had that, right?"

"Yes."

Amid questions about how serious their relationship was, Geragos won an admission from Amber that Scott had never formally professed his love for her—although she maintained he conveyed the same sentiments with other words. In the end, he may have solidified the impression that Amber was gullible and a bit desperate for a husband and father for her child. He might have convinced some jurors that Scott did not kill Laci to run off with Amber. However, he did not explain away his client's incriminating statements, which littered the six weeks of taped phone calls.

Next, the State called a string of lower-profile witnesses. District Attorney Investigator Steven Jacobson testified about the wiretaps placed on Scott's phones. Jurors received thick copies of transcripts to follow along with the many calls played in court. Among them was the voicemail to Scott from Sharon Rocha on January 11, 2003, in which she happily reported that the sonar scan of the San Francisco Bay turned up a boat anchor and not Laci's body. Scott could be heard letting out a quiet whistle in response to the news.

Another revealing moment was the conversation with realtor Brian Argain in which Scott spoke of selling or renting the Covena Avenue home, claiming that, "There's no way if Laci comes back that we're gonna stay there."

"Yeah, I don't blame you whatsoever, I'd be the same way," Argain responded.

The many pages of transcripts also made it clear to jurors that Scott had lied to family and friends repeatedly about where he was calling from. The investigators' work made it clear that Scott was often hundreds of miles away from his claimed locations when he placed the calls. Scott's calls also made it clear that he wasn't a grieving husband—he could be heard joking, hammering out business proposals, and planning evening's out at local bars.

"There were a lot of victims in this," juror Bertalis, the youth football and baseball coach, said later. "A lot were deceived."

Checking cell phone logs, Jacobson found over 250 calls between

Scott and Amber during a three-month period, from November 19, 2002, to February 19, 2003. He acknowledged that there could have been other calls placed from pay phones that were not counted. While Geragos tried to convince jurors that Amber was pursuing Scott, the prosecutors were able to show that Scott had placed a majority of those calls.

During the trial, prosecutors also presented their theory of how Scott transported his wife's body to the marina on Christmas Eve without detection. Over defense objections, DiStaso introduced a number of photographs of a pregnant woman named Kim Fulbright, an employee in the district attorney's office in her thirty-eighth week of pregnancy who was almost identical in size to Laci Peterson. The photos showed Fulbright lying inside the large green plastic toolbox that Scott kept in the bed of his pickup, and concealed on the floor of the Gamefisher, to dispel the defense's argument that it would be impossible to hide Laci's body from view.

Under cross-examination, Fulbright conceded that she could not fit inside the boat without bending her legs.

Dog handler Eloise Anderson, whose trailing dog Trimble performed the search of the Berkeley Marina, testified about her findings. Anderson reported that Trimble had found a trace of Laci's scent leading away from shore onto one of the Marina's three boat ramps. Following Anderson's testimony were more law enforcement officers, and then Scott's father, Lee Peterson.

"I'm proud to say Scott's my son," the elder Peterson told the court.

Prosecutors asked Scott's father about his two phone calls with Scott on December 24. At no time during those two calls, jurors learned, did Scott mention his new boat or the fishing trip he'd supposedly taken that day. During cross-examination, Lee sought to portray Laci as someone who had an easy time getting around, contrary to what others had told the court. He recalled the family's trip to Carmel, testifying that his daughter-in-law had done a fair amount of walking—and shopping. She even managed a steep three-quarter-mile incline from the beach to the hotel, Lee reported.

"At any point, did Laci complain?" defense counselor Pat Harris asked the ashen-haired Peterson.

"I think we all complained a little bit . . . we stopped two or three times, and everybody got to the top of the hill all right."

Lee described Scott as an avid fisherman. "Scott's the fisherman," he claimed. "I'm more the golfer." Jurors would hear more from the elder Peterson during the penalty phase of the trial.

Sharon Rocha excused herself from the courtroom during the testimony of Dr. Brian Peterson, the pathologist who had performed the autopsies on Laci and Conner. Her departure was not lost on the jurors, several of whom were seen wincing as the gruesome photos were displayed in court. It was also widely reported that the otherwise stoic defendant shed tears when gruesome photos of his wife and unborn son were shown to jurors.

Dr. Peterson told the court that it was his conclusion that Conner was not born through normal vaginal birth or Cesarean section. He maintained that the baby was still in utero when Laci died and her body dumped in the bay. Sometime afterward, as Laci's body was decomposing, the uterus ruptured and expelled the fetus through the abdominal wall in what is known as a coffin birth.

Dr. Peterson conceded that he could not determine Laci's cause of death, but he did cite strangulation, smothering, and poisoning as three types of modus operandi that leave little or no clues.

When it was his turn Geragos immediately jumped up, drawing the jury's attention to Dr. Peterson's original finding that Conner was a full-term baby. He also harped on the point that Dr. Peterson's report stated that he couldn't rule out the possibility that Conner had taken a breath.

On Day 54, prosecutors called Detective Craig Grogan to the stand. Grogan knew the pressure was on, and he was determined not to fumble during Mark Geragos's cross-examination. He had done his homework. Studying Geragos's tactics with other witnesses, he noticed that the attorney deliberately sought to rattle witnesses by rapidly firing questions at them. Grogan resolved to think through his responses slowly and methodically, and resist the temptation to snap back at the defense attorney. Grogan was also thoroughly prepped for his testimony by Deputy District Attorney Birgit Fladager, who joined the team mid-trial while Dave Harris battled the flu. Fladager garnered praise for her articulate, bright, and pointed examination of witnesses.

Over the course of the trial, the police perceived a pattern with Geragos. He would drop a bombshell on Thursdays, and every Monday he would be in chambers fighting about something. Sources told me that it was Geragos who had wanted Fridays off, but the other side also found the extra day useful to prepare for the coming week.

Grogan proved to be an excellent foil for Geragos. During his eight days on the stand, the detective effectively put the pieces of the circumstantial puzzle together for the jury. He was focused and came across as a man who was simply doing the best job he could.

Grogan explained the resources that were used during the course of the investigation. There were 42,000 pages of discovery, including 115 audiotapes and seventy-four videotapes; more than 10,000 tips, with well over seventy-four reported Laci sightings and at least ninety sightings of Scott's truck and boat on December 24. Three hundred officers and ninety agencies were involved in the investigation, the detective said.

Grogan's testimony was presented chronologically and in great detail. One of the highlights was his list of forty-one reasons police believed Laci Peterson's body would turn up in the San Francisco Bay, and not in a lake or other waterway.

"Before we get into those specific reasons, let me ask you this question: Why is it that you, at that point, had the idea that she was going to be found in some body of water?" Fladager asked, leading the detective.

"Because of the cement debris in the warehouse, the circles on the flatbed trailer in the warehouse, and the boat that he had in the warehouse that no one seemed to know about, except for the person that sold it to Mr. Peterson, the defendant, and possibly Laci Peterson," Grogan responded.

"So this list that you came up with, what were the reasons that you came up with for why Laci Peterson would eventually be found in the bay?"

"Well, we looked at the fact that Mr. Peterson did have a parking stub from the Berkeley Marina that's dated 12/24, and the timing is consistent with his statement. We had the cell site information that showed his location on December 24. It did show that he did make phone calls from over in that area, and it did appear that he was there.

"The dog track at the Berkeley Marina that indicated that Laci Peterson's scent was there. . . . The defendant told us that he was at the Berkeley Marina. He had a fishing license, two-day fishing license that was purchased on December 20, and filled out for the twenty-third and twenty-fourth. . . . The fishing tackle in the boat, at least the majority of the fishing tackle, if not all, was fresh water tackle."

"On January 11, when everyone was waiting to see the Side Sonar image that eventually ended up being an anchor . . . Sharon Rocha called him and left him a message, and he whistled when he heard it was an anchor.

"At that point, he had already made three trips—three subsequent trips to the Berkeley Marina since the December 24 visit, which seemed odd. And it directed us back there.

"Another thing that we considered was the fact that right after the defendant found that his wife was missing from the house, that he told people that he was golfing that day. And [we] considered that as possibly what his initial alibi was meant to be."

"The initial alibi was golfing?" Fladager asked.

"Yes. . . . Initially his plan was to say that he was golfing on that day, and for no one to ever know that he had the boat, or that he made the trip to San Francisco Bay."

Later, foreman Steve Cardosi told journalists that the jury was convinced that Scott had, in fact, switched his alibi. "One of the maintenance men at the Berkeley Marina saw him back his boat into the dock and they were laughing at him," the firefighter told Larry King after the verdict was rendered. "So I think he was an intelligent guy. He knew that somebody saw him there. And he better admit to being there. And I don't think he ever thought his wife's body and the body of his baby would ever be found."

When Fladager asked Grogan for more clues, he was ready. "The fact that there were umbrellas in the back of his truck wrapped in a tarp," he offered. "That those umbrellas are approximately the same height as Laci Peterson."

"What conclusion did you draw from that? Why was that significant?"

"Well, it would enable him to explain to anyone seeing him load something in his truck."

Grogan went on to cite "the fact that we had already conducted some searches of the lakes around bridges, and we had not found Laci up to that point. The fact that we tested the water in the bow of the boat, and it came back as saltwater and not freshwater. Also, looking at the computer searches that we conducted of the defendant's computers at his shop, and the fact that he was researching the San Francisco Bay. I have to add that he also had sites for fishing locations that were freshwater, and lakes throughout California, but the San Francisco Bay. Berkeley Marina did appear in there as well.

"The fact that he didn't clean up the mess at the shop, that led me to believe he never intended for anyone to come back there and look at the boat."

"Your next reason?"

Grogan coolly continued. "The fact that he had no real activity on the phone that morning."

"On December 24?"

"On December 24, and then after around two o'clock, when, by his statement he's leaving, he starts to make phone calls. And he leaves a message at the house that he's at the bay, or just fishing, and he's going to be late coming home.

"After that call, then he stops to get gas on his route back. But he buys thirteen dollars' worth of gas. Which I think is not a significant amount of gas in the truck."

"Okay. And your next reason for believing that Laci Peterson would turn up in [the] San Francisco Bay?"

"I have that there is deep water current nearby, where the map on his computer that he was looking at does show a deep water current in that area."

"All right. What's another reason?"

". . . the fact that he paid cash for the boat, and he didn't register the boat."

"Next reason."

"The boat cover."

"What was significant about the boat cover?"

"You have to ask why it's in the truck on the twenty-fourth in the evening. Did he take it to the bay? And, if so, why? Was it tied on the boat and covering the boat? Was it taken off the boat before he left, why not leave it in the warehouse? Why put it in the truck? Was he using the boat cover for some other purpose to cover something maybe in his boat? And then the fact that we find the boat cover in the shed on the search warrants on the twenty-sixth and twenty-seventh with a leaking gas blower on top."

"Okay," Fladager continued. "And do you understand the condition of the boat cover at that time was neatly folded, or in some other condition?"

"It was not neatly folded."

"What was another reason for your belief?"

"Looking at the driving Mr. Peterson was doing that was captured on the tracker, in Bakersfield around the time of this anchor found at the bay, and when it's identified, it's erratic. It's just kind of strange."

"What was your ultimate conclusion?" Fladager asked.

"The ultimate conclusion was that Laci Peterson's body was in [the] San Francisco Bay, and that we needed to search there, to focus our efforts on that search."

The bodies washing up in the San Francisco Bay turned out to be critical for jurors. "If these bodies had been found anywhere else other than [the] San Francisco Bay, and for that matter, right where Scott Peterson had described he'd been fishing on Christmas Eve, we wouldn't be having this conversation," juror Greg Beratlis told the press after the verdict.

Geragos managed to win a few more points by having the detective admit that Scott was relatively cooperative in the days following Laci's disappearance.

Grogan also acknowledged that portions of what Scott told police at the start of the investigation were accurate—specifically that Scott used his computer on the morning of December 24, and that several witnesses saw him at the marina that day. But he stopped short when Geragos tried to suggest that Scott's trips to the marina were searches for those witnesses.

If Scott were really looking for those witnesses, Grogan shot back, he would have stayed for more than just a few minutes, gotten out of his vehicle, and attempted to locate the harbormaster or other workers during his three trips.

On the stand, the detective admitted learning that Laci did not like her Land Rover, having referred to it as "a piece of shit," lending credence to the fact that Scott wasn't as cruel as he appeared when he sold the SUV in late January 2003.

"You learned that Laci did want a larger home and a new vehicle?" Geragos posed.

"Yes."

According to the police report, the real estate broker related that Laci had inquired about purchasing a home in the $400,000 to $600,000 range. Investigators knew the Petersons had planned to move to San Luis Obispo when their son was old enough to start school, and that Scott dreamed of buying an olive ranch. Apparently, Laci could not wait. I firmly believe that financial profit was not a motive for the murders, but freedom from Laci's clear intention to increase their standard of living may well have played a role.

Grogan also testified to a conversation he had with Scott's sister, Anne Bird, in February 2003, in which she described how she and Scott had talked about his affair with Amber Frey. According to Bird, Scott said that Laci had found out about his mistress.

"Scott said Laci was extremely pissed off and they were going to get through it, but Laci was upset?" Geragos asked the detective.

"Yes."

"And Laci insisted they not tell their parents about it?"

"Yes, that's what Anne said . . ."

"Scott admitted that he had screwed up and made a huge mistake in seeing Amber Frey?"

"Yes," Grogan responded.

Despite Geragos's tough questioning, Grogan proved unflappable. When the detective left the stand, jurors had a much clearer picture of the prosecution's argument. Grogan had managed to weave the pieces of evidence into a strong circumstantial case.

After nineteen weeks and 175 witnesses, the prosecution rested its case.

Geragos had made a number of promises in his opening remarks—that he would produce witnesses who saw Laci walking her dog after the time police believed she died, and a defense expert who could prove that Conner had been carried to term. If that was indeed the case, then Laci was not killed on Christmas Eve, as the prosecution insisted. Most memorably, he promised to prove his client was "stone cold innocent." But Geragos was unable to deliver.

The defense expert on Conner's gestational age calculated that the baby survived at least five days after Laci's Christmas Eve disappearance, and maybe into January. Dr. Charles March's conclusion was undermined, however, when he acknowledged that his judgment was based on his ideas of "realistic" behavior by women at baby showers. March assumed that because Laci never mentioned her pregnancy at her friend Renee Tomlinson's baby shower on June 8, 2002, she must not have taken a pregnancy test until the following day. Only then did she call her friend to relate the good news.

He then assumed June 9 was the first day she could detect her pregnancy and thus the date of conception was May 26, 2002, six days later than the date reached by the State's experts. Based on his thirty years of experience with female patients, March maintained that he was making correct assumptions. "I mean, women talk all the time," he testified. "The chances that a woman hosting a baby shower would not announce on the day of a shower that she was pregnant and have everybody rejoice in two pregnancies—that's not realistic at all."

At one point, after Assistant District Attorney Dave Harris pressed him about date discrepancies in his report March looked meekly at the prosecutor and implored him to "cut me some slack." Several jurors laughed aloud, while others shook their heads in disbelief. "This witness was pummeled like a fighter on the ropes," said former prosecutor Chuck Smith about the prosecution's cross-examination of Dr. March.

Geragos's other thirteen witnesses contributed little. Five police officers delivered secondhand reports about Laci sightings. No one who claimed they saw Laci after ten o'clock on the morning of December 24 ever testified. Geragos also called three experts, one in cement, another in finance, and a third in dog tracking. Scott's parents followed.

Jackie Peterson testified about a large amount of money she had given Scott. On April 8, 2003, she said, she withdrew ten thousand dollars to buy Scott's truck for his brother John. Jackie claimed there was a snafu at the bank. She insisted that she didn't have her account number handy, and inadvertently withdrew the money from an account she had given to Scott and Laci years earlier. This was the explanation she offered for giving Scott money for the truck and an additional ten thousand dollars to replace the funds she "accidentally" withdrew. Jackie's claims sounded highly illogical, bordering on the absurd.

Lee's testimony failed to prove significant. He said Scott was staying in San Diego in the week of April 17, 2003, when Laci and Conner were identified. He was unable to say whether Scott had considered going back to Modesto when the DNA results were announced.

After six days of testimony, much of it unimpressive, the defense rested.

After a brash opening statement, and his effective cross-examination of the State's witnesses, Geragos's case-in-chief was a major disappointment. As many legal experts have observed, sometimes it is better simply to rest at the end of the prosecution's case and assert that the charges have not been proven beyond a reasonable doubt. The defendant has no obligation to put a case before the jury, but if the defense team chooses to do so, there are expectations that emerge. People naturally expect the defense to present evidence that might prove the defendant not guilty. Geragos could offer no such evidence, and when he rested, his case was in shambles.

DiStaso had won little praise from observers during the early stages of the Peterson trial, but he had a reputation as a "good closer"—someone who could make a solid and convincing closing argument to a jury. When it came time for DiStaso's final remarks, he lived up to expectations.

"It's no question about how we got here. You can not deny one particular fact; the defendant went fishing, and Laci Peterson washed ashore, Conner Peterson washed ashore. . . . The only person that we know without any doubt that was in the exact location where the bodies washed ashore is sitting right there. That alone is proof of guilt beyond a reasonable doubt in this case. You can take that to the bank."

"The defendant strangled Laci Peterson on the night of December 23, or the morning of December 24. . . . I don't know; I don't have to prove that to you. Strangling and smothering is not going to leave a lot of evidence. . . . He wrapped her in a blue tarp, backed his truck up to the gate . . . he carries Laci out, puts her in the back of the truck . . . who's going to suspect him? Everyone thinks he's the perfect husband, the perfect gentleman. You know, show me something that's perfect, and I'll show you something that's not.

"There are two lives going on with Scott Peterson. Let's talk about Scott's reality. . . . Scott Peterson created a fantasy life for himself. . . . In his mind, the only way to continue that life was to have a plan. He didn't want that dull, boring life, with a wife and kid. . . . So, in November, he starts making a plan. . . . I don't think he killed his wife because he was going to marry Amber Frey. Amber Frey to him was freedom; that's what he wanted. He's not stupid; he knows there will be some hoopla over Laci missing. But he had no idea it was going to snowball into this huge mass . . .

"For some reason, and much to this man's detriment, this case blew up, didn't go away. But he didn't know that back in November, when he was setting this crime in action. This is the life that Scott wanted . . . not that boring old married life. . . . He didn't want a baby. The reason he killed Laci Peterson was because Conner was on the way. When it was just Laci, he could lead the two lives. . . . When it was just Laci, it was okay for him; if she found out he was only hurting her. No big deal for Scott Peterson. But when Conner comes along [he] can't divorce her . . . he can't lead the big, freewheeling bachelor life if he is paying alimony or child support. . . .

"He didn't want to be tied to that kid for the rest of his life; he didn't want to be tied to Laci for the rest of his life; so he killed her.

"There's no big mystery here," DiStaso closed. "As we've said all along, this is a circumstantial case. . . . The best way is to look at it like a jigsaw puzzle; take each piece of evidence and see where it fits. Each piece I've talked about today fits only in one direction—that is that this man is guilty of murder."

On Wednesday, November 3, 2004, Mark Geragos stood before the jury to deliver his closing remarks. The swagger he brought to the courtroom months ago had gradually faded away with his case. According to my sources, Geragos held court in a local bar many nights during the trial, flanked by admirers eager to be in his company. Yet as he paced the courtroom, trying to expose flaws in the prosecution's case, his performance was lackluster.

He began with a question as he gestured at Scott. "I just want to go over to my client here and ask if you hate him? We've heard four hours of 'This guy is the biggest jerk to walk the face off the earth, the biggest liar to ever walk the face of the earth . . . and you should hate him, because if you hate him, you'll convict him.'"

"Within one hour . . . *one hour* . . . [the police] decided that the person who had done this was Scott Peterson," he said. "This turns traditional police work on its head. They've come up with him, and now they try to fit the facts to it.

"I'm not asking you to nominate Scott as husband of the year," Geragos had the audacity to tell the jurors. "But I tell you, on most accounts he treated Laci with respect. He cheated on her, and he's a fourteen-carat-gold asshole for doing it. . . . But he had a relationship that, by all accounts, was working."

As I sat in the courtroom that day, I cringed at Geragos's remarks.

"I think the stark reality is that this is a guy who literally got caught with his pants down, but he fully expected [Laci] to come home."

"When you take an oath here . . . the judge will tell you you're supposed to examine the facts, the evidence and come to an opinion based on the facts and evidence, not emotion . . . the fact is, there is no evidence that Scott Peterson was involved in this crime. . . .

"If you are swept up in feeling these emotions, 'I don't like Scott Peterson,' you have to set those things aside. . . . The fact of the matter is, beyond any reasonable doubt, Scott Peterson didn't have anything to do with this. We ask you to return a verdict of not-guilty in this case."

Since the burden of proof rests with the state, DiStaso got the last word.

"There are only two possible things that happened here; either he killed them and put the bodies in the bay, or someone else did it to frame him. Now it's getting harder, because the police are searching the bay. So the people who have held Laci for three days would have to drive to the marina, while the police are out there searching and dump the bodies in the same place he was fishing. December 28 would be the first time these people would read about the Berkeley Marina . . . they'd have to hold her for four days before these people have any idea where this defendant went." By the time he concluded, DiStaso had made it clear that the kidnapping theory was preposterous.

Deliberations began that afternoon, with jurors sequestered at a nearby hotel. After sitting through seventy-four days of testimony, the six men and six women finally had the case. Deliberations had been under way for about twenty-six hours when jurors asked to view Scott's fourteen-foot aluminum boat. Judge Delucchi granted the request, and to my surprise he even allowed two jurors to climb aboard. While inside, they began to rock the boat back and forth. The judge quickly put a stop to their "experiment," but Geragos was outraged. He insisted that the judge reopen the case, so he could play his own videotaped demonstration showing attempts to dump a body from such a boat. If this was not permitted, he would settle for a mistrial.

Throughout the case, I felt that Delucchi had been particularly lenient with the defense team. This is not always a bad thing from an appellate viewpoint. No judges wants to be reversed by a higher court for failing to give the defendant a fair trial. Since prosecutors have no right to appeal an acquittal, they cannot make the same complaint on behalf of the state. However, there were times I thought he went too far, admonishing the prosecutors unnecessarily in front of the jury while allowing Geragos to joke and move about the room as if he owned the space.

Nevertheless, I believed that most of the judge's evidentiary calls were correct. That was certainly the case when he denied Geragos permission to air his demonstration tape and overruled his request for a mistrial.

Law enforcement sources told me that the videotape was an attempt to reenact Scott's disposal of Laci's body. To make the demonstration authentic, the man playing Scott strapped weights to his waist to simulate Peterson's actual weight. But the demonstration proved either funny or dangerous when, after standing up to heave the body overboard, the man tumbled into the water and the weights begin pulling him under. The next thing on the tape was the sight of the cameraman dropping his equipment to assist in the rescue.

As deliberations continued inside the San Mateo County Courthouse, a controversy was swirling several blocks away. Just hours after jurors viewed Scott's Gamefisher, a boat of the same size and make turned up in a parking lot several blocks from the courthouse. What appeared to be a dummy wearing coveralls was propped inside the craft, with concrete anchors tied to its arms and legs. Mark Geragos had actually bought the building and parking lot, giving him an unrestricted right to mount his display. Ostensibly, he had rigged up the boat to protest the judge's ruling and possibly sway public opinion. Yet his plan backfired when the site quickly became a makeshift memorial for Laci and Conner. By evening, dozens of mourners bearing candles, flowers, cards, and signs turned out to pay their respects to the victims. "Justice for Laci and Conner," read one sign; "Rot in Prison," read another.

"The message was supposed to be that Scott didn't do it and to reach the community by showing this evidence that wasn't allowed at trial and trying to get community sympathy for Scott," Robert Talbot, a professor at the University of San Francisco School of Law, told the press. "What it brought up was how strongly people feel about Laci's death and how, generally, the community feels like Scott did it."

To me, the stunt was tacky at best. At the time I wondered aloud whether it might constitute a violation of the gag order, as certain actions can equal speech under the law. I also believed that this was ethically reprehensible conduct that might be grounds for a grievance with the state bar association. Later in the evening the boat was towed away, but by then Geragos's actions had already provided lively fodder in legal circles and media broadcasts.

The jurors had been deliberating for about thirty-two hours when Judge Delucchi announced that he was replacing Juror #7, a woman in her mid-fifties, with Alternate Juror #1, a woman named Richelle Nice. A thirty-something mother of four with several tattoos, Nice was dubbed "Strawberry Shortcake" by reporters because of her fuchsia-colored hair. There was speculation that Juror #7 was removed because she had gone to the Internet to research something about the case, but the reason was never confirmed. In theory, the substitution required the remaining jurors to begin deliberations anew.

Another shocking twist came the following morning, when Delucchi dismissed a third juror. Juror #5, the doctor/lawyer who had replaced Justin Falconer during the trial, had been elected foreperson when deliberations began, but clearly something was going on in that jury room. Apparently, the juror asked Delucchi to release him from the case. While the exact reason is still unknown, some speculated that he refused to take a vote without reviewing every piece of evidence, and rumor had it that rebellion was afoot in the jury room. Another report suggested that the foreman could no longer deliberate honestly because public pressure might affect his verdict. We probably will not learn the specifics until transcripts of Delucchi's conversations with jurors #5 and #7 become public. While this was a controversial move and certainly grounds for appeal, I expect the judge was very careful to get justifiable reasons on the record.

Alternate Juror #3, an older man whose future son-in-law was once employed by Scott and Laci Peterson, then joined the jury. That same day, the jurors elected a new foreperson, firefighter/paramedic Steve Cardosi. The frustrated jurors started over a second time. Remarkably, the panel remained balanced with six men and six women.

After deliberating for seven hours and fourteen minutes, this "third jury" announced that it had reached a verdict. As the jurors filed in to deliver their decision, several looked directly at Sharon Rocha; one even gave her a nod.

Sharon and Brent huddled close, clasping hands, as the foreperson handed the verdict form to the clerk. Laci's mother wore a shocked look as the verdict was read. Scott Peterson was guilty of murder in the first degree for killing her only daughter, and guilty of murder in the second degree for her grandson, baby Conner.

In California, murder in the first degree has two possible sentence recommendations—death, or life in prison without the possibility of parole. Grabbing her son's hand, Sharon and Brent sobbed quietly, as did the group of Laci's friends who had gathered for the verdict. On the other side of the aisle, Jackie Peterson sat with a few family members. Although her head was bowed, no tears fell from her eyes. The only person crying on Scott's side of the courtroom was a legal assistant who worked for his lawyers.

By contrast, Scott Peterson sat stone-faced at the defense table. Conspicuously absent were his lead defense attorney, Mark Geragos, and his father, Lee Peterson. I was very critical of Geragos over his decision to skip the verdict. Away in Los Angeles on another case, Geragos had warned the court that he might be unable to get back to Redwood City in time to sit with his client. Yet I know very few judges who would insist that an attorney appear in their courtroom on another matter knowing he was awaiting a verdict in a capital case. Furthermore, if Scott was found guilty, Geragos would have to face that jury in the penalty phase and explain why he was too busy to show up for his client's day of reckoning.

For Lee Peterson, who was reportedly in San Diego at the time with other family members, the situation was no doubt very different. Perhaps Lee was not up to the crushing pain that a father must feel as his son is convicted of murder. Still, it was painful to watch as Jackie Peterson was left to face her son's conviction without him.

Scott's first-degree murder conviction told us that the jury believed that he had planned the crime. The finding of second-degree murder in Conner's case was puzzling to some. Several jury members later explained that they believed the target was Laci. While Scott should have known that her death meant the same for Conner, they did not believe he premeditated the killing of his child.

Meanwhile, outside the courthouse, throngs of people had gathered to await the verdict. Newspapers appeared almost instantly after the decision was read in court, their headlines proclaiming Scott Peterson GUILTY.

"What was sickening to me was all the bystanders cheering," said juror Julie Zenartu.

# CHAPTER TWENTY

# THE PENALTY PHASE

On Monday, November 22, 2004, Judge Delucchi announced that the penalty phase of the trial would be delayed until November 30. There were legal matters to be resolved.

Geragos, it seemed to me, was in a real quandary. During the trial, he had told jurors that Scott Peterson was a cad, a cheat and "a fourteen-carat-gold asshole." Now he had to convince them to spare his client's life. Could this jury ever show leniency to his client, after Geragos had offered so little reason to believe him at trial? Would they ever listen to people who knew Scott as gentle, helpful, and sincere? How would they respond to a plea for Scott's life that did not include an expression of remorse by his client?

Geragos tried a Hail Mary pass. He asked Judge Delucchi either to grant a change of venue or to pick an entirely new jury in Redwood City to pass judgment on Scott. "I believe [there had been] irreparable harm to any kind of a fair process in a penalty phase," the defense lawyer insisted. He pointed to the large crowds that had assembled outside the courthouse to hear the verdict, some shouting derogatory taunts at Jackie Peterson as she departed the courthouse that day. "This court saw what happened," he argued. "I can only liken it to what happened in the Fifties in the South, to young black men accused of raping white women. I fully expected people to start building a gallows across the street."

Not surprisingly, Judge Delucchi denied both motions. Granting them would have led to an enormous expenditure of time and money.

Any new jury would essentially have to hear the case over again to deliberate the punishment fairly. It would be an extraordinary remedy for any judge to grant. "This is a problem without a solution; a change of venue is not going to change anything in this case . . . so we're going to have to go with this jury," Delucchi concluded.

Geragos bought a few more days by appealing this decision to the Court of Appeals. He lost. On Monday, November 29, the California Supreme Court also denied Geragos' petition for a review and request for a stay. There was nowhere else to go but back to the jury that convicted Scott.

Unlike the trial, Judge Delucchi permitted video cameras and microphones into court for jury instructions. Silence fell over the courtroom as jurors filed in just before 11:30 A.M. Once seated, the judge explained their role.

"In determining which penalty to be imposed," he told them, "you shall consider all of the evidence. You shall consider, take into account and be guided by the following factors; the circumstances of the crime, the presence or absence of criminal activity by the defendant, other than crimes for which the defendant has been tried which involve use or attempted use of force or violence, the presence or absence of any prior felony conviction other than the crimes for which the defendant has been tried in present proceedings, whether or not victim was a participant in the defendant's homicidal conduct, whether or not the defendant acted under extreme duress under substantial domination of another person, the age of the defendant at the time of the crime, whether or not the defendant was an accomplice to the offense, and any other circumstance, which extenuates the gravity of the crime and any sympathetic or other aspect. You may also consider any lingering or residual doubt as to the defendant's guilt. Lingering or residual doubt is defined as a state of mind between reasonable doubt and all possible doubt. You may consider lingering doubt as a factor."

Prosecutor David Harris delivered the prosecution's opening remarks. Rising to his feet, the soft-spoken lawyer addressed the jury: "The circumstances of this crime are like ripples on water. When the defendant dumped the bodies of his wife and unborn son into the bay, those ripples spread out, and touched many lives . . . you'll hear from Brent Rocha, Amy Rocha, Ron Grantski and Sharon Rocha . . . these witnesses will tell you who Laci and Conner were; they'll talk about the joy that Laci brought into their lives . . . you've hear about her as a person, what she meant to this family, the lose they all suffered . . .

"You'll hear how it was for a mother, waiting every single day to find out what happened to her daughter, to her grandson . . . never knowing what had happened for a hundred and sixteen days . . . the entire time with the defendant, the one that caused those ripples in the pond, in their midst . . .

"You'll hear about their guilt because they didn't protect Laci from the one person they didn't think she needed protection from. . . . There's a hole in their hearts that can never be repaired.

"I'm going to argue to you that, based on the circumstances of this crime, the only just punishment is death."

After lunch, jurors filed back into the courtroom. They watched as Brent Rocha made his way to the witness box.

"Laci was your sister?" Harris addressed the poised young man.

"Yes."

"Tell us in your own words about your sister."

"We grew up together, both got married, and were beginning to move on to the next phase of starting our families. She was a very energetic person, very kind," Brent choked back tears. "To sit here and try to describe her is very difficult to do.

"We always talked when we were growing up about how nice it would be to have kids at the same time, so we could stay close as a family. . . . My first child was born in 2001, and I know at that time she was interested in starting her family as well."

"Why was it you wanted to have your kids at the same time?"

"Not so much as we wanted to have them at the same time, we wanted to be together as a family, just be together."

"Was she looking forward to it, when she found out she was pregnant?"

"Oh, very much so. I don't think I've ever heard her more excited than the day she called me up to tell me she was pregnant," Brent recalled.

"Why?"

"She was having problems getting pregnant," he said. "We were very happy for her. She was really excited. She had everything ready; she was so prepared, the nursery was perfect."

"At some point in time around Christmas Eve 2002," the prosecutor asked, "did you get notified Laci was missing?"

"Yes, by Scott."

"What was it like?"

"That night, I was in shock. It was cold. You're in disbelief. You can't believe you're going through this right now," Brent told the jury.

"Do you miss your sister?"

"Yes, I miss my sister. I miss her very much. I try to remember the good memories we have with each other, but they are overshadowed all the time by what happened to her, how she died, by maybe her knowing who did it. . . . I miss her terribly."

"How has Laci and Conner's death affected you?"

"Numerous ways. You wake up in the middle of the night; think about it constantly. My kids won't have any cousins. Laci was my only full sibling. It's a big part of the family that's missing now.

"Laci was the person that coordinated the holidays. She was the one that did Christmas. She brought everyone together. We haven't done that since she's gone. She was kind of the life of the holidays. . . . I still can't imagine the rest of my life going on without her."

Laci's half sister, Amy Rocha, shared Brent's sentiments. She told jurors how Laci assumed the role of family matriarch when her grandmother Helen Rocha passed away in 1999.

"She pretty much just took over the holidays," Amy told the hushed courtroom. "She made sure we all got together."

"How are the holidays now that Laci is gone?" Harris asked.

"They'll never be the same," Amy answered.

"I first met Laci when I went to pick Sharon up for a date at her house," Laci's stepfather, Ron Grantski, recalled. "She was about a foot and a half tall, and came running up to the door to open the door. She never stopped running, and she always had something to say. . . . She lit up any room, and she was always the center of attention. She was the love of many people's lives. She will be missed.

"She never studied, as far as I could see, but got straight As. It really bothered me because I had to figure out that was definitely smarter than me," Grantski smiled. "I miss telling her that, and I miss the grandson we were supposed to have. If you look at her and her mother, they had that same smile. It's one of the things that attracted me to Sharon, that great big beautiful smile. And Laci had it, too. She was always with a smile.

"I wish I could be the one gone and not her," Grantski said, his voice breaking. "Part of my heart is gone."

Laci's mother, Sharon Rocha, was the final witness called by the prosecution to give a victim impact statement. To many, her testimony was also the most poignant.

"Tell us about Laci," Harris asked the victim's mother, her face worn and tired.

"Laci was just somebody that people gravitated to. She had a personality that made people feel comfortable. She was an upbeat person. She was more of a leader than a follower. She was involved. She followed her heart. She would fight for her beliefs, and when she wanted something she went after it. She was a strong-willed person. She wasn't dependent on other people. She was very independent actually."

As we had learned throughout the trial, Laci was her own woman. While she had at least one direct encounter with Scott's infidelity, she seemed determined to keep her family together. He seemed quiet and pliable; she was gregarious and resolute. He did not want a child; she did. He was a fertilizer salesman; she wanted a half-million-dollar home in San Luis Obispo. Ultimately, Laci wanted a family and Scott wanted to be free. The marriage was tumbling toward disaster, with no one but Scott the wiser.

On the same screen used to project the autopsy photos, the jurors now saw a picture show about Laci Peterson. The first snapshot was of Laci smiling for the camera. "Is that how Laci was when she grew up?" Harris asked Sharon Rocha.

"Laci was like that from the time she was born. She didn't let things get her down. A lot of things that would have upset other people would upset her, but she didn't dwell on the negative."

"Did she start forming friendships at an early age?

"As soon as she could talk, yes."

"Those friends, some of those friends still around?"

"Yes, some of them are here today that she's known since she was a little girl.

"Describe these friendships Laci developed."

"Her friends were her loyal friends. They were a group that were all loyal to each other, all very much the same . . . happy girls, great attitudes, a lot of fun to be around."

"When she was going through school, was she involved in activities?"

"Yes, in a lot of clubs, organizations. She worked when she was in college at the shop in the horticulture department. She worked for a florist."

"Did Laci have an interest in flowers?"

"That was her major, horticulture. She loved flowers and plants. Laci took an early interest in plants. She liked weeds. She had a talent for putting things together and making them grow. . . . At one time, after getting back to Modesto, she talked about opening an herb shop, but I reminded her she was in Modesto, not San Luis Obispo, so things were a little different."

Displaying a series of photos of a young Laci Peterson, Harris asked her mother to describe them to the jury.

"This was her graduation from junior high school, she just had her braces removed just a couple of weeks before that.

"That was in May 2000, just before she moved up here. They moved back up here in June. That was taken on the beach at San Simeon. Scott took the picture. That was taken at a restaurant in San Luis Obispo; Jackie took that picture. We had lunch together."

"We see, in those pictures, Laci's big smile. Was that just part of her personality, the way she always was?"

"Always. I can hear her giggling. She didn't just smile, she giggled. She would laugh at herself."

Flashing another photo on the overhead screen, Sharon explained, "That was Mother's Day, 2002; that was about a week after Laci's birthday at her house."

"Who is in the picture?"

"Myself, my mother, and Laci."

"It was taken on Mother's Day. Did all of you mothers come together?"

"Yes all of us, also Jackie and Lee were there."

"This Mother's Day . . . how was it different?"

"I laid on the floor and I cried most of the day because [Laci] should have been there and she should have been a mother also, and that was taken away from her." Turning to Scott, she shouted, "She wanted to be a mother!" Seated only a few feet away, Scott merely stared vacantly. "Divorce is always an option, not murder!"

The courtroom was stunned, silent, as her words spilled out. The defendant did not flinch.

"You said Laci loved children," Harris continued. "Did she talk to you about becoming a mother?"

"She talked a lot about becoming a mother. Before they moved back to Modesto, we were talking about childbirth. She was asking me what it was like. She was really looking forward to it."

"It was a couple of years before she became pregnant," Sharon continued. "[On] the day she learned Brent and Rose were going to have a housewarming, she called me later that evening and was crying. She said Scott wasn't ready yet, but she really wanted to be pregnant and have a baby the same time as Rose did."

Sharon fought back tears as she described her daughter's excitement at the prospect of motherhood. "She would call me every time she went to the doctor and let me know the results. She gave me a copy of the sonogram. It's the only picture I have of the baby, and he was a baby. You could see his little body."

Sharon turned to the snapshot of her pregnant daughter on the large screen. "That was taken on December 14, and the next day,

December 15, was the last day I saw her. She wanted me to put my hand on the stomach and feel the baby kick. I didn't feel it, but I kept my hand on her stomach the rest of the evening, and I put my face on her stomach and I talked to him. She was anxious. She was ready to have him."

"On Christmas Eve 2002," Harris asked, "when you got the phone call that Laci was missing, tell us how you felt."

"I was scared to death because I knew she wouldn't just be missing. Laci just didn't disappear. I knew something had happened to her. It was cold that night and I had my friend Sandy take me back to my house and get blankets and coats for everyone, and I got one for her because I knew she would be freezing when we found her."

"Did Laci come home?" Harris asked Sharon, now visibly upset by the memory.

"No, I never saw her again. I never saw her after December fifteenth."

"After Laci went missing, did you sleep?"

"No, we came home that night, Brent and I and Ron stayed up all night in the living room. I didn't sleep for weeks. I couldn't get comfortable and be warm and not know where she was."

"Did you try to stay awake for long periods of time?" Harris asked.

"Yeah, I felt I needed to be awake just in case she called so I could go to her as soon as she called. I was afraid to go to sleep, afraid I would have nightmares about what happened to her. I knew she wouldn't be sleeping because she would be afraid. She would be scared. . . . I think about her every day. Did she know she was being murdered? Did she know what was happening to her?"

"During the time that she was missing, did you have to go out in the public and make statements try to get support to help find her?"

"Yes, we did it all the time. I begged for whoever had her to bring her home, to let her go, tell us where she was." Sharon looked straight at Scott. "And there was somebody who knew all along and you wouldn't tell us! Instead you just let us go through this every day!"

"When you finally found Laci and Conner . . . ?"

"The day they were found I wasn't feeling well. I was at home. I heard footsteps coming up to my door, and I didn't answer the door because I knew.

"I hadn't heard anything, but I just knew, and then when they went to the backyard to the back door I knew I had to answer the door. And I knew in my soul, I knew they had been found. Then later, when I was told it would be several days before they were identified, and I asked why, because they could use dental charts, I was told she didn't have a head, and I didn't believe it.

"I just dropped to the floor. It never occurred to me what condition she might be in."

At times, it seemed the entire courtroom was crying along with Sharon Rocha. In the jury box, jurors and alternates clutched tissues and dabbed at their tears. Yet Scott's face was empty. He seemed unmoved by his mother-in-law's powerful words.

"When you were told Laci and Conner been recovered from the bay, was there something about that that upset you because of Laci?" the prosecutor asked.

Staring back at Scott, Sharon gasped. "Laci always got motion sickness, and you knew that, and that's the place you took her. . . . You put her in the bay, and you knew she'd be sick for eternity, and you did that to her anyway!"

"Did it take the authorities several days before they finally notified you that the body was Laci?"

"Yes, she was found on Monday," Sharon recounted. "They identified her on Friday, but I knew it was her, I knew it was her from the beginning.

"I knew that I needed to spend some time with her and to have the opportunity to say goodbye to her alone and I knew she was in the casket and I knew the baby was there and I knew she didn't have arms to hold him either." Tears streamed from Sharon's eyes. "She should have had her arms and her head, her entire body! It just haunts me all the time, but I just hope she didn't know what was happening."

Sharon's testimony left many in the courtroom in stunned silence.

"A short time after that, was there a memorial service?

"On her twenty-eighth birthday. She would have been astounded to see there were so many people interested in her, concerned about her. We were told there were over three thousand people there."

"How are you doing? How has this affected you . . .?"

"Every morning when I get up I cry. It takes me a long time just to be able to get out of the house. I keep thinking, 'Why did this happen?' I miss her. I wanted to know my grandson. I wanted Laci to be a mother. I wanted to hear her be called 'Mom.'

"When I go to buy birthday cards, Mother's Day cards, I just can't stand it. I always look at the ones from daughter to mother or mother to daughter.

"I don't sleep well. I think about her all the time." On several occasions, she said, she had even managed to forget that Laci was no longer alive. "I remember the first time it happened, I was outside, locked the door, heard the phone ring, thinking it was Laci. I hadn't heard from her in a long time. It should be her, and then I realized it wasn't. It would never be her . . .

"I remember walking into the house. I walked into the entryway, [and] I just stopped because she turned around and said 'Hi, Mom.' It was as though she was right there. I saw her a lot of times. . . .

"When I have a question about something that's been going on," Sharon said, "I think, 'Well, I'll just ask her and she'll tell me.' But I can't. . . .

"Laci didn't deserve to die."

Just before 3:30 P.M., court was adjourned for the day. As the jurors filed quietly out of the courtroom, some thought back to the autopsy photos they had seen earlier of Laci and Conner; others later reported that they were unable to escape the thought of Laci in her coffin, with no arms to hold her baby.

When the jurors returned the following morning, they heard not from Mark Geragos, but his partner, Pat Harris. "For the past four or five months, we've sat here and we've basically gone through a man's life, in very minute detail," he said. "We know what would seem to be practically every detail of this man's life. . . . What I'm here to tell you is that the next week will prove that wrong. We don't know who Scott Peterson is.

"It will be our job to show you. When we show you the thirty years before this, I think you'll agree that this is a life worth saving. . . .

"One of the things we are going to do is go into a lot of depth about his parents' background. Why is that relevant? The answer is, we're all products of our parents, none more so than Scott Peterson. . . . The way Scott acted is not the way they acted. They are emotional people."

Scott's father spoke first. Lee told the court that he was with family in San Diego on the day of the verdict, and together they watched as it was read on TV. "As soon as they read the verdict, they all burst into tears."

Asked to describe his relationship with Scott, he said, "I have great respect for him. I just love him very much." The elder Peterson told jurors about his life, coming to America as a young boy and his hardworking parents. Scott, he said, followed in those footsteps. During college he had moved out, telling his parents, "You guys have done enough for me, and I want to support myself. I'm going to be totally on my own." Lee contended that Scott "did it [himself], every inch of the way . . . he always had at least two and sometimes three jobs."

"What effect would having your son get the death penalty have?" Pat Harris asked.

Lee reported that he was "frightened, depressed," over the jury's verdict. "Losing someone you loved and now having you son in this kind of jeopardy, it's not something I ever thought I'd have to go through. . . . I just can't imagine anything worse."

Of course, the Rochas could.

"I can't describe exactly how we would go on," Scott's half sister Susan Caudillo sobbed on the stand to the thought of her brother being handed the death penalty. "I know it would kill my parents. . . . I see the pain in their faces every day, [and] it keeps getting worse. . . .

"We've gone through so much as a family, but we're sticking by [Scott] one hundred percent. But I don't think my parents will make it if he goes."

Scott's older half brother John, who was six when Scott was born, recalled their childhood. "My first memory is of Scott in the hospital: he was sick so I was not allowed to see him," he said. "When we got older, we lived in a nice area, with a lot of hills and bushes and boulders. We'd build forts back there. . . . I'd make Scott the lieutenant and I'd be the president. And if he told on me, I'd demote him to private. . . ."

"Should your brother be sentenced to death?" Harris posed.

"I can't even imagine; I'd be wrecked. He's my little brother. I love him."

In addition to Scott's siblings, a number of aunts, uncles and cousins spoke on Scott's behalf. One who did not appear was Anne Bird. "Don't you want to save your brother's life?" Jackie Peterson reportedly asked Anne when she learned that her newfound daughter would not take the stand at the Penalty hearing.

Anne had been ready to testify if called by the prosecution in the guilt-innocence phase of the trial. One of the things the state considered offering was her information about Scott's use of her house, and his strange admission that he borrowed a shovel from the Lake Arrowhead cabin and never returned it. Early on, Bird had counted herself among Scott's supporters, but as she learned more about the case, and hosted Scott as a houseguest, she changed her mind. Anne told me that she was concerned about testifying against her brother. She claimed that Jackie Peterson carried an old Colt .45 in the glove box of her car, and once almost shot her husband, Lee, in a hotel room when she mistook him for an intruder.

According to Anne, Jackie once asked her, "What is your problem with Scott?"

"All the lies," Anne replied, referring in part to the Amber tapes in which he claimed to be in Europe while still in California.

"Well, he's been all those places," Jackie told her.

However, the prosecution considered Anne a high-risk witness for both sides, and she was never called to testify.

In addition to Scott's family members, myriad individuals offered anecdotes about Scott: his high school coach, a Cal Poly professor, his former boss at the restaurant where he worked in San Luis Obispo. Not one of them could imagine Scott committing these crimes.

"I can't reconcile the accusations with the person I've known," one said. "The Scott Peterson I know is the kind of person you respect and admire," said another. "He is the absolutely last person I would ever think would be suspected for something like this," offered a third. Such sentiments were heard over and over, as thirty-nine people took the stand. Yet no one seemed to have a deep connection with Scott. They could talk about what he did, but none of them was able to convey what he thought, how he saw the world, or who he really was. None of them knew about Amber and the others, and none of them had seen this coming.

The final witness was Scott's mother. Jackie Peterson began, "We all lost Laci. We all loved her."

She told jurors how her father was murdered when she was two, and how she and her brothers had lived in a Catholic orphanage because her mother was too ill to care for them. She said her life changed completely when she married Lee Peterson.

"He gave me the family I always wanted. We called ourselves 'The Brady Bunch,' there were so many of us." Then Scott was born. "I would always say he was a joy from the moment he was born, he was always a good student, all through school, I had teachers tell me, 'I wish I had a whole room of students like Scott.'

"I beg you to consider how he helps people," she said, "and he can do a lot of good things with his life. All his world has been taken away . . . he was stalked by the media, harassed by the police, and painted as a devil in public. He's not that; he's always been nurturing and kind. . . .

"I really feel that if you were to take Scott away from us . . . they were like a family—Scott, Laci, and Conner. It would be a whole family wiped off the face of the earth. It would be like Laci never existed. Both Sharon and I would lose a whole family . . . such a waste. It's irreversible."

On the eighth day of the penalty phase, the attorneys had their last chance to speak to the jurors set to decide Scott's fate. Dave Harris quickly said the obvious. "These thirty-nine witnesses . . . didn't really know what they are talking about." He described the lies, the manipulation, and betrayal that Scott imposed on them all.

"Laci was an anchor around his neck . . . so he put one around hers. This is someone who had everything, and he threw it away. He had a plan, and he executed it.

"Leaving his wife's body to rot on the bottom of the ocean . . . leaving his own son's body to be treated as trash . . . someone who shows no mercy, so heartless, so cruel deserves death."

Pat Harris stepped up first for the defense. He had taken the lead in this stage of the case and would begin the plea for Scott's life. He had to address the apparent Jekyll and Hyde that had been portrayed throughout the trial.

"Every single [defense witness] says 'respectful, generous.' You're going to have to make the decision: Was it phony? Was it made up? As a twelve-year-old, a fourteen-year-old, he was fooling all these people? Or are these character traits that he truly does have?"

"This is a person who's continually helped people," he told the jury. "This is an opportunity to salvage something positive out of a life that's virtually gone now.

"I wish there was a phrase I could give you that would turn this around, make you believe that there is good in this person . . . this is not a monster. I don't have that phrase; I don't have the ability to do it . . . that's up to you."

Maybe Mark Geragos had the magic to sway the panel. Could he find that phrase that would turn things around? He began with an apology. "I have nightmares about this case. I feel like I let my client down, feel like I let the family down, feel like I let you down, for not being able to convince you. . . . I say that as kind of a confession to start off with, because I'll also . . . tell you the truth. I did not prepare a penalty phase. I did not do it. The day the verdict came down, I was in another courtroom, and I did not expect that you guys were coming back that day. I apologize for that; I want you to know that was not meant as any sign of disrespect. I also want you to know that part of the reason you were cooling your heels for two weeks was so I could go out and find mitigating witnesses."

I listened, somewhat shocked. Was Geragos trying to inject an appellate point on ineffective assistance of counsel? Was he setting himself up as the fall guy to win Scott a new trial? I knew that Judge Delucchi had given him ample time to prepare during that two-week break, but this "admission" was astounding. Geragos also chose phrasing that was unflattering to Scott, stressing that he had to "go out and find mitigating witnesses." After all, they certainly had not rallied behind Scott throughout the trial. Anne Bird later told me that several family members who testified had been pressured to do so. And while childhood and college friends, an old principal and a golf coach joined the chorus, where were the people Scott seemed close to when all of this occurred? Where were Heather and Mike Richardson, the couple he called and visited repeatedly during the search for Laci? Where was his good friend Guy Miligi, or his fishing buddy, Greg Reed?

Nevertheless, Geragos pressed on. "You may consider lingering doubt as a factor in mitigation . . . that state of mind between beyond a reasonable doubt and all possible doubt . . . that lingering doubt alone may be enough to spare his life.

"Somebody said that life without parole would be, to them, worse than death. Understand what it is. . . . Prison is an awful, awful place. . . . Scott would be placed in a cell roughly the size of a king-size bed for the rest of his life; he will die in that cell. He will have a bed, and a cold metal toilet. And he will stay in that cell every single day until he dies."

"The State is asking you to be the one who sanctifies the death. There's no reason to have any more death. . . . All that's being asked of you is to punish him with life without parole. . . . To kill him at this point serves absolutely no purpose. All I'm asking you to do is hang on and vote for life."

Geragos knew that in California, if the jury was deadlocked in the penalty phase of the trial, the district attorney could seat another jury and again pursue the death penalty. But he might hope that a hung jury in Redwood might convince prosecutors to agree to a life sentence.

However, that was not to be. After eight hours and twenty-three minutes over a three-day period, the jury returned a unanimous verdict—death for Scott Peterson.

As the decision was read, Scott did not shed a tear. Seated with his attorneys he remained cold and impassive, as he had throughout the trial. His family behind him remained silent. Only Sharon Rocha's gentle sobs broke the hush.

Several people in the courtroom noticed when Ron Grantski turned to Lee Peterson and mouthed, "I'm sorry."

"Fuck you," the elder Peterson mouthed back.

Following the decision, jurors went to a room in the courthouse where three of them agreed to speak to the press. The media was impressed by their candor, their honesty, and their obvious commitment to a fair trial for Scott Peterson. All twelve had agreed that *innocent until proven guilty* was their mantra throughout the process. They also agreed that the totality of the evidence was overwhelming. As difficult as it was, each believed their decision was the right one.

"I think the Sharon Rocha testimony was probably the most . . . not even probably. For me, [it was] definitely the most moving testimony of the penalty phase," said jury foreman Steve Cardosi. "She said things in there that I will never forget, such as *Laci doesn't have arms to hold her baby. Laci got motion sickness, and Scott placed her in basically a watery grave. She's going to be seasick for eternity.* I will never forget those things. My heart goes out to her."

"I don't know why the trial has attracted so much publicity," juror Richelle Nice said. "I don't even know why I got so connected to it. But I will forever feel a connection with Laci and with the two families Scott tore apart for no good reason."

Ah, but Scott Peterson felt he had a very good reason. It was the most important reason in the world—himself. In his mind, he was that charming, romantic, world-traveling playboy. His should have been a life filled with champagne and strawberries, not lawn mowers and diapers. He was determined to remain on the pedestal that he occupied for so long as a boy.

What right did Laci have to demand that he become a responsible father? Yet, strong-willed, and decisive, she had clearly become the boss in their family. He was never going to be the provider she wanted, and he didn't intend to face that reality. He knew he was "real smart," and he felt shouldn't have to prove it to anyone. He should be admired simply for being Scott.

Whatever his rationale, onlookers were left wondering: *Why didn't we ever see any strain, or fear or anguish, throughout this ordeal?* We didn't see these reactions because they didn't exist. To exhibit worry, concern, or grief for someone you care about, you have to be able to feel love. To express shame, guilt, or fear, you have to believe there are moral or legal rules that apply to you. Psychiatrists know that sociopaths, contrary to expectations, are often very calm, easygoing, and relaxed in times of intense pressure or grief, because they do not feel what others are feeling. Remember the testimony: Scott *never* got upset, not as a kid, not playing golf and not over his missing wife and child.

What tears we saw from Scott Peterson, I believe, were shed either as an effort to manipulate others, or for himself.

Scott firmly believed that he could win this deadly game. He planned his crime carefully. As a pathological liar, he had his delivery down pat. He had fooled so many for so long that he must have assumed a few cops and reporters would be easy. He knew the masses would grieve right along with this handsome young husband who'd "lost" his wife.

Unfortunately, another characteristic of the sociopath is an inability to develop realistic long-term plans. Scott was never able to see past late January, when he thought the search would end. He would return to wooing Amber, the naive, admiring young mother.

Unable to accept responsibility for his actions, and free from the moral and legal limits that most of us recognize, he could not imagine an outcome other than complete freedom. On the day of his arrest, he played gleefully with the cops that pursued him. In his first days behind bars, he wrote Amber and Anne Bird about all the "good" things he would do when released.

On January 16, when Sharon Rocha and Ron Granski begged Scott to tell them where to find their beloved daughter, he never denied his involvement. He only repeated that he, too, wanted her back. Yet he made one comment that stood out in my mind.

"My world is done without Laci and my child."

With those words, Scott intended another lie. Instead, he may have delivered his own epitaph.

# EPILOGUE

s this book goes to press, Scott Peterson remains ensconced in
the Stanislaus County Jail, awaiting his formal sentencing by
Judge Delucchi on March 11, 2005. The judge is not mandated
to impose the jury's recommendation of death, and could impose a
life sentence instead. However, it is very unlikely he will substitute
his own judgment for theirs. In this event, Scott will move to death
row at the infamous San Quentin prison, to join three other inmates
who murdered their pregnant wives.

While Amber Frey had a book on the stands by January 5, 2005,
Sharon Rocha has stepped back from the public eye. However, the
Rocha family has filed a civil lawsuit against Scott, seeking a
multimillion-dollar judgment for the wrongful death of Laci Peterson.
A judgment in their favor is virtually assured. I doubt they expect to
collect a dime, but the judgment would remain on file in the event
Scott ever tried to profit from the crime.

As of this date, Mark Geragos continues to represent Scott. I do
not believe any lawyer or firm involved in a death penalty trial
should undertake the appeal. These entities have a vested interest in
the outcome and would be reviewing the record, in part, for their
own mistakes. An appeal, ideally, is an opportunity for a fresh, independent appellate expert to examine the transcript for possible errors. I expect that Scott's representation will change after the
defendant's motion for a new trial is denied by Judge Delucchi.

In the meantime, Geragos is soliciting "investigative" funds to find the "real killer" and free Scott. A message posted on Geragos's website reads: "For Scott to get the justice he deserves, the investigation must continue. Unfortunately, this does not come without a price. . . ." and then gives an office address. This is certainly a page from the Simpson playbook—although the last time I interviewed O. J., he readily admitted that he was doing nothing to "find the real killer."

When the publicity dies down, I suspect this Web page will disappear.

In January 2005, I was contacted by a seventeen-year-old from North Dakota who believes that Scott Peterson is his father. While his mother is deceased, he says that friends and relatives have dropped a few intriguing hints about a one-night rendezvous in San Diego. He began his quest by contacting Scott's half sister, Anne Bird, who forwarded the letter to Jackie and Scott.

When I sat down to interview Anne, she showed me Scott's response to the boy's plea, written from jail on January 9. In responding to the letter, Scott writes: "What a weird ass letter you received." He never denies the allegations, and adds only one more line, asking, "Why would someone do such a thing." Sound familiar? He moves on to more mundane matters for a few short lines, then closes.

Scott may spend the rest of his life on death row. The appeal process is arduous, and death penalty politics may be shifting. Nevertheless, through all those remaining days, his world will be limited to a tiny cell, a TV, and limited contact from the outside world. Maybe he can relive those fairytales about his adventures in Paris.

Should Scott Peterson have received the death penalty? I understand how the jury reached its conclusion. The crime was monstrous. The pictures of Laci and Conner when they washed ashore will linger in the minds of those people forever. Scott's cold, callous behavior throughout the case helped seal his fate. By the end of this trial, he was reviled, justifiably, by everyone on that jury. Had Scott appeared more emotional, less calculating—indeed, had he taken the stand during the penalty phase—I believe his life would have been spared.

Frighteningly, pregnant women are murdered all too often. For sheer cruelty, few crimes exceed the murder of one's own wife and unborn child. Yet it is also my conviction that the death penalty should not be treated lightly—that we should take care to enforce some sort of continuum when these penalties are assessed. The crime of murder is a violent, evil act. In no way does this lessen the impact of Laci and Conner's deaths, but is it right to punish a Scott Peterson in the same way that we punish the most egregious murderers of all—the predators, the terrorists, the serial killers?

My own thoughts about the death penalty have evolved since I joined the Dallas County District Attorney's Office in 1978. When I arrived there, I was a proponent of capital punishment. I left in serious opposition to it. I was witness to the Randall Dale Adams case, which gave rise to Errol Morris's documentary *The Thin Blue Line*. Three times this man was convicted of capital murder before the truth was discovered and he was exonerated. One of the last capital cases I saw tried before I left the district attorney's office was that of Joyce Ann Brown. One very certain eyewitness watched this woman gun down her husband in their fur salon. Only it was not Ms. Brown, as was discovered by accident when another woman was arrested in New Mexico and confessed to the crime *nine years later*. Had this not occurred, Joyce would have joined other innocent people on death row.

Certainly most prisoners who have been executed were guilty, but not all of them. I concede that, for many, the moral/religious maxim "an eye for an eye" is not open to debate. Those who firmly believe in this justification for capital punishment are perfectly justified in that conviction.

As a pragmatist, however, I would also point to some other, less emotional considerations. It costs more to try a death penalty case through to execution than it does to house an inmate the rest of his or her life. Studies show that the death penalty is no deterrent to anyone but the person who is ultimately executed. The states that carry out executions most frequently are also the most violent in the country. Remember, as well, that human beings are fallible creatures. We can never make the criminal justice system foolproof. Intentionally or not, people will make mistakes, and forensic science is a tool, not a guarantee.

Personally, I consider life without parole to be much more severe than simply going to sleep on a gurney. Over a decade ago, I interviewed Charles Walker, the first man to be put to death in Illinois after the state reinstated its death penalty statute. (The state has since enacted a moratorium on executions, after discovering a large number of cases where inmates were falsely convicted through prosecutorial or law enforcement misconduct. Some of these people were clearly innocent.) Walker told me that he was ready to die because he could no longer stand to look at the shadows of the bars on the wall. He wanted to be put out of his misery.

The nation remains deeply divided over this issue. However, many people moderate their stance if assured that life without parole really means that the inmate will never again walk the streets. If we lock a killer away for twenty-four hours a day, seven days a week, and simply throw away the key, I believe that justice has been served.

As for Scott Peterson, whatever the court decides, we can be certain of one thing. He will live in an earthly hell for the rest of his life.

# ACKNOWLEDGMENTS

I am intimately familiar with our criminal justice system, having served as a prosecutor and judge and now a journalist. It is rare to obtain the kind of access that gives rise to such an in-depth look at an investigation and trial. Without Cole Thompson's tireless pursuit of every fact and detail, this book would not have been written. Lisa Pulitzer spent months working overtime to organize volumes of material into a manageable chronology. The value of her work cannot be overstated. My thanks, as well, to Barbara Young, who served as Lisa's right hand during this immense assignment.

So many people contributed to this work. While some of them must remain nameless, I can thank others personally. Dr. Vincent Di-Maio lent his forensic expertise to our investigation and Anne Bird gave her personal insights. Court TV's amazing correspondent, Beth Karas, and reporters Harriet Ryan and Bryan Lavietes were the network's eyes and ears in the Modesto and Redwood City courtrooms. KOVR reporter Gloria Gomez was very generous with her time and talent as I covered the story.

My dear friend and literary agent, Jan Miller, again worked her magic, and Michael Broussard was always just a phone call away. Publisher extraordinaire Judith Regan and my editor, Cal Morgan, were thoroughly committed to making this book the best it could be. I am blessed to work with such supportive people at Court TV—Henry Schleiff, Art Bell, Marlene Dann, Emily Barsh, Sean Giangeruso, and my wonderful staff at *Catherine Crier Live*. Special thanks to my assistant, Barbara Stansell, who successfully juggled too many tasks, D. J. Haverkamp, who kept order in the midst of chaos, and to the world's best publicist, Heidi Krupp, who gives all my projects her extra attention.

Finally, to my heart and soul, Jim Logan, who makes it all worthwhile.

# APPENDIX

## From *The State of California v. Scott Peterson:*
## THE UNSEEN EVIDENCE FILES

Janet Ilse, holding the twelve dozen roses Scott Peterson brought her on their first date. She later gave this photo to police as evidence of their relationship.

Scott with McKenzie, the dog Laci gave him before they were married. He often brought McKenzie along on his dates with Janet.

Scott (*above, at right*) and Laci (*below, center*) with friends

Scott and Laci as a young couple

Scott with Amber Frey at the holiday party, December 14, 2002. *Inset:* The Star Theater 2 home planetarium Scott gave Amber as a Christmas present.

The Berkeley Marina, where Scott launched his fishing trip on December 24

# BILL OF SALE

1991 14 FOOT GAMEFISHER BOAT WITH ACCESSORIES

15 HORSEPOWER GAMEFISHER MOTOR

1989 SHORLINE TRAILER

$1400.OO

*Bruce F. Peterson*

Bruce F. Peterson                    12/09/2002

The paper trail: Scott's bill of sale for the Sears Gamefisher boat, and Laci Peterson's jewelry repair receipt (*inset*).

Scott at the New Year's Eve vigil

Scott's green Ford 4 x 4, which he used to drive to the marina

The bloodstain found on the interior door, later determined to be Scott's

A photo of Scott and Laci found at their home by police

The pool in the Petersons' backyard

Images from the Petersons' home: The living room (*above*) and kitchen (*below*)

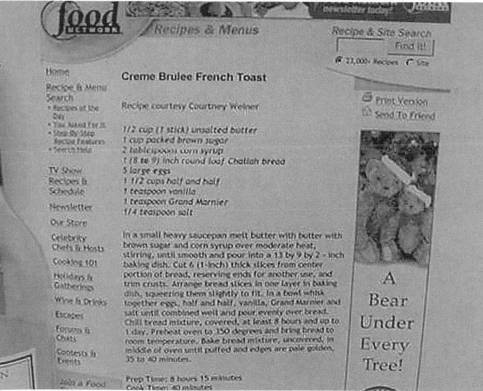

*Above:* Laci loved to entertain, as the cookbooks on her shelf (including two by Martha Stewart) attest. *Below:* The French toast recipe Laci was planning on serving for Christmas brunch.

Twin bathrobes in the Petersons' home

Children's books (*above*) and books on pregnancy and motherhood, found in the Petersons' home, suggest how excited Laci was about having her first child.

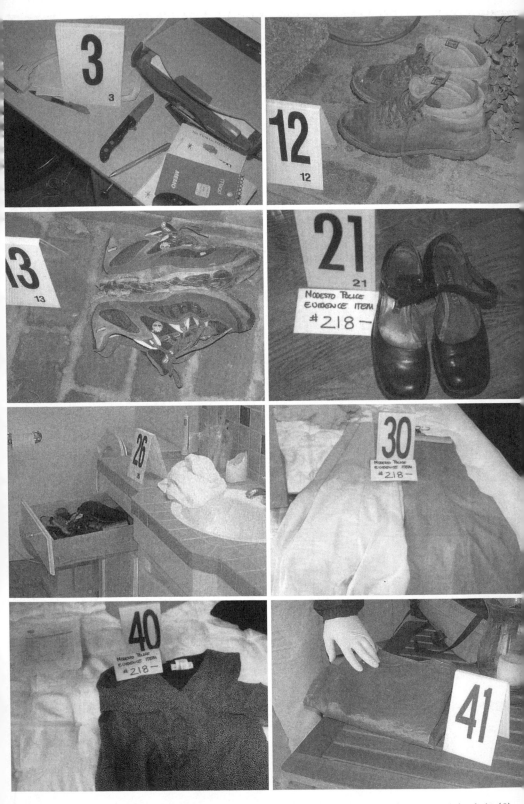

Evidence photos taken at the Petersons' home, including the blue tarp (# 41) and McKenzie's leash (# 48)

Item #57: off white comforter cover

close-up digital photo of the brown stains on side B.

- These stains did not ~~transfer~~ transfer ~~red~~ well onto moist swab in LMG testing

- purple, orange and green post-it flags were put next to the ~~red~~ brown stains for photo.

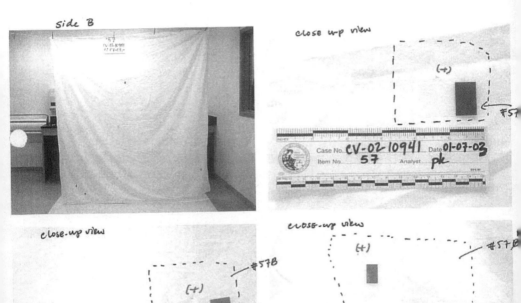

side B

close up view

Case No. CV-02-10941   Date 01-07-03
Item No.   57   Analyst  pk

close-up view

#57B

(+)

Case No. CV-02-10941   Date 01-07-03
Item No.   57   Analyst  pk

close-up view

#57B

(+)

(+)

Case No. CV-02-10941   Date 01-07-03
Item No.   57   Analyst  pk

(+) = LMG

DEFENDANT'S EXHIBIT
DLM-7
SC 55500 A
PENGAD 800-631-6989

A forensic investigator's worksheet detailing the bloodstains found on the Petersons' duvet cover. The symbol (+) indicates a positive finding for blood.

above view of the boat
with black stickers ph arrows
pointing toward stains
tested with LMG.

O = LMG (+) stains.

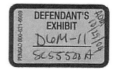

← closed up of
stains between
the rear and
middle seats
of the boat

DEFENDANT'S
EXHIBIT
D6M-11
SC55503A

A worksheet detailing the investigators' write-up of Scott's boat

overall rear of truck →

← overall top view
from rear of truck

The rear of Scott's rental truck, also examined for evidence

rear of the truck
(~~track~~ bed ) with
~~tail of ga~~
tailgate

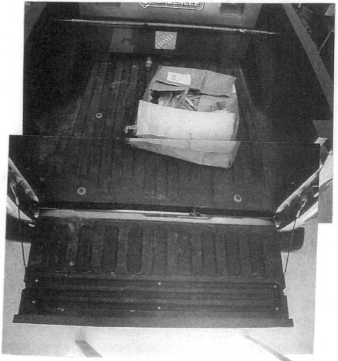

← rear of the truck
with expended
shotshell & truck hitch
collected by MoPD.

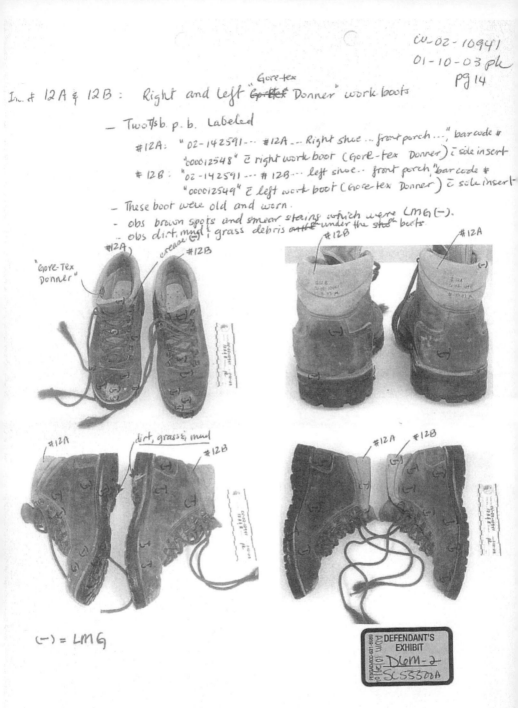

CV-02-10941
01-10-03 pk
pg 14

In. # 12A & 12B: Right and Left "Gore-tex Donner" work boots

— Two t/s b. p. b. Labeled

#12A: "02-142591 ... #12A ... Right shoe ... front porch ...," barcode #
"000012548" c̄ right work boot (Gore-tex Donner) c̄ sole insert

#12B: "02-142591 ... #12B ... left shoe .. front porch," barcode #
"000012549" c̄ left work boot (Gore-tex Donner) c̄ sole insert

— These boot were old and worn.
— obs brown spots and smear stains which were LMG (−).
— obs dirt, mud, grass debris on the & under the stuff boots

"Gore-Tex Donner"    #12A    #12B    #12B    #12A

#12A    dirt, grass & mud    #12B    #12A    #12B

(−) = LMG

DEFENDANT'S
EXHIBIT
D6M-2
SC55500A

Scott's work boots, which tested negative for blood

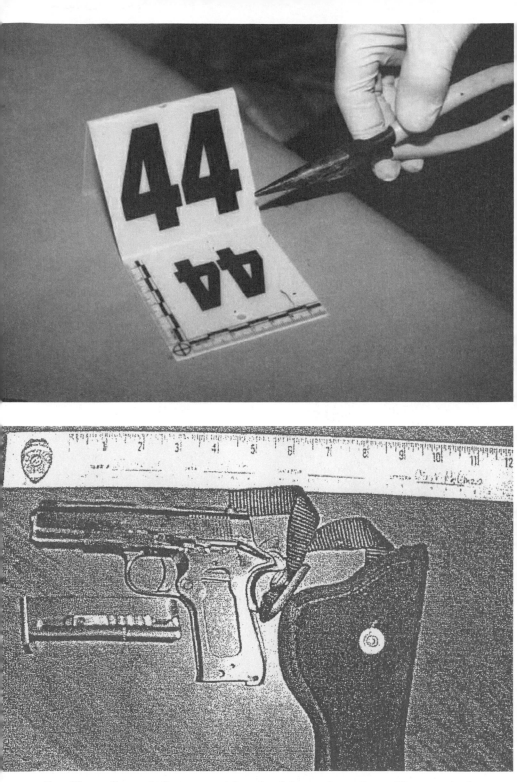

*Above:* The needle-nosed pliers recovered from Scott's boat at the warehouse. These contained a hair consistent with Laci's, one of the few pieces of forensic evidence in the case.
*Below:* The Llama .22 caliber handgun police found in his glove compartment.

Cell-tower information allowed the prosecution to map out Scott's travels for the jury. As the call transcript indicates, on January 11 he called his mother from Berkeley while pretending to be in "west Fresno" (*opposite*).

## RECORDED PHONE CONVERSATION BETWEEN JACKIE PETERSON AND SCOTT PETERSON: January 11, 2003 at 1048 hours

| | |
|---|---|
| Scott Peterson: | Hey mom |
| Jackie Peterson: | Hi, are you there? |
| Scott Peterson | Yeah |
| Jackie Peterson | Where are you? |
| Scott Peterson | What's that? |
| Jackie Peterson | Where are you? |
| Scott Peterson | west Fresno |
| Jackie Peterson | Oh, Okay. Can you...Um, Donna asked that you call her. Would you mind calling her? |
| Scott Peterson | Why? |
| Jackie Peterson | Um, she just wants to talk to you. |
| Scott Peterson | Let me get her number. |
| Jackie Peterson | Okay, you ready? |
| Scott Peterson | yeah |
| Jackie Peterson | ▉▉▉ |
| Scott Peterson | yeah |
| Jackie Peterson | ▉▉▉ |
| Scott Peterson | ▉▉▉ yeah |
| Jackie Peterson | ▉▉▉ |
| Scott Peterson | ▉▉▉ got it. |
| Jackie Peterson | Yeah, okay |
| Scott Peterson | Okay, thanks |

# Scott Peterson's Interest in Selling his and Laci's Home

523 Covena Avenue, Modesto, California

Brian Argain

| | |
|---|---|
| 1/22/03 at 5:39 pm | Scott called Brian and discussed the sale of his house.<br>Scott: "I'd like to put it on the market right now."<br>Scott: "Can I sell it furnished?" |
| 1/23/03 at 5:42 pm | Scott called Brian and left a voicemail message wanting to talk to him about the house. |
| 1/27/03 at 5:41 pm | Brian called Scott and asked Scott if he wanted him to talk to his manager. |
| 1/29/03 at 3:32 pm | Brian called Scott. Brian told him after talking to his manager he would need to talk with his attorney in order to sell it.<br>Scott: "Hey, what about renting it?" |

C-1

As this exhibit shows, Scott also called real estate agent Brian Argain repeatedly to inquire about putting his house on the market—only a few weeks after Laci disappeared.

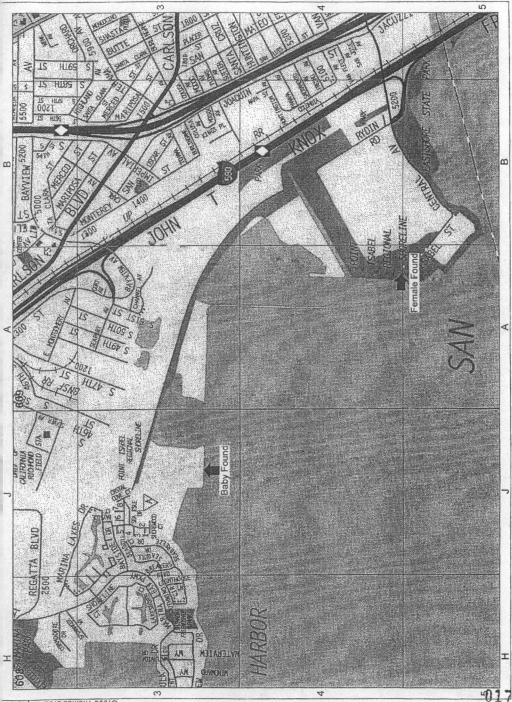

The northern shore of the San Francisco Bay, showing the locations where Laci's and Conner's bodies were found

00052

| BAY: | LAKE: |
|---|---|
| ① TICKET | ① CEMENT IN TRUCK |
| ② GAS | ② ALIBI LEADS TO BAY |
| ③ CELL SITES | ③ 22 HR OPEN 13 TIME FRAME. |
| ④ DOG TRACK | |
| ⑤ TARP | ④ LAKES INTE NET |
| ⑥ CLAIM/STATEMENT | |
| ⑦ BOAT | ⑤ CLOSER |
| ⑧ FISHING LIC | ⑥ LOW RISK WITS |
| ⑨ FISHING TACKLE | ⑦ NOT FAMILLAR W/ OCEAN |
| ⑩ ANCHOR | ⑧ DIFFICULT TO DUMP BODY. |
| ✳ ⑪ WHISTLE | ⑨ BROAD DAYLIGH |
| ⑫ 3 VISITS RENTAL CARS | ⑩ BUNDLE EXPOSED |
| ⑬ GOLFING SWITCH | |
| ⑭ GOLFING STATEMENT PRIOR | |
| ⑮ NO ONE KNOWS ABT BOAT | |
| ⑯ UBRELLAS IN AM | |
| ⑰ BODY NOT FOUND IN LAKES. | |
| ⑱ SALT WATER | |
| ⑲ DEEP WATER CURRENTS | |
| ⑳ CURRENT CHART + BAY (INTERNET) | |
| ㉑ DIDN'T CLEAN UP SHOP | |
| ㉒ DIDN'T WANT NEWS SPREAD ABT BOAT "NOT GOING TO TELL BOSS"? | |
| ㉓ PAID CASH FOR BOAT | |
| ㉔ BOAT NOT REGISTERED | |
| ㉕ BOAT COVER WHY? COVER BODY? | 024101 |
| ㉖ MEDUNIC IRRATIC DRIVING ROVERSELLO | |

Detective Craig Grogan's list of forty-one reasons he believed that Laci's body would show up in the San Francisco Bay (versus ten reasons it might show up in an area lake)

00053

(28) X MAS EVE LOW RISK OF OTHERS AT DOCK.
(29) RESEARCHED OTHER BOAT LAUNCH AREAS.
(30) FINANCIAL PROB'S / $1400 BOAT.
(31) MEDIA COVERAGE ABT RUSSIAN BODYS.
(32) GUN IN GLOVE BOX
(33) WET CLOTHES.
(34) SCUFFED KNUCKLE
(35) NO REASON TO GO FISHING INSTEAD OF GOLFING
     IF HE DIDN'T HAVE TO CHANGE STORY BECAUSE
     OF WITS.
(36) QUOTE JUST WANTED GET BOAT IN WATER.
(37) FISHING TACKLE NOT FOR SALT WATER
(38) DOESNT KNOW WHAT FISHING +
(39) DESCRIBES ISLAND

MANNER OF DEATH ?
         1. UNCONCIOUS - (NO INJURIES)
         2. SUFFOCATION (BLOOD)

40 TEST BOAT NEVER USED OCEAN
41. WEATHER CONDITIONS BAY.

024102

# CONTRA COSTA COUNTY
# OFFICE OF THE SHERIFF - CORONER
# CORONER'S REPORT

**CLASSIFICATION:** Homicide/Unknown Means   **CASE:** 03-0808

**DECEDENT:** PETERSON            LACI            DENISE
                _Last_            _First_         _Middle_

**DATE REPORTED:** 04/14/2003      **TIME REPORTED:** 1610 HOURS

**DATE OF DEATH :** 04/14/2003 - Found   **TIME OF DEATH :** Unknown HOURS

**AKA:** _____  Other I.D.:  CDL # A8874209

**DOB:** 05/04/1975  **AGE:** 27 YEARS (UNDER 1 YEAR: ___ MONTHS ___ DAYS)

**SEX:** Female  **RACE:** Caucasian  **EST HGT:** 5'1"  **EST WGT:** 57

**HAIR:** Brown  **EYES:** Brown  **SOCIAL SEC#:** _____

**USUAL ADDRESS:** 523 Covena Ave.

**CITY STATE ZIP:** Modesto, Ca. 95354   **PHONE#:** _____

**IDENTIFIED BY:** Angelynn Moore  **DATE:** 04/18/2003  **TIME:** ___ HOURS

**ADDRESS and PHONE#:** DOJ DNA Lab, 1001 W. Cutting Bl. Richmond, CA 94804

████████████████████

**OTHER INVESTIGATING AGENCY:** East Bay Reg. Park PD

**AGENCY FILE#:** 03-0414009  **ASSIGNED OFFICER:** Detective I. Frazier

## NEXT OF KIN

Sharon Rocha                         Mother
_NAME OF LEGAL NEXT OF KIN_       _RELATIONSHIP TO DECEASED_

**ADDRESS:** 1017 Mark Lee Way

Modesto, Ca. 95354

**RESIDENCE PHONE #:** ████████  **BUSINESS PHONE#:** _____

_AUTHORIZED ALTERNATE NEXT OF KIN_      _RELATIONSHIP TO DECEASED_
**ADDRESS:** _____

**RESIDENCE PHONE #:** _____  **BUSINESS PHONE#:** _____

**LEGAL NOK NOTIFIED BY:** Detective C. Grogan  **AGENCY:** Modesto PD

**NOTIFIED DATE:** 04/18/2003  **TIME:** 1850 HOURS  **HOW:** In Person

**REPORTED BY DEPUTY CORONER:** L. Martin        017319

CCC SHERIFF CORONER'S REPORT                              Page 1

The coroner's report on Laci Peterson, noting the cause of death as "Homicide/Unknown Means"

NAME:    PETERSON, Laci
AKA: DOE, Jane

REPORT OF AUTOPSY 2003-0808

POSTMORTEM AT:  Central Morgue

DATE: 04/14/03  TIME: 1830 Hrs.
Finish Time: 2200 Hrs.

PLACE OF DEATH:  Richmond, California

FOUND DATE: 04/14/03  TIME: Unk. Hrs.

AGE:                                    SEX:  Female                            RACE: Caucasian

## AUTOPSY DIAGNOSES

1) Female body with:
   A.    Absence of each radius, each ulna, and both hands
   B.    Absence of both feet and left tibia and fibula
   C.    Absence of head and cervical vertebrae 1-6
   D.    Absence of thoracoabdominal viscera

2) Gravid uterus; fetus, placenta, and umbilical cord absent, with opening near fundus. Cervix intact and closed.

3) Extensive changes of immersion, postmortem animal feeding, tidal effect and decomposition; estimated postmortem interval: months

4) Multiple rib fractures (left 5 and 6, right 9)

CAUSE OF DEATH:       Undetermined

COMMENTS: The absence of body parts in this case may simply be attributable to postmortem change, animal feeding, and tidal action; there is no evidence of tool marks on remaining bones of the extremities or on the thoracic vertebral column.   Toxicology testing performed on skeletal muscle is positive only for caffeine and PEA (decomposition product).

Date: 05/14/2003

BLP/ica

Brian L. Peterson, M.D.
Forensic Pathologist

Laci's autopsy report, noting the condition of her body at the time it was found. The cause of death remained "undetermined."

# CONTRA COSTA COUNTY
# OFFICE OF THE SHERIFF - CORONER
# CORONER'S REPORT

**CLASSIFICATION:** Homicide/Unknown Means   **CASE:** 03-0799

**DECEDENT:** PETERSON___ CONNOR___ ___
                Last            First           Middle

**DATE REPORTED:** 04/13/2003   **TIME REPORTED:** 1915 HOURS

**DATE OF DEATH :** 04/13/2003 - found   **TIME OF DEATH :** Unknown HOURS

**AKA:** ___ Other I.D.: ___

**DOB:** ___ **AGE:** ___ YEARS (UNDER 1 YEAR: ___ MONTHS ___ DAYS)

**SEX:** ___ **RACE:** ___ **EST HGT:** ___ **EST WGT:** 3.5

**HAIR:** ___ **EYES:** ___ **SOCIAL SEC#:** ___

**USUAL ADDRESS:** ___

**CITY STATE ZIP:** ___ **PHONE#:** ___

**IDENTIFIED BY:** Angelynn Moore **DATE:** 04/18/2003 **TIME:** ___ HOURS

**ADDRESS and PHONE#:** DOJ DNA Lab, 1001 W. Cutting Bl. Richmond, CA 94804

██████████

**OTHER INVESTIGATING AGENCY:** R.P.D.

**AGENCY FILE#:** 03-38939 **ASSIGNED OFFICER:** Officer Opdyke

## NEXT OF KIN

Sharon Rocha___ Grandmother___
*NAME OF LEGAL NEXT OF KIN*   *RELATIONSHIP TO DECEASED*

**ADDRESS:** 1017 Mark Lee Way
Modesto, Ca. 95354

**RESIDENCE PHONE #:** ██████████ **BUSINESS PHONE#:** ___

*AUTHORIZED ALTERNATE NEXT OF KIN*   *RELATIONSHIP TO DECEASED*
**ADDRESS:** ___

**RESIDENCE PHONE #:** ___ **BUSINESS PHONE#:** ___

**LEGAL NOK NOTIFIED BY:** Detective C. Grogan **AGENCY:** Modesto PD

**NOTIFIED DATE:** 04/18/2003 **TIME:** 1850 HOURS **HOW:** In Person

**REPORTED BY DEPUTY CORONER:** C. Martinez   017368

CCC SHERIFF CORONER'S REPORT   Page

Conner's coroner's report. His body weighed 3.5 pounds.

## CONTRA COSTA COUNTY CORONER'S OFFICE

## WARREN E. RUPF, SHERIFF-CORONER

NAME:  PETERSON, Connor
AKA:  DOE, Baby Boy

REPORT OF AUTOPSY 2003-0799

POSTMORTEM AT:  Central Morgue

DATE: 04/14/03 TIME: 0810 Hrs.
Finish Time: 0835 Hrs.

PLACE OF DEATH: Richmond, California

FOUND DATE: 04/13/03 TIME: Unk. Hrs.

AGE:  SEX: Male  RACE: Caucasian

### AUTOPSY DIAGNOSES

1) Phenotypic male fetus, estimated gestational age 9 months (33-38 weeks based on anthropologic measurements)

2) No gross external or internal anomalies

3) Moderate postmortem decomposition with apparent additional postmortem injuries to torso; no evidence of animal feeding

CAUSE OF DEATH:  Undetermined

COMMENT: Moderate decomposition without evidence of postmortem animal feeding suggests relative protection of this body prior to its discovery.

Date: 05/14/2003

Brian L. Peterson, M.D.
Forensic Pathologist

BLP/ica

017375

Conner's autopsy report

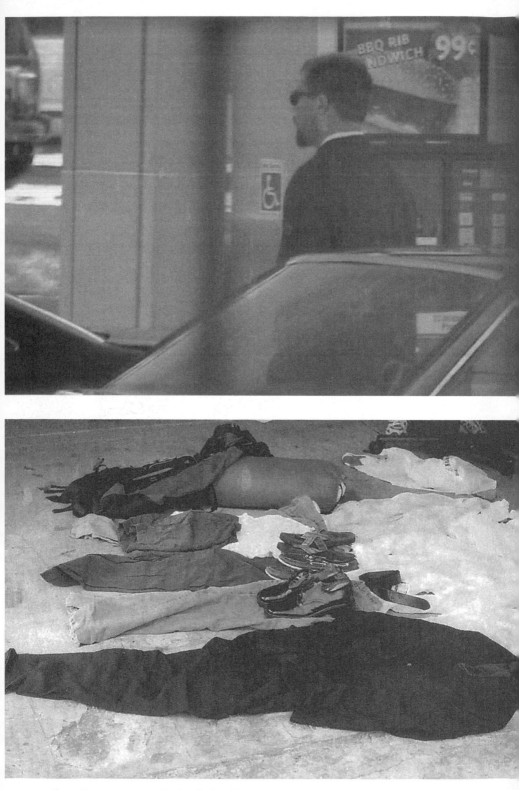

*Above:* Scott at a gas station just before his arrest
- The clothes and belongings he had with him

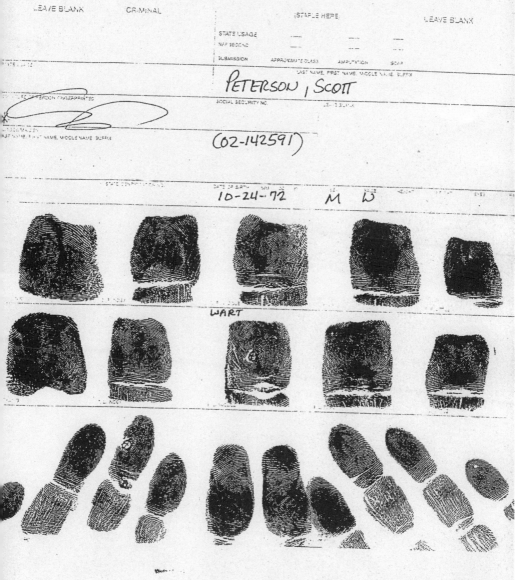

Scott's fingerprints

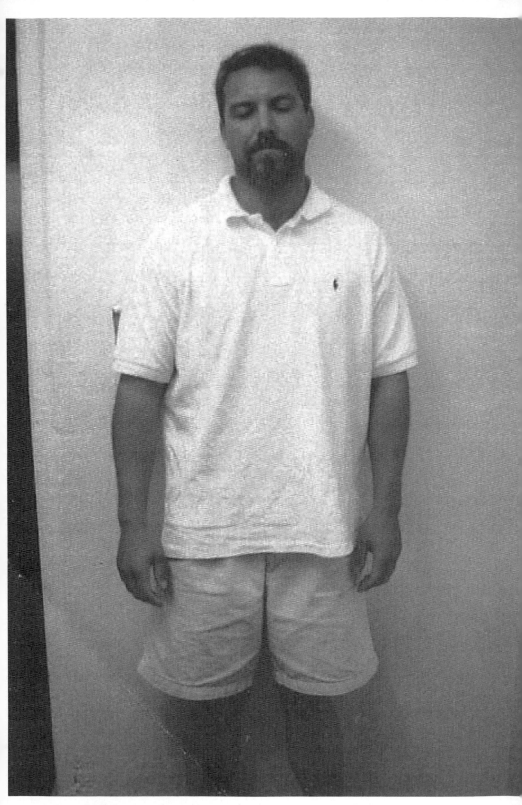

Scott after his arrest

**D** PETERSON, SCOTT LEE AKA — BOOKING NUMBER 558289

ADDRESS: 523 COVENA AVE, MODESTO CA. PHONE 505-0337 SOID NUMBER 242127

OCCUPATION: — BUSINESS ADDRESS: REFUSED — EMPLOYER: —

DOB 10/24/72 · AGE 30 · RACE W · SEX M · HGT 6-0 · WGT 200 · HAIR BLN · EYES BRN · BUILD MED · COMP LHT · OCL/ID A5077297

CLOTHING: BLUE SWEATER, WHT POLO SHIRT, WHT SHORTS, NIKE T-SHOE

SIGNATURE OF ARRESTING CITIZEN

| Code | Name (Last, First, Middle) | | | | Residence Address | Residence Phone |
|---|---|---|---|---|---|---|
| | Occupation | Race | Sex | Age | Date of Birth | Business/School Address | Business Phone |

| Code | Name (Last, First, Middle) | | | | Residence Address | Residence Phone |
|---|---|---|---|---|---|---|
| | Occupation | Race | Sex | Age | Date of Birth | Business/School Address | Business Phone |

Date & Time of Offense: 12/23/02 / 12/24/02 · Location of Offense: 523 COVENA AVE, MODESTO · LOCATION OF VEHICLE: ☐ NONE ☐ TOWED BY ☒ LEFT AT SCENE ☒ REL TO JOE PETERSON

Location of Arrest: SAN DIEGO / CALLAS/TORREY PINES RD

48 HRS. EXPIRES - DATE/TIME: 04/18/03 - 1110 / 04/22/03 - 1110 · DATE/TIME REC'D AT JAIL · VEHICLE DESC./LIC.

ARRESTING OFFICER: CRAIG GROGAN · ID# M682 · AGENCY MODESTO P.D. · 02-142591 · ARREST NO.

☒ WARR ☒ FEL ☐ MISD — 187 PC (2 COUNTS) PROBABLE CAUSE WARRANT OF ARREST

CHARGE: ☐ ON VIEW ☐ 11 & 82 ☐ CITZS ☐ WARR ☐ FEL ☐ MISD

CHARGE: ☐ ON VIEW ☐ 11 & 82 ☐ CITZS ☐ WARR ☐ FEL ☐ MISD

CHARGE: ☐ ON VIEW ☐ 11 & 82 ☐ CITZS ☐ WARR ☐ FEL ☐ MISD

**NARRATIVE / FACTS ESTABLISHING PROBABLE CAUSE FOR ARREST:**

ON FRIDAY 04/18/03 AT 1110 HRS, DOJ SPECIAL AGENT SUPERVISOR ERNIE LIMON, SPECIAL AGENT PETER SHEAR AND OFFICER CLAUDE JUBRAN COMPLETED A FELONY TRAFFIC STOP AND ARREST AT MY REQUEST. SCOTT LEE PETERSON WAS ARRESTED FOR AN OUTSTANDING PROBABLE CAUSE WARRANT IN SAN DIEGO CO. CA. PETERSON WAIVED BOOKING IN THAT JURISDICTION AND WAS TRANSPORTED TO STANISLAUS COUNTY JAIL FOR BOOKING.

COPIES TO:

I declare under penalty of perjury that the foregoing is true and correct to the best of my information and belief.

Executed on 4/18/03 at Stanislaus County, CA. BY: _____ IBM# 10259

ON THE BASIS OF ☒ the foregoing declaration, ☐ telephone declaration, I HEREBY DETERMINE THAT: ☒ there IS ☐ there is NOT probable cause to believe this arrestee has committed a crime.

Date: 4/19/03 Time: 1450 Magistrate: _____

ORIGINAL JAIL COPY

prebooking from 107

The prebooking sheet for Scott's arrest, signed by Detective Craig Grogan

BOOKING REGISTER
STANISLAUS COUNTY JAIL
MODESTO CALIFORNIA 95353

BOOKING DATE 04/19/2003 00:09      BOOKING..: 558289
ARREST DATE 04/18/2003 11:10      FILE NO..: 02-132591

PETERSON, SCOTT LEE                  ID NUMBER: SC242127
523 COVENA AVE         MODESTO, CA  95354

RACE....... W  SEX......... M     AGE........ 30  D.O.B.. 10/24/1972
HEIGHT..... 6 00  WEIGHT...... 180  HAIR....... BRN  EYES... BRN
BIRTHPLACE. CA  CITIZEN.... US  MARITAL STATUS... SINGLE
SOC SEC NO..               DRIVERS LICENSE.
OCCUPATION.. SALES          EMPLOYER.. TRADE CORP/MODESTO

*    EMERGENCY NOTIFICATION INFORMATION    RELATION ——— TELEPHONE——
PETERSON, LEE                    FATHER

ILLNESS/INJURY: REFER TO MEDICAL PRE-SCREEN/CLRD. BY MEDICAL & INTAKE

*  BOOKING CHARGE(S)         HOW
#  ——————————CODE    CTS F/M ARR ——BAIL—— ——FINE—— ——WARRANT——
01 187 PC           2 F  RAM  NO BAIL        RAMEY
   MURDER                      COURT: STAN.SUPERIOR

      TOTAL FINE $    0    TOTAL BAIL $ NO BAIL

ARREST LOCATION : CALLAS / TRODEY PINES RD  SAN DIEGO, CA 92121
VEHICLE LOCATION: REL TO JOE PETERSON    SAN DIEGO, CA 92121

**    LAW ENFORCEMENT PERSONS               NO.  AGENCY
ACCOMPANYING OFFICER..
ARRESTING OFFICER......GROGAN, CRAIG DETECTIVE MPD    M682  MPD
BOOKING OFFICER........PORTER, ROSANNE LEGAL CLK III    SA02

PETERSON, SCOTT LEE                 ID NUMBER: SC242127
CHARGE(S): 187 PC             FINE:    0 BAIL: NO BAIL
P R O P E R T Y         CASH:    0.00    BOOKING..: 558289

BRN BELT, BRN SUNGLASSES, MISC.PAPER, VISA CARD.,NOPT
WHT SHIRT, KHAKI SHORTS, _blue sweats_ (B)
BLU/GRY TENNIS SHOES, ,NOCT

I CERTIFY THAT THE ABOVE IS A CORRECT ITEM LIST OF MY PERSONAL PROPERTY.

          SIGNATURE X
RD _____ CLASS _____ IBM# _____  * * * * END OF BOOKING REGISTER * * * *

Scott's booking register. Note that his marital status is given as "single."

02- 142591

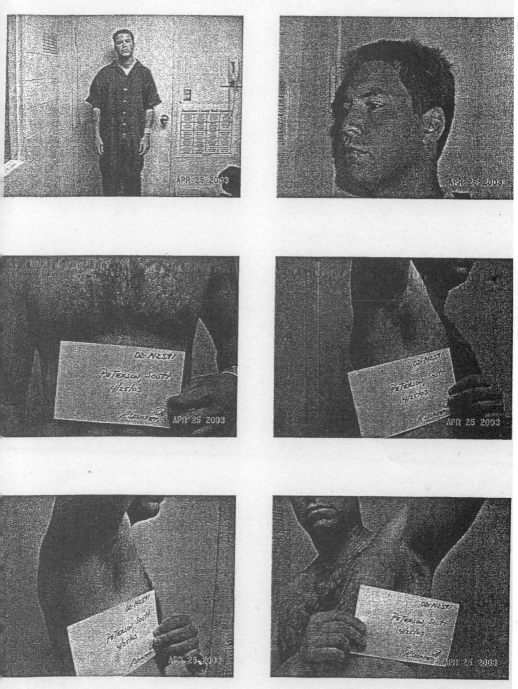

Photos of Scott taken at the Stanislaus County Jail, April 25, 2003

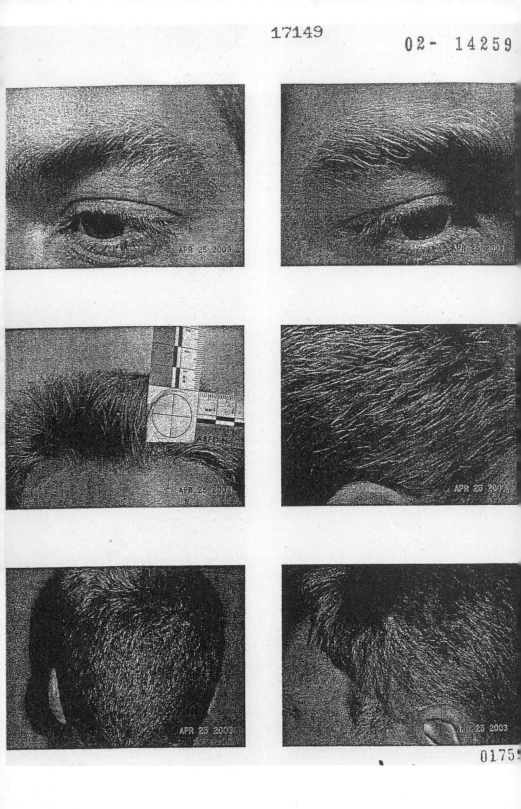

Photos of Scott taken at the Stanislaus County Jail, April 25, 2003

# INDEX